# Sorry States

A VOLUME IN THE SERIES

Cornell Studies in Security Affairs

*edited by* Robert J. Art, Robert Jervis, *and* Stephen M. Walt

A list of titles in this series is available at www.cornellpress.cornell.edu

# Sorry States

*Apologies in International Politics*

JENNIFER LIND

Cornell University Press

*Ithaca & London*

First published 2008 by Cornell University Press
First printing, Cornell Paperbacks, 2010


*Library of Congress Cataloging-in-Publication Data*

Lind, Jennifer M.
   Sorry States : apologies in international politics / Jennifer Lind.
     p. cm.—(Cornell studies in security affairs)
   Includes bibliographical references and index.
   ISBN 978-0-8014-4625-2 (cloth)
   ISBN 978-0-8014-7628-0 (pbk.)
   1. Apologizing—Political aspects. 2. Reconciliation—Political
aspects. 3. Reparations for historical injustices. I. Title. II. Series.
   BF575.A75L56   2008
   327.1'7—dc22
   2008013106

Cloth printing       10  9  8  7  6  5  4  3  2  1
Paperback printing  10  9  8  7  6  5  4  3  2  1

# Contents

# Acknowledgments

While I was researching this book, I came across a haunting photo of West German Chancellor Willy Brandt kneeling before the Warsaw Ghetto Memorial in 1970. I photocopied it and tacked it up on my bulletin board. Moving from school to school, office to office, I brought the photo with me. It was a hopeful, noble symbol that helped sustain me through a project in which I was constantly forced to confront acts of reprehensible evil. I would read with distaste the statements of West German politicians who—emphasizing the need for economic recovery and democratic stability rather than justice—argued that the country should move forward rather than confront its dark past. Some people, I lamented, just don't get it.

This project began when I realized just how prevalent the issue of war memory was in East Asian politics and how little international relations scholars had explored the topic. I decided to write a book that would use social science tools to evaluate the connection between a country's remembrance of past violence and reconciliation with its former adversaries. Like everyone else, I already knew the answer: as a bumper sticker recently told me, "No peace without justice!" Obviously countries could not move their relations forward unless perpetrators atoned for the crimes they had committed. What a book! Maybe I could get on *Oprah*.

I still remember the day that I realized that this was not the book I would write. Having started the project convinced that countries must atone for past wrongs, over time I realized that my evidence was not pointing me in this direction. I did find substantial evidence that denials of past violence were poisonous for a country's foreign relations. But I also found that countries have been able to heal their relations despite offering little or even no contrition. Peace and reconciliation were possible, I realized, amid glaring, screaming injustice. Even worse, I noticed a pattern (in Japan and elsewhere) in which countries that offered contrition to foreign victims experienced an explosion of controversy that was *harmful* to foreign relations. Contrition, in other words, could be counterproductive to international reconciliation.

I fought my findings every step of the way. That one day that I finally relented, I looked up at the photo of Willy Brandt on his knees and realized that my book would be arguing in favor of those West German conservatives whose advice I had previously scorned—and arguing *against* gestures such as his famous *Kniefal*. I put my head down on my desk in despair as I realized what I had to do. So much for *Oprah*.

It would have been much more satisfying to write the book that I had wanted to write; the one that everyone wanted to read. But instead I wrote this one, and I share it here with you.

THIS book would not have existed, in any form, without the support of many people. In particular I am forever grateful to my advisers at the Massachusetts Institute of Technology. I thank Barry Posen for his tremendous support, his tough comments, and his wise advice. His perpetually raised eyebrow constantly motivated me (and still does). I am also grateful to Stephen Van Evera, not only for his extensive feedback but also for those long and fascinating conversations that led to my interest in the topic of this book. I also benefited greatly from incisive comments and guidance from Thomas Christensen and Richard Samuels. All of these advisers helped me not only by providing generous and thoughtful criticism of my project but also by setting the very highest standards in their own research. I also thank Suzanne Berger, Melissa Nobles, and Roger Petersen at MIT for their advice and support. I am very grateful to my graduate student colleagues David Art, Eugene Gholz, Kelly Greenhill, Yinan He, Sara Jane McCaffrey, David Mendeloff, and Christopher Twomey.

I owe my colleagues and friends a tremendous debt for their willingness to read and comment on my work: for identifying problems and helping me think through solutions. Thanks to Stephen Brooks, Jennifer Dixon, Taylor Fravel, Stuart Kaufman, Ned Lebow, Michael Mastanduno, Robert Ross, Anne Sa'adah, Allan Stam, Benjamin Valentino, and William Wohlforth. Audiences at the University of Chicago's Program on International Security Policy, the John M. Olin Institute at Harvard University, and U.C. Berkeley gave me valuable feedback. Thanks to Stephan Haggard and Ellis Krauss at the University of California–San Diego for the opportunity to present my work there and for their support and encouragement. I am especially grateful to the members of Dartmouth's International Relations Faculty Working Group for their extremely helpful comments on an earlier version of this manuscript. Many thanks to Kenneth Yalowitz and the John Sloan Dickey Center for International Understanding for funding the immensely valuable manuscript review seminar and to Robert Jervis and Jack Snyder for traveling to Hanover to participate. Their tough but encouraging feedback greatly improved this book.

I am grateful to many people who gave me vital advice and logistical help for my fieldwork. I am eternally indebted to David Kang and Victor Cha, not only for their substantive discussions about this project but also for their many introductions in Korea. Thanks also to Peter Beck for his valuable advice. I thank Chung-in Moon of Yonsei's Graduate School for International Studies (GSIS) for giving me an academic home in Seoul and for his guidance on this project. I also wish to thank the GSIS Center for International Studies and Institute for Modern Korea Studies. For their kindness and thoughtful comments I particularly thank Professors Jung-hoon Lee, Chung-min Lee, and Kim Taeho. I am very grateful for help from Jisook Han, Seo-hyun Park, Hyeran Jo, and Jung-ran Joo. Many thanks to Jung-hae Kim, Noriyuki Katagiri, and Jennifer Xi for superb research assistance.

Chikako Kawakatsu Ueki and Yoshibumi Wakamiya provided tremendous support during my trips to Japan. My Japanese "parents," Reiko and Ikuo Suzuki, could not possibly be more generous or kind, and to them I will always be grateful. Thanks also to Yumiko and Fumihiko Aoki for their friendship. Suzanne Berger and Sylvain Ferrari of the MIT France Program and Anne Sa'adah at Dartmouth provided essential guidance for my fieldwork in France. In Paris I benefited enormously from the help of Ariane Chebel d'Apollonia and Etienne de Durand.

For my fieldwork in France and the Republic of Korea, I owe the greatest debt to all of the extremely busy and talented people who graciously agreed to be interviewed. Our conversations were some of the most fascinating of my life, and I feel lucky to have experienced them. Your contributions reach far beyond the data you provided; your kindness and encouragement meant so much.

This book was made possible by the generous financial support of several institutions. For early funding of this project I thank Kenneth Oye, Stephen Van Evera, Bill Keller, and Carolyn Makinson of the MIT Center for International Studies and Harvey Sapolsky of the Security Studies Program. I also thank the MacArthur Foundation for its support of this project through MIT's Center for International Studies. Dartmouth's Dickey Center generously provided funds for book production. I benefited greatly from the opportunity to pursue this research during postdoctoral fellowships at Dartmouth's Government Department and Nelson A. Rockefeller Center and the University of Pennsylvania's Christopher H. Browne Center for International Politics. I also thank Avery Goldstein, Ian Lustick, Edward Mansfield, and Rogers Smith of the University of Pennsylvania for their advice and their kindness. For helping me turn a big lumpy stack of papers into this book, I express my sincere thanks to an anonymous reviewer, to

Bruce Acker, and to Cornell's Roger Haydon and Teresa Jesionowski. Many thanks also to Stephen Walt and Robert Art for their support.

My family has been behind me the whole way. I am so grateful to my mom, Cathy, for her love, support, and continual interest in my work. Thanks to my dad, Don, for encouraging me into graduate school in the first place and for having faith in me all along. And thanks to Eleanor and Ian, just for being you.

It is not possible to adequately thank my husband, Daryl Press. When he said "better or worse," he had no idea that "worse" would include reading endless drafts of theory chapters. Thanks to Daryl for all of his superb criticism and advice, which helped this book immensely. And above all thanks to him for his steadfast support and faith.

I dedicate this book to Daryl, with love and gratitude.

JENNIFER LIND

*Hanover, New Hampshire*

# Sorry States

# Introduction

True reconciliation does not consist in merely forgetting the
past.
                                                —Nelson Mandela

Carry the battle to them. Don't let them bring it to you. Put
them on the defensive. And don't ever apologize for anything.
                                                —Harry S Truman

The elderly Korean woman was very slight, with salt-and-pepper hair
pinned back. She stood with head ducked, behind a bank of microphones,
her shy eyes peering up at her audience. Kim Hak-soon told an astonished
world how during World War II she was sent to Manchuria as a "comfort
woman" of the Japanese Imperial Army. Raped twenty, thirty times a night
by Japanese soldiers, she toiled in menial labor all day, received little food,
and endured terrible beatings. She watched soldiers beat to death and
offhandedly execute many women imprisoned alongside her. "Just hearing
the word, Japan, makes my heart break," Kim said. "I want an apology after making it crystal clear what happened. I want to convey the historical
fact to younger generations."[1]
     When Kim came forward in 1991, the world was more receptive than
ever before to such a plea. For centuries countries had impenitently invaded, raped, pillaged, and plundered; governments offered apologies
only for minor breaches of protocol. For example, the United States apologized to Britain in 1928 after the Coast Guard seized a British ship suspected of smuggling liquor in Bahamian waters. As late as World War I,
countries neither sought nor offered apologies for human rights abuses.
Following World War I, the victors demanded massive reparations from
Germany, and included in the Treaty of Versailles a "war guilt" clause that
forced the Germans to accept responsibility for starting the war. They bitterly resented this clause and fought its inclusion until the last moment of
the negotiations.[2]

However, since World War II apologies for human rights violations have grown increasingly common. Governments, religious institutions, and private firms have apologized and paid reparations for past abuses. As such gestures have grown more frequent, a chorus of voices—victims, activists, scholars, and the international media—increasingly demand them.[3] National governments lobby one another to recognize past abuses. The U.S. Congress recently debated resolutions that urge Japan and Turkey to acknowledge past human rights abuses; the French National Assembly also scolded Turkey and passed a bill criminalizing denial of genocide. The European Union and the United Nations pressure members to admit and atone.[4]

As the issues of memory and apologies grow more prominent, scholars increasingly cite their importance in international reconciliation. Observers contrast the cases of Germany and Japan: after World War II, West German leaders issued apologies and paid extensive reparations. West German textbooks, museums, and monuments detailed and repudiated Germany's horrific crimes. The Federal Republic of Germany also experienced a dramatic reconciliation with its former adversaries. A half-century after the war, images of Nazi terror have been replaced by images of the solid German bureaucrat and loyal ally standing hand-in-hand with François Mitterrand at Verdun Cemetery. As one French scholar put it, "The idea of conflict between us is absolutely unthinkable."[5]

By contrast, the world criticizes Japan for failing to come to terms with its past. Tokyo's apologies have been perceived as too little, too late. Even worse, its politicians repeatedly shock survivors and the global community by denying past atrocities; its history textbooks whitewash its wartime crimes. Japan sees itself as a pacifist, cooperative, and generous global citizen, with a strong antiwar and antinuclear identity. But after sixty years,  Japan's neighbors still see bayoneted babies. Relations between Japan and its former victims remain fraught with distrust.

The German and Japanese experiences have led many analysts to argue that international reconciliation requires that countries come to terms with past violence.[6] This view is bolstered by many scholars of transitional justice who argue that *within* states, truth-telling and legal prosecutions for human rights abuses promote democratic consolidation and postconflict stability.[7] Yet international relations scholars so far have not systematically tested the effects of apologies and other acts of contrition. Is it true that they reduce fear and promote reconciliation between states? To explore this question, this book outlines a theory of "remembrance" and reconciliation and tests it empirically in the cases of Japanese-South Korean relations and Franco-German relations since World War II. It also examines the role of remembrance in Japanese relations with Australia and China and in British relations with Germany.

## The Argument in Brief

This book supports some of the claims made by advocates of international contrition but raises profound doubts about others. First, as many analysts have argued, denials of past aggression and atrocities do fuel distrust and elevate fears among former adversaries. Japan's unapologetic remembrance—for example, frequent denials by influential leaders and omissions from Japan's history textbooks—continues to poison relations with South Korea, China, and Australia more than sixty years after the war. By contrast, Bonn's willingness to accept responsibility for the crimes of the Nazi era, and the absence of denials or glorifications among mainstream West Germans, reassured Germany's World War II adversaries. To this day France and Britain monitor German remembrance for signs of revisionism and are reassured by their absence. All this evidence suggests that avoiding denials and glorification of past violence facilitates reconciliation.

This book, however, refutes the view that international reconciliation requires apologies and other contrite gestures. Many bitter enemies—including West Germany and France—successfully reconciled with very little contrition. In the early years after the war, Bonn expressed modest contrition. Although it offered a lukewarm apology and paid reparations to Israel, West German commemoration, education, and public discourse ignored the atrocities Germany had committed, and instead mourned *German* suffering during and after the war. Nevertheless, during this era of minimal contrition West Germany and France transformed their relations. By the early 1960s, the French viewed the West Germans as their closest friend and security partner. Bonn's remarkable expressions of atonement—wrenching apologies, candid history textbooks, and memorials to Germany's victims—had not yet occurred.

Other World War II enemies reconciled without expressing virtually any remorse for their actions. Both the British and Americans reconciled with West Germany without apologizing for fire-bombing German cities, a campaign that killed hundreds of thousands of civilians. Japan and the United States built a warm relationship and solid security alliance in spite of the fact that neither government has apologized for its wartime atrocities: e.g., Pearl Harbor, Japan's mistreatment of POWs, and the U.S. counter-city bombing campaign that culminated in the atomic bombardment of Hiroshima and Nagasaki. Indeed, both sides justify their wartime actions as necessary given the strategic circumstances of the time.[8] Furthermore, after the war the European partners of Italy and Austria ignored the blatant dodging of culpability in these former Axis countries. International reconciliation is possible—even in the aftermath of horrendous crimes—with little or no contrition.

3

Finally, this book highlights an issue that has been neglected in debates about international reconciliation: the potential dangers of contrition. As seen in Japan and elsewhere, expressions of contrition typically prompt a backlash from conservatives. They offer a competing narrative that celebrates—rather than condemns—the country's past and justifies or even denies its atrocities. Thus contrition can be counterproductive: observers will be angered and alarmed by what the backlash suggests about the country's intentions. Such anger can mobilize nationalistic sentiment in the victim country, creating a spiral of acrimony that makes reconciliation even more elusive. The great irony is that well-meaning efforts to soothe relations between former enemies can actually inflame them.

## Plan of the Book

Reconciliation requires that countries stop perceiving one another as a threat. What is the link between contrition and how threatening a country appears to others? Political scientists argue that countries assess threats by evaluating two aspects of potential adversaries: their capabilities and their intentions. This book examines whether a country's "remembrance"—for example its leaders' statements, textbooks, museums, and so forth that teach its people about the country's history—affects how former adversaries view its intentions. Do states that glorify or deny past violence appear to have hostile intentions? And do states that admit and atone for past violence appear benign?

Chapter 1 outlines a theory that connects remembrance to intentions and threat perception. It defines relevant concepts (e.g., What is "remembrance"? What is an "apology?"), and lays out rules for measuring them. Numerous other factors can shape perceptions of intentions and threat (regime type, territorial claims, institutional membership, and capabilities), and these need to be monitored in order to test the effects of remembrance on threat perception.

Chapter 2, the first of three empirical chapters, examines the influence of Japan's remembrance in its postwar relations with South Korea. In the early years after the war, the Japanese glorified their colonial policies in Korea, focusing only on their economic development and ignoring their severe cultural, political, and physical repression of the country. They forgot their wartime atrocities such as the "comfort women," mass rapes and massacres, the counter-civilian bombing of Chinese cities, and their use of slave labor. Only later, when Tokyo began normalizing relations with its neighbors, did it begin to offer token apologies. Japan's real awakening came in the 1990s, when the country began to confront its World War II crimes. But as Tokyo offered more contrition, many politicians and intellectuals spoke out in favor of a more "patriotic" historical narrative. Opponents of contrition frequently justified or denied Japan's atrocities.

4

Japan's unapologetic remembrance had a powerful effect on Koreans. In the early postwar period, South Korean leaders sought Japanese apologies as a precondition for reconciliation. They expressed alarm about Japan's intentions when they observed denials; they expressed cautious optimism after apologetic gestures. But the recurring pattern of apology-then-backlash led South Koreans to conclude that Japanese contrition was insincere and that Tokyo continued to harbor hostile intentions. Of course remembrance is not the only factor that determined South Korean threat perception: Japanese capabilities (specifically the constraint of the U.S.-Japan alliance) played a powerful role. However, Japan's denials fueled Korean distrust of Tokyo's intentions, which makes Koreans highly sensitive to changes in the balance of power.

In contrast to Japan, the Federal Republic of Germany has come to terms with its past violence to a historically unprecedented degree. As Chapter 3 demonstrates, this introspection did not begin immediately after the war. Although Bonn quickly accepted official responsibility for Nazi era crimes and paid reparations to Israel, for nearly two decades West Germans forgot German atrocities and instead remembered Germany's *own* suffering (e.g., the plight of veterans, expellees, and POWs; and the viciousness of Allied fire bombings and the Soviet invasion of Germany). It was not until the 1960s that West Germany started to examine its horrific crimes against the Jews and its neighbors. West and then unified Germany would eventually engage in the most profound self-reflection the world has ever seen.

West Germany's initial acceptance of its war guilt facilitated Franco-German reconciliation. The French feared that the West Germans would create a postwar mythology that justified or denied Nazi-era crimes, which would fuel a revival of xenophobic nationalism and militarism. To prevent this, France (along with the other Allies) implemented education reforms during the occupation of West Germany that encouraged candid remembrance. Throughout the postwar era, the French continued to monitor West Germany's national debates about the war: they praised its candor and expressed wariness at perceived revisionist trends.

Although the French valued Bonn's acknowledgment of past atrocities, they did not require much in the way of contrition in order to reconcile with West Germany. Their rapprochement was well underway before West Germany began to atone to any significant extent. In the immediate aftermath of war, the French public felt deep loathing toward Germany and terror at the prospect that it would ever be reunified or rearmed. But by the end of the 1950s, the French began to see West Germany as their closest security partner. By this time, Bonn had recognized and paid reparations for Nazi-era crimes, but its remembrance remained evasive, self-exculpatory, and preoccupied with its own suffering. This case—like the Japan-South Korea case—shows the importance of avoiding poisonous denials and acknowledging past atrocities. But it also shows that countries can reconcile in the absence of much contrition.

I conduct three additional and brief case studies in chapter 4, which bolster the findings of the two primary case studies of this book. History haunts not only Japan's relationship with South Korea, but also its relations with the People's Republic of China and Australia. The Chinese castigate and demonstrate in response to perceived Japanese whitewashing. The Chinese people and elites lament Tokyo's unapologetic remembrance and say that it makes them distrust Japan. Australians similarly condemn Japanese denials, and speculate that they send dangerous signals about the country's future intentions. Furthermore, in Britain's relations with West Germany, evidence shows that in the early days after the war, the British worried about the return of German nationalism. Later they carefully watched German debates: the British were reassured by Bonn's willingness to confront the past, and were reassured by the absence of nationalist themes.

The comparison of Japanese and German remembrance raises a new, important puzzle that I discuss at length in the book's conclusion. Japan's modest efforts to apologize and pay reparations repeatedly triggered sharp outcry among conservatives, who justified and even denied past atrocities. Japanese contrition—because of the nature of the debates it triggered—had the effect of alarming Japan's neighbors. In Germany, by contrast, far more ambitious efforts at contrition did not provoke a similar backlash. Many West German conservatives preferred to emphasize a more positive national history, but opponents of contrition did not deny or glorify Nazi crimes. The French thus viewed West German struggles with the past as healthy, cathartic experiences for the country's democratic development— and as a positive signal of its intentions.

Whether or not contrition promotes international reconciliation thus seems to depend on the nature of the national debates that it provokes. In the conclusion I argue that backlash is a predictable response to efforts to apologize. This is evident not only in Japan, but also in the United States, France, Austria, Great Britain, and Australia. The conclusion describes the links between contrition and backlash and provides an explanation for why West German debates played out so differently.

## Implications for Policy and Scholarship

Should countries apologize for past human rights abuses? This is a normative question, which ultimately this book cannot answer. Offering victims the contrition they deserve is laudable, and this book shows that denials of the violence they suffered are detrimental to international reconciliation. However this study uncovers risks associated with contrition, and shows that more is not always better, or even necessary, for countries to repair their relations.

Findings from this book suggest the need to balance the demands of foreign and domestic audiences. If leaders seek to reconcile relations with past adversaries, they should encourage remembrance in ways that reduce the risk of domestic backlash. Countries might stage bilateral commemoration that emphasizes shared tragedies or triumphs rather than one country's victimization at the hands of the other. Alternatively, multilateral settings can provide political cover to perpetrator countries by deemphasizing any single country's guilt. International textbook commissions—used in Europe and more recently in Asia—offer a way for countries to negotiate their historical narratives.[9] The key attribute of such strategies is that they balance the need to acknowledge past violence against the need to prevent damaging backlash.

This book also has implications for recent strategies adopted by the international community. National governments, international institutions, and NGOs are increasingly pressuring countries guilty of human rights violations to atone. "Naming and shaming" has met with success in some issue areas, and analysts should think about how it might be usefully applied in this realm.[10] Pressuring countries to atone has the benefit of raising awareness of past human rights violations, both globally and within the culpable country. At the same time, it is likely to create backlash within the targeted country, which damages relations with former victims. If international pressure alienates moderates and empowers the nationalist Right, this backlash may also have domestic political effects that the international community might find troubling. As noted above, this does not mean there is no role for the international community with respect to encouraging remembrance. Its institutions can provide forums in which countries are encouraged to confront their pasts in a more multilateral, and less accusatory, fashion.

In addition to its policy implications, this book contributes to scholarship on international relations and justice. It informs theoretical debates about how states perceive threats. Providing empirical support for the role of intentions in threat perception, it demonstrates the importance of a previously understudied signal of intentions (remembrance). More broadly, this book contributes to a growing literature that has begun to empirically test the effects of ideas on international security outcomes.[11]

This book also makes contributions to the study of political memory and international justice. It creates an analytic framework for conceptualizing and measuring remembrance that can be used to answer a plethora of other research questions in international relations and in the study of civil wars and transitional justice.[12] Scholars of transitional justice have debated whether or not leaders responsible for human rights violations should be prosecuted for their crimes after they have left office. Contrary to the "legalist" school that favors prosecutions, my findings support the arguments of scholars who highlight the destabilizing "spoiler" effects of legal prosecutions and thus recommend amnesties.[13]

This book uncovers a powerful dilemma, and offers an imperfect solution. A country's acknowledgment of its past atrocities is important to move relations forward with its former adversaries. However, coming to terms with the past is an unpredictable process that is as likely to antagonize as soothe relations with former victims. To be sure, a policy that compromises remembrance and justice in service of political reconciliation—in order to preemptively silence nationalist ire—will offend activists and individual victims such as Kim Hak-soon, the survivor of the sex slave program whose heartbreaking call for recognition opened this chapter. However, if the goal is international rather than individual healing, remembrance that is sensitive to the risks of backlash will be the most effective at promoting reconciliation.

# CHAPTER ONE

# Remembrance and Reconciliation

The past is never dead. It's not even past.
—William Faulkner

Criticism of Japanese impenitence and praise for German contrition rest on an implicit and untested claim that remembrance affects international reconciliation. A theory linking remembrance to reconciliation—one that has clearly defined variables and causal mechanisms and makes testable predictions—is necessary to test this claim.

Countries might experience different stages of reconciliation ranging from a tense ceasefire to a true reconciliation that reflects friendship and trust. An essential first step toward the latter outcome is an absence of threat perception. In other words, before countries can start thinking of one another as friends, they must cease to see each other as enemies. The question of how countries might reach a deeper level of reconciliation (i.e., a strong sense of community and affinity) is beyond the scope of this work.[1] Rather, this book examines the momentous transformation from a state of fear and hatred between countries to a normal state of relations unencumbered by distrust. I posit that unapologetic remembrance (i.e., forgetting, denying, or glorifying past atrocities) elevates threat perception and inhibits reconciliation. Conversely, apologetic remembrance (or "contrition") reduces threat perception and promotes reconciliation.

International relations scholars are divided on what drives threat perception. Neorealists argue that states perceive threats primarily from material capabilities: military power, national wealth, and geography.[2] Leaders make little effort to divine a state's intentions—and do not factor them heavily into threat assessments—because intentions cannot be reliably judged and may quickly change. Others argue that the neorealist emphasis on material capabilities is too narrow: that perceptions of a country's intentions also affect how threatening it appears.[3]

Scholars have highlighted several factors that convey information about a state's intentions. Democratic peace theorists focus on *regime*

9

*type;* according to John Owen, for example, "Liberals believe that they understand the intentions of foreign liberal democracies, and that those intentions are always pacific toward fellow liberal democracies."[4] Because democratic countries have greater trust in one another, they are less likely to experience the suspicion and fear that underpins the security dilemma.[5] The benign effects of the democratic peace, however, would not be evident during a democratic transition: because democratizing states are prone to conflict, other countries are likely to be wary of their intentions.[6]

Scholars have also argued that a country's membership in *international institutions* signals information about its intentions: these institutions increase transparency, reduce miscalculations, and raise alarms when any one member adopts a more aggressive posture. In contrast to ad hoc interaction, writes Celeste Wallander, "an established framework of negotiation makes it easier for states to evaluate patterns of policies and thus intentions."[7] Constraints imposed by institutions—for example, demilitarized zones, ceilings on armed forces, or restrictions on weapons purchases—decrease state power in the short term. Although a country still could decide to withdraw from an institution and build up its military power, the institution creates a potentially important time delay between potential and mobilized power. A state's willingness to accept such constraints thus signals that it probably does not intend to pursue aggression in the near future. In these ways, institutions promote trust among members.

Membership in institutions that do not impose real constraints on member behavior—"talk shops"—may contribute somewhat to a country's cooperative image but generally convey little information about intentions. If membership is without cost and might improve a country's image, peaceful and potentially aggressive countries alike would be willing to join; membership would not distinguish between them. Membership in institutions that make substantive demands on their members—and have mechanisms for monitoring compliance—provides a more reliable signal of a country's intentions.

States also judge each other's intentions on the basis of *territorial disputes.* Although such disputes might be resolved peacefully, the threat always exists that the claiming state might attempt to seize territory by force. Thus the owner of disputed territory will be suspicious of the other's intentions.[8] Countries without land at stake in the dispute might also distrust the claiming state's intentions: Neighbors may fear that the existence of the dispute increases the likelihood of conflict; that the claiming state may expand its war aims beyond the acquisition of that one piece of territory; or that the use of force might have other unpredictable and destabilizing regional consequences.

## The Link between Remembrance and Intentions

As a state evaluates another country's intentions, it is likely to observe how that country remembers past violence. Remembrance might affect perceptions of intentions through at least three processes. First, remembrance can be viewed as a "costly signal" that a country does not intend to adopt an aggressive posture. Building on a large economics literature, international relations scholars distinguish between "cheap talk" and signals that are more credible because they require the sender to pay real costs or make real sacrifices (either economically or strategically).[9] Most previous studies of costly signaling have focused on signals related to material power (e.g., disarmament). In principle, however, countries could also send costly signals through their ideas.[10] According to this reasoning, if contrition is costly for aggressive countries, it will convey credible evidence that a country is no longer aggressive.

This mechanism posits that remembrance is a costly signal because of its link to domestic mobilization. Mobilizing a country for war requires not only weapons and troops but also support within the military and the general public.[11] To prepare a society to fight, leaders rally nationalistic and patriotic sentiment; in doing so, they often vilify the adversary while glorifying their own state's history, motives, and current goals.[12] Historically, countries that have been intent on aggression have mobilized their publics by whitewashing and glorifying their country's past violence and scapegoating the intended victim as the cause of the country's ills.[13]

Contrition complicates such rallying efforts by teaching the population about their country's past violence: conferring respect upon the victim, and delegitimizing violence against it. In countries schooled about their own past wrongs, "permissible lies" within public discourse are less common and less tolerated; whitewashed, mythologized versions of the past will encounter opposition.[14] Nationalists wanting to mobilize the public will be forced to reeducate them in order to swing public opinion in favor of war. Reeducation may confront opposition from actors within the media, academe, or other independent evaluative institutions; at the very least, it delays mobilization.[15] For this reason, countries that remember and atone for past violence are signaling that they are unlikely to adopt aggressive strategies. Contrition thus constitutes a costly signal because, as Robert Jervis has written, it is "behavior that is felt to be too important or costly in its own right to be used for other ends."[16]

It is important to note that this argument pivots on the assertion that contrition interferes with domestic mobilization. This may not be so; or the time delay required for reeducation may be negligible. In other words, if public opinion is easily and quickly malleable, a regime may be able to quickly reverse it.[17] It is also possible that apologetic views of past violence can coexist with a willingness to use force in defense of national interests or security. Because many—if not all—expansionist wars have been fought in the name of self-defense, contrition would not be much of a limiting factor if this were so. Finally, contrition would not inhibit domestic mobilization if it triggered domestic backlash. If the public opposes contrition, voters might choose to empower rightist politicians under the mandate of "restore our national pride" and "stop kowtowing to foreigners." Such was the fear of a 1943 British Foreign Office policy paper, which argued that efforts to reeducate Germans would backfire because such interference would only "harden their unrepentant hearts."[18] If contrition provokes backlash, it could actually *increase* (not decrease) a state's level of nationalistic mobilization.

Contrition could convey information about a country's intentions through a second mechanism quite different from costly signaling. A growing body of international relations theory observes that interactions between countries are shaped by the way they perceive each other's identities, as formed in particular historical and regional contexts. Countries do not view each other as "billiard balls" with identical or inscrutable intentions; rather, they learn through repeated interactions whom they can trust and whom they must fear.[19] States that treat each other well can, over time, learn to trust each other; they can develop shared understandings and a sense of "we-feeling."[20] According to this view, countries expect goodwill from those they consider friendly and expect hostility from those they view as enemies; they also interpret others' behavior in a manner that is consistent with—and hence reinforces—these expectations.[21]

Remembrance may be a critical factor that shapes how states perceive each other's identities.[22] As Consuelo Cruz points out, "*How* we remember shapes *what* we imagine as possible." If a country justifies or glorifies violent policies, others will fear that the country still considers them viable tools of statecraft. Refusals to offer contrition also convey disdain for the other country's suffering and indifference toward bilateral relations. On the other hand, repudiation of past violence shows that the country considers such behavior outside the "field of imaginable possibilities" for national policy.[23] Contrition suggests that the country holds different values today than it did when it committed the acts. By offering recognition and respect for the other state's suffering, a country shows it wants to restore good relations. Apologies and other acts thus can demonstrate the way a former adversary has changed, pave the way for the former victim to forgive, and help construct a new image of a former enemy.[24] In these ways contrition may help transform the images the two countries have of each other—and the nature of their relations—from adversarial to friendly.

It is possible, however, that contrition does not alter states' identities as expected. Whereas some scholars emphasize the potential for identities to evolve, others emphasize that they are deeply rooted, self-reinforcing, and thus hard to dislodge.[25] Friendly acts from a trusted ally reinforce positive feelings; the same friendly acts from an enemy often trigger suspicion. In this light, contrition from a former adversary may be seen as strategically motivated: designed to improve its international image, or perhaps to lull the former victim into complacency. Unless contrition is repeated, institutionalized, and sustained for decades, it may lack the power to transform deeply held antagonistic images.

Alternatively, remembrance could influence perception of intentions through its cognitive or emotional effects on observers. The way a country remembers or forgets past violence leads others to have positive or negative feelings about that country. Neta Crawford argues that if a state is viewed positively, observers frame its ambiguous behavior as "neutral, positive, or motivated by circumstances other than hostile intentions." Conversely, resentment about the way a country denies or forgets its past violence may lead to negative evaluations of ambiguous behavior. A desire for cognitive consistency is said to exacerbate this tendency.[26]

According to this mechanism, remembrance—specifically, unapologetic remembrance—influences perception of a country's intentions because of its powerful effects on the cognition or emotions of observers. Contrition acknowledges the suffering and the humanity of victims. Apologies, reparations, and so on are signs of respect: they reflect a belief that a country is too important to treat poorly. By contrast, a country's denials, glorification, or whitewashing of past atrocities signal contempt for a people, for their country's status, and for the future of the bilateral relationship. This affront triggers emotions of anger and wounded pride among victims, creating hostility toward the other state that will influence assessments of its policies or military capabilities.

This mechanism (unlike the others) should not be expected to work in both directions. In other words, although unapologetic remembrance should be expected to generate a powerful negative response, feelings of goodwill generated by contrition are unlikely to be as intense. Victims feel that they deserve recognition of their suffering; receiving it is seen as proper and right. It is precisely the perceived violation of this social norm that creates such strong emotion when such gestures are withheld.

The mechanisms described here link remembrance to threat perception in very different ways; through costly signaling, through an evolution in countries' intersubjective identities, or through the emotional and cognitive responses of observers. The empirical cases in this book test these causal processes as they evaluate the connection between remembrance and threat perception.

CONCEPTUALIZING REMEMBRANCE

What constitutes "remembrance"? Countries remember past violence through both official and unofficial channels. Because other countries are interested in assessing a government's intentions (i.e., whether or not a regime might pursue aggression), observers will assess government policies related to remembrance. Government policy is also the most transparent and accessible indicator of how a country remembers. But observers will also be interested in gauging the views of the broader society. If the population remembers the past in ways very differently than its government, leaders will have to work harder to gain popular support as they pursue their policy goals. Moreover, the views of wider society are relevant because a regime may be one election or coup away from leaving office.[27]

*Official Remembrance.* Governments reveal their interpretations of past violence through numerous instruments. Leaders' statements are one example. One might contend that statements are not a credible signal; for example, they may not reflect popular sentiment, they might be offered for strategic reasons, or they might only be fleeting gestures. However, such statements should not be dismissed: They influence a country's official historical record and provide leadership in other areas in society (for example, setting agendas for scholarly research and civic activism, shaping textbook coverage, and influencing litigation). Reactions to statements also serve as credible signals; if a politician is fired or demoted as a result of something he or she said, this action clarifies what a government believes are acceptable views about the past. An example is the 2002 resignation of Trent Lott as U.S. Senate majority leader after his statements that appeared to express support for racial segregation.

Remembrance that will influence observers' views the most is that which is institutionalized within laws or policies. Institutionalization reflects a certain level of national support for a given historical interpretation (because it requires laws to be passed) and shows that the interpretation will be transmitted to future generations. The historical interpretation, in other words, is not only currently prevalent but is likely to be around for some time. One example is national *reparations* paid to former victims. Parliamentary reparations require agreement among a majority of elected officials; their support for such legislation likely reflects confidence in their constituents' support. The U.S. government's decision to pay reparations to Japanese-American citizens interned during World War II constitutes official government condemnation of the wartime policy of internment; it confirms the existence of the event and clarifies it as unjust for the official historical record.

Governments may also decide to hold perpetrators of past violence accountable in *legal trials.* Some scholars argue that trials reduce the chance that a country will engage in future violence through preemption (the removal of potential recidivists from society through imprisonment) and through deterrence (e.g., of potential human rights violators through threat of future punishment).[28] Trials help establish an official historical record by

14

uncovering and disseminating evidence about past violence. Israeli leader David Ben-Gurion advocated the 1961 trial of Holocaust planner Adolf Eichmann for this reason; indeed, it was only after this trial that a more comprehensive understanding of the Holocaust became widely publicized within Israel and throughout the world.[29]

Governments also remember the past through *commemoration:* national monuments, museums, ceremonies, and holidays. By deciding to erect a monument, build a museum, or commemorate a national holiday in honor of a person or event, a government confers recognition and honor. Because commemoration is scarce—countries can have only so many monuments in their capital cities and a limited number of national holidays—and because numerous candidates compete for memorialization, the people and events that a country chooses to honor are important indicators of prevailing political opinion and national priorities.[30]

One of the most important ways countries institutionalize remembrance of past violence is through history *education.* Leaders' statements may be ephemeral and may not represent the views of the country as a whole; textbooks, on the other hand, are the central vehicle through which a government transmits national identity to a country's young people.[31] Charles Merriam notes that although citizens are educated in many ways, public education is designed to be the most systematic and organized effort to influence the next generation.[32] According to David Mendeloff, textbooks shape a country's view of itself and others. "Answers to central questions such as 'Why have we gone to war in the past, and who was to blame?' 'Why have other countries attacked us?' and 'Why have we attacked other countries?' define a nation's self-image, and its image of others. These are essentially simple, yet fundamental questions that lie at the core of a nation's self-image."[33] As noted earlier, historically regimes intent on aggression have used their educational systems to deploy nationalist myths that whitewash past aggression and scapegoat intended victims. Because of the link between history education, national self-image, and national policy, battles over textbooks—between groups with different visions of patriotism and different policy goals—are common all over the world.[34] The centrality of textbooks to national identity and policy make them an important indicator of a country's intentions. In sum, governments shape national remembrance through all of these various policy instruments, which are highly credible indicators of how the current government interprets past violence and, because of institutionalization, show how the country is likely to remember its past for years to come.

*Remembrance in Wider Society.* To get the most representative picture of a country's attitudes, observers will also assess how the broader society remembers past violence. Although official policies strongly affect how people remember, a government does not have complete control over national discourses; leaders who try to "instrumentalize" remembrance may spark public debates that evolve in unanticipated and disadvantageous ways.[35] It is precisely this imperfect control that makes remembrance in wider society a highly credible signal of national sentiment. As Robert Jervis maintains, a signal is more credible when a government is unable to control that aspect of its behavior.[36] Wider society both reacts to government policy and engages in its own discussions of the past; in such debates, participants delineate the acceptable range of discourse about past violence.

To assess societal views, I examine the statements and writings of mainstream opinion leaders: members of the political opposition and public intellectuals. I do not incorporate the views of actors on the fringes that exist in every society (e.g., neo-Nazis on the far Right; anarchists on the far Left). Rather, I endeavor to assess the range of respectable opinion within a society.

To be clear, remembrance as I define it is only a subset of phenomena that could be categorized as "national" or "collective" memory.[37] This book explicitly focuses on (1) official statements and policies about past violence and (2) statements by individuals in wider society; and tests their effects on observers' perceptions. My coding of remembrance does not attempt to capture the full complexity of a country's collective memory or strong variations in views, feelings, or sense of culpability within the society. Rather, I seek to determine whether the most observable expressions of the ways a people remember past violence affect others' perceptions of their country's intentions.

## WHAT IS "APOLOGETIC"?

Different cultures have different protocol surrounding apologies—both in what offenses require an apology and how apologies should be offered. Americans, for example, do not offer apologies with the deep bow required of a Japanese. But social psychologists have identified core components of apologies that transcend cultures; an apology requires admitting past misdeeds and expressing remorse for them.[38]

The most apologetic remembrance is that which thoroughly addresses both admission and remorse. The events in question are enumerated and explained in detail; agency is clear (i.e., *I* did this to *you*); remorse is conveyed through the tone, scale, or symbolism of the gesture. An example of an apology is a statement by F. W. de Klerk in 1993: the South African leader acknowledged that apartheid had forced people from their homes, restricted their freedom and jobs, and attacked their dignity. He said that he and his party "deeply regretted" the misery of apartheid.[39] Remembrance might be somewhat apologetic: it might convey some regret while offering a vague or incomplete list of past violence. For example, Serbian President Svetozar Marovic stated in 2003, "I want to apologize for all evils that any citizens of Serbia and Montenegro inflicted upon or committed against anyone in Croatia."[40] This statement reflects remorse but specifies no wrongdoing. Moving toward the middle of the continuum, countries might acknowledge that they committed harmful violence against another country, but not apologize for having done so (i.e., admission without remorse).

On the other side of the spectrum is unapologetic remembrance, which either fails to admit past wrongdoing or fails to express remorse for it. The classic nonapology among scandal-ridden politicians or corporate leaders is: "If my remarks gave anyone offense, I regret it." U.S. Senator Robert Packwood—accused of sexually harassing a dozen female staffers—said in 1994, "I'm apologizing for the conduct that it was alleged that I did." Unapologetic remembrance might justify past violence (admission without remorse), or deny it (no admission, no remorse). Unapologetic remembrance may glorify past actions (admission and praise rather than remorse). Or countries may simply not remember past violence at all; they might obscure the past through "passive collusion" not to discuss a particular episode in public. Such amnesia may include focusing on one's own suffering rather than on the suffering of victims.[41]

Unapologetic remembrance in all of its guises—historically the norm—remains common across the world. Amnesia was rampant in Western Europe after World War II; Tony Judt argues that countries substituted forward-looking "founding myths" about the idea of Europe for painful memories of collaboration and culpability. Turkey does not recognize as a genocide the ethnic cleansing and killing of a million Armenians from 1915 to 1917 (indeed, calling these killings a "genocide" is punishable under Turkish law). Iranian president Ahmadinejad calls the Holocaust a "myth." For many years, American education glorified westward expansion and mythologized that Native Americans died from disease instead of war and ethnic cleansing. Contemporary Russian textbook guidelines celebrate Joseph Stalin as "the most successful leader of the USSR" while ignoring his mass deportations and killings of millions of people. Chinese textbooks laud Mao Zedong's leadership and neglect to mention the tens of millions of Chinese people who perished in the famines and forced relocations caused by his policies.[42]

Assessing the quality of a country's remembrance during a given time period requires a method of aggregating official and societal remembrance. Remembrance is most *apologetic* when a government pursues a wide spectrum of apologetic policies (e.g., statements, reparations, commemoration, and education), and the statements and actions of wider society also reflect contrition. Remembrance is somewhat apologetic when a government admits and repudiates past violence through a few isolated policies (e.g., a major treaty or apology), and the wider society endorses these policies.

A country's remembrance is somewhat *unapologetic* if minimal government efforts to atone are met with uninterest or skepticism in society. Lack of interest might stem from people's preoccupation with their own suffering or from the belief that the country, and its relationships with others, is better served by looking forward rather than backward. Still further toward the unapologetic end of the spectrum is a society that responds to government contrition with denunciations and outright denials. At the most unapologetic extreme, neither the government nor the broader society admits or repudiates past violence; they may deny that it occurred or glorify it as heroic.

The theory developed here makes predictions about the effect of remembrance on threat perception. The more that a country's remembrance is apologetic, the more positively others should view its intentions. *Ceteris paribus,* a country's intentions should be judged as friendly if a government pursues a range of apologetic policies and if the broader society endorses and defends such contrition. If official contrition meets with indifference or skepticism among the population, this should neither be particularly reassuring nor alarming. Remembrance *should* be alarming, however, if official contrition provokes justifications, denials, or glorification in wider society. For in this scenario contrition is associated only with the present regime; an unrepentant (and potentially hostile) government is a mere election or coup away. A country's intentions will appear the most hostile when *both* official and societal remembrance denies or glorifies past violence.

## AVOIDING CODING PITFALLS

To assess the extent to which a country is apologetic about past misdeeds, I code its official and societal remembrance. Critics of this approach may maintain that this method misses a critical dimension: the *victim's* perspective. An apology is an inherently intersubjective act, one might argue; only a victim can decide when a gesture is apologetic.

Although it is reasonable to speculate that a victim's willingness to accept an apology influences the likelihood of reconciliation, using aspects of the victim's *response* to an apology to measure the *existence* of an apology invites serious problems of inference. Namely, evidence disconfirming the connection between apologies and reconciliation would be systematically overlooked. For example, imagine that victims typically reject apologies, and apologies therefore have little effect on reconciliation. But if scholars only considered remembrance to be "apologetic" when the victim accepts apologies, they would overlook a great deal of disconfirming evidence by treating most cases—those in which the apology was rejected by the victim—as if no apologies had been offered in the first place. In other words, allowing victims to determine when an apology has been issued would conflate *acceptance* of an apology with the *issuance* of an apology, biasing findings in favor of the theory that apologies facilitate reconciliation.

One might also argue that remembrance should be judged based on the motivations behind it. For example, one might dismiss Japan's post-World

War II reparations to Southeast Asia as not apologetic because Tokyo was only seeking to build markets for its exports. The problem with this method, however, is that it is impossible to reliably ascertain the intentions behind a given policy at the time: let alone decades later. The criteria described here for evaluating remembrance, especially the use of societal responses to government policy, are likely to distinguish cynical gestures from sincere ones.

Finally, one might criticize the narrowness of my definition of remembrance. After all, countries also show their interpretations of the past through the activities of citizens' groups and in their art, literature, and film; such activities are not represented in my coding. There are good reasons to include such factors; doing so paints a richer picture of memory within a country. There are also downsides to including these factors, however. More nuanced codings are more difficult to replicate and more difficult to aggregate. The advantage of my approach is that—by including both official and societal elements—it captures a broad segment of remembrance within a country; however, by relying on the most observable indicators of memory, it lends itself better to replication.

## Methods

One essential step toward reconciliation between former enemies is a substantial reduction in the level of threat they perceive from each other. To explore the link between remembrance and threat perception, I evaluate (1) the extent to which remembrance affects perceptions of a country's intentions and (2) the extent to which remembrance—relative to other signals of intentions and to capabilities—drives overall threat assessment.

To evaluate how one country perceives another country's intentions, I examine the *statements* made by the general public and elites and look for indications of trust or suspicion. For public "statements" I rely on public opinion polls and media coverage;[43] for elite statements I consult archival documents, secondary sources, memoirs, and elite-authored scholarly articles and op-eds. To assess contemporary perceptions, I conducted interviews with government officials, academics, journalists, and think-tank analysts. In the written documents and interviews, I look for evidence that the author or interviewee believes the other state has benign, uncertain, or hostile intentions toward his or her country. Indications that a person feels affinity, trust, or a general sense of community with a former enemy state suggest that they perceive benign intentions. At the opposite end, observers perceive hostile intentions when they say they dislike and distrust a state.

To examine how strongly remembrance affects overall threat perception I look at public and elite *statements* (using sources similar to those above) to determine whether or not people believe the other country to be a security threat. I also assess *state policy* (defense policy, diplomacy, etc.) for what it conveys about threat perception. For example, against whom is the state configuring its military forces? Against whom, and with whom, does it seek alliances? I evaluate whether a state's diplomacy tries to punish, isolate, or support the other country, and whether its policies reflect concerns about relative gains.

In countries with *low* threat perception, the public and elites express no concern about a military conflict between the two states; no one expects disputes to escalate to the military level. People do not fear the other country's military or economic gains. State policy reflects similar equanimity; the state does not configure military forces or cultivate allies to defend itself against the other country. At the other extreme, *high* threat perception is evident in statements expressing the fear that the other country is an imminent threat. People worry that bilateral disputes will be resolved through force. State policy is adversarial: The state configures military forces against the other country; it finds allies to protect itself; through diplomacy it attempts to weaken and alienate the other country. In between these two extremes are countries with *moderate* threat perception; public and elite statements express uncertainty about whether or not the other state is a security threat; state policy reflects hedging, with perhaps some sensitivity to relative gains. Diplomacy may be cooperative in some areas and competitive in others.

One criticism of this method—specifically of the use of policies to measure perceptions of intentions and threat—is that governments adopt policies for a multitude of reasons. A government's decision to procure certain military capabilities, to pursue hard-line or conciliatory diplomacy toward another state, or even to use military force might be motivated by domestic factors rather than by its perceptions of another state.[44] For example, perhaps a country's decision to acquire aircraft carriers reflects not fear of a nearby maritime power but rather the navy's influence in the domestic policymaking process. Or a regime's competitive diplomacy—for example, opposing another state's leadership in international institutions, lobbying for sanctions against it, or canceling summits or other diplomatic activities—may not be the result of distrust or threat perception: rather, it may stem from the government's desire to scapegoat the other country for its own domestic political purposes.

The possibility that policies may not accurately reflect a government's perceptions of threats and intentions from another power is an important caveat when relying on policies as an indicator of sentiment, and I discuss it further in the cases of South Korea and China (chapters 2 and 4). However, I use multiple indicators to assess perceptions of intentions and threat: in effect "triangulating" perceptions by relying not only on policies but also on private and public statements of leaders and on popular sentiment. Although it may be true that some policies are undertaken for reasons unrelated to levels of distrust, the use of multiple indicators—particularly statements conveyed in private communications such as interviews—increases our confidence that this evidence is a legitimate signal of perceptions of intentions and threat.

## TESTING THE THEORY

To test the effects of remembrance on perceptions of intentions and threat, I rely on congruence procedure using multiple within-case observations as well as extensive evidence about the reasoning of government officials, journalists, scholars, and the public.[45] For the congruence testing, I divide the post-World War II era into smaller time periods, which creates more observations on the independent variable (remembrance) and thus more tests of the theory. To draw valid inferences from the evidence, I define the periods so that they do not span a time during which there was significant fluctuation in the value of the key independent variable. For example, consider a situation in which a country's remembrance was *unapologetic* between 1940 and 1950 and its intentions were seen as hostile; remembrance was *apologetic* between 1950 and 1960 and intentions were seen as friendly. It would be unsound to create a period that spans 1940–1960, because this would lead the values to be "averaged out," obscuring otherwise clear congruence between remembrance and perceptions of intentions. In general, periods should be defined to encompass a time in which the independent variable did not vary significantly; as long as this is the case, periods may be further subdivided without biasing findings.

After dividing the post-World War II era into smaller time periods, I code remembrance and threat perception and compare their covariation over time to determine whether more apologetic remembrance corresponds with more benign perceptions of intentions and with lower levels of threat perception.

One cannot draw conclusions from congruence procedure alone because, as noted, other factors influence threat perception. Understanding the relative influence of remembrance thus requires monitoring changes in *alternate variables*. With this in mind I monitor territorial claims, regime type,[46] institutional membership, and capabilities.

I define capabilities as the power that one state can bring to bear against another. Power includes *potential power*, which I define as wealth (measured by GDP) and population; it also includes *mobilized power*, defined as military expenditure and the number of standing military forces. The capabilities a state can bring to bear are also affected by *constraints*. Constraints include the presence of an occupier, an "offshore balancer," or a balancing coalition.[47] Another constraint might be the existence of a threat that ties up military forces on one front or otherwise consumes resources, reducing the state's ability to menace others. A strong constraint would be the presence of an occupier's or offshore balancer's military forces stationed within a country and the existence of an institutionalized security agreement. The strength of constraints imposed by other security threats is measured in terms of the military power of those other states; namely, State A is more constrained in its ability to menace State B if facing other powerful adversaries. In sum, a country with a high level of capabilities enjoys a high level of both potential and mobilized power that is unconstrained by either security threats or the presence of foreign military forces. As I test for the effects of remembrance, I monitor changes in capabilities—as well as changes in alternate variables affecting perceptions of intentions—to determine whether these other factors might be driving fluctuations in threat perception.

To bolster the congruence testing, I examine the reasoning of government officials, journalists, scholars, and members of the public as they explain their views about the former adversary's intentions and threat. If remembrance really does affect perceptions of intentions, then observers should say so: in other words, they should specifically link their views of the other state to its remembrance of past violence. People should say, for example, that a country's denials, glorifications, and justifications of past violence make it appear hostile today. Conversely, they should connect their trust of a former adversary to that country's contrition.

Different versions of the hypothesis that remembrance affects threat perception are possible. One formulation (which I call the "strong" version) expects that a country's remembrance will dominate other signals that influence threat perception. This version of the theory would work through the cognitive/emotional mechanism discussed earlier. It predicts that if a country denies or glorifies its past atrocities, the outrage these denials create will overwhelm efforts to coolly assess capabilities, territorial issues, and so forth. In other words, because observers are so angry about a country's denials, they exaggerate the malignance of its capabilities or policies. According to this version of the theory, unapologetic remembrance should correlate with distrust and high threat perception. Discussion of remembrance should also be a major theme in observers' reasoning.

A "weak" version of the theory expects observers to evaluate remembrance along with a myriad of other factors as they assess threat. This version of the theory might work through the other mechanisms posited earlier (i.e., related to domestic mobilization or identity). It predicts that if a country's remembrance is unapologetic, *ceteris paribus*, distrust and threat perception will be elevated. However, if other factors are reassuring, threat perception will not necessarily be high. Conversely, if a former adversary has shown a great deal of contrition, but has also amassed powerful offensive military capabilities and pursued hard-line policies in its territorial disputes, it may be perceived as threatening. In other words, contrition will be reassuring, but not to the extent that it outweighs concerns about other alarming signals.

The strong version of the theory fails if an unapologetic country is not feared. However, the weak version of the theory is not falsifiable using congruence evidence alone. Given a contrite country, either low or high threat perception would be consistent with the theory. The weak version of the theory can, however, be falsified using process tracing: it fails if observers discussing the other state do not link their perceptions to remembrance, but instead discuss alternate variables.

This book conducts two case studies: the effects of Japan's remembrance on its relations with South Korea and the effects of German remembrance on Franco-German reconciliation. I selected the Japanese and German cases for several reasons. They are the classic cases through which the topic of apologies has entered the lexicon of international relations, and they provide substantial variation in remembrance. In addition, choosing to study Japanese and German remembrance controls for many factors: both countries suffered defeat during World War II, both gradually gained autonomy after a period of occupation, and both were allied with the United States in the Western alliance system. Finally, Germany is the strongest regional power in Europe, and Japan is its Asian counterpart: studying these countries is important simply because they are great powers that play a pivotal role in regional stability in Asia and Europe.

I selected *South Korean* perceptions of Japan and *French* perceptions of Germany on the basis of several criteria. First, South Korea and France were significantly victimized. One would expect such countries to be highly attuned to threats—or lack thereof—from their former adversaries. Second, these dyads are strategically significant: relations between France and Germany and between South Korea and Japan have important regional security implications. Finally, the cases are "study-able" from the standpoint of availability and accessibility of evidence.

This research design might prompt a variety of critiques. One criticism might be that the two cases are too disparate for a comparison to be useful. Although the French were brutalized in many ways, they suffered less during their occupation than did Koreans. The Germans did not attempt to eradicate French identity and culture. The occupations were also very different in length: Whereas Korea experienced thirty-five years of Japanese colonization, France was occupied for four.

No comparison of cases is perfect: Korea probably suffered more material and emotional hardships than did the French. But in some ways French reconciliation with Germany should have appeared a more remote possibility than Korean reconciliation with Japan. The French had recently fought three wars with Germany. Following World War II, they knew about the atrocities the Germans had committed across Europe. In 1945 there was little reason to hope the Germans would change their ways, and apparently no limit to the cruelties the Germans were willing to commit. For all the French knew, the Germans might try to do in the future to the French what they had done to the Jews and Slavs. Only the benefit of hindsight makes the Germans look easy to forgive by comparison to the Japanese; in 1945, it would have been quite natural to expect that Franco-German relations would be poisoned for decades.

Future studies might build on this project, use my data on German and Japanese remembrance, and evaluate the theory in countries that experienced extreme brutality. In the case of Germany, such countries might include Russia and Poland. These studies would have merit, but there are good reasons to begin, as I did here, with France. First, because of restrictions on the media throughout the Warsaw Pact, German contrition was not widely reported; contrition cannot reconcile enemies if their leaders, journalists, and other opinion elites are denied critical information about another country's contrite behavior. Second, efforts to measure perceptions of intentions and threat would be difficult in cases involving Cold War enemies. At various times in the Cold War, Warsaw Pact countries sought to portray West Germany as a hotbed of neo-Nazi militarism; at other times, they sought to reach out to Bonn to divide it from NATO. Both of these motivations complicate efforts to measure true sentiments in Russia or Poland about a German threat. Finally, studies that track the perceptions of Cold War enemies will inevitably risk conflating the animosities arising from Cold War disputes with the hatreds stemming from past atrocities. To be clear, evidence from these cases may be illuminating and should be gathered; however, there are strong reasons to begin the process of theory testing with cases that minimize these problems.

One might also critique this research design because of concerns about selection bias. Indeed, the cases studied here are not typical; they involve some of the most egregious violence in world history. This fact biases some of the empirical conclusions. The good news is that the direction of the bias is predictable, and it works to reinforce my findings. Specifically, domestic backlash to contrition will be more likely if a country's culpability is ambiguous (and certainly if it is manufactured); denials will be less likely if events are widely known and well documented. Furthermore, egregious violence is more difficult to glorify than morally ambiguous actions. Thus by studying Korean and French perceptions of Japanese and German remembrance of violence during World War II, I study a set of events for which domestic backlash should be relatively unlikely to occur. My finding that contrition tends to trigger backlash is therefore reinforced by the egregious nature of the violence committed by Japan and Germany. I discuss this issue in greater detail in the conclusion.

One might also criticize this research design by arguing that any generalization about remembrance and reconciliation will be impossible from the small number of cases examined. For example, one might argue that findings from the Korea-Japan case are idiosyncratic: that is, related to factors unique to the Korea-Japan historical experience or to factors unique to either country, such as domestic politics or culture. With this in mind, I examine three additional cases—Chinese and Australian perceptions of Japan and British perceptions of Germany—to see whether my findings appear to be upheld elsewhere. These cases provide broader support for my findings.

As a "small-n" case study, the results from this project cannot serve as the last word on the effects of remembrance on interstate reconciliation. Further testing is needed to determine whether its findings and implications are broadly generalizable in relations between states and whether the findings might also apply to relations between subgroups.[48] Nonetheless, this book makes important contributions to literature on both memory and international relations. It offers a conceptualization and operationalization of national remembrance and apologies; it theoretically develops and outlines mechanisms through which remembrance might affect reconciliation; it empirically tests a theory of remembrance and reconciliation in prominent case studies; and it explores the plausibility of findings in additional cases.

# CHAPTER TWO

# An Unhappy Phase in a Certain Period

> The war inflicted horrific, indescribable suffering on many
> people in Asia and throughout the world. Reflecting deeply on
> the agony and sorrow of those people, I wish to express my
> deep remorse and humbly offer my heartfelt condolences.
>
> —Japanese Prime Minister Murayama Tomiichi,
> August 1994

> I do not think Japan intended to wage a war of aggression. . . .
> It was thanks to Japan that most nations in Asia were able to
> throw off the shackles of colonial rule under European
> domination and to win independence.
>
> —Sakurai Shin, member of the Murayama Cabinet,
> August 1994

In the late 1990s, relations between Japan and the Republic of Korea (ROK) warmed perceptibly. Shared fears of North Korea prompted increased political and military cooperation; opportunities for economic exchange soared with the ROK's repeal of a long-standing ban on Japanese cultural imports such as movies and music. And their joint hosting of the 2002 World Cup tournament prompted the *New York Times* to enthuse that the formerly tense relationship reflected "a new spirit of respect and reconciliation."[1]

Less than a year later, relations had soured again. Japan's Ministry of Education had approved a textbook that many Koreans thought whitewashed past aggression. Prime Minister Koizumi Junichiro visited the Yasukuni Shrine, which honors, among others, war criminals convicted by the Tokyo Trials. Such Japanese remembrance led South Korean President Kim Dae-jung to lament in his Liberation Day anniversary speech, "How can we make good friends with people who try to forget and ignore the many pains they inflicted on us? How can we deal with them in the future with any degree of trust?"[2]

Chapter title from Emperor Hirohito's apology to South Korea, 1984.

The study of the effects of Japan's remembrance on its relations with South Korea can logically be divided into three time periods: (1) an early phase (1952–64), in which the Japanese generally forgot or glorified their violence in Asia; (2) a middle phase (1965–89), in which Tokyo began to delve into issues of war responsibility; and (3) a late phase (1990–2000s) marked by the onset of an intense national debate in which remembrance of war and colonization has become prominent in Japan's domestic politics and foreign relations.

Strong evidence shows that Japan's remembrance has fueled Korean suspicions of its intentions. Throughout the postwar period, Japanese remembrance has been unapologetic, and Koreans have distrusted Japan. Furthermore, in Korean newspapers, opinion polls, and my interviews with elites, Koreans directly link their distrust of Japan to its denials and glorifications of past violence. Wariness of Tokyo's intentions has not necessarily translated into high threat perception; in later periods, Korean fears were dampened by constraints on Japanese capabilities (namely, the U.S.-Japan alliance). But distrust of Japan—driven in great part by Japanese remembrance—feeds Korean apprehension of a potential U.S. withdrawal from Asia, after which Koreans fear the strategic independence of a hostile Japan.

This case study also reveals a striking finding about the domestic dynamics of remembrance. Japanese denials, and the whitewashing of history textbooks, often occurred as a reaction to government contrition. In particular, official apologies and education reform prompted some politicians to justify or deny past violence and galvanized conservative groups to write textbooks that glossed over less-flattering events. A widespread conventional wisdom holds that if Japan would just apologize, its relations with its neighbors would improve. This chapter shows, however, that it is not an *absence* of official contrition that has damaged Japan's relations with South Korea: rather, it is backlash from contrition. This finding raises important questions about the utility of contrition in Japan's foreign relations and in international reconciliation more broadly.

## Japanese Aggression in Asia

One of the few beautiful vistas in Seoul's unpicturesque downtown is a statue of Admiral Yi Sun-shin, breathtakingly framed by a backdrop of rugged mountains. Sword in one hand, other arm akimbo, Yi stands defiant. He is accompanied by a small replica of a "turtle boat," which contributed to Yi's important naval victories. Japanese forces, led by Toyotomi Hideyoshi, had invaded in 1592 and rampaged throughout the country; they were finally expelled by Yi's turtle boats and the intervention of Chinese Ming army forces.[3] But the Japanese returned. Its leaders viewed control of Korea, as well as of Manchuria, as important to establish economic security and to protect Japan from the threat of Western colonization. Japan

27

pushed its rivals off the peninsula by defeating China in 1896 and Russia in 1905. It formally annexed Korea as a colony in 1910, and would rule there until its World War II defeat.[4]

Korea experienced political, physical, and cultural oppression as a Japanese colony. The authorities banned public assembly and abolished Korean newspapers and political organizations. Over a million frustrated Koreans took to the streets in nationwide demonstrations on March 1, 1919. This was violently suppressed by the colonial police; death toll estimates range from the official Japanese figure of approximately 500 killed to the Korean estimate of 7,500, plus thousands more wounded and arrested. To quash the independence movement, colonial police arrested its leaders and their family members; they were tortured, raped, imprisoned, and often executed. Repression of Korea extended into the cultural sphere; in an effort to impose a Japanese identity, Koreans were required to adopt Japanese names, to speak Japanese, and to worship the emperor and adopt Shinto (the Japanese national religion).

In the 1930s, as war with China strained Japan's resources, its colonial policies grew more severe. Korean food and resources were diverted to Japan and other territories while Koreans suffered increasing deprivation. Tokyo deported 750,000 Koreans to Japan and other colonies to work as forced laborers; they were undernourished, overworked, beaten, and often killed. Many perished in American conventional or nuclear bombardment. Korean men were conscripted to fight in the Japanese Imperial Army. From its colonial and conquered territories, Tokyo mobilized approximately 200,000 girls and women (most of them Korean) to provide sex for its soldiers. The "comfort women," as the Japanese call them, were often deceptively recruited by the promise of a well-paying factory job or were abducted from their homes by colonial police. Shipped to "comfort stations" at the front, the women were raped upwards of thirty times a day; survivors describe how women were beaten or savagely murdered for escape attempts or if they became diseased or pregnant.[5] Women who managed to survive not only this but the chaos of the war's end were tormented by shame and chronic medical problems; many were unable to bear children.

Korea's suffering was only part of the devastation caused by Japanese aggression. Fifteen million Chinese perished in the Sino-Japanese war, which officially began in 1937 and lasted until Japan's defeat in 1945. The Japanese Army unleashed chemical and biological warfare against Chinese soldiers and civilians. Army doctors set up a research facility in China, called Unit 731, in which they dissected and killed Chinese civilians and prisoners of war (POW) in medical experiments and training. In occupied cities, Japanese soldiers plundered, killed, and raped with abandon (most notoriously, the Nanjing Massacre and the Rape of Manila). Japanese strategic bombing campaigns devastated Chinese cities, killing more than 260,000 noncombatants. Famine and epidemics spread throughout Asia. Local economies were devastated; millions of refugees fled their homes.[6]

The Japanese people also suffered greatly in their attempt to dominate Asia. Once the region's most powerful military and economy, Japan lay devastated in 1945, stripped of sovereignty and occupied by the United States. Three million Japanese had perished in the war, including nearly two million civilians; over four million people lay wounded or ill. As John Dower has powerfully chronicled, not only did Japan leave "a trail of un-speakable cruelty and rapacity," but "they also devoured themselves. Japa-nese died in hopeless suicide charges, starved to death in the field, killed their own wounded rather than let them fall into enemy hands, and mur-dered their civilian compatriots in places such as Saipan and Okinawa. They watched helplessly as fire bombs destroyed their cities. . . ."[7] Over-seas, perhaps three million Japanese citizens living in the empire were ex-pelled from their homes after the defeat; in the chaos these refugees struggled to make their way to Japan. Japanese POWs starved and died un-der brutal conditions in Russian camps. The American firebombing of Tokyo killed 80,000 people; the U.S. bombarded Hiroshima and Nagasaki with nuclear weapons, killing 80,000 and 40,000 people, respectively, and causing tens of thousands more people to suffer wounds and radiation poi-soning. Japan's urban areas were 40 percent destroyed, and 30 percent of its urban population was homeless. The early days after the war were a des-perate struggle for survival among millions of shattered families, orphans, widows, and dazed veterans.

### Shaping Japanese Remembrance: The American Occupation (1945–52)

Policies during the American Occupation set the stage for Japan's later re-membrance. Scholars have rightfully criticized the policies of the Supreme Commander of the Allied Powers (SCAP) for encouraging Japanese amne-sia;[8] however, in one area (education reform), the United States did encour-age Japan to acknowledge its past violence. Americans viewed Japan's highly centralized educational system (administered under the 1890 Imper-ial Rescript on Education) as instrumental for inculcating hypernationalism and militarism within the Japanese people. According to one Occupation of-ficial, the rescript was the "bible" of emperor worship, from which "mili-tarists and ultranationalists drew most of their ammunition."[9] Following the war, SCAP instituted a range of education reforms. It decentralized educa-tional administration to local authorities, abolished the teaching of moral education and emperor idolatry, and fired and hired teachers.[10] Under American pressure, the Japanese Diet in 1947 passed the Fundamental Law of Education and the School Education Law. The former was considered a "constitution" for Japanese education, a declaration of educational values designed to replace the 1890 rescript. It addressed issues such as equal opportunity and coeducation; it stated that "Education shall not be subject to improper control, but it should be directly responsible to the whole people."[11]

SCAP sought to influence educational content as well as structure. The head of the Occupation, General Douglas MacArthur, noted in his 1945 education directive "the important psychological task of reminding the Japanese people of the total devastation brought on by the Pacific War." To this end, SCAP printed and distributed fifty thousand copies of the textbook *History of the Pacific War* and ordered Japan's Ministry of Education to stop printing textbooks until the Occupation authorities could approve new ones. SCAP approved the use of textbooks that hammered home the lessons of a misguided war, instigated by reckless leaders, which had brought devastation to Asia and misery and defeat to the Japanese nation. This message was further disseminated in a public information campaign aimed at promoting widespread awareness of Japanese war atrocities. SCAP ordered that a series of articles and reports about Japan's aggression and war crimes should be published in newspapers and broadcast on radio programs.[12]

Ultimately, many education reforms unraveled amid strong opposition from Japanese conservatives. After the defeat, Imperial education minister, Ota Kozo, mourned "the people's insufficient dedication to the emperor, along with their failure to bring into full play the spirit nurtured by their imperial education." (In other words, Japan lost the war because the people had not been nationalistic *enough*.) Ota's successor, Maeda Tamon, drew the same conclusion: Japan's new education system, he argued, should be founded on the Imperial Rescript on Education, the most important virtue of which "was the harmonious relationship it prescribed among the people and their loyalty to His majesty." Furthermore, lacking expertise and funding, local school boards demurred to Tokyo; Ministry of Education guidelines for curricula and textbooks were "swallowed whole," leaving the ministry essentially in charge.[13] The recentralization of education precipitated a noticeable decline in textbook coverage of Japan's wartime violence. But it should not be forgotten that American Occupation reforms had sought to democratize Japanese education, promote the influence of local education authorities, and encourage candid remembrance of the war.

These efforts notwithstanding, American Occupation policies fostered Japanese amnesia in many ways. Although Occupation-era textbooks portrayed the war as a tragic mistake, the American narrative downplayed Japanese culpability and deflected attention from Japan's worst atrocities. Psychological warfare officials and Occupation authorities alike crafted a mythology of Japanese victimhood in which the public had been duped by a militarist clique into launching an ill-fated war.[14] This view was evident in the 1945 Potsdam Declaration, which argued that "self-willed militaristic advisers" had "deceived and misled the people of Japan."[15] The military clique thesis absolved the Japanese people of guilt and nurtured their already prevalent sense of self-pity. In referencing the war, the Americans rejected the imperial moniker of the "Greater East Asian War"—Tokyo's rallying call against Western colonization—in favor of the term "Pacific War." This narrative diverted postwar memories away from Japan's colonization, atrocities, and war on the Asian continent and toward the maritime battles against the Allies—which had culminated in Japan's atomic bombardment (i.e., Japanese victimization).

Postwar policies of justice would also promote Japanese amnesia. In the International Military Tribunal for the Far East (known as the "Tokyo Trials"), the United States orchestrated trials of Japanese war criminals. For two-and-a-half years, these trials identified and sentenced planners of Japanese aggression; a few were put to death. However, many scholars have maintained that the Tokyo Trials were flawed by procedural misconduct, omissions and hypocrisy. For example, scholars have criticized the failure to try the emperor and other war criminals, the lack of Japanese staff, and the absence of Chinese or Russian participation. Emphasizing Japanese misdeeds in the Pacific War, the Tokyo Trials ignored forced conscription and labor of Koreans and Taiwanese, the sex slaves of the Imperial Army, and the grotesque medical experiments conducted by Unit 731. Washington agreed not to prosecute the heads of Unit 731 in exchange for their findings; U.S. officials covered up both the existence of the program and the amnesty deal.[16] Such flaws and omissions, scholars argue, discredited the evidence of war crimes that the trials did uncover, tainted the concept of postwar justice, and restored the legitimacy of the very leaders the trials had sought to impugn.

The dawn of the Cold War, which caused a "reverse course" in American Occupation policy, also encouraged Japanese amnesia. Initially planning to de-fang and enfeeble Japan, Washington instead decided to reconstitute it as a strong anti-Soviet ally. Reconstruction required rearming a country that Washington had only recently disarmed, and squirming around an American-authored constitutional prohibition (Article 9) that prohibited Japanese ownership of military forces. Reconstruction required political, military, and industrial leadership, but the people with this expertise had been recently purged or imprisoned for their campaign of imperial expansion.

Faced with the choice between justice and reconstruction, the United States chose the latter. Government officials were de-purged and reinstated; most prisoners were released, pardoned, and returned to positions of authority. The most notorious example is Kishi Nobusuke, the minister of Commerce and Industry in Tojo Hideki's wartime cabinet, who had been instrumental in the colonization of Manchuria and organized the program of forced labor. Kishi was released after three years in jail; he later became a key figure in forming the Liberal Democratic Party (LDP) and became prime minister in 1957. Kishi's release enabled the creation of a conservative dynasty: his son-in-law (Abe Shintaro) and grandson (Abe Shinzo, elected prime minister in 2006) became powerful political leaders.

American plans for Japanese reparations also shifted under the reverse course. In 1945–46, U.S. reparations commissioner Edwin Pauley recommended a steep reparations bill; he advocated dismantling Japanese industrial equipment and redistributing it to other East Asian nations to promote regional recovery.[17] Subsequent government reports about the reparations issue warned that removing industrial facilities would undermine the objectives of the Occupation and would overburden the American taxpayer. Ultimately Washington devoted the maximum amount of Japanese capital toward reconstruction; the United States waived its own reparations and deflected compensation demands from Japan's victims. The 1951 San Francisco Peace Treaty stipulated that reparations should not be paid to the extent that they damaged the recovering Japanese economy. The two countries most victimized by Japan in the war—the Koreans and the Chinese—received no reparations. Korea—part of the Japanese Empire—was deemed an enemy combatant and thus ineligible.

Emerging Cold War fault lines diminished focus on Japan's atrocities in Asia. The People's Republic of China was proclaimed in 1949; although the Chinese had been the most savaged by Japan, the United States blocked Beijing's participation in the 1951 San Francisco Peace Treaty and denied China reparations. In Japanese domestic politics, Washington feared the empowerment of the pacifist and procommunist Left (the socialist and communist parties, teachers, and labor unions). This led Washington to subvert the Left in favor of Japanese conservatives: the people most implicated in the war and the least inclined to remember or atone for atrocities. Occupation and Japanese authorities cooperated in conducting a "red purge" from industry and the bureaucracy. Ironically, the institution that had been tasked with the mission of investigating war criminals was repurposed for monitoring Japanese leftists.[18] Although the Left had opposed Japanese imperialism and was more likely to favor justice and remembrance, in the emerging Cold War they had become, in Washington's eyes, the enemy.

## The Initial Post-Occupation Phase, 1952–64

### MEMORIES OF A GLORIOUS PAST

In the early postwar years, Japan was self-preoccupied with the ravages of defeat and the challenges of recovery. Official policies of remembrance reflected the view that Japanese colonization of its East Asian neighbors was necessary and justified by the threat of Western incursion into the region; and it was glorified as economically advantageous for the former colonies. Textbooks portrayed the Japanese people and emperor as victims of a small clique of militarists. Advocates of contrition in wider society were rare; the Japanese people mourned their own losses as they recovered and rebuilt.

*Japan's Official Remembrance.* Japanese leaders conducting normalization negotiations with the ROK were unapologetic about past violence in Korea. Diplomats from the two countries met in four negotiation conferences starting in 1953. When the Koreans used the term "enslavement" to describe the Japanese occupation, the chief Japanese negotiator in normalization talks, Kubota Kenichiro, dismissed such language as the "product of wartime hysteria." Saying that Japanese investment had spurred Korean development, Kubota asserted that "he did not consider the Japanese occupation an 'entirely unmixed evil.' "[19] Indeed, Kubota said, "Japan also had the right to demand compensation from Korea because for 36 years Japan has changed Korea's bare mountains to a flourishing country with flowers and trees." He commented that "Korea would have been taken over either by Russia or China and Korea would have been in a much worse situation if Japan had not colonized it." Incensed, the Korean delegation walked out of the conference. They returned after four years of diplomatic back-and-forth in which negotiators insisted that Kubota retract the statement and apologize.[20]

Tokyo did not discipline Kubota as an embarrassing loose cannon; on the contrary, other officials rallied to his defense. "Perfectly rational," said Foreign Minister Okazaki Katsuo; "We did not utter anything wrong, and there is absolutely no reason for us to apologize for what we have conveyed."[21] The Japanese Foreign Ministry scolded Seoul as "solely responsible for the dissolution of the conference by intentionally distorting the private talks." Other Japanese statements from this period reflect similar amnesia: When a Korean diplomat suggested, "Let us bury the hatchet," a Japanese negotiator wondered, "What are the hatchets to bury?" In 1958, LDP politician Ono Banboku suggested that Japan coordinate its diplomacy toward the ROK and Taiwan, another former colony. "If feasible," Ono said, "it would be nice to form the United States of Japan with the ROK and Formosa." Also in 1958, Japanese envoy Yatsugi Kazuo reportedly issued an apology to Seoul on behalf of Prime Minister Kishi. Summoned by indignant Diet members to explain himself, Kishi assured them he had not apologized: "I am not familiar with what Mr. Yatsugi said in Keijo." (Keijo was the Japanese colonial name for Seoul.) Former prime minister Yoshida Shigeru made his views clear in a conversation with a Korean diplomat. Yoshida told Kim Dong-jo that as a foreign ministry official, he had frequently visited Seoul during the occupation and had been pleased by "how well the Government-General was ruling Korea." Yoshida said, "I do not understand why Koreans hate the Japanese so much and voice such strong anti-Japanese sentiments." Statements of Japanese political leaders were thus unapologetic about the colonization of Korea; they tended to justify or even glorify it, and did not acknowledge Korean suffering.

Japan's reparations policies did not reflect admission and remorse for wartime atrocities. Tokyo concentrated on Japanese (rather than foreign) victims. Three million Japanese who had become refugees or had been ethnically cleansed from the dissolved empire and had arrived penniless in Japan were politically mobilized and were demanding state assistance. The Japanese government compensated them as well as veterans and victims of the atomic bombings (*hibakusha*). As for foreign victims, Tokyo negotiated several bilateral settlements: with Burma (1955), the Philippines (1956), Indonesia (1958), South Vietnam (1959), and Thailand (1963). Totaling about US$1 billion (about US$6 billion in 2007 dollars), these funds were not linked to specific wrongdoing.[22] Compensation was offered in the form of Japanese grants, loans, products, and services; it was used to build factories, dams, power plants, and railways. Because these funds were tied to products or services provided by Japanese vendors, they were widely interpreted as a Japanese effort to gain an economic foothold in Southeast Asia. As a U.S. State Department report noted, "With an eye to increased trade opportunities in Southeast Asia, Japan intends to make considerable sacrifices to obtain a normalization of relations throughout the area."[23]

Individual victims of Japanese atrocities received no reparations. After the war's end, Korean victims of forced labor immediately began demanding unpaid back wages. Many of the corporations which had relied on forced labor had retained unpaid wage deposits, but these never found their way to workers. In 1946 Tokyo paid out indemnities not to the workers but to the corporations who had brutalized them; thirty-five companies shared an indemnity of fifty-six million yen (about $560 million) for losses sustained during the war. Mitsubishi and Mitsui, which had relied the most on forced labor, received the largest shares (14 percent and 5 percent, respectively).[24]

Former laborers who remained in Japan never received government compensation; beginning in the 1970s they initiated lawsuits, which led nowhere, to demand that they receive the same compensation as Japanese nationals. Tokyo actively denied the existence of forced laborers; the Kishi administration claimed that "voluntary contract labor" had worked in wartime factories. Although the Ministry of Foreign Affairs had in 1946 drafted a comprehensive study of Chinese forced labor, the Kishi administration testified to the Diet that the study had been destroyed. During the war, Kishi himself—as minister of Commerce and Industry as well as vice minister of Munitions—had authorized the wartime forced labor program.[25] In sum, during this period, Tokyo paid compensation to national governments in Southeast Asia. But individual victims (such as the sex slaves, forced laborers, POWs, or victims of Unit 731) received no reparations; Tokyo forgot or denied the atrocities they had endured.

The Japanese government made no efforts to bring to justice the perpetrators of past aggression and atrocities. Politicians devoted their energy to freeing people who had been convicted by the Tokyo Trials. The Diet passed resolutions demanding their release. In 1957, one of Kishi's primary political goals was to secure the release of war criminals. Kishi persuaded the Eisenhower administration to expedite the release of prisoners convicted for crimes such as murder, rape, and torture. After prisoners were set free, Tokyo paid back salaries and restored pensions for the prisoners because they had not been tried under Japanese law and the government would not treat them as common criminals.[26]

Japanese education policy during this period also reflected little admission or remorse for past violence. Through new legislation and through bureaucratic regulation, the Japanese government unraveled many SCAP education reforms. LDP leaders accused the leftist-pacifist teacher's union of fomenting a communist agenda; conservatives argued that Japanese education needed to foster patriotism and "defense-mindedness." Ironically, this conservative agenda was supported by Washington, which was now encouraging Japanese rearmament. Conservatives sought to diminish local controls over education (to minimize the influence of liberal teachers) and to recentralize education policy within the Ministry of Education. The LDP succeeded in passing new legislation (amid strong public and political opposition) to appoint rather than elect local school boards.[27] The LDP failed in its efforts to tighten textbook screening through legislation but succeeded in enacting the desired measures through bureaucratic regulation. Later, the 1963 Textbook Law decreed that country-level school boards rather than schools would select textbooks and placed new restrictions on publishers in textbook submissions. Thus during this period, the LDP reversed American reforms aimed at decentralizing education policy.

Once the Ministry of Education had regained control, it began rejecting textbooks that depicted unsavory Japanese wartime behavior. Texts were screened not only for factual accuracy but for their "level of patriotism." In 1956 the ministry rejected eight books on the grounds that they had too many negative comments on Japan's wartime conduct; the following year, it nixed eight more for their "slanted" discussions (despite the fact that they exceeded the number of points required for approval). Textbook author and historian Ienaga Saburo noted, "The certification has become stricter year by year." Ienaga's textbook *A New History of Japan* (*Shin nihonshi*) was rejected in 1963 as "too gloomy" and "excessively critical" of Japan's actions in World War II.[28] Ienaga was told to delete pictures of maimed soldiers and

35

of Hiroshima as well as descriptions of rapes by Japanese soldiers, the Nanjing Massacre, and Unit 731. The word *shinryaku* (invasion or aggression) was to be replaced with *shinshutsu* (advance). Regarding the issue of rape, the Ministry stated: "The violation of women is something that has happened on every battlefield in every era of human history. This is not an issue that needs to be taken up with respect to the Japanese Army in particular."[29] Ienaga commented that such screening clearly showed "the tendency of the Education Ministry to control the content of historical education." Ienaga filed his first lawsuit against the Japanese government in 1965, launching what would become a decades-long legal battle against the Ministry of Education. In this lawsuit he argued, "Government certification of textbooks is used to weed out, or force revision in, all books that fail to conform to an orthodox ideology," which was a violation of free speech and of the Fundamental Law of Education of 1947.[30]

Publishers adapted to Ministry of Education screening, and textbook coverage of the war grew increasingly vague. Writes James Orr, the elementary school text *Hyojun Shogaku Shakai* "presented what can only be characterized as a patriotic narrative of Japanese continental aggression." The textbook *Nihon Shoseki* describes Japan's imperial era to junior high school students as follows: "Thinking to liberate Southeast Asia from Western colonial control, [Japan] built a 'Greater East Asia Co-prosperity Sphere' encompassing all of East Asia, with Japan as its leader who could freely use the region's resources."[31]

Historical studies commissioned by the Japanese government also reflect unapologetic interpretations. A thirty-five-volume study called "Historical Research on Japanese Overseas Activities" dismissed accusations of Japanese colonial exploitation of Korea as "absurd and lamentable," "defamatory," and disproved by Korea's economic progress. In 1949 the Foreign Ministry also released a report on the Japanese colonies that stated that Japanese governance in these areas should not be seen "as so-called exploitation by a colonial power. On the contrary, these territories when the Japanese took over were the most underdeveloped regions, and each region's economic, social and cultural advancement should be attributed to the Japanese. This fact is already acknowledged by the learned people of the world—including the natives of the land." The report rejected charges of Japanese "exploitation" of the region, dismissing such talk as "coming out of ignorance or strictly for the purpose of political propaganda." It condemned the ethnic cleansing of "Japanese inhabitants who made earnest living in these areas," as a gross violation of the "normal international protocol." Finally, the report argued that because Japan acquired its territories "through methods deemed legitimate by international convention," Tokyo "strongly objects to the notion that it had obtained these territories [through criminal measures]." Thus during this early period, Japanese education and official histories glossed over Japanese abuses and glorified colonization. [32]

During the early postwar years, as noted, Japanese commemoration emphasized Japanese rather than foreign victims. Starting in 1963 Japan held an annual "National War Dead Memorial Service" on August 15 (the day of the surrender). Chief Cabinet Secretary Kurogane Yasumi told the press that the ceremony showed "the entire nation's sober desire to offer its sincere tribute to the more than 3 million whose sacrifice has given us today's peace and development." At the ceremony, "the emperor read a message of regret, condolence for bereaved families, and appreciation to the dead." [33] Foreign victims are not commemorated on this or any other day.

Hiroshima's monuments and museum focused entirely on Japanese victimhood. In 1952 the Hiroshima Peace Park was established, featuring the preserved ruins of the "A-bomb Dome": a building gutted in the attack. The Hiroshima Peace Memorial Museum was installed in 1955. Emphasizing the days after August 6, 1945, the museum omitted mention of Japan's invasions in East Asia. Exhibition scripts in both Hiroshima and Nagasaki emphasized Japan's commitment to the "Peace Movement"—that is, the "anti-nuclear" movement. During this period, many Japanese felt that Japan could atone for its past aggression "by drawing on its atomic bomb experience to become a champion of a non-militarized, nonnuclearized world": this view of course privileged the memory of Japanese victims of the atomic bombings. For example, immediately after the surrender, Tokyo's Information Bureau encouraged national repentance "by taking a leading role in prohibiting the future use of nuclear weapons." [34]

Every year on the August 6 anniversary, the Hiroshima Peace Park hosts ceremonies mourning the atomic bombing. In 1958, schoolchildren and community members of Hiroshima installed the Children's Peace Statue to honor children killed by the atomic bomb: in particular a young girl, Sasaki Sadako, who had died at age twelve of leukemia. Sadako had thought that if she folded 1,000 paper cranes, she might be cured. To honor her and the other victims of the bombing, children all over Japan, and throughout the world, fold paper cranes and send them to Hiroshima, where long strings of them are displayed in a profusion of color around Sadako's statue. The inscription on the statue reads, "This is our cry, this is our prayer, peace in the world."

*Wider Japanese Society.* Unapologetic remembrance in official government policy was echoed among the population. The devastated Japanese public felt intense antiwar sentiment—giving rise to what analysts would call a "culture of antimilitarism." [35] This sentiment, however, did not stem from a confrontation with Japan's war crimes, but rather from a pervasive sense of victimization. The Japanese people adopted what Steven Benfell has called

37

the "renegade view" of the war: a military cabal had hijacked Japan and launched it into a misguided policy of imperialism.[36]

The opposition Left was working hard to prevent Japan's remilitarization, and in doing so argued for the need to remember the horrors of war—and to avoid any policy that might lead Japan down that path. To this end the Left did invoke Japan's role as a victimizer of other nations and encouraged remembrance of that history. However, Japanese leftists also embraced the military clique thesis. They were ideologically sympathetic to the view that the masses had been deceived by the ruling bourgeoisie and were thus victims as much as any other. Emphasis on Japan's victimhood in the atomic bombings also played into the Left's call for demilitarization and distance from the U.S.-Japan alliance.[37]

When the Left did call for greater self-reflection, Cold War politics often got in the way. Advocates of contrition (for example, among the teachers' unions) were stigmatized by the public because of their communist affiliations. Similarly, traumatized veterans began speaking out in the late 1950s about the wartime atrocities they committed. Such testimony met with harsh criticism, which dismissed the veterans as brainwashed by Chinese communists.[38]

Broader societal debates about war remembrance also reflected the renegade view. A best-selling two-volume book about the Showa era (1926–89)"rounded up the usual suspects: the military clique . . . operating in concert with certain right-wing thugs and academic ideologues, plus a few industrialists and politicians." Its coverage of the war era, as John Dower has noted, evinced no interest "in exposing the nature of Japan's aggression or its victimization of others (the Nanjing Massacre was not even mentioned) or in exploring broader issues of 'war responsibility.' "[39] Japan's victim narrative was bolstered by numerous memoirs written by soldiers recalling the suffering they had endured (rather than inflicted).[40] Politician Ashida Hitoshi, a moderate conservative, summarized public opinion when, in response to calls for national self-reflection, he urged people to focus on those who were truly guilty. "If you were to say that the nation's masses were responsible for defeat, you would definitely raise their ire," Ashida said.[41] Nongovernmental associations formed by the Japanese public during this time also reflect self-preoccupation: the Japan War Bereaved Families Association (Nihon izokukai) and the Association of Shinto Shrines (Jinja honcho) lobbied for reparations for domestic victims.

Despite the pervasive sense of victimhood, some opinion leaders thrust the topic of its war responsibility into the Japanese popular mind-set. Scholars began compiling, studying, and publishing records from the Tokyo Trials. One of the first writers on war responsibility was journalist Cho Fumitsura, who argued that the people must recognize their complicity in order to "establish a genuine democracy based on the principle of responsibility."[42] Scholar Maruyama Masao faulted the Emperor for

Japanese imperialism, and the Japanese Communist Party for its failure to stop it. He lambasted the "system of irresponsibility" in which elites after the war shifted blame onto others.[43] Other intellectuals debated war responsibility upon the 1955 publication of the book *Showa-shi* [A History of Showa]. Although Japanese opinion leaders struggled with the issue of war responsibility, these debates did not result in a broader confrontation with Japan's past atrocities.[44]

In sum, both official and societal remembrance in Japan was largely unapologetic. At the official level, if colonization and war were discussed, they were justified or glorified. Wider Japanese society did engage in debates about the war, but in doing so emphasized its own victimhood, mourned its own war dead, and forgot foreign victims.

## COMPETING THEORIES AND PREDICTIONS

Koreans assessing Japan in the 1950s and early 1960s could have studied a range of signals emanating from Tokyo: none was reassuring. As described above, neither the Japanese government nor wider society remembered or regretted Japan's past violence in Korea. The Japanese viewed their colonization as beneficial to Korea and paid little attention to atrocities there or elsewhere. As summarized by U.S. Ambassador to Japan Edwin O. Reischauer, the "Japanese officials and public simply do not feel they owe any apology to Korea."[45]

Other factors should also have contributed to Korean suspicion. Japan and Korea both claimed sovereignty over a group of islets (Tokdo in Korean; Takeshima to the Japanese) located halfway between the two countries. These tiny, rocky, uninhabited islands are perceived as valuable for the surrounding natural resources and fishing rights that their ownership confers. Additionally, in the late 1940s Japan and Korea nearly came to blows over fisheries; Korea proclaimed a boundary line (the Rhee Line), and impounded Japanese fishing vessels and imprisoned Japanese sailors who crossed it. In response, Japan began sending naval patrols to escort its fishing vessels. The Americans feared this would lead to an armed confrontation between the two nations and intervened to prevent escalation.

These ongoing disputes were not alone in promoting Korean distrust of Japanese intentions: Other factors that elsewhere have smoothed relations between former adversaries—for example, mutual democratization and membership in international institutions—were absent. In the 1950s neither country was a mature democracy, so the potentially stabilizing effects of the dyadic democratic peace were not present. Furthermore, neither country was a member of multilateral institutions that could significantly constrain its behavior or create transparency about its intentions.[46] In sum, during this period, Japanese signals about its intentions should all have appeared worrisome.

Japan's capabilities, though recently dealt a major blow by the military defeat, should have also appeared threatening to Korea. Japan already out-matched the ROK in military power. Not only did Tokyo outspend Seoul on defense by roughly four to one, Japan also enjoyed a vast lead in potential power; it had four times the population and twenty-four times the eco-nomic output as South Korea.[47]

To make matters worse, in the 1950s it did not appear at all certain that the U.S.-Japan alliance would continue to constrain Japanese foreign policy. Japan signed a security treaty with the United States in 1951, and U.S. forces were stationed in Japan in large numbers, but Korean leaders had se-rious doubts about the staying power of the alliance. Alignment with the United States was hotly contested in Japanese politics; in fact, the renewal of the U.S.-Japan security treaty in 1960 triggered massive protests across the country and brought Japan to the brink of civil war.[48] Koreans also wor-ried about American staying power, fearing that Washington planned to withdraw its troops from East Asia and shift the burdens of regional secu-rity to Japan. Japan was also relatively unconstrained by regional security threats. None of the communist states (the Soviet Union, North Korea, or China) had significant power-projection capabilities to threaten Japan; the vast majority of Soviet military power was positioned in the European the-ater.[49] Japanese relations with neighboring communist regimes were not in-evitably hostile. During the 1950s, powerful factions within the LDP were cultivating close relations with Beijing and Moscow. In other words, Japa-nese neutrality—and thus the termination of the U.S.-Japan alliance—was a real option at the time. Therefore, because of signals of hostile Japanese in-tentions (including its unapologetic remembrance), as well as fears of un-constrained Japanese power, Korean fears of Japan should have been elevated during this period.

## KOREAN PERCEPTIONS, 1952–64

South Korean statements from the 1952–64 period reflect profound dis-trust of Japanese intentions, as well as fears of a resurgent threat. President Syngman Rhee told U.S. President Eisenhower that Koreans were "caught between our fear of Japan on one side, and of the Communists on the other," arguing that "Japan has nothing whatsoever to offer the peoples of Asia, either substantively or psychologically. We all have learned by harsh experience the ruthlessness of Japan's ambitions."[50] Rhee frequently argued that Japan was the most menacing country in East Asia. He told U.S. Secre-tary of State John Foster Dulles that the Korean people were more worried about Japan than the Soviet Union, because Japan desired to revive its colo-nial policies. In a letter to Dulles in 1954, Rhee said that if the United States tried to rehabilitate Japan, then Asians "would rather join with the Soviets to resist the Japanese." Rhee similarly wrote to Eisenhower: "We are conscious of continuing pressures to align ourselves more closely with Japan, economically and militarily. But the totality of our national fears is of such a nature that this whole situation impels many of our people to consider the possibility of accepting reunification on Communist terms as the only form of safety which they may expect from a renewal of Japanese dominion over our nation." Similarly, while campaigning for reelection, Rhee called Japan "a greater menace than the Communists."[51]

Suspicion of Japan extended beyond the notoriously anti-Japanese Rhee. ROK Foreign Minister Pyun Yong-tae accused the Japanese of manipulating the United States "to rearm the island with a view to using her in the coming armed conflict with Russia." He warned, "Uncle Sam must be on guard not to be taken in by the kissing of his hand by the Japanese. They usually kiss a hand they cannot bite."[52] In talks with American officials, Pyun "stressed the danger . . . that the Japanese Government was intent, in the long range, upon reasserting its influence in Korea."[53]

Scholars in Korea exhibited similar distrust. In the words of Lee Hui-sung, "Some Japanese may tell us that our fears and suspicions are imaginary and absurd. But those who advance this view may not have a full knowledge about the history of Japanese-Korean relations."[54] Korean scholar Chong-Sik Lee reported that Koreans "share the feeling that the Japanese are not to be trusted" and harbored "deep-seated suspicion or fear of Japanese motives." Lee summarized Korean thinking as follows: "Most Korean leaders refuse to believe that Japan has undergone any fundamental change in the postwar period. As far as the Koreans are concerned, the reform programs of the United States Occupation forces barely scratched the surface of Japanese society and the Japanese leaders are still obsessed by the mentality of the colonialists."[55] During the short-lived government of John M. Chang, initial overtures toward rapprochement with Japan triggered a widespread and nationally destabilizing anti-Japanese student revolt.[56]

Not only did Koreans distrust Japan, they perceived a resurgent Japanese security threat. Diplomacy toward Japan was adversarial and fearful of Japan's relative gains. Alarmed at the prospect of Japanese rearmament, and hoping to achieve military parity, South Korean leaders pressured American officials against rearming Japan and lobbied for American weapons transfers to Seoul. Rhee protested that Washington was cultivating "Japanese imperialism" under its protection and warned that the United States should prevent Japan from returning to "its old militaristic ambition." A U.S. official reported "ROK appeals that . . . its army, air force, and navy be at least as strong as their projected Japanese counterparts." He noted that Korean fears regarding its naval inferiority vis-à-vis Japan were understandable and emphasized that "we have agreed to help [South Korea] in supporting naval forces."[57]

Seoul was so fearful of Japan, it was unwilling to even normalize diplomatic relations. Korean leaders believed that Tokyo would exploit any cooperation to its advantage, and to Korea's peril. Negotiations for normalization dragged over fourteen years and were conducted in an atmosphere of intense hostility. Normalization was only achieved in 1965 because of pressure from Washington and the willingness of Korean President Park Chung-hee to push for an agreement despite widespread domestic opposition.[58] Park sought Japanese reparations in order to finance national economic development and as a source of cash to support his political patrons. He faced a nation extremely hostile to the idea of normalization; as negotiations progressed, Korean students and intellectuals formed a national protest movement in March 1964. Korean cities were paralyzed by demonstrations; in June Park declared martial law and brought four army divisions into Seoul to restore order. When Park brought the treaty with Japan before the National Assembly for ratification, Park's entire cabinet resigned in protest; the opposition parties also resigned en masse. Nevertheless, Park rammed the treaty through the National Assembly in a secret session in which the opposition was not present. The vehement resistance of most Koreans to even minimal cooperation with Japan reflects strong fear.

*Korean Reasoning.* Koreans frequently linked their distrust and fear to Japan's statements, policies, and actions related to remembrance. Leaders repeatedly declared that they could not trust Japan if it continued to forget or glorify its past violence. President Rhee said, "We are trying to forget and will forget the past. If the Japanese would meet the Koreans with truthfulness and sincerity, friendly relations would be renewed."[59] In a confidential memorandum to his negotiators, Rhee told the diplomats to determine: "Have the Japanese abandoned their arrogant and domineering attitude toward us? Have they finally and completely renounced their expectation of dominating us? These are the fundamental issues which, from our point of view, have to be decided before there is any hope of bringing the two nations together. . . ." Rhee argued that in order to understand Japanese intentions, "What we most need from Japan . . . is concrete and constructive evidence of repentance for past misdeeds and of a new determination to deal fairly with us now and in the future," and "convincing evidence that this change of heart has occurred and has become deeply rooted in Japan."[60] When a Japanese religious leader wrote an open letter in the *Mainichi Shinbun* seeking forgiveness for Japan's misdeeds toward Korea, Rhee responded with his own open letter in that newspaper. He wrote: "I am ready for restarting new relations with Japan if the Japanese show the same cooperative spirit. . . . Your apology for the forty years of Japanese rule over Korea drew my serious attention because it was, in fact, the first statement of such nature I have ever heard from prominent Japanese people. In the absence of such expressions as yours, one could understand why we Koreans have believed that the Japanese intent is not to be friendly toward the ROK, but to redominate Korea. . . ."[61] In a meeting with Japanese Prime Minister Yoshida Shigeru, Rhee pressed Yoshida "to express that the militarists were responsible for everything and from now on there will be no militaristic aggression on Korea." Rhee said, "Some such statement would help the Koreans who still suspect and fear Japanese ambitions and attempts to control Korea again."[62]

The stridently anti-Japanese Rhee was not alone in seeking Japanese recognition of past wrongs against Korea. In the words of scholar Chong-Sik Lee, "Many Koreans felt that Japan owed Korea an apology for the atrocities committed by the Japanese colonialists in Korea. The Koreans feel that the Japanese people, particularly the leaders, are morally responsible for the suffering of the Korean people in the past and that the Japanese leaders should atone for these offences by showing at least a more conciliatory, if not submissive, attitude."[63] The Korean National Assembly adopted a resolution in 1961 demanding that normalization with Tokyo be accompanied by a Japanese apology. Foreign Minister Lee Dong-won also told an American official that such a gesture was a vital prerequisite for normalization.[64] In 1964, shortly before the normalization treaty was signed, ROK President Park Chung-hee said, "The Japanese people, especially Japanese leaders, should reflect on what they did to us during the past 36 years. It is the consensus of our national sentiment that Japan's normal reflection on and legal expression of its regret for its past aggression should precede any cooperation with Japan on our part."[65]

Koreans were alarmed by Japanese statements of denial and glorification. Korean officials condemned the statements of lead Japanese negotiator Kubota Kenichiro during normalization talks in 1953. Kubota had said that Korea would have been worse off had Japan not colonized it; that if Japan had not colonized Korea, then Russia or China would have; and that the Koreans were the ones who should be paying Japan compensation because Japan had modernized Korea's economy.[66] The Korean delegation walked out of that meeting and refused to return until Kubota retracted his statements. After four years elapsed, Kubota issued a retraction, and the South Koreans returned to the conference. Seoul's unwillingness to normalize with Japan, reflected in their reaction to the Kubota statement—at a time when the ROK was in desperate need of capital and allies—reflects the importance of remembrance to Koreans.

Disputes over territory also fueled Korean distrust. American officials mediating the fisheries dispute over the Rhee Line reported "Korean alarm with respect to [Japanese] fishing and patrolling activities close to [the] Korean coast."[67] A Korean political group (the National Independence Federation) reported that Japan's desire to expand the Rhee Line closer to the Korean coast "is nothing but proof that Japanese imperialistic ambitions have not expired."[68] A newspaper editorialized that Japanese designs on the islets reflected Japan's goal to expand its influence, arguing, "As past history teaches us, it was when Japan gained the command of the sea that Japanese imperialism started its invasion activities in earnest." Government officials also expressed concerns about Japanese territorial claims; Rhee asserted that Japanese fishing in Korean waters reflected that they "probably would like to extend themselves even to Seoul. They had a good time for forty years in Korea." The ROK foreign minister wrote a letter to the U.S. embassy in which he expressed fears about the "very grave [situation] being created by [the Japanese government] sending massed fishing fleets to seas adjacent to [Korea] under convoy of patrols." The South Korean Foreign Ministry said that Seoul would never have allowed U.S. military command of the area had it known that the United States would prohibit Korean vessels from operating while a "freed" Japan would "ruthlessly and provokingly threaten" Korea.[69] Rhee's alarm led the Commander-in-Chief of the United Nations Command to recommend barring Japanese fishing vessels from coastal waters, after which Rhee expressed relief that Korea need no longer fear Japanese naval patrols.

Koreans also expressed suspicions of Japan based on its claim of the Tokdo/Takeshima Islands. Saying that Japan had used the islands as "stepping stones for aggression on the continent of Asia," a Korean political group sought to clarify Korean ownership of the islets in order to "deny Japan a bridge to the Asian continent."[70] Korean newspapers editorialized about Japan's "sinister designs" and warned that if Koreans forgot the past, this would lead to "the repetition of [Japan's] past sins." Disputes over fisheries and territory thus fueled Korean distrust during the early period.[71]

Koreans perceived a threat not only because they viewed Japan's intentions as hostile, but because they feared Japan's capabilities: specifically, Japan's unconstrained power. Seoul's fears of a U.S. pullout from the region were displayed in its continual seeking of assurances that the United States would guarantee its security. Rhee constantly pressed American diplomats to clarify that the Mutual Defense Treaty between the U.S. and ROK would "guarantee the ROK against Japanese aggression." The State Department assured him that "The Mutual Defense Treaty with Korea applies to attacks from any quarter," and that "we can assure the Koreans that we will not tolerate in the future the resumption of any aggressive or oppressive measures by the Japanese in economic, political, or military fields concerning Korea."[72] In a 1954 letter to President Eisenhower, Rhee lobbied for a nonaggression pact between the United States, ROK, and Japan. He argued, "Should any of the three become an aggressor, the other two would combat that aggression. Such an accord, seriously entered into by the three nations, should assure their peaceful and friendly relationship for the foreseeable future. Once this were signed, Korea may be prepared to negotiate a commercial agreement with Japan and enter into amicable social and cultural exchanges."[73]

Koreans also worried that Japan-ROK normalization would precipitate a U.S. pullout, leaving them alone with an unfettered Japan. Foreign Minister Pyun noted that "the possible courses for America to pursue in the Orient may include leaving it to the domination of Japan, a course already tried. . . ."In an article entitled "Is Uncle Sam to Usher the Japs Back?" Pyun speculated that the United States "may bid Korea good-bye at any moment."[74] Such concerns extended into the Park Chung-hee era; Foreign Minister Lee Dong-won echoed this fear that normalization with Japan would precipitate a U.S. military withdrawal.[75] In a discussion with President John F. Kennedy, the Korean Ambassador "raised the question of whether or not our interest in the ROK-Japanese settlement presaged a reduction of U.S. commitments and an attempt to shift the responsibility to Japan."[76] Another Korean ambassador sought further assurances from Washington, reporting "apprehensions among the Korean people" that after normalization, "the role of the United States of America in supporting Korea would be shifted to Japan."[77] Yun Po-son, a former ROK president, quipped that giving Japan responsibility over Korea was like expecting "a loan shark to do philanthropic work."[78]

Korean fears of a U.S. exit registered among American officials. A U.S. State Department report noted Rhee's conviction that a group of U.S. officials "wants to give Korea back to Japan." President Eisenhower protested, "the United States sent its men . . . to protect Korea [in 1950]." He said he "could not conceive how we could be accused of trying to make Koreans bow their necks to the Japanese."[79] After a trip to Seoul, U.S. Secretary of State Dean Rusk relayed the Korean view that normalization "may result in a reduction of United States assistance to Korea." The State Department reported one "widespread fear" that upon normalization, the United States would "attempt [to] shift [the] burden of Korea to Japan and perhaps 'abandon' Korea."[80]

After sixty years of American internationalism and interventionism, readers might be perplexed by Korean insecurities. However, Koreans in the 1950s had grounds to doubt the American commitment. A half century earlier, the 1905 Taft-Katsura agreement had facilitated Japan's annexation of Korea: Washington had given Japan a free hand on the Korean Peninsula in exchange for Japanese noninterference in the American colony in the Philippines. And in the early 1950s, prominent American leaders were dismissing Korea as tangential to American interests. General Douglas MacArthur made statements to this effect in 1949; Dean Acheson gave his notorious security perimeter speech in 1950—the speech later believed to have encouraged Pyongyang and Moscow to launch the Korean War. Korean suspicions at the time were in fact totally justified. U.S. government documents later published show that during this time, Washington had indeed envisioned passing off what it termed its "unstable stepchild" to Tokyo.[81]

Fearing a U.S. pullout, Koreans strongly objected to increases in Japanese power. Leaders urged American officials against the strategy of rebuilding and rearming Japan as a Cold War ally. "Instead of rearming Japan," Rhee argued, "the United States should support South Korea." He complained to Dulles, "It was not wise to build up Japan economically and militarily"; Foreign Minister Pyun seconded this view, arguing that Koreans were concerned by the U.S. economic and military reconstruction of Japan. Rhee wrote to President Eisenhower, "American development of renewed power in Japan cannot but be regarded by all Oriental peoples as hastening the time when they must once again prepare to resist or be victimized by a resurgence of Japanese imperialism."[82]

American officials recognized Koreans fears of Japanese military power during this period. Dulles attempted to placate Rhee by saying that the United States-Korea Mutual Defense Treaty would protect Korea from Japan as well as from the Soviet Union, that the United States also wanted to prevent Japan from again becoming "a dominant power," and that Japanese-Korean cooperation was needed for the security of the Western Pacific. He contended that Rhee must abandon his antagonism toward Japan because of its strategic importance.[83] Another American official noted that "the Korean emotional reaction to Japan" was understandable, but that today "it is necessary for the United States and Korea, both of which suffered from Japanese imperialism, to recognize the realities of the present-day world and look to the future." Another U.S. official reported President Rhee's complaints that U.S. rearmament of Japan "will lead to the imperialism he fears."[84]

Korean debates also reflect concern about Japan's economic power. Although normalization promised increased opportunities for bilateral trade and Japanese aid, Koreans feared that Japan would profit more from their interaction. By the end of the 1950s the Japanese economy had recovered and was beginning its stunning growth; Korea, on the other hand, languished. President Park Chung-hee commented that many Koreans "expressed concern at possible Japanese economic aggression if relations were normalized, especially in view of past history."[85] An American CIA report noted, "Koreans distrust the Japanese and . . . fear that Japan's economic strength might lead to renewed domination by Tokyo."[86] Secretary of State Rusk noted, "The Koreans fear that an influx of the Japanese capital into Korea may result in what may be called "an economic invasion" by Japan."[87]

In sum, Koreans distrusted and feared Japan during this period. Korean threat perception was based on the perception of hostile Japanese intentions, rooted in Japan's unapologetic remembrance, and in territorial disputes over fisheries and the Tokdo/Takeshima Islands. Koreans also feared Japanese capabilities. Korean statements clearly indicate—and the testimony of American officials further confirms—their agitation at the reconstitution of Japanese power and at the prospect of a U.S. withdrawal from Japan.

## Middle Period (1965–1980s)

### STIRRINGS OF REMEMBRANCE

Japanese amnesia and glorification gave way to more self-reflection about past violence from the mid-1960s to the late 1980s. Tokyo pursued "apology diplomacy" as it sought to renew relations with former victims. Nevertheless, whitewashing and denials of past atrocities remained widespread.

Starting in the 1960s, Japanese leaders began issuing tepid apologies. As part of diplomatic normalization with Korea in 1965, Foreign Minister Shiina Etsusaburo read a statement that noted an "unhappy phase" in Japanese-Korean relations for which Japan "felt deep regret and deep remorse."[88] This statement conveys remorse but falls short on the "admission" dimension because it does not describe what transpired during the "unhappy" period or who had been responsible. The Japanese apparently also did not consider the foreign minister's statement to be particularly significant; the national newspapers covered the normalization agreement but barely mentioned Shiina's statement.[89]

Tokyo also agreed to compensate Seoul for damages incurred during colonial rule. Tokyo's initial negotiating position had been that it was *owed* reparations by the ROK. Eventually the Japanese agreed (1) to relinquish all claims against Korea, (2) to return art and other cultural artifacts taken during the occupation, and (3) to compensate the ROK with $300 million in outright grants, plus $500 million in loans ($200 million from Tokyo and $300 million in private commercial credits).[90] Importantly, Seoul agreed to relinquish any further reparations claims against Japan.

This compensation suffers along the dimensions of admission and remorse because not only was it not linked to any specific wrongdoing, Japanese officials even refused to characterize it as "reparations." Foreign Minister Ohira Masayoshi said that if the ROK insisted on receiving "reparations," then Japan would pay no more than $70 million in grants (the amount Tokyo had initially estimated for Korean property claims). Ohira suggested calling the payment "congratulatory in recognition of Korean independence." The Korean side (represented by Korean CIA Director Kim Jong-pil) agreed to the settlement as long as Seoul could inform the Korean public that Japan had paid "reparations."[91]

Other Japanese leaders issued subsequent—and similarly weak—apologies during this period. ROK President Chun Doo Hwan's visit to Tokyo in 1984 marked the first Japan-ROK summit. During Chun's visit,

Japanese Emperor Hirohito said: "I feel great regret that there was an unhappy phase in relations between our two countries in a certain period of this century despite the close ties between us. I believe that such things should not be repeated."[92] Like the Shiina statement, the emperor's apology did not acknowledge the violence that occurred during the "unhappy period" or who was responsible for it. The following day, Japanese Prime Minister Nakasone Yasuhiro made a second statement: "Unfortunately the fact cannot be denied that Japan caused great suffering to your country and your people during a certain period this century. I would like to announce that the Japanese government and people express deep regret for the wrongs done to you and are determined to strictly caution themselves against repeating them in the future." The prime minister's statement went further than the emperor's because it clarified Japanese culpability, but remained vague about the "wrongs" committed. The joint communiqué issued after the summit did not include a written Japanese apology.[93]

A subsequent Nakasone apology, given before the United Nations in 1985, continues in a similar vein. Nakasone said that Japan "profoundly regretted the ultra-nationalism and militarism it unleashed," and the "untold suffering the war inflicted on peoples of the world."[94] Nakasone also regretted the suffering inflicted on Japan's "own people" and noted that "having suffered the scourge of war and the atomic bomb," the people of Japan would never allow a militarist revival. This apology spends as much time regretting Japan's victimhood as its aggression, and reflects little in the way of admission. In sum, Japanese apologies from the middle period represented a change away from glorification of colonialism and showed some remorse. However, they admitted no specific misdeeds.

As some Japanese leaders offered apologies, other members of the government denied or glorified past violence. During a 1982 history textbook dispute, angered by perceived Chinese interference in Japan's domestic affairs, Interior Minister Matsuno Takayasu maintained that the term "invasion" was not used at the time of the war so should not be used in textbooks. He also denied that Japan had committed atrocities, arguing that "8,000 Japanese soldiers were killed and 12,000 Chinese died in Nanjing. There was no massacre at all."[95] Another cabinet official was angered by Nakasone's conciliation in the textbook dispute. Education Minister Fujio Masayuki wrote a controversial essay about Korea in which he argued, "Japan's annexation of Korea rested on mutual agreement both in form and in fact. As such, the Korean side also bears some responsibility for it. . . . Can we be sure that China or Russia would not have meddled in the Korean peninsula if Japan had not annexed it?" Fujio commented, "A large portion of the blame should be allocated toward Korea also."[96] In response to the uproar that these remarks provoked from Seoul, Nakasone fired Fujio (who had refused to retract his statement or resign his post). The Japanese foreign minister apologized to his South Korean counterpart, expressing "deepest regret and sincere apology" for Fujio's statement. Prime Minister Nakasone also said, "I deeply apologize to the Korean people and President over former education minister Fujio's remarks, which seriously hurt the feelings of the Korean people."[97]

A second episode occurred in 1988 after controversial statements were made by a member of Prime Minister Takeshita Noboru's cabinet. Okuno Seisuke objected to an exhibition on the Nanjing Massacre to be held in Japan, arguing that it should not be permitted because the facts surrounding the event were unclear. Okuno also defended Japanese actions in the 1930s. "It was the Caucasian race that colonized Asia," he argued: "If anybody was the aggressor, it was the Caucasians. It is nonsense to call Japan the aggressor or militaristic." Okuno claimed that Japan's war in Asia was a war of "Asian liberation" that aimed to form a republican system "comprising the Japanese and Koreans, then Manchurians, Hans, and Mongolians. . . . The people, long colonized by whites, needed to be liberated to give them stable livelihoods." Okuno commented that Japan was blamed for the war not because it had started it, but because it had lost it.[98] Prime Minister Takeshita demanded a retraction; when Okuno refused, he was asked to resign. These episodes sent a mixed signal about Japanese remembrance. To be sure, the resignations and dismissals clarified that the Japanese government did not view such statements as acceptable for its political leaders. At the same time, these events showcased the fact that numerous high-level Japanese leaders held strongly unapologetic views about the past.

Japanese education policy evolved significantly during this period. Wielding greater political influence in the 1970s, the Japanese Left encouraged education about colonization and war. Legal decisions also facilitated increased textbook coverage. Historian Ienaga Saburo won a landmark court victory in 1970; the Tokyo District Court ruled that the Ministry of Education had violated constitutional rights of freedom of expression "by extending its certification of textbooks to substantive content." The ruling upheld the ministry's right to certify textbooks but restricted textbook screening to "indicating typographical errors, misprints, and clear errors of 'historical fact.' " It "explicitly warned against scrutinizing an author's selection of illustrative material or his interpretations and conclusions."[99]

As a result, the Ministry of Education was forced to relax its screening procedures and accept a broader range of material, including descriptions of Japanese atrocities. In 1973 the ministry approved an Ienaga textbook containing descriptions of colonial policies in Korea and the war with China. James Orr writes that instead of celebrating Japan as an inspiration to Asian liberation movements, Japanese textbooks increased their descriptions of popular opposition to Japan's colonization of the Korean Peninsula. The junior high school textbook *Atarashi Shakai* [New Society] (1974) notes that Japan "tried to force the Koreans to assimilate by teaching the Japanese language and forbidding the teaching of Korean history." This text discussed the Korean March First independence movement, noting that it spread because of "suffering under Japanese colonial rule." In elementary school texts, coverage of Asian liberation movements and the suffering of Asian victims began appearing.[100]

Increased focus on atrocities angered conservatives, who decried such discussions as unpatriotic. Empowered by sweeping electoral victories in 1980, LDP Diet members pressured Ministry of Education bureaucrats to tighten their screening standards to reduce discussion of atrocities. As a result, in one case a screener ordered Ienaga to rewrite his textbook in ways that would gloss over Japanese atrocities, among them the Nanjing Massacre. The screener commented, "Readers might interpret [Ienaga's] description as meaning that the Japanese Army unilaterally massacred Chinese immediately after the occupation. This passage should be revised so that it is not interpreted in this way."[101] The screener also instructed Ienaga to remove passages about the medical experiments conducted by Unit 731, citing insufficient evidence of its existence.

Such changes prompted two international disputes in the 1980s. In 1982 the Japanese media reported that government textbook screeners were requiring all 1983 high school textbooks to describe the Japanese invasion of China as an "advance" rather than aggression. Such reports were later revealed to be erroneous (*Sankei Shinbun* and *Asahi Shinbun* later issued apologies for misleading coverage). However the bottom line is that media coverage (accurate or not) prompted intense scrutiny of Japanese textbooks, which were judged as unsatisfactory by Japanese liberals and by other countries. For example, Seoul protested the description of the March First independence movement (described as a "riot") and objected to the statement that Koreans had been "encouraged to worship at Shinto shrines." Chong-Sik Lee comments, "[Ministry of Education] censors had tried to mitigate Japanese responsibility for such events as the Nanjing Massacre of December 1937, the massacre of Koreans during the March First movement in 1919, and the conscription of Korean laborers during the early 1940s. Japanese atrocities were often treated as reactions to provocations, and descriptions of harsh treatments of victims were modified or deleted. The number of victims was often deleted for reasons of 'uncertainty of reports.' "[102]

Controversy over Japanese history textbooks was reignited in 1986 when the Ministry of Education approved a book that many critics said whitewashed Japan's past violence. Angered by the Suzuki government's conciliatory gestures toward China and the ROK during the 1982 dispute, Japanese conservatives organized the "National Congress for the Defense of Japan." Chaired by Japan's former UN ambassador, this group mobilized to write "a history textbook on its own to oppose prevalent school textbooks" that were "written by leftist scholars."[103] The group produced the textbook *Shinpen Nihonshi* [New Edition: Japanese History], which critics said whitewashed Japan's aggression in Asia. The book argued that Japan's war had been a war of liberation for Asian countries. It referred to the Nanjing "Incident," said that Japan "turned Korea into a protectorate," and lauded the Imperial Rescript of Education—the nationalism of emperor worship taught in Imperial Japan—as "national morality" from "ancient times."[104] Ministry of Education approval of this textbook infuriated Seoul and Beijing and touched off the second textbook dispute in 1986.

Japanese government policies during these textbook disputes reflected some contrition. In 1982, the Ministry of Education stood firm in response to criticism; Education Minister Ogawa Heiji told a press conference that the ministry had no intention of changing the texts and condemned Seoul and Beijing's "interference in Japan's internal affairs." However, the Foreign Ministry and Prime Minister Suzuki Zenko agreed that the books should be rewritten in order to reduce anti-Japanese sentiment abroad. Textbook revision standards were also changed, and an "Asian Neighbor's Clause" was added to Ministry of Education guidance: a requirement that proposed texts "show the necessary consideration for international understanding and international harmony in their treatment of the events of modern and contemporary history between [Japan and its] Asian neighbors."[105] Despite Tokyo's assurances that disputed passages would be changed, they continued to appear in subsequent texts.

Tokyo's handling of the 1986 dispute also reflects some contrition. Prime Minister Nakasone responded to domestic and international protests in a conciliatory fashion by creating an Ad Hoc Council on Education that discussed proposals for deregulating the textbook approval process. (Ultimately no reform was undertaken.) Nakasone also prodded the Ministry of Education to change some of the controversial passages.[106]

In sum, Japan's treatment of its past within history textbooks reflects more acknowledgment of past atrocities and more sensitivity to the concerns of neighbors. Overall, however, Japanese education was largely unapologetic: discussions of past misdeeds—if not totally absent—were often cursory at best.

Japanese commemoration continued to focus exclusively on Japan's war dead. This period witnessed the new significance of Tokyo's Yasukuni Shrine, a Shinto religious memorial honoring Japan's war dead. According to Shinto beliefs, because they died for the emperor, those enshrined at Yasukuni would become gods. Associated with the themes of emperor worship, racial superiority, and militarism, the shrine would become even more controversial after 1978, when fourteen men whom the Tokyo Trials had convicted as "Class-A" war criminals were enshrined there. ("Class-A" was the designation for people charged with "crimes against peace": i.e., those who had planned and implemented Japan's colonization and invasions.) As Ian Buruma writes, the shrine symbolized "all the bad things postwar

Japanese were supposed to forget as quickly as possible and keep away from their children, lest nasty things happen all over again."[107]

Although previous Japanese leaders had avoided the shrine because of its controversial symbolism, this changed in the 1980s. After the war, prime ministers would visit, but would go privately rather than in an official capacity. Emperor Hirohito had gone to the shrine since 1952, but ceased visiting after the fourteen men were enshrined there. But in 1985, Nakasone would be the first to visit in his official role as prime minister: on August 15, he gave a ritual offering of an expensive tree branch, purchased with public funds.

Nakasone's visit touched off intense domestic debate, student protests in China and the ROK, and condemnation from Beijing and Seoul. Critics argued that the shrine honors men who had orchestrated international aggression and gross human rights abuses; furthermore, domestic critics charge that official visits undermine Japan's constitutional separation of secular and religious authority. In response to domestic and international outrage, Nakasone agreed not to visit the shrine the following year. His chief cabinet secretary said, "We must stress international ties and give appropriate consideration to the national sentiments of neighboring countries."[108] Later, Prime Ministers Takeshita Noboru and Kaifu Toshiki also abstained from visiting.

In sum, official Japanese remembrance grew somewhat contrite from the mid-1960s through the 1980s, displaying increased sensitivity to the effects of remembrance in Japan's foreign relations. The increase in official contrition was far from stunning; apologies were lukewarm, commemoration ignored Japan's victims, and textbooks continued to omit a great deal about Japan's past. But Japan's official remembrance had grown more contrite relative to the silence and glorifications of the earlier period.

*Controversy over the Past in Japanese Society.* Discussion of past misdeeds grew more common, and more contentious, in Japanese society. Liberals, for their part, began to push for greater acknowledgment of past aggression and atrocities. The Vietnam War—and particularly American strategic bombing of North Vietnam after 1965—led Japanese liberals to confront Japan's history as an aggressor. In a movement known as *Beheiren,* Japanese liberals denounced American aggression and Tokyo's support for the war. Calls for solidarity with the North Vietnamese often invoked themes of shared victimhood: that is, Japan should oppose the war because it too had suffered American strategic bombing. But leaders of *Beheiren* also discussed the need for Japan to remember its own past as a "victimizer." *Beheiren* leader Oda Makoto urged the Japanese to "always be aware of and critical of our own experience (or potential) as assailants." He argued that "the only way for us to truly achieve the universal principle [of peace] is to keep criticizing the conduct of others as assailants, at the same time highlighting similar conduct by our own people." Oda and other *Beheiren* leaders, said liberal intellectual Konaka Yotaro, had for the first time prompted Japanese people to realize: "We had victimized Korea in the past and were victimizing Vietnam in the present." *Beheiren's* calls for greater candor about the past were complemented by an increasing number of memoirs and confessions by Japanese soldiers, who began discussing the acts they had committed during the war.[109]

As liberals explored the idea of Japan as victimizer rather than victim, they also pushed for greater coverage of war and colonization within history textbooks. Ienaga Saburo's battle in the Japanese courts, for example, was described above. Additionally, *Asahi Shinbun* and other liberal media outlets aggressively covered the issue of Japanese history education in the 1980s. Indeed, it was the Japanese media that brought the issue of national history education into the international spotlight and prompted the dispute with Japan's neighbors in 1982. Although Japan's critics condemned what they viewed as a disturbing nationalist trend, many people ignored the fact that powerful liberal forces in Japan were attempting to counter this trend, and indeed had instigated the debate in the first place.

While Japanese remembrance evolved during this period, societal debates reflected the prominence—if not dominance—of unapologetic views. This was evident in the controversies over remarks by Fujio and Okuno. To be sure, liberals condemned their statements. The Socialist Party, the Social Democrats (*Minshato*), and the Communist Party demanded that Nakasone fire Fujio. Furthermore, the dismissals, retractions, and apologies that followed their remarks should be viewed as important official condemnation of denials of Japanese culpability.

At the same time, it is important to note that many other people clearly tolerated—or even endorsed—such unapologetic interpretations about Japan's past. In both cases, the *Komeito* Party murmured criticism but did not demand any action, and LDP reaction was mixed, with some joining in the leftist rebuke and others defending Fujio and Okuno. Right-wing organizations sprang to their defense; before Fujio was fired, supporters drove cars with loudspeakers shouting "Don't quit!" in front of his ministry office.[110] It is also important to note that the cabinet dismissals were not career-ending events. Fujio and Okuno resumed their seats in the Diet and continued to be reelected and to enjoy influential political careers. When Okuno retired in 2004 due to old age, he was the longest-serving Diet member.

Finally many prominent Japanese leaders embraced the symbol of the Yasukuni Shrine and engaged in other commemorative events that honored the country's veterans and war victims. Deference to the neighbors—for example, Nakasone's decision to abstain from visiting the shrine—was clearly unpopular among many LDP conservatives. Nine of Nakasone's cabinet ministers visited (including Education Minister Fujio) in 1986. Sixteen of twenty Kaifu cabinet members went in 1989, along with a delegation of 184 Diet members.[111] Glorification of the country's own war dead—and a lack of attention to Japan's victims—was thus prevalent in Japanese society.

## COMPETING THEORIES AND PREDICTIONS

As Koreans evaluated various signals of Japan's intentions, they once again would not have felt reassured. Official policies had grown more contrite, but Koreans could also see that prominent elements in wider Japanese society still disputed the notion of Japanese war guilt and the basic facts about past atrocities. Moreover, the disagreement over the Tokdo/Takeshima Islands persisted into the 1980s; the condition of mutual democratization was still not present;[112] and—as before—neither country was a member of multilateral institutions that might have encouraged restraint and transparency. It is not surprising then that according to these criteria, Japan's intentions would have continued to appear hostile.

Changes in capabilities during this period, however, would have been reassuring: Korea's relative position improved markedly. In the 1960s, Korea under President Park Chung-hee embarked on a project of national economic development. The success of his export-led growth strategy earned Korea the moniker of one of East Asia's "tigers."[113] Although Japan's economy also continued to grow, Korea's development narrowed the wealth gap between the two states. The ROK also increased its military power; the ratio of Japanese to Korean military spending fell from 5:1 to 2.6:1 (by 1990, Tokyo spent $41 billion on defense, compared to the ROK's $16 billion). Korea maintained its favorable ratio in the number of mobilized military forces, in the range of 650,000 compared to Japan's 250,000.[114]

Koreans also had grounds to feel more secure because of American military protection. Importantly, diplomatic normalization with Tokyo in 1965 had not resulted in an American military withdrawal from Asia. That year President Johnson had praised normalization between the two countries and repeatedly pledged continued U.S. military support of Korea.[115] In 1967 Washington and Seoul deepened their alliance further by signing a Status of Forces Agreement. Moreover, the 1960 renewal of the U.S-Japan Security Treaty reinvigorated an alliance that Koreans had feared would break down. In Japanese politics, alliance with the United States became accepted—even by the formerly hostile Left—as the cornerstone of Japan's foreign policy. Thus during the middle period, Korea's overall position vis-à-vis Japan improved.

In the 1970s, American policies again stirred fears of impending withdrawal. President Nixon's July 1969 speech in Guam (known as the Guam Doctrine) promised ongoing U.S. support for friendly states but exhorted Asian allies to bear the major responsibility for their defense. This and his policies of "Vietnamization" represented a U.S. effort to encourage regional allies to assume more of the burden of the East Asian anticommunist effort. Many Koreans were concerned by Nixon's policies, and later by Jimmy Carter's campaign promise to withdraw numerous American troops from the Korean Peninsula.[116] At the same time, both Nixon and Carter emphasized to Seoul that changes in American policy did not include plans for a U.S. termination of its security commitment to the ROK.[117] Most important, no one was discussing the termination of what the Koreans viewed as the most vital protection against Japanese military resurgence: the U.S.-Japan alliance. Defense of Japan remained a cornerstone of the American global fight against communism, and during the 1980s the alliance would grow stronger than ever.[118]

Tokyo also grew more constrained during this period because of the growth of Soviet military power in the Pacific. Previously, Japan had enjoyed a favorable military balance and political climate. Superpower détente and the U.S. normalization of relations with China had enabled Tokyo to normalize and improve relations with neighboring communist regimes.[119] However, Japan's security environment worsened in the mid-1970s: the Soviet Union began building up its military presence in the Pacific theater and appeared more threatening after its 1979 invasion of Afghanistan.[120] Growth in North Korean conventional military power also exacerbated the communist threat in East Asia.

In sum, based on remembrance and territorial claims, Koreans distrusted Japanese intentions during this period. However, Korea should have felt less threatened by Japan because Seoul had narrowed the power gap between the two countries and because of increasing constraints on Japanese power (a sturdier alliance and stronger security threats).

KOREAN PERCEPTIONS, 1965–89

Although normalization ushered in a productive period in Japan-ROK relations, Korean distrust of Japanese intentions persisted. Poll data reflect strong animosity; respondents to a 1975 *Chungang Ilbo* newspaper survey ranked Japan as one of Koreans' least-liked countries (behind Communist China and the Soviet Union). A 1972 *Shin Dong-a* poll reflected fears of a revival of Japanese militarism, with 90 percent of respondents reporting that memories and scars of Japanese colonization remained acute. Over half of Koreans reported in 1978 that they viewed Japan as untrustworthy; 34 percent were undecided.[121] Words people associated with the Japanese were militarism, colonial rule, forced oath to emperor, forced Japanese names, forced Shinto worship, and racial discrimination. A similar poll conducted in 1985 reveals the persistence of such negative images. The *Kyonghyang Shinmun* newspaper reported in a 1982 poll that only ten percent of respondents viewed Japan as "a friendly country."[122] One newspaper wrote that the legacy of Japan's colonial rule had "grossly embittered the Koreans and thus sowed the seeds of longstanding national antagonism against Japan." As Chong-Sik Lee confirmed, there was "no genuine friendship between the two peoples"; he noted that Koreans believed that "the only interest Japan has in Korea is to aggrandize itself by exploiting whatever opportunity Korea provides."[123]

During this period, American calls for greater Japanese burden sharing in the U.S.-Japan alliance were met with wary approval from Seoul. Although Koreans accepted the need to enlist Japan to help counter an increasingly serious communist threat in the region, profound Korean distrust is evident in Seoul's qualified approval of Japanese military activities: a more active Japan was regarded as positive if, and only if, it operated within the U.S.-Japan alliance. "The Japanese defense buildup effort and regional security role," wrote a Defense Ministry official, "can contribute to Korean security and stability if the U.S. remains a mighty Pacific power, [and] if Japan increases her defense capability in such a way as to augment the U.S. regional strategy." He argued that if plans for "an increased military role for Japan" were part of "the American strategic design either to reduce their defense burden or to fill a power vacuum in Northeast Asia . . . it might cause a sense of insecurity in both Korea and Japan over the years to come." After announcements of increased Japanese military roles, an ROK government spokesman noted that Seoul "plans to closely watch Japan's defense maneuvers."[124]

Scholars exhibited similar wariness. One noted that Japan should only "augment U.S. military capabilities, if and when some of the U.S. military units now deployed in the Western Pacific have to be shifted elsewhere in an emergency. It should not replace the U.S. presence in the area. Also, Japan's Self-Defense Forces should be integrated into the U.S. defense network."[125] Scholar Soong-Hoom Kil wrote, "South Korea has expressed concern . . . about the possibility that Japan might undertake a military buildup either under U.S. pressure or under her own nationalistic mood." A Japanese buildup was a subject of concern because "South Korea recalls how a militarily strong Japan was a direct threat to her."[126] Such statements reflect lingering distrust; Koreans still viewed Japan as a potential future threat to Korea.

*Korean Reasoning about Japan's Intentions.* After normalization, Koreans appeared to be willing to move forward on issues related to history; Shiina's apology (however tepid) won praise as a reassuring sign that bilateral relations were entering a new era.[127] Seoul devoted its energies to cultivating stronger political relations, trade ties, and Japanese investment. The disputes that arose in the 1970s centered not on issues of history but on South Korean dissatisfaction with Japan's insufficient support to defend it against the North.[128]

In the 1980s, however—after revelations about Japanese history textbooks and insensitive remarks by prominent leaders—South Koreans once again expressed concerns that Japan had not satisfactorily come to terms with its past. Many Koreans protested that Tokyo was sending mixed signals: while some leaders apologized, others justified or denied past violence. Seoul lodged a diplomatic protest in 1986 after Fujio's statement that Japan's annexation of Korea had been peaceful and legitimate. Foreign Minister Choi Kwang-soo told the Japanese foreign minister, "Fujio's outrageous remarks have created a serious and important problem in the basic relations between the two nations and have greatly stirred up the Korean people's sentiments against Japan." The issue at hand was not so much Fujio specifically, commented Prime Minister Roh Shin-yong, but a broader problem with Japanese attitudes.[129] The Korean media agreed that the controversy was "more fundamentally" about the Japanese predilection "to justify and even glorify their past wrongs." Calling Fujio's remarks "abusive," "absurd," "astonishing," and "outrageous," an editorial commented, "There have been many claims, and indeed hopes, along with lingering misgivings, that post-war Japan has been rebuilt into a 'new Japan' based on democracy, and ... devoid of its past militarism and colonialism which had devastated so many Asian countries. However, belying the claims ... were repeated absurd remarks by none other than an incumbent Cabinet minister of the Japanese government." Another newspaper called Fujio's statement "a shrewd 'venture' by Japanese conservatives to restore Japan's pre-war 'glory.' "[130]

In two disputes over history textbooks, Koreans argued that whitewashing of past atrocities reflected hostile intentions. ROK Education Minister Yi Kyu-ho chided Japan for trying to "gloss over or beautify its past crimes." Yi commented, "South Korean concern about the reported erroneous historical descriptions in Japanese textbooks with regard to Korea-Japan relations is not for 'reminiscent resentment' but for the maintenance of friendly relations between the two countries in the days to come."[131]

Dismay about Japanese history textbooks appeared across Korean society. Opposition politicians joined the government in condemning Tokyo's "attempt to whitewash Japan's atrocities during its colonial rule of Korea." Scholars expressed outrage: "Not only are the Japanese unrepentant," one lamented, "but also many are proud of their 'accomplishments' in Korea." Another scholar wrote that Japan's whitewashing of history textbooks made Koreans wary of "Japan's basic stance toward its Asian neighbors as well as Tokyo's ulterior motives in revising the textbooks."[132] The media closely monitored and criticized Japan over the textbook issue. A *Kyonghyang Shinmun* editorial warned, "Japan's arrogant attitude toward Korea implies a likelihood of Japan's repetition of [its] crimes." Another editorial said that the issue at hand was not quibbling about specific text but evidence of a widespread "preposterous, imperial view of history." The editorial noted that "distortions of facts" in Japanese textbooks were manifestations of a new "militarist trend" and maintained that the books must be rewritten to check this trend. Finally, hostility toward Japan was evident in the anti-Japanese petitions and rallies held all over the country, protesting

" 'distorted' Japanese history textbooks and the remarks made by Japanese Cabinet ministers in support of them." The Japanese ambassador to South Korea received death threats, and his embassy received a bomb threat.[133] Tokyo's unapologetic remembrance thus contributed significantly toward Korean distrust of Japan.

Although Koreans continued to suspect Japan's intentions—largely, as noted, due to unapologetic remembrance—their fears of Japan relaxed in this period. Seoul abandoned its attempts to keep military parity with Japan, which had initiated a military buildup in the late 1970s. South Korean force structure (such as the Force Improvement Plan of 1975) reflects a preoccupation not with a maritime threat from Japan but with the North Korean ground threat. Seoul announced that the Force Improvement Plan sought to "[secure] a defense capability to repel North Korean aggression."[134] Whereas in the previous period (1952–64), Korean officials had frantically tried to dissuade American leaders from empowering Japan with new military capabilities or missions, now they accepted and even encouraged a more active Japanese posture. When Japanese Prime Minister Suzuki agreed in 1981 to take on more responsibilities within the U.S.-Japan alliance, the *Korea Herald* reported, "We were pleased." Japan's move to patrol the sea lanes out to 1,000 miles was called "a positive response" to pressure for burden-sharing from Washington. Media coverage after the January 1983 meeting between U.S. President Ronald Reagan and Prime Minister Nakasone was similarly enthusiastic; an article in the *Korea Herald* discussing the potential dangers of Japan's new roles noted only potential Soviet (not Korean) concerns.[135]

South Korean leaders also approved of a more active Japanese military. President Chun Doo Hwan commented, "Japan should reinforce its defense capabilities not only to protect its territory but also to safeguard the peace of the region and to ensure the sea lanes will be kept open."[136] After the 1983 U.S.-Japan summit, a Japanese official noted that his country's new military roles would include blockading the Korea Strait in case of Soviet aggression. Media coverage reflected no uproar about this announcement; the South Korean government only requested prior consultations before Japan would launch "military operations on the high seas between the two countries," although it noted, "Seoul is not in a position to meddle in Japan's military maneuvers."[137]

A significant increase in bilateral cooperation during this period also reflects diminished South Korean threat perception. Cooperation extended beyond the 1965 diplomatic normalization. An ROK Ministry of National Defense (MND) official noted "a phenomenal expansion in Korean-Japanese military contacts."[138] The Korean media urged a more robust bilateral relationship with Tokyo; one article speculated hopefully about "the prospect of security cooperation between Korea and Japan." Another noted that to cope with changes on the Korean Peninsula and in Asia Seoul should create "a trilateral security system among the U.S., Japan, and

Korea." Similarly, in a historic 1979 visit to Seoul, Japanese Defense Agency head Yamashita Ganri became the first high-level military official to conduct talks with the ROK. At this meeting, defense chiefs discussed closer security ties. Overall, South Korean media coverage welcomed closer relations with Japan, arguing for increased trilateral cooperation with Tokyo and Washington. An article urged the Japanese to make "substantial contributions to the regional security system in logistical support and exchanges of military intelligence," as well in defense industries.[139]

Bilateral cooperation continued to grow in the next decade. In 1983 the two countries held their first-ever presidential summits. That year, after the USSR shot down a Korean Air Lines jumbo jet, the government sought "increased defense cooperation with the United States and Japan to check the Soviet military expansion in the Far East," and cited its "strong desire to strengthen tripartite cooperation." An article noted that although "Japan has been reluctant to have any form of military connection with Korea," perhaps the incident of Soviet aggression would lead it to reconsider.[140] As Soong-Hoom Kil argued at the time, "Korea and Japan exist in the northeast Asian context. When looked at from this broader perspective, the two countries are required to bury ill feelings and work hard in close cooperation in two important enterprises, one vis-à-vis the Soviet Union and the other vis-à-vis North Korea.[141] Despite lingering distrust of Japan, fears of a Japanese threat had dropped relative to the 1952–1964 time period.

*Korean Reasoning about a Japanese Threat.* Korean fears of Japan during the 1965–89 period were eased because of stronger constraints on Japanese capabilities: most important, the U.S.-Japan alliance appeared more durable. Koreans had feared Japan's neutrality; one article said Koreans were "deeply grateful" that the LDP overcame strong leftwing opposition and successfully renewed the U.S.-Japan Security Treaty in 1960. Koreans welcomed the 1970 decision to automatically reapprove the treaty every ten years.[142]

Because Koreans viewed the U.S.-Japan alliance as the major constraint on Japan's ability to threaten the ROK, they favored policies to strengthen it. Amid increased American calls for greater burden sharing, Koreans supported Japan's military buildup and new military roles because such actions mollified Washington. After a meeting of the U.S.-Japan security consultative committee in 1976, one newspaper noted, "Korea expects Japan will develop U.S.-Japan security relations and U.S.-Japan-Korea cooperation by strengthening its Maritime and Air Self-Defense Forces." As a later article pointed out, "the growing Soviet military buildup in the region" necessitated "a substantive boost in Japan's defense capabilities . . . to safeguard the U.S.-led defense framework in northeast Asia and the western Pacific." Tokyo's announcement that it would blockade the Korea Strait in the event of war with the Soviets was not considered threatening because the policy was adopted as part of regional defense and within the U.S.-Japan alliance. "Japan's plan for blockading the straits," one newspaper reassured, "should be understood from such a viewpoint." Another article called the new role of sea-lane patrol "a positive response to Washington's desire that Japan take up the defense of a large area of the western Pacific."[143] A scholar explained Japan's recent increase in military activities: "It is the Reagan administration, with an eye toward the Soviet Union, that is pushing Japan to increase military spending and assume a greater defense role."[144]

Not only did Koreans feel more secure that Japanese capabilities were constrained, they also expressed confidence in the U.S. defense of South Korea. During the 1960s and 1970s, Koreans worried that Vietnam war-weariness would weaken the U.S. commitment to Seoul.[145] But they were relieved when, first, the 1965 normalization between Korea and Japan did not lead to the dreaded U.S. pullout and, second, when Washington and Seoul took a number of steps to solidify the U.S.-ROK alliance. For example, Foreign Minister Lee Dong-won commented that the 1967 Status of Forces Agreement put an end "once and for all to the pending negotiations of many past years" and confirmed strong bilateral ties. Prime Minister Chung Il-kwon similarly noted that the agreement signaled a strengthened U.S. commitment. Subsequent leaders were pleased by later events such as the 1978 establishment of a general headquarters for U.S. and Korean forces; President Park said the move was an expression of firm U.S. resolution to defend South Korea.[146]

In sum, Korean perceptions of Japan evolved from 1965 through the 1980s: Japan was no longer seen as a security threat. Koreans felt more secure because of changes in Japanese capabilities: most important, they perceived Japanese power to be credibly constrained by the U.S.-Japan alliance. But Koreans still evinced strong distrust of Japan's intentions, speculating that it might someday again threaten the peninsula. Such distrust was linked to Japan's unapologetic remembrance. Koreans argued that Japanese denials and glorifications of past violence showed Japan had not rejected its violent past. Interestingly, during this period the Tokdo/Takeshima dispute did not significantly affect Korean perceptions; the issue died down after Seoul and Tokyo "agreed to disagree" within the 1965 normalization treaty.

## Late Period (1990–2000s)

### THE PAST EMERGES

Before 1990, Japan's wartime past had lurked in the background; during the 1990s it burst into the Japanese national consciousness. It marched with banners on city streets; it blared from activists' loudspeakers; it crowded newspaper headlines; and it poured out of memoirs. Forgotten victims attracted attention (the "comfort women," slave laborers, and victims of the biological warfare Unit 731). Mark Selden and Laura Hein write that starting in the 1990s, the Japanese "produced stacks of testimony, including books, documentary films, and archival research, on previously suppressed or ignored aspects of the war. That testimony has also clarified how difficult the war years were for most Japanese, so that memory of Japanese suffering has grown along with knowledge of suffering of others at their hands."[147] During this period, official remembrance grew more apologetic; however, government contrition fueled increased controversy within Japanese society. The trend toward greater self-examination sparked a backlash in which opponents of contrition frequently denied or justified Japan's past actions. This backlash was part of a more general nationalist trend in Japanese politics.

*Official Remembrance since 1990.* Leaders issued numerous apologies during this period. Although several of them resembled the tepid statements of the previous era, others conveyed a great deal of admission and remorse. In 1990 Prime Minister Kaifu Toshiki and Emperor Akihito (who had succeeded his father after Emperor Hirohito died in 1989) both apologized to Korea. The emperor was attempting to compensate for the vagueness of Hirohito's 1984 statement. Akihito said, "When I think of the sufferings your people underwent during this unhappy phase, brought on by my country, I cannot help feeling the deepest regret."[148] For his part, Kaifu was the first Japanese official to voice the word "apology" (*owabi*). He said, "I would like to take the opportunity of Your Excellency's visit to express my sincere remorse and honest apologies for the fact that there was a period in our history in which Japanese actions inflicted unbearable suffering and sorrow on the people of the Korean peninsula." Prime Minister Miyazawa Kiichi offered another apology in 1991. He said, "I would like to state frankly that the people of Asia and the Pacific have experienced unbearable torment and grief caused by Japan. We would like to, once again, convey our feelings of regretfulness and reflection. Also, we look straight in the face of our past atrocities and would like to convey the proper interpretation of the history to preclude this kind of misdeed from ever repeating itself again. And as a member of the international society, it is incumbent upon the Japanese to take the full responsibility for our past wrongdoings."[149]

Prime Minister Hosokawa Morihiro offered a landmark apology in 1993. The leader of a multiparty coalition government, Hosokawa symbolized the end of a half-century of LDP rule, and both his leadership and his apology were viewed as a new beginning. He was the first Japanese leader to characterize Japan's past actions in Asia as an "aggressive war" (*shinryaku senso*). His apology reflected very high admission and remorse. Hosokawa said, "During Japan's colonial rule over the Korean Peninsula, the Korean people were forced to suffer unbearable pain and sorrow in various ways. They were deprived of the opportunity to learn their mother tongue at school, they were forced to adopt Japanese names, forced to provide sex as 'comfort women' for Japanese troops, forced to provide labor. I hereby express genuine contrition and offer my deepest apologies for my country, the aggressor's, acts." Hosokawa was also the first prime minister to invite representatives from other nations to participate in the annual National Memorial Service for the War Dead on August 15; in his speech he referred to Asian war victims as well as Japanese.[150]

Murayama Tomiichi offered two important apologies in 1994 and 1995. Japan's only socialist prime minister offered his "deep remorse" and "heartfelt condolences" for the "horrific, indescribable suffering" endured by Asians in the war.[151] A year later (on the fiftieth anniversary of the surrender), he issued what would become a milestone apology:

> During a certain period in the not-too-distant past, Japan, following a mistaken national policy, advanced along the road to war, only to ensnare the Japanese people in a fateful crisis, and, through its colonial rule and aggression, caused tremendous damage and suffering to the people of many countries, particularly to those of Asian nations. In the hope that no such mistake be made in the future, I regard, in a spirit of humility, these irrefutable facts of history, and express here once again my feelings of deep remorse and state my heartfelt apology. Allow me also to express my feelings of profound mourning for all victims, both at home and abroad, of that history.

Notable in Murayama's statement was the first use of the words "profound remorse" (*tsusetsu na hansei*) and "heartfelt apology" (*kokoro kara no owabi*).

To commemorate the fiftieth anniversary of the World War II surrender, the Japanese Diet in 1995 debated and passed a resolution of apology.[152] Debate over this resolution was intense, and produced a statement that satisfied no one. The resolution admits to essentially nothing: as if Tokyo were an uninvolved party, it extends "condolences" to those who "fell in action" (rather than those whom the Japanese killed). Diluting the focus on Japan's colonization and aggression, the resolution mourns victims "of wars and similar actions all over the world": not only Japan's victims from the era in question, but also victims of "many instances" of violence "in the modern history of the world." It does, however, "recognize that Japan carried out" aggression and colonial rule in the past and expresses "a sense of deep remorse." The Diet resolution reads:

*The 1995 Diet Resolution*

RESOLUTION TO RENEW THE DETERMINATION FOR PEACE
ON THE BASIS OF LESSONS LEARNED FROM HISTORY

The House of Representatives resolves as follows:

On the occasion of the 50th anniversary of the end of World War II, this House offers its sincere condolences to those who fell in action and victims of wars and similar actions all over the world.

Solemnly reflecting upon many instances of colonial rule and acts of aggression in the modern history of the world, and recognizing that Japan carried out those acts in the past, inflicting pain and suffering upon the peoples of other countries, especially in Asia, the Members of this House express a sense of deep remorse.

We must transcend the differences over historical views of the past war and learn humbly the lessons of history so as to build a peaceful international society.

This House expresses its resolve, under the banner of eternal peace enshrined in the Constitution of Japan, to join hands with other nations of the world and to pave the way for a future that allows all human beings to live together.

(Source: Ryuji Mukae, "Japan's Diet Resolution on World War Two:
Keeping History at Bay," *Asian Survey* 36, no. 10 (October 1996), 1011–1030)

The next major Japanese apology came in 1998 at a summit between ROK President Kim Dae-jung and Japanese Prime Minister Obuchi Keizo. The Koreans insisted on a Japanese apology within the text of a planned joint declaration. Tokyo eventually agreed, on the condition that Seoul explicitly accept the apology and pledge to move relations forward. The declaration stated:

Reviewing bilateral relations between Japan and Korea in the present century, and recognizing with profound humility the historical fact that, for a time in the past, Japan by its colonial rule inflicted great damage and pain on the Korean people, Prime Minister Keizo Obuchi expressed deep remorse and most sincere apologies for this. President Kim Dae-jung in good faith accepted and appreciated Prime Minister Obuchi's expression of his view of history and stated that the current of the times was such that the two nations are required now to live down the unhappy phase of their past history and to make their best efforts for reconciliation and for good neighborly and friendly relations.

Obuchi also met with Chinese Premier Jiang Zemin that same autumn, and the two sides planned to issue a joint declaration. Ultimately, the declaration was never signed due to disputes over whether it would include a Japanese apology and a Chinese acceptance of that apology. Obuchi verbally repeated the Murayama expression of "remorse" and extended a "heartfelt apology."[153]

Subsequent apologies were offered by the Koizumi government. Prime Minister Koizumi Junichiro apologized for Japanese aggression during a 2001 visit to the Yasukuni Shrine.

During the war, Japan caused tremendous sufferings to many people of the world including its own people. Following a mistaken national policy during a certain period in the past, Japan imposed, through its colonial rule and aggression, immeasurable ravages and suffering particularly to the people of the neighboring countries in Asia. This has left a still incurable scar to many people in the region. Sincerely facing these deeply regrettable historical facts as they are, here I offer my feelings of profound remorse and sincere mourning to all the victims of the war.[154]

In September of that same year, on the occasion of the fiftieth anniversary of the signing of the San Francisco Peace Treaty, Foreign Minister Tanaka Makiko offered an apology in her speech. "We have never forgotten," she said, "that Japan caused tremendous damage and suffering to the people of many countries during the last war. Many lost their precious lives and many were wounded. The war has left an incurable scar on many people, including former prisoners of war. Facing these facts of history in a spirit of humility, I reaffirm today our feelings of deep remorse and heartfelt apology expressed in the Prime Minister Murayama's statement of 1995."[155]

In November, Koizumi issued another apology in Seoul. He visited the Seodaemun Prison History Hall, a facility used during the Japanese occupation to imprison, torture, and execute Korean independence activists and other opponents of Japanese authority. The buildings now host a museum detailing Japanese atrocities during the occupation that includes execution facilities and macabre exhibits of torture and rape rooms. Koizumi laid a wreath at a memorial for Korean independence leaders; he said he felt "heartfelt remorse and apology for the tremendous damage and suffering Japan caused the South Korean people during its colonial rule."[156] Koizumi's remarks and his visit to this site, which drew worldwide attention to Japanese atrocities, reflect significant admission and remorse.

Koizumi also apologized in April 2005 at the Asia-Africa summit in Jakarta. In front of a group of world leaders, he acknowledged, "Japan, through its colonial rule and aggression, caused tremendous damage and suffering to the people of many countries. . . ."[157] He said, "Japan squarely faces these facts of history in a spirit of humility. And with feelings of deep remorse and heartfelt apology always engraved in mind, Japan has resolutely maintained, consistently since the end of World War II, never turning into a military power but an economic power, its principle of resolving all matters by peaceful means, without recourse to the use of force.[158] In sum, most prime ministers since 1990 have offered apologies—some of them remarkably contrite—for Japan's past aggression.

DURING this period, Tokyo also paid compensation to previously neglected victims: the sex slaves of the Japanese Army. Initially the Japanese government had said that women had provided sex for Japanese soldiers in World War II, but said that they were prostitutes (and thus willing participants) working for private individuals. For example, as Japanese official Shimizu

Tadao commented, the women "had just been taken around with the Forces by private operators, so frankly speaking, I do not believe it is possible to obtain any results by investigation as to the true facts of the matter." Prime Minister Miyazawa had also said that no documentary evidence confirmed government involvement.

After Japanese scholar Yoshimi Yoshiaki discovered and published archival documents proving government administration of the program, the Japanese government apologized to the women and to Seoul. Chief Cabinet Secretary Kato Koichi said in 1992 that a government inquiry revealed Tokyo had established and managed the "comfort women" program. Vague on the issue of forcible recruitment, Kato said that Tokyo "had been involved in . . . the control of those who recruited comfort women." Kato apologized, saying,

> The Government again would like to express its sincere apology and remorse to all those who have suffered indescribable hardship as so-called "wartime comfort women," irrespective of their nationality or place of birth. With profound remorse and determination that such a mistake must never be repeated, Japan will maintain its stance as a pacifist nation and will endeavor to build up new future-oriented relations with the Republic of Korea and with other countries and regions in Asia.[159]

At that time Tokyo offered no compensation.[160]

Prime Minister Miyazawa also apologized during a visit to South Korea, where he expressed a "heartfelt apology for the Japanese government's involvement in the conscription of tens of thousands of Korean women for forced sex for Japanese soldiers during World War II. . . ." On his last day in office, Miyazawa apologized again, offering "sincere apologies and remorse" to the women.[161] Twelve years later, Chief Cabinet Secretary Hosoda Hiroyuki met with a group of survivors and issued an apology, saying, "I apologize from the bottom of my heart for disgracing women's dignity during the war."[162]

In 1995 Tokyo announced that a foundation known as the Asian Women's Fund (AWF) would provide sex slave victims with "sympathy money" (*mimaikin*). The AWF was funded from public and private sources; it received its operating budget from the Japanese government. Announcing the formation of the AWF, Prime Minister Murayama said: "Established on this occasion and involving the cooperation of the Government and citizens of Japan, the 'Asian Women's Fund' is an expression of atonement on the part of the Japanese people toward these women and supports medical, welfare, and other projects." He noted, "To ensure that this situation is never again repeated, the Government of Japan will collate historical documents concerning the former wartime comfort women, to serve as a lesson of history."[163] Each survivor was eligible for compensation in the amount of

2 million yen (about U.S. $17,000) and a letter from the Japanese Prime Minister expressing "apologies and remorse."

Many people have been highly critical of the AWF. Survivor Jan Ruff O'Herne commented, "This Fund was an insult to the 'Comfort Women.' . . . [We] refused to accept it. This fund was a private fund, the money came from private enterprise, and not from the government. Japan must come to terms with its history, and acknowledge their war time atrocities." Similarly, survivor Yi Ok-seon said that the AWF was Tokyo's attempt "to shut the mouths of the comfort women." Scholar Norma Field argues, "In proffering money donated privately for 'sympathy,' the government is in effect canceling its confession of wrongdoing."[164] As these critics have claimed, the AWF certainly lacks the power of parliamentary reparations; however, Tokyo's support of the foundation, the official apologies that accompanied the compensation, and the educational efforts associated with it demonstrate more contrition toward the sex slave victims than in the past.

ALTHOUGH Tokyo has never indicted individuals for war crimes, litigation has resulted in some official admission of Japanese atrocities. Starting in the 1990s, individual victims of Japanese atrocities—particularly victims of forced labor, "comfort women," and former POWs—increasingly began pursuing litigation against the Japanese government and companies. On the one hand, plaintiffs were generally unsuccessful. Approximately sixty war-related lawsuits had been filed as of late 2007, but the courts most often have thrown them out or ruled against the plaintiffs. Many lawsuits were dismissed because the statute of limitations had expired or because when national governments normalized relations with Tokyo, they waived the right to make future reparations claims. Nevertheless, district courts have at times awarded settlements to plaintiffs. For example, a 2002 decision by the Fukuoka District Court described Mitsui's policies as "evil" and ordered the company to pay compensation; in 2004, the Niigata District Court found the Japanese government and Rinko Corporation responsible for damages. For the most part, however, such verdicts were subsequently reversed, for the aforementioned reasons, by higher courts. In an important decision in April 2007, the Japanese Supreme Court rejected two compensation claims (for forced laborers and the sex slaves).

Such litigation, however, reflects a greater admission of Japanese guilt than in the previous era. Victims have heard Japanese atrocities acknowledged by courts and have received some compensation. In September 2004 a court-mediated settlement was reached between former slave laborers and the corporation Nippon Yakin Kogyo. In November 2000, Kajima Corporation settled out of court, agreeing to set up a foundation to compensate Chinese forced laborers and their families and to pay out about $5 million. Although judges normally rule against plaintiffs, they have frequently encouraged greater admission of Japanese culpability for the events in question. In a 1995 lawsuit filed by eight Chinese victims of Unit 731, the courts ruled against the plaintiffs but stated that the Japanese government was indeed culpable of the atrocities of which it was accused. The Fukuoka High Court overturned a decision that required Mitsui to pay compensation to former slave laborers, but in its 2004 ruling it decried the behavior of both the Japanese state and the company as "an outrageous transgression of human dignity." The court explicitly stated that the Chinese men were seized through violence or deception and forced into slave labor.[165]

In 2007, although the Supreme Court rejected compensation claims by forced laborers and the sex slaves, its decisions stated and the facts of the atrocities and condemned them. The court recognized that the two plaintiffs had been violently abducted; it also recognized the "extremely large mental and physical suffering" of slave laborers and urged Nishimatsu Construction to "provide relief to the victims."[166] As William Underwood has pointed out, although victims are unlikely to receive compensation, litigation has helped establish an "invaluable historical record" of the basic facts of Japanese war crimes such as the Nanjing Massacre, forced labor, strategic bombing, Unit 731, and the "comfort women."[167]

JAPANESE commemoration has changed little since the 1965–89 period; for the most part, museums, monuments, and ceremonies continue to remember domestic rather than foreign victims. The Yasukuni Shrine acquired a new political prominence as prime ministers and other powerful leaders resumed visits. In 1994, Minister of International Trade and Industry Hashimoto Ryutaro visited the shrine with several other cabinet members on the anniversary of the surrender. Hashimoto was also the leader of Japan's "bereaved families' association" (*Nihon izokukai*), dedicated to honoring the memory of Japan's war dead. Hashimoto returned two years later as prime minister, visiting on his birthday in July in what he said was a purely personal capacity. Prime Minister Koizumi visited the shrine repeatedly. As noted above, during his August 2001 visit he issued an apology to Japan's past victims, saying it was contrary to his wish if his visit would "lead people of neighboring countries to cast doubts on the fundamental policy of Japan of denying war and desiring peace."[168]

Koizumi's visits to the shrine were supported by many LDP members, many of whom visited themselves. Abe Shinzo (LDP secretary general and Koizumi's successor) said in 2005, "It's the duty of the nation's leader to offer prayers to the souls of people who lost their lives for our country." Cabinet member Aso Taro commented that he had been visiting the shrine for a long time and viewed it as perfectly natural. Secretary General Takebe Tsutomu of the Liberal Democratic Party said, "Those who want to visit the shrine can do so—to console the souls of the war dead and make a pledge not to fight a war again. Under the Constitution, freedom of religious belief is guaranteed."[169] Ninety-six Diet members (largely from the LDP) visited the shrine in April 2006; among them, Koga Makoto said, "It is quite natural to pay respect for those who devoted their precious lives to the state of Japan." Earlier, 233 lawmakers had passed a resolution declaring their strong opposition to a proposal that the government construct an alternate, secular war memorial. They argued such a memorial was unnecessary because the Japanese government "[has] not considered the Class-A war criminals as criminals."[170] In 2001, Koizumi also drew fire from conservatives for not visiting on August 15 (the day of the surrender): *Sankei Shinbun* wrote that he "would lose the trust of the people," who had hoped "for the appearance of a strong-willed leader."[171]

Museums reflect amnesia about or glorification of Japanese atrocities and colonization. The refurbished Yushukan museum (next to the Yasukuni Shrine) glorifies Japanese colonization and omits the violence associated with it. Its exhibits portray Tokyo as a liberator of Asian nations, forced into a defensive war by European and American colonizers who had attempted to strangle Japan by cutting off its raw materials.[172] "Chinese terrorists" are blamed for Japan's invasion of China. The attack on Pearl Harbor is described as the inevitable result of American pressure. The Yushukan museum describes the Nanjing Massacre—which historians estimate as having killed 100,000–300,000 Chinese—as the "Nanjing Incident." The exhibit reads: "The Chinese troops were soundly defeated, suffering heavy casualties. Inside the city, residents were once again able to live their lives in peace." The exhibits do not mention the 200,000 women forced into sexual servitude of the army, forced laborers, the grotesque medical experiments of Unit 731, abuse of Allied POWs (such as the Bataan Death March), Japanese strategic bombing of Chinese cities, or Japanese use of chemical or biological weapons against Chinese noncombatants. A curator explained such omissions by arguing that the "debate over what really happened is still under way." The exhibits honor the *Kaiten* human-torpedo operators (suicide bombers), who are celebrated as gods (*kami*), with displays of their personal effects and final letters to their families. The chairman of the Japan Veteran's Association commented, "The original purpose of the museum was to pay tribute to the souls of the war dead, by displaying their belongings. That way, their children can live with pride."[173]

Two Tokyo museums remember the war by emphasizing hardships suffered by the Japanese people. The National Memorial Museum for Peace (*Heiwa kinen tenji shiryokan*) emphasizes the hardships of Japanese soldiers at the front. It describes in particular the campaign after the Soviet offensive in Manchuria and notes the plight of POWs who suffered in Soviet detention camps after the war. The other, the glossy Showakan museum, commemorates the imperial Showa era of Hirohito's reign (1926–89). Opened in 1999, the museum is publicly funded, although it was first proposed, and is

Prime Minister Koizumi at Yasukuni Shrine. AP PHOTO/SHUJI KAJIYAMA.

administered by, the Japan War Bereaved Families Association (*Nihon izokukai*). Intense controversy surrounded the museum's construction. Plans to include exhibits about the Nanjing Massacre were scrapped; historians on a government advisory committee resigned in protest, saying that the government was planning to use the museum to "justify Japan's road to war." A group of thirteen organizations protesting the museum's "one-sided" view filed a lawsuit to stop construction.[174]

The *Showakan* features photos and belongings of Japanese people during the war. It briefly details the American firebombings of Tokyo and other cities and shows the number of casualties. Other than that, the museum focuses primarily on the tenacity of Japanese citizens amid the hardships of war, notably the "rubble women," whose bravery and hard work brought the nation from defeat to reconstruction. The museum does not describe the war in Asia. A government official in charge of the project said the museum's objective was to "collect, preserve, and exhibit information about Japanese life during and after the war": particularly the suffering endured by the families of the war dead.[175]

JAPANESE education has been one of the most contested realms in the country's debate about the past. Since 1990, textbooks have continued to omit and gloss over many of Japan's worst human rights abuses. Many atrocities go unmentioned in textbooks, including Japan's strategic bombing campaigns in China (which killed 266,000 people); biological warfare; Unit 731's medical experiments on Chinese POWs and civilians; and the mistreatment of Allied POWs.[176] Vague discussions of other atrocities, such as the sex slaves, convey little of their true horror. For example, one text's discussion of the sex slaves says cryptically, "[Japan] rounded up the young women under the name of volunteer corps for the war."[177] According to one junior high textbook, Japan did not colonize Korea; instead, "Japan entered into a treaty with Korea to take charge of its foreign affairs and control its domestic affairs and police."[178]

One of Japan's most controversial textbooks is known as the Fusosha textbook (after its publisher). This book states that Japan's annexation of Korea was necessary "to protect Asia from Western imperialists." Specifically, Japanese control of Korea was necessary to prevent a hostile power from seizing it and establishing an "ideal base for that country to control Japan."[179] As the contents of the book became publicized, domestic and international criticism led Japan's Ministry of Education to require numerous changes in this as well as other textbooks up for approval. The Ministry said it "requested the revisions to 'balance' the contents of the textbook in line with a clause in the criteria for textbook screening" (the Asian Neighbor's Clause, adopted in 1982). After these changes, the Fusosha text was approved and released. However, revealing the polarization about the wartime past within Japan, left-leaning teachers and school districts in Japan ultimately chose not to use it (the Fusosha textbook was adopted by fewer than 0.1 percent of Japanese schools).[180] As the Fusosha and other texts show, Japanese textbooks fall short of presenting candid and complete descriptions of past violence. Trends in Japanese education—the revision in 2006 of the 1947 Fundamental Law on Education and the disappearance in several textbooks of reference to the "comfort women"—also suggest that political leaders are encouraging textbook coverage that is more "patriotic."[181]

At the same time, overall coverage of the war and of Japan's atrocities and aggression has increased since 1990. After the 1996 settlement of lawsuits brought against the government by textbook authors, the Ministry of Education permitted mention of the sex slaves and (the following year) of Unit 731.[182] The textbook *Nihonshi* says, "In occupying [Nanjing], the Japanese army killed large numbers of troops who had already surrendered, prisoners of war, and other Chinese, and engaged in looting, arson, and rape in an episode that was to incur international criticism as the Nanjing Massacre. The number of those who died within a few weeks . . . totaled from 100,000 to 150,000." Another text notes, "Japan, without a formal declaration of war, embarked on an overall war of aggression against China."[183] Some books detail policies during the Korean occupation; a junior high school text reports, "Japan was to rule Korea by military force as a colony, inflicting indescribable suffering on the Korean people." The text *Osaka Shoseki* says, "The new government stationed Japanese troops and police throughout the peninsula to suppress the resistance. In schools Korean children were forced to learn Japanese language and history." Another text comments that through such policies Japan "sought to deprive Koreans of their ethnic awareness and pride." One textbook features a sidebar about a Korean slave laborer's experience, and concludes, "violence [against the workers], together with accidents and malnutrition, led to the death of an astonishing 60,000 people out of the approximately 700,000 Koreans brought forcibly to Japan."[184]

During this era, the Japanese government also increased its educational cooperation with Seoul. In 1997 Tokyo had refused to collaborate with Seoul in a UNESCO-backed joint textbook panel. But after the controversy over the Fusosha textbook, Koizumi agreed that Japan would participate. And in 2002, Japan, China, and the ROK formed a multilateral research organization to study history issues; the result was *The Modern History of Three Countries in East Asia,* published in all three states in summer 2005.[185]

In sum, vagueness and omissions persist within many Japanese textbooks, and many other policies (notably commemoration) reflect amnesia or justification of past violence. However, official remembrance from 1990 to 2007 has grown more contrite than in earlier periods; Japan compensated the sex slave victims; textbook coverage of the war expanded; and Japanese prime ministers have issued numerous impressive apologies.

*Wider Japanese Society.* The increased prominence of Japan's past galvanized both liberals and conservatives to greater activism. Whereas liberals supported contrition and pressed Tokyo to be much more remorseful than it had been, conservatives argued against focusing on war and atrocities. They clashed in numerous debates during this period.

One of the most controversial topics was the "comfort women." In the 1990s, Japanese liberals celebrated Tokyo's acknowledgment of the atrocity, and pushed for greater contrition toward survivors. As noted above, activists created the Asian Women's Fund, funded in large part by charitable donations from the Japanese people. Additionally, in Tokyo in December 2000 a Japanese civic group (Violence against Women in War Network, Japan) organized a "people's tribunal" regarding the sex slaves. The Women's International War Crimes Tribunal assembled seventy-five survivors to testify in front of an international group of prosecutors and judges, many of whom had served in international tribunals in Europe and Africa.[186]

Liberal efforts to raise awareness of the sex slave issue (particularly within Japanese history education) were highly incendiary to conservatives. Conservative opinion leaders routinely denied or downplayed the atrocities. Most notoriously, Okuno Seisuke stated in June 1996 that Tokyo had not coerced the women: "They worked for financial reasons and were not forced to do so." Okuno maintained that the brothels had been privately owned, rather than operated by the Japanese government. A decade later, the issue would resurface when the U.S. Congress debated a bill pressuring Tokyo to apologize to the sex slaves: Prime Minister Abe Shinzo made a statement denying Japanese government coercion of the women.[187]

Japanese society also clashed about how to remember victims of forced labor. On the one hand, increased discussion of this atrocity was due in great part to efforts by Japanese liberal activists and the media. As noted earlier, litigation had contributed to greater admission in the courts. However, litigation also showcased profound denial. As William Underwood emphasizes, in court Mitsubishi Materials (the successor company to Mitsubishi Mining, which during the war had relied extensively on forced labor) condemned the perspective that considered Japanese actions as war crimes and engaged in historical revisionism. Mitsubishi's defense team denied the use of slave labor and argued that the company's innocence was proven by the fact that company officials were not punished during the American Occupation. Underwood notes that the testimony of slave labor survivors and the corporations who used them are making completely opposite claims about historical truth.[188]

The Japanese media promoted greater awareness of the slave labor issue. The Ministry of Foreign Affairs had repeatedly rebuffed attempts to access slave labor records: it claimed that although it had compiled a report about slave labor activities in 1946, all copies had been destroyed. As late as May 11, 1993, a ministry official testified to the Diet that he had heard of the report, but because "it does not now exist . . . we cannot say anything with certainty." He said that the Ministry of Foreign Affairs "has employed various means and done all it can," but "such documents no longer remain."[189] Six days later, NHK television described a five-volume Foreign Ministry report about Chinese forced labor: records that confirm that nearly 39,000 Chinese men were brought forcibly to Japan between 1943 and 1945 in order to perform harsh physical labor in brutal conditions. On average, one-sixth of them perished, although at some particularly brutal sites the death rate was fifty percent. NHK followed up with an hour-long television special called "The Phantom Foreign Ministry Report" and published a book the following year. The revelation of the Foreign Ministry report would raise national awareness of the issue and would motivate many Japanese and Chinese activists to search for more victims.[190]

LIBERALS and conservatives also contested the proper place of the Yasukuni Shrine. After Prime Minister Koizumi announced plans to visit in 2001, over 100 lawmakers met to oppose the gesture. Social Democratic Party leader Doi Takako likened the visit to laying a wreath at Hitler's grave and questioned, "What would the countries that suffered under his hand feel?" The Democratic Party's Kan Naoto said, "A visit to Yasukuni Shrine, which enshrines Class A war criminals, by an incumbent prime minister would restore the honor of such people." Leaders of the other two parties in the coalition government with the LDP met with Koizumi to urge him to abstain from visiting. Noda Takeshi of the New Conservative Party told Koizumi, "While the Prime Minister is the leader of Japan, you are also a leader of Asia. I want you to make a decision after seriously considering the matter from a higher and broader perspective." Fuyushiba Tetsuzo of the New Komeito Party agreed: "Relations with neighboring Asian nations will be the core for the 21st century."[191]

Subsequent visits by Koizumi sparked similar criticism. When Ozawa Ichiro assumed leadership of the Democratic Party of Japan in 2006, he criticized Koizumi, saying: "Yasukuni Shrine originally was not a place where people with the greatest responsibility for leading Japan into wars were honored." Ozawa emphasized the need for Japan and China to develop "a friendly relationship based on trust and cooperation." Also that year, Hatoyama Yukio of the Democratic Party of Japan called Koizumi's visit "absurd" and "irresponsible"; he said the visits damaged Japan's relations with neighboring nations and violated the constitutional separation of state and religion.

Over a hundred Japanese lawmakers—from the LDP, Komeito, and Minshuto—formed a parliamentary group to lobby for the construction of an alternate secular memorial to honor Japanese war dead. "We should urgently create a state memorial," said Komeito leader Kanzaki Takenori, "where anyone both at home and abroad can pay homage without worry." Advocates of such a plan proposed expanding Tokyo's Chidorigafuchi National Cemetery: Created in 1959 to house the remains of unidentified soldiers from World War II battlefields, the cemetery is Japan's equivalent of a "tomb of an unknown soldier."[192]

Other elites criticized the increasingly frequent Yasukuni visits. The head of Soka Gakkai (the Buddhist group backing New Komeito) called on Japanese leaders to respect the pacifism enshrined in the constitution. A pacifist association for war bereaved families said, "We strongly protest against the shrine visit." Writer Tanaka Nobumasa wrote prolifically on the issue; he argued that Japanese court decisions have deemed official shrine visits unconstitutional and urged Japanese leaders to remember that "the constitutional prescription of freedom of religion and the principle of separation of politics and religion were adopted in response to the harsh history of oppression and exclusion of minorities under state Shinto." He further noted the importance of repenting for war, saying that when Japan vowed "Never again," this meant that it must abandon "the idea of special facilities for singing the praises of the Japanese war dead."[193] In sum, as conservatives increasingly embraced the Yasukuni Shrine as a patriotic symbol, some elites fought back. The Japanese public was roughly divided on the issue: before Abe took power in 2006, a poll showed 40 percent of respondents supporting a visit, with 40 percent opposed, and 20 percent having no opinion.[194]

Liberal activism led to local commemoration that reflected more concern with Japan's past atrocities. Established in 1991, the Museum of Peace Osaka International Center (known as Peace Osaka), describes not only suffering at home, but also Japanese invasions and colonization in Asia, the Nanjing Massacre, Unit 731, forced labor, and strategic bombing campaigns. The exhibit script asserts that the public must understand the horrors of war in order to understand the meaning of peace and to live within the international community. In Tokyo, the metropolitan government decided to build a similar museum to honor the victims of the Tokyo fire bombings. Rather than focus exclusively on Japanese victims, however, the organizing committee planned to set the context with discussion of Japan's initiation and conduct of the war. Finally, the Hiroshima Peace Memorial Museum was renovated in 1995: within a new wing was a room dedicated to Japan's role in World War II. Hiroshima Mayor Hiraoka Takashi, who instigated the addition, said, "For the Hiroshima message of peace to be better heard overseas, it was necessary for us to face the dark sides of our history." The new room includes discussion of Hiroshima as a key center in Japan's military-industrial complex; and it reports on the Nanjing Massacre and Korean and Chinese slave laborers, many of whom perished in the atomic bombings.[195]

As liberals pushed for greater focus on Japan's past atrocities, conservative intellectuals and politicians objected that such a move was unpatriotic. Regarding the proposed changes to museums, *Sankei Shinbun* editor Ishikawa Mizuho opined that Peace Osaka used "false and horrible pictures" to "self-abuse" Japanese people. Tokyo University professor Fujioka Nobukatsu (leader of a conservative textbook group) dismissed Japan's war crimes as "wartime propaganda" or "rumor" and decried national "self-flagellation" at taxpayer expense. Noted author Ara Kenichi lambasted the exhibits at Peace Osaka as "distortion of the facts" and dismissed museum activists as "communists." LDP politicians supported these protests and pressured the museum to withdraw graphic photographs. Several photos were withdrawn in response, although most exhibits remained. Calls from some civic groups to add a "victimizer's corner" to the Hiroshima Peace Memorial Museum provoked angry backlash from nationalist groups, who argued that such coverage would be tantamount to admitting that Japan was responsible for the war. Ultimately, a modest amount of coverage of Japanese wartime aggression was included in the 1995 renovation. In Tokyo, Professor Fujioka was also active in opposing discussions of Japanese atrocities; he asserted that the real war crime was the U.S. bombing of Japanese cities. He argued that Tokyo museums present Japan's "face" to the world, and as such should not include content that suggested U.S. bombing raids on Japan might have been justified. Amid such protests, the Tokyo museum project was cancelled.[196]

JAPAN's national debate about the past was particularly contentious during the period of a coalition government from 1994 to 1996. Socialist Murayama Tomiichi presided as prime minister over a cabinet filled with conservative LDP politicians. In 1994 Justice Minister Nagano Shigeto touched off controversy when he called the Nanjing Massacre "a fabrication" designed to tarnish Japan's image. Nagano also justified Japan's war in Asia as a war of Asian liberation. "I still think it is wrong to define [the Greater East Asia War] as a war of aggression," he said. "Because Japan was in danger of being crushed, the country rose up to ensure its survival. We also sincerely believed in liberating Asia's colonies and establishing the Greater East Asia Co-Prosperity Sphere. . . . The objective of the war was a justifiable one, which was permissible in those days."[197] The South Korean press and government condemned Nagano's statements, as did Japanese opposition leaders; he was forced to resign.

Cabinet member Sakurai Shin glorified Japanese aggression in a statement just two days before Prime Minister Murayama's apology on August 15, 1994. "I do not think Japan intended to wage a war of aggression," said Sakurai. "It was thanks to Japan that most nations in Asia were able to throw off the shackles of colonial rule under European domination and to win independence. As a result, education also spread substantially . . . and

Asia as a whole was energized for dramatic economic reconstruction." Murayama called the remarks "inappropriate," forced Sakurai to issue a public retraction, and apologized on his behalf.[198]

Under Muruyama's leadership, Japan engaged in one of its most contentious national debates: over the proposed resolution of apology by the Japanese Diet. In 1991, on the fiftieth anniversary of the attack on Pearl Harbor, the Socialist and Komeito opposition parties proposed a Diet resolution apologizing for the war. An absence of LDP support scuttled the plan. In 1995, however, the Socialists—now with a prime minister in office—proposed another such resolution. The Socialists envisioned that through it Japan would offer a very contrite statement to mark the fiftieth anniversary of the war's end. LDP conservatives wanted no part of it, but the Socialists threatened to pull out of the ruling coalition.[199] Their debates produced the above-cited resolution of 1995. Despite being watered down, the Diet resolution was nonetheless so offensive to conservatives it was approved in a session boycotted by over half of the members of the Diet, and was never approved by the Upper House.

Angered by the Diet resolution, conservative politicians formed parliamentary groups to commemorate the war in a more patriotic fashion. The LDP's large Dietmembers League for the Fiftieth Anniversary of the End of the War staged various events in August 1995 and invited officials in neighboring countries to "thank the war dead and praise Japan for its contribution to the independence of Asian countries."[200] These groups drew on support from a variety of nationalist citizen organizations, including the powerful National Shrine Association (*Jinja honcho*) and War Bereaved Families Association (*Nihon izokukai*).

During the Diet resolution debate, numerous conservatives justified or denied past Japanese violence. Watanabe Michio, a former deputy prime minister and minister of foreign affairs, denied that Japan had taken over Korea by force in 1910. He objected to the proposed resolution, saying in June 1995 that "Japan governed Korea for 36 years, but you would look in vain to find any reference to 'colonial rule.' Both sides have now recognized the legitimacy of the annexation treaty, agreed that there would be no reparations to be paid but cooperative financing to be provided . . . and that's exactly what we've been providing." At a subsequent press conference, Watanabe rejected the term "colonial policy" to describe Japan's actions toward Korea and clarified further his view that "the annexation was completed peacefully, a different matter than colonization by the use of force."[201]

Further controversy was triggered by Prime Minister Murayama's 1995 apology, which prompted an outcry from within his own government. Education Minister Shimamura Yoshinobu—briefed about the apology the prime minister intended to give—preempted Murayama's statement with unapologetic remarks. Shimamura maintained that because two-thirds of the Japanese people were born after the war, "We are entering an age of complete innocence," and thus "it makes little sense to keep harping on the past and apologizing for one particular incident or another."[202] Shimamura added, "Doesn't it take two to wage a war . . . that is, mutual use of aggression?" Another cabinet minister, Eto Takami, objected to Murayama's apology in off-the-record statements that a magazine later published. Eto commented, "Prime Minister Murayama was wrong when he said that the annexation of Korea had been an act of coercion. . . . In those years, the weak got taken advantage of, and nothing could be done about it." Eto also said, "Not all that Japan did during the colonial years was bad." The remarks nearly resulted in Seoul recalling its ambassador and canceling a bilateral summit scheduled for that month.[203] Eto was later forced to resign.

Statements justifying or denying Japan's past violence continued into the next decade. In 2001, the former head of the Japan Defense Agency, Norota Hosei, told LDP supporters that Japan was not to blame for entering World War II. Blaming oil and other embargoes, Norota said, "Japan had no choice but to venture out southward to secure natural resources. . . . In other words, Japan had fallen prey to a scheme of the United States." At this time, Norota was an LDP member and chair of the Diet's Budget Committee. In 2004, Education Minister Nakayama Nariaki said that he wanted to reduce discussions of atrocities in Japanese textbooks (in particular, the "comfort women" and forcible abductions from occupied Japanese territories). Nakayama's remarks sparked demonstrations in Korea and criticism from Seoul; he subsequently apologized. Aso Taro, another cabinet official and future foreign minister, commented in 2003 that Koreans had willingly adopted Japanese names during colonization; he apologized after this prompted outcry in Seoul.[204]

As in the previous period, liberals and conservatives each sought to impose their narratives of the war on Japanese history textbooks. Dismayed by increased coverage of atrocities, conservatives mobilized to write books that offered what they called a more patriotic historical interpretation. Objecting to "perverse, masochistic historical views" in contemporary texts, Professor Fujioka organized a group in 1995, and he subsequently authored a series of books criticizing the "Tokyo Trials view of history." Featuring inspiring stories about ordinary Japanese people, the first two volumes were bestsellers, as were serialized versions in the *Sankei Shinbun* newspaper.[205]

Conservatives were chagrined by the 1996 court ruling that permitted mention of the sex slaves in junior high school history books. Some argued that the sex slaves had been willing prostitutes; others continued to deny Japanese government involvement in the program. Others did not object to teaching about such atrocities but argued that junior high was too young an age for it, preferring that it be taught only at high school and college levels.[206] Kanji Nishio, the leader of the Association to Create New History Textbooks (*Atarashii Rekishi Kyokasho wo Tsukuru-kai*) said, "Why should

Japan be the only country that should teach kids—twelve- to fifteen-year-old kids—bad things about itself?" He said it was "ridiculous, and very sad and tragic that Japan cannot write its own patriotic history."[207] Kanji's group produced the Fusosha textbook discussed earlier, which triggered tremendous domestic and regional controversy.

Liberals criticized what they viewed as growing nationalism in Japanese education. In 2001, prominent intellectual Oe Kenzaburo (a 1994 Nobel Laureate) lamented evasion in history textbooks, asserting that they distorted "invasions and savagery by Japanese militarism." He warned that the texts would "sow a mentality of national isolation" and urged his countrymen to remember that Japan was a global citizen. Koizumi's coalition partners were similarly critical; Foreign Minister Tanaka argued that one controversial book "distorts the facts"; Komeito urged that Japanese textbooks set the record straight. A group of intellectuals mobilized to criticize what they called "regressive" history textbooks and commented, "We have grave concern that most of these textbooks can hardly be considered appropriate to teach the future generations the truths of history and that they are likely to deepen the distrust of Asian peoples toward Japan."[208]

One journalist summarized Japanese remembrance during this period as follows: "For every sincere expression of contrition for Japan's conduct in World War II, there has always been a headband-wearing revisionist or a bigoted old-boy politician ready to declare that the Nanjing Massacre never happened or that Korean comfort women were 'volunteers.' "[209] Conservative voices denounced official apologies and offered a different interpretation of past events that emphasized the threat Japan faced at the time and the developmental benefits to colonies from occupation. Education was a major front in the battle for ownership of the Japanese past.

## COMPETING THEORIES AND PREDICTIONS

Official Japanese remembrance grew noticeably more contrite after 1990. Leaders offered numerous apologies—some of them reflecting profound admission and remorse—and textbook coverage of past violence increased. In wider society, many liberals worked doggedly to increase remembrance of and contrition for past atrocities. However, these trends were countered by widespread evasion and denials: conservatives challenged not only the wisdom of contrition, but also the basic facts of Japan's past violence. Evidence that powerful elements in Japanese politics and society were defending past atrocities should have been unsettling for Koreans.

The continuing dispute over the Tokdo/Takeshima Islands should have also sent a worrisome signal to South Korea. Japan grew more vocal about its claim; in spring 2005, Japan's education minister urged that students be taught that the islands are Japanese territory, and he approved the Fusosha textbook (which described the islands as Japanese territory). Japan's ambassador to the ROK reiterated Tokyo's claim to ownership of the islands, and a Japanese local government established Takeshima Day to underscore Japanese sovereignty.[210] One would expect the reinvigorated island dispute also to elevate Korean distrust of Japan.

Membership in multilateral institutions should not be expected to significantly affect Korean perceptions. Although East Asian institutions have increased in number and prominence, they remain largely informal and do not impose constraints on members' behavior.[211]

One factor that should have reassured Koreans during this period is regime type; by the late 1990s, both countries had developed into mature democracies. Some scholars would have expected bilateral relations to *worsen* in the late 1980s and 1990s because of South Korea's democratic transition: such times are ripe for nationalistic posturing and even war.[212] But after Korea's transition (i.e., heading into the 2000s), democratic peace theory predicts that mutual perceptions should improve.

The balance of capabilities did not change significantly during this period; Japan continues to have substantial—but constrained—power. Japan retains its advantages in long-term power (population and wealth). The balance of mobilized power also favors Tokyo: Although Korea fields more standing military forces, the ratio of Japanese to Korean military spending is about 3.6 to 1, and Japan wields impressive maritime capabilities.[213]

As in the previous period, however, Japanese power continues to be highly constrained by the U.S.-Japan alliance. Koreans and others grew nervous about the alliance's future after the end of the Cold War, but Tokyo and Washington reinvigorated their relationship in the early 1990s. The diplomatic fallout from perceived Japanese lethargy in the 1991 Persian Gulf War spurred leaders from the two countries to renegotiate Japan's alliance roles in case of a second Korean war. Japanese responsibilities were clarified in the 1996 Guidelines for Defense Cooperation; ten years later, the Defense Policy Review Initiative further coordinated alliance policy to better meet regional and global security threats. Tokyo's response to the attacks of September 11, 2001 (the dispatch of naval support ships to the Indian Ocean to support the U.S. invasion of Afghanistan) and its participation in the U.S. occupation of Iraq are frequently cited as signs of the alliance's rejuvenation.[214]

Japanese power has also been constrained in the late period by the existence of security threats. After the fall of the Soviet Union, Japan faced a decreased but still worrisome threat environment. Pyongyang hurls apocalyptic rhetoric at Tokyo; it threatened to attack Japanese cities with ballistic missiles, and in 1998 test-fired a rocket over Japanese airspace. North Korea reneged on arms control agreements and tested a nuclear weapon in 2006. Although China continues to lag militarily behind Japan in many aspects of military power, China's potential power is high relative to Japan's, and it could someday pose a significant regional threat.[215] Thus the boon to

Japanese security from the disappearance of the Soviet threat has been mitigated by an increasingly menacing North Korea and the growth of Chinese power. On the basis of capabilities, Koreans should therefore conclude that Japan has advantages in relative power but that constraints on Japanese power reduce its ability to threaten the ROK.

## KOREAN PERCEPTIONS, 1990S–2000S

Since the 1990s, South Koreans have continued to distrust Japan. Poll data reflect strong hostility: in a 1996 poll, South Korean respondents ranked their feelings about seventeen countries, assigning points on a scale from zero (dislike) to 100 (like). They gave Japan 41 points, above North Korea (last at 27), but in the company of Libya and Iran (41 and 42 points, respectively).[216] A 2001 poll showed that the most popular countries were Australia and the United States (each selected by 19 percent of respondents), Canada (12 percent), Switzerland (11 percent), and France (4 percent). The most disliked countries were Japan (63 percent), *followed by* North Korea (11 percent), the United States (7 percent), and China (3 percent). A *Dong-a Ilbo*/Harris Poll conducted in 2001 showed 42 percent of respondents reporting an unfavorable view of Japan compared to 17 percent with a favorable view. Next to North Korea—viewed by 54 percent as the greatest current security threat to the ROK—Japan drew the second-largest number of votes (21 percent), with China receiving only 8 percent.[217] Most South Koreans (71 percent of respondents to a 2001 *Chosun Ilbo* poll) reported feeling no sense of closeness to Japan. Korean perceptions show no sign of improving; in 2005 89 percent said they were pessimistic about Japan-ROK relations, with only a tiny minority (9 percent) expressing trust in Japan.[218]

South Korean media coverage also conveys profound suspicion. "Japan has failed to win the trust of Asians," argued one commentator. "We are not alone in being concerned," noted another article, "in watching where Japan, a country with vast potential power, may be headed. The whole world is watching."[219] According to an article in the *Hankook Ilbo*, Japan is suspected "of edging toward resurrecting militarism." "The root of reconciliation between Japan and the rest of Asia," lamented another, "remains as remote as ever."[220]

South Korean media coverage after North Korea's 1998 test launch of a rocket over Japan reflected profound distrust. Japan was criticized in spite of the fact that it had been the victim of a provocative act by a shared adversary, and in spite of its relatively modest response (Tokyo agreed to codevelop theater missile defenses [TMD] with the United States and decided to procure its own military reconnaissance satellites). A *Dong-a Ilbo* article asserted that the North Korean rocket launch was a "pretext" for Japan to expand its military role and revise its constitution. Japanese concerns about North Korea, noted the article, "cannot fully explain the strengthened role and capabilities of the [Japanese military], which are now underway at a rapid pace." Another paper editorialized, "Japan is suspected of persistently trying to transform itself into a militarily strong country."[221] The *Korea Herald* warned that after the rocket launch, Tokyo's reactions "may portend events of more grave significance for its neighbors than the mere self-defense of the island nation." The episode caused "extraordinary anxiety and apprehension for many Koreans," who were said to hear "resurgent imperial trumpets growing ever noisier from across the sea."[222]

As before, Korean distrust did not translate to high threat perception. Koreans, particularly elites, did not regard Japan as a security threat. One professor noted, "Japan is not a source of threat from the ROK perspective." Another said, "I don't see a Japanese threat because they don't have the military capability right now." Kim Jae-chang, the director of the Defense Ministry's study group on military modernization (Revolution in Military Affairs) commented, "Certainly I don't see Japan as a threat today." An analyst at the Korea Institute for Defense Analyses (KIDA) commented that Japan did not pose a threat to South Korea as long as Tokyo continued its policy of "defensive defense." Another analyst similarly noted, "If Japan's policies of self-defense change then, this will be a threat to the ROK, but they aren't right now."[223]

Current policies also do not reflect perceptions of a Japanese threat. South Korean military force structure is overwhelmingly geared to combat a North Korean ground threat; its maritime forces are weak. ROK military forces are concentrated in ground weaponry and personnel; out of 687,000 active duty military personnel, 560,000 are ground troops.[224] The ROK is strong in tanks, artillery, and anti-armor assets. In addition, Seoul has expanded its security cooperation with Tokyo. The ROK and Japan began holding joint exercises; since 1999 they have conducted biannual search-and-rescue drills. Most Korean analysts cite the need for a trilateral framework with the United States or for stronger regional multilateral security institutions; they say that closer ties would reduce tensions and promote regional stability.[225] In sum, distrust of Japan's intentions does not translate to perceptions of a Japanese security threat.

Because they distrust Japan, however, Koreans remain wary of a future Japanese threat. South Korean defense planning for the postunification era has reflected such concerns. In August 2000 the Ministry of National Defense issued a report, "National Security and the Defense Budget in the 21st Century," that described necessary ROK military modernization.[226] The document asserted that the future Korean military should be smaller but more modern, with high technology weaponry and the ability to exploit information technology. It said that the ROK faces a short-term threat from North Korea and long-term threats from regional powers. The MND argued that Korea cannot match the strength of Japan or any of the other great powers—nor would it be desirable to try. However, according to the MND, Korea needs to have minimum adequate strength to deter these forces.

Korean long-term defense planning reflects an emphasis on *maritime* rather than ground power. Military reform includes the creation of a more balanced force, with less emphasis on ground capabilities and more emphasis on air and naval forces. An MND official argues, "Our military is not balanced; it's too heavy on ground forces. So it's natural in this situation to start to develop our navy."[227] ROK maritime modernization projects include advanced destroyers (the 3,900-ton KDX destroyer, the nearly 5,000-ton KDX-II destroyer, and the Aegis-capable KDX-III destroyer for advanced air defense). Furthermore, the ROK Navy seeks to purchase "a submarine capable of operating further from South Korean shores."[228] Observers of trends in Korean defense note the shift toward maritime power. One article comments, "Most of the weapons systems South Korea is looking to buy are not focused exclusively on North Korea, but have more strategic applications to defend against a possible Chinese or Japanese threat."[229] *Jane's Defence Weekly* noted South Korea's "effort to develop a more balanced force, with increased emphasis on maritime and air capabilities that would find limited application in an intra-Korean conflict."[230] As President Roh Moo-hyun put it, "Northeast Asia is still in an arms race, and we cannot just sit back and watch."

To be sure, increased South Korean interest in the maritime sphere could be the result of South Korean wariness about the rise of China. Beijing has been engaged in military modernization since the 1990s, and has dramatically improved its maritime capabilities.[231] South Korean elites do express a great deal of uncertainty about China, but they also specifically cite Japan as a possible security threat in the future. The MND "National Security and the Defense Budget in the 21st Century" identified Japan and China as potential regional threats, noting Japanese development of an Airborne Warning and Control System (AWACS), Aegis, TMD, and the advanced F-2 fighter. One Korean military analyst writes, "It is well known that Japan has the technological capability and the financial resources to go beyond its agreed task of protecting waters within a perimeter of 1,000 nautical miles from the island of Honshu."[232] Many proponents of the ROK's submarine program argued that the program was motivated by concerns about a potential Japanese threat. Analysts have also pointed out that the KDX destroyers and the long-stalled submarine projects were approved only after a 1996 crisis with Japan over Tokdo/Takeshima in which the ROK navy was unfavorably compared to Japanese naval forces. Many analysts specifically linked Korea's need for the Aegis-equipped KDX-III destroyer to the territorial dispute with Japan.[233] Thus, ROK military planning cites specific concerns about a future Japanese threat.

Many Korean analysts also discuss an *indirect* threat from Japan. In interviews, elites argued that Korea must not get caught in the great-power crossfire; they frequently highlighted nineteenth century Korean history, in which China, Russia, and Japan competed for influence on the peninsula and razed Korea in the process. Elites describe Korea as an "avenue," "boulevard," or "thoroughfare" that great powers cross in order to fight each other. Kim Jae-chang, director of the Defense Ministry's Revolution in Military Affairs Group, argued that Korea must have the military capability to deter great-power intervention. He said,

> When Korea is unified someday, we will face the same threats we faced before: Korea will be between powerful continental and maritime powers. If Korea is strong enough, it will work as a stabilizer between two great powers; if it is not strong enough, then it will again be used as an avenue (one direction or another) between the great powers. This is the threat to us. I explain our military plans by saying we don't want Korea to be this avenue anymore, so we need to be strong enough to deny an attempt by either side.[234]

Korean analysts maintained that another indirect threat to Korea is disruption of the sea-lanes, which could adversely affect Korean trade; expanding the navy is essential to ensure that the sea-lanes remain open. According to Seo-hang Lee of the Sejong Institute, "The defense of major maritime trade routes has been greatly emphasized in recent years. Korea's economic viability depends almost entirely on sea-borne foreign trade. . . . [This has] contributed greatly to greater interest in defense of sea-lanes. . . ." [235] Admiral Kang Tok-dong commented, "Korea needs to place top priority on building up its navy to secure sea lanes in the event of a crisis in the Pacific or a threat from a neighboring power."[236] With this maritime mission in mind, analysts argue for reforming the ROK military. A former MND vice minister commented that after unification Korea will be "surrounded by great powers" and "we have to be wary of them." He noted that Korea "will have this huge number of ground forces that will no longer be meaningful in the new situation. So we need to modernize our forces."[237]

Although many Korean elites claimed that either Japan or China might threaten Korea in the future, the Korean public appears convinced that the country's next threat is Japan. As Lee Sook-jong, a public opinion analyst, wrote, "Regardless of age or education, fully half of all South Koreans view Japan as the most likely threat to South Korea's security." Lee noted that in response to questions about future security options (e.g., ally with the United States, unilaterally reinforce South Korea's own self-defense capability, or pursue regional security), the most commonly expressed opinion was that Japan posed the greatest danger to the ROK and that Korea should increase its self-defense capability.[238] In a 1996 *Chungang Ilbo* newspaper poll, when asked which country would be most likely to threaten the ROK in the future, 60 percent of Koreans answered Japan and 18.9 percent answered China, followed by the United States and Russia at 6.8 and 4.9 percent, respectively.[239] Respondents to a 1996 RAND poll reported that the "greatest future danger to Korea's military security" was Japan (54 percent), followed by China at 33 percent of respondents. Also in the RAND poll, a large majority of Koreans (87 percent in a 1999 version of the poll) said that if Japan were to acquire nuclear weapons, Korea should as well. Similar views persisted into the next decade: a 2005 poll by the *Hankook Ilbo* and *Yomiuri Shinbun* reported that 58 percent of Koreans viewed Japan as a threat.[240]

*South Korean Reasoning about Japan's Intentions.* South Korean distrust of Japan is driven in great part by Japanese remembrance. Koreans often react positively to Japanese apologies and other gestures; however, they express dismay when such apologetic sentiments are later contradicted, and say that these mixed signals show that Japan cannot be trusted.

It is important to note that Koreans sometimes do praise Japanese apologies as grounds for optimism. ROK Foreign Minister Han Sung-joo called the 1993 summit between Prime Minister Hosokawa and President Kim Young-sam "an important starting point for spiritual reconciliation between the people of the two countries" and said Japan's "correct view of history" would stabilize bilateral relations. Commentator Yi Dong-min wrote that the summit "may well go down in history as the meeting that helped the two countries close the book on the dark past and turn their eyes to the future." In 1998 the Korean media celebrated "Prime Minister Obuchi's expression of great remorse for his nation's actions" as "momentum to put an end to the long-running controversy."[241]

As in the previous period, however, Koreans cited inadequate apologies as grounds to distrust Japan. Koreans received Emperor Akihito's 1990 apology with confusion. To express his "deepest regret," the emperor used the word *tsuseki* (*T'ongsuk* in Korean), an infrequently used combination of Chinese characters that made puzzled Koreans reach for their dictionaries. His choice of this strange word did not sit well with his Korean audience, who did not understand what the emperor had said and were exasperated that he could not just clearly say "We apologize." Polls showed that over 70 percent of Koreans remained unsatisfied.[242]

Furthermore, most Koreans resented Japanese policy toward the former sex slaves. Koreans received the Miyazawa apology with satisfaction but reacted bitterly to Tokyo's refusal to pay official reparations. Miyazawa's visit to Seoul was disrupted by anti-Japanese rallies: protesters threw eggs at the Japanese embassy. An association of bereaved family members of war victims issued a statement: "We express indignation over the visit of the Japanese prime minister at a time when no compensation and no apology was made for Korean patriots tortured and killed by Japanese imperialists." The Foreign Ministry said, "A true future-oriented and mutually beneficial relationship between Korea and Japan can be achieved only when Japan correctly recognizes past history and remorsefully reflects on its deeds." An editorial noted that although Japanese leaders apologized, their "words were hardly matched by any concrete actions," and the case of the sex slaves was "disappointingly no exception." Scholar Kim Kyong-min opined, "Japan has tried to distort the history of its aggressive war and deny culpability in the issue of its sex slaves. Under these circumstances, who would trust Japan?" The general public is similarly dissatisfied; as late as 2005, 87 percent believed Japan had not adequately expressed contrition or compensated survivors.[243]

Koreans had viewed the 1995 Diet Resolution as an opportunity for Japan to clarify once and for all its views about its past; they argued that the debate showed the strength of unapologetic sentiment in Japan. Argued the *Dong-a Ilbo*, a parliamentary resolution was important "to put a stop to all the confusion arising from the occasional gaffes by cabinet members, contradicting the many apologies made by Japanese prime ministers and the emperors." An article in *Hankook Ilbo* wondered "how genuine Japan's self-reflection is," noting,

South Koreans demanding Japanese apologies to the "Comfort Women." AP PHOTO/YUN JAI-HYOUNG.

In the past, Japan sought to cloud the wrongs of its colonial and war legacy with ambiguous phraseology. Repeatedly, one heard opaque references to "a sense of painful regret," "aggressive conduct," "a sense of reflection," or "profound apology," all of which seemed an exercise in word games. As if these circumlocutions were not enough, Japan has come up with one rationale after another to excuse its past actions. . . . Japan's evasive attitude toward the war has incurred the wrath, rather than the understanding of the world community. This is the root of why reconciliation between Japan and the rest of Asia remains as remote as ever.[244]

Before the vote on the Diet Resolution, the *Hankook Ilbo* editorialized, "If Japan puts an apology into its resolution against war, this will contribute to securing peace in the Asia-Pacific area in the future." The editorial implored Japan to "be frank." Another *Hankook Ilbo* article dismissed the resolution as "an empty shell," and "a bag of excuses," and wrote, "Nowhere in the document can we find any indication of a sincere desire to apologize and repent." President Kim Young-sam commented that he was "perplexed" that the Diet should attempt of its own accord to pass such a resolution but end up with a "washed out and inadequate" version.[245]

Korean enthusiasm about Japan's contrition was further undermined by widespread denials in Japanese society. As Hahnkyu Park of KIDA summarized: "The acrimonious debate about the resolution and the compromise among political parties only yielded a lukewarm 'sense of remorse' which reinforced Asian suspicions that Japanese attitudes about its militarist past had not really changed." Japan "has failed to win the trust of Asians," argued journalist Nam Si-uk, because of its "anachronistic tendency to justify Japan's colonial domination over Korea." President Roh Moo-hyun declared in 2005, "We call on Japanese leaders not to make new apologies but to make actions suitable for the apologies already made."[246]

Koreans inferred hostile intentions from the justifications and denials of Japanese leaders. Democratic Liberal Party spokesman Pak Pom-chin rebuked "history-distorting remarks" by Education Minister Shimamura as a serious setback to regional relations. Prime Minister Yi Hong-ku condemned Watanabe's 1995 statement that Japan had not taken over Korea by force. He said the South Korean government and people "cannot but express shock and worry over the absurd remarks made by the former Japanese foreign minister" and called the remarks "an obstacle to the future of South Korean-Japanese relations."[247] South Korean scholars showed similar outrage. Lee Chul-seung wrote, "Japan is apparently haunted by its illusion of building a Greater East Asia Co-Prosperity Sphere, which was a defining element of its militarist past. If not, how can Japan claim that its 1910 annexation of Korea was valid without squarely facing up to its past wrongdoings and atoning for its misdeeds?" A KIDA analyst argued that although in many ways "Japan is a different country" since World War II, a number of

Japanese elites evidently "still think Japan is a divine country, and its colonialism was justified."[248]

The South Korean media extensively covered Japanese leaders' statements. The dailies overflowed with denunciations of Watanabe. *Hankook Ilbo* asserted that bilateral relations would sour because of Japan's "double-faced attitude, which officially apologizes for the annexation but denies it when our back is turned." "Japan is a secret and organized country," argued the conservative *Chosun Ilbo*. "Thus, the ROK should constantly seek to keenly disclose Japan's attempts to hide, distort, and fabricate history." The moderate *Dong-a Ilbo* wrote that the countries could only improve their relations if "offenders apologize for what they have done and if the victims offer forgiveness." After Justice Minister Nagano's 1994 statement, one newspaper editorialized, "If Japan does not face historical facts squarely and teach historical truths to its younger generation, how can we build a sense of trust toward Japan as a partner in the Asia-Pacific era?" Another editorial said that while some Japanese "pretend to be remorseful," others, "particularly intellectual and ranking government officials, do not hesitate to distort historical truths." It continued, "Such perversion itself is the very reason Japan's neighbors are suspicious about Japan; they see the distortions as reflecting the minds of the Japanese. . . . This is all the more so at a time when Japan is suspected, more or less, of edging toward resurrecting militarism." Reactions among the South Korean public were no less condemning. After their statements, Nagano and Watanabe were both burned in effigy by protestors, and students threw Molotov cocktails at the Japan Cultural Center in Seoul.[249]

Koreans were also alarmed by Japan's resurrection of symbols from its imperial past: the Kimigayo national anthem and the Hinomaru flag. Koreans, claimed one editorial, "see an unrepentant nation being given a green light to rebuild its war-making capabilities inspired by the ode sung by legions of imperial soldiers." The editorial commented that the symbols reflected "the nationalist 'desire' of the Japanese ultra rightist forces," who want to rearm Japan. Commentator Kim Young-ho similarly characterized the adoption of the symbols as a "revival of militarism and nationalism."[250]

South Koreans also monitored developments in Japanese education and said that attempts to omit or gloss over past violence signaled a pernicious nationalist trend. During the debate over the reissue of the Fusosha textbook, Koreans argued that Japan was "reviving its military ambitions." The Korean ambassador to the UN Human Rights Commission, Choi Hyuk, called Japan's textbooks "a factor of serious concern for Korea" and said at a meeting of the commission, "If we don't learn the lessons from the mistakes of history, we are doomed to repeat them." Seoul refused to support Tokyo's bid for a permanent seat on the UN Security Council. South Korea's UN Ambassador Kim San-hoon commented, "A country that does not repent for its historical wrongdoings and does not have the trust of its neighbors cannot play a leadership role in international society." According to poll data, 92 percent of the Korean public also opposes a Japanese Security Council seat on these grounds. Similarly, ROK Prime Minister Lee Hae-chan reacted coolly to a Koizumi apology and noted Korean alarm about Japanese textbooks. "A country that distorts history and does not reflect upon it cannot open the future," he said. "A country that wants to stand in a leadership position in an international organization such as the United Nations needs to do so with trust and morality."[251]

Koreans were equally alarmed during the initial debate about the Fusosha textbook in 2000. President Kim Dae-jung highlighted the issue in his Liberation Day speech the following year, imploring Japan to face its history and arguing, "How can we deal with them in the future with any degree of trust?"[252] As a result of Tokyo's refusal to decertify the controversial textbooks, Seoul temporarily reimposed bans on imports of Japanese cultural goods (films, music, and computer games); these restraints had been lifted after Prime Minister Obuchi's 1998 apology. Seoul also canceled diplomatic visits and joint military exercises. Korean scholars were incensed: one commented that he was concerned about a future threat from Japan "because of the emergence of the right wing there. In the education problem we see something very wrong with Japan." Won-deog Lee wrote, "Japanese repeated attempts to distort its history . . . portend the revival not only of Japanese militarism, but also of its nationalistic sentiments reminiscent of the days of Japanese imperialism."[253]

Media coverage of the 2000 textbook dispute conveyed similar alarm. An editorial in the *Korea Herald* commented that "another attempt to whitewash historical facts is raising its ugly head in Japan," that approval of the book showed "the lingering influence of militarist sentiment." Koreans, argued another Korea Herald article, could not afford to overlook the lessons of the past; doing so "may turn out to be a naïve illusion leading to a repetition of the same mistakes and tragedies." A *Dong-a Ilbo* op-ed asserted that nationalism displayed in the history textbooks will "place Japan on a more militarist footing." "In an era of globalization, Japan has chosen chauvinism," lamented the *Chungang Ilbo*, "reversing the trend in its recent history of reconciliation and peace with its neighbors."[254]

Koreans also worried about Japanese officials visiting the Yasukuni Shrine. Presidential spokesman Kim Man-soo said the 2005 Koizumi visit "undermines peace and cooperation in Northeast Asia and isolates Japan in the international community." The spokesman for the opposition Grand National Party called the visit evidence of Japan's "extreme-rightist identity, which will make Japan the enemy of the world." Koizumi's 2005 visit to the shrine, asserted one article, "glorifies [Japan's] historical wrongdoings"; after his 2002 visit, an editorial wondered, "How can Japan be trusted in international society?"[255] Korean lawmakers passed a resolution condemning the shrine visit and the textbook ruling; they lambasted Koizumi's 2001 visit as evidence of "nostalgia for neo-militarism," and "tantamount to declaring another round of World War II." Parliamentarians issued a letter of protest to the Japanese embassy in Seoul, demanding an apology and a pledge that Japanese leaders abstain from future visits. Korea's ruling party chairman said that the shrine visit evinced "resurgent militarism"; former Foreign Minister Han Sung-joo also worried that it signaled "a Japanese turn toward militarism."[256]

The Korean people shared their leaders' dismay; crowds of angry protestors greeted Koizumi on his 2001 visit to Seoul. A civic group said the Japanese leader "resurrected the specter of imperialism by paying homage at Yasukuni Shrine and disregarded the Korean people's demands for truth and repentance." Twenty South Korean men staged a macabre protest in which, draped in South Korean flags, they each cut off a finger to protest Koizumi's visit.[257] Koreans were so embittered by the Yasukuni and textbook issues, they ignored Koizumi's remarkable trip to Seoul's Seodaemon Prison History Hall and the apology he offered there. An article in *Dong-a Ilbo* decried, "We cannot but ask again why he visited. It is true that the recent South Korea-Japan relationship is more strained than ever before." Koizumi's visit to the Yasukuni Shrine only illustrated "a vast difference in Japan's words and deeds," argued an article in *Choson Ilbo*. It said that Koizumi was "opportunistically" pursuing simultaneous policies of "reflections and apologies" on the one hand and "distortions and official homage" to war criminals on the other.[258]

In sum, since the 1990s, Koreans have reacted with shock and outrage to words and deeds by Japanese politicians that have glorified, denied, or justified past violence. Koreans view such statements as reflections of Japan's true hostile intentions. Thus, although Koreans recognize and appreciate contrite gestures, Japan's unapologetic remembrance has eroded any positive effects and has sustained Korean distrust.

*Territorial Claims.* Although the Tokdo/Takeshima issue died down after the 1965 normalization settlement, the issue later reappeared and would fuel Korean distrust of Japan. Elites continue to assert Korean ownership of the islands and to suspect Japan's intentions. Korean legislators established a "Tokdo Devotees Group" and enacted a resolution demanding that Japan drop its claim to the islands;[259] politicians also take high-profile trips to the islands to show their commitment. After a local Japanese government assembly passed an ordinance establishing "Takeshima Day," Seoul issued a protest, to which Koizumi responded only with a call to deal with the situation in "a forward-looking manner." The Korean government responded by saying, "A series of actions taken by Japan of late has caused us to raise a fundamental question as to whether Japan has the will to coexist with its neighbor as a peaceful power in East Asia."[260] A defense analyst argued, "Japan would seem less threatening if it stopped claiming that Tokdo was part of Japan." Another think-tank analyst complained, "Japan believes it owns Tokdo. We think there's no dispute. This is one reason why we distrust them."[261] During this period the ROK's annual Defense White Papers featured pictures of ROK military aircraft flying patrols over Tokdo/Takeshima; they appeared in the section discussing Japanese defense policy. The caption in the 1990 White Paper read: "Japan seems to be on its way to becoming a military superpower as it expands its military strength." The photos of Tokdo/Takeshima, according to a Defense Ministry spokesman, "are intended to show Korea's sovereignty over the islands and the Armed Forces' willingness to defend them when challenged."[262]

The Korean media and public reject any legitimacy on the Japanese side. An editorial condemned "Japan's absurd claim" as an issue that would "only serve to heighten suspicion among its neighbors." Another accused Japanese "neoconservatives" of "replaying their ancestors' model of 100 years ago, when they were poised to become a world power."[263] The Korean public was as impassioned on the subject of the islands as were media headlines; the island dispute frequently motivated protests in downtown Seoul. After remarks made by Japanese Prime Minister Mori Yoshiro about Japan's claim to Tokdo/Takeshima, "Protestors characterized Mori's remarks as being driven by Japan's militaristic ambitions to invade other territories." A national headquarters for protecting Tokdo was established by prominent citizens.[264] Korean tourists organize sightseeing trips to Tokdo and try to build buildings and monuments there. At a soccer match in 2004 between the two countries, a South Korean forward celebrated a goal by pulling off his jersey to reveal an undershirt with the words, "Tokdo is our territory," prompting jubilation among Korean fans. In sum, Korean elites and the public show a strong commitment to the island claim and cite Japan's claim as evidence of its hostile intentions.

As noted, whereas South Koreans continue to distrust Japanese intentions, since 1990 they have not viewed Japan as a security threat. Low threat perception depends almost entirely on the constraint of the U.S.-Japan alliance. Korean leaders bluntly say they do not currently perceive a threat because the alliance serves as a "cork" in the Japanese bottle.[265] One analyst called the alliance a "safety valve to prevent Japan from emerging as a military power." Japanese capabilities are high, according to a Foreign Ministry official, "but we don't worry about them as long as U.S. leadership is maintained."[266] In its 1990 and 1991 Defense White Papers, Korea's Ministry of National Defense declared, "Japan's expanding role for regional peace and stability is increasingly becoming cause for concern to its neighbors. As

long as it is pursued within the framework of the U.S.-Japan security cooperation, however, the larger Japanese role will contribute directly and indi-
rectly to the balance of military power, the protection of [sea lines of
communication] and war deterrence in the region."[267] Scholar Park Yong-
Ok wrote that a Japanese military buildup would promote regional security
"if the U.S. remains a mighty Pacific power, if Japan increases her defense
capability in a way as to augment the U.S. regional strategy, and if the
Korea-U.S. military cooperative relationship is firmly maintained." Survey-
ing the Korean-language international relations literature on Japan, Choon
Kun Lee and Jung Ho Bae concluded, "The majority of [international rela-
tions] experts in Korea recognize the limits of Japanese military power under the context of the U.S.-Japan alliance."[268]

Elites agree that if Japan were to end the U.S.-Japan alliance, they would
fear the buildup of Japanese power that would certainly ensue. As an official at the Ministry of Foreign Affairs and Trade argued, "If U.S. forces
leave, then Japan will want to build up its military, and we'll be in trouble. . . . As long as the U.S. relationship is maintained, I don't worry about
Japan."[269] Park Yong-ok contended that a United States reduction in its
military presence "so as to encourage a rapid expansion of the Japanese
military capability and regional role" would negatively affect both Korean
and regional security. According to scholar Rhee Kyu-ho, "The presence of
U.S. forces in Japan at present is not so much to protect Japan as to contribute to the stability of the entire Asian region by restraining Japanese
power and applying political control over it." The U.S. military presence,
he said, is regarded "as a restraint against the revival of Japanese militarism or imperialism. This is why plans to scale down the U.S. military
presence tend to heighten fears that Japan may become a military superpower."[270]

Elites express cautious optimism about the future of the United States in
East Asia. They have been gratified by American policies that strengthen
the alliance with Japan, seeing these as signs of renewed commitment. As
Rhee Sang-woo noted, "Koreans anticipate that for the next few decades
the U.S. will persist as the hegemonic power in East Asia."[271] However,
many statements reflect uncertainty. "America's role in the region is gradually decreasing," commented In-taek Hyun and Masao Okonogi. They argued that in many post–Cold War conflicts, the United States followed a
wait-and-see policy before committing forces; "Nobody can guarantee,"
they warned, that the U.S. would not take such an approach to the Korean
Peninsula: South Korea "must try to persuade the United States to maintain
its military presence in the region and play a positive role as stabilizer."[272]
Another scholar, Woosang Kim, speculated, "Would the United States
maintain her policy of active engagement in the region or change it to the
policy of isolationism?" Byung-joon Ahn feared "the power vacuum that

may result from disengagement of the U.S. military presence," and that "China and Japan may well fill the vacuum should [it] materialize." As a Foreign Ministry official summarized, "Our threat perception in the future depends on how U.S. policy in the region evolves."[273]

Because Koreans see the U.S.-Japan alliance as the key constraint on Japanese power, they support measures to strengthen it. A major U.S.-Japan policy initiative was the Guidelines for Military Cooperation, revised in 1997. In it, Japan specified several rear-area support missions it would perform in the event of a second Korean war. Seoul expressed cautious approval; it urged Tokyo and Washington to consult Seoul and urged Japan to maintain transparency in its defense policies. The Foreign Ministry issued a statement saying the guidelines "will contribute to peace and stability on the Korean Peninsula, because the declaration made it clear that the United States will continue to maintain its role in securing peace and stability in the Asia Pacific region." The guidelines, said a Foreign Ministry spokesman, "will serve to quell the move toward revision of [Japan's] Constitution by strengthening the joint security alliance." He argued that "the more military commitments the United States makes in Asia, the less possibility of Japan actively operating militarily in Asia" and that "what we should worry about is, on the contrary, the possibility of the United States retreating from Asia." Another Foreign Ministry official, Yu Kwang-sok, noted that Japan's expanded military role was aimed at reinforcing U.S. forces stationed in Japan and South Korea—forces that guard against a potential attack from the North. "In that sense," Yu said, "we cannot deny the fact that the revision of the U.S.-Japan defense guidelines will help secure peace and stability on the Korean peninsula."[274]

Scholars echoed government support for an expanded Japanese role under the guidelines. Former Foreign Minister Han Sung-joo wrote that the guidelines would put U.S.-Japan relations "back on a cooperative track" and that the new U.S.-Japan security declaration would positively affect regional security. Scholar Woosang Kim argued, "The proposed revision should be understood as aiming to further solidify the U.S.-Japan alliance, which is indispensable for establishing a durable regional security order"; and a researcher at South Korea's Sejong Institute said, "As long as the alliance lasts, then we don't see a threat from Japan. The passage of the guidelines is a good thing, because it is a reflection of a strong U.S.-Japan relationship."[275]

## Trying to Cover Up the Sky With Their Hand

This case study offers three major findings about remembrance in the Japan-ROK relationship. First, although South Koreans praised official apologies, they were offended and alarmed by Japan's justifications, glorifications, and denials of past violence. As a frustrated South Korean President Roo Moo-hyun said in 2007, Japan's attempt to dodge and deny its wartime atrocities was like trying to cover up the sky with their hand.[276] The recurring inflammatory statements emanating from Tokyo, apparently endorsed by large swaths of the Japanese public, led Koreans to suspect that Japanese contrition represented only a pleasant patina designed to assuage the neighbors in order to conceal the fact that Japan's beliefs and intentions remain fundamentally the same as they had been in the 1930s.

South Korean dismay about Japanese remembrance—and the resulting distrust of Japan—is intense and real. However, the second finding is that when Koreans sat down to make national policy, they recognized that despite their suspicions of Japan, Tokyo was in no position to threaten them. Korean fears were kept in check by Japan's limited capabilities: most powerfully, the constraining effects of the U.S.-Japan alliance. Koreans did fear Japan during the 1950s, when leaders in Seoul expected the United States to withdraw its military presence from the region. However, events in the 1960s proved reassuring. Most important, Washington and Tokyo agreed to renew their security treaty automatically, every ten years, without a potentially divisive debate on either side of the Pacific. In sum, despite their enduring distrust of Japan, South Koreans have realized that their historical enemy is contained: there is little to fear from Tokyo.

## CONTRITION AND BACKLASH

Many observers have expressed dissatisfaction with Japanese contrition and dismay about Tokyo's repeated denials and justifications of its past violence. But they have overlooked a surprising pattern. The third finding from this case is that many of the "gaffes" that have so angered Japan's former victims were in fact *caused* by Japanese contrition. In other words, efforts to apologize galvanized Japanese conservatives to deny, justify, or glorify Japan's past behavior. For example, the Suzuki administration's conciliatory behavior in the 1982 textbook crisis—its willingness to revise textbooks and to institute the "Asian Neighbor's Clause"—led a group of Japanese conservatives to write and publish a history textbook that whitewashed past aggression. Ministry of Education approval of this book for publication in 1986 touched off the second textbook dispute. Prime Minister Nakasone's conciliatory behavior in that dispute then prompted the 1986 denial by Education Minister Fujio Masayuki.[277] Similarly, Okuno Seisuke's denials in 1988 were triggered by an exhibition in Tokyo about the Nanjing Massacre.

The pattern of contrition-then-backlash continued into the next two decades. Prime Minister Murayama Tomiichi's 1994 apology triggered Sakurai Shin's statement that Japan had not committed aggression. The cause-and-effect relationship between apologies and denial was never more evident than in the case of the 1995 Diet Resolution; LDP members of the coalition government, and powerful members of the Diet, hastened to distance themselves from the Socialist Murayama and his resolution. Debate over the resolution directly prompted unapologetic statements by Eto, Sakurai, Shimamura, and—the most damaging for South Korea-Japan relations—Watanabe. Later, in the exact pattern observed in the 1980s, Ministry of Education approval of the mention of the sex slaves in textbooks triggered conservatives to mobilize and write the Fusosha textbook with the goal of presenting a less "masochistic" interpretation of Japanese history. The approval and reapproval of this book later touched off disputes over textbooks in 2001 and 2005.

In a new twist, *foreign* pressure on Japan to apologize also incited denials. The U.S. congressional debate over House Resolution 121 (which urged Tokyo to apologize to the sex slaves) prompted Prime Minister Abe Shinzo to do the opposite: he denied Tokyo's culpability in the forcible abduction of the "comfort women."[278] Thus, in Japanese politics apologies and denials do not simply coexist: apologies (or proposed apologies) frequently *cause* denials. To be sure, unapologetic sentiments were widespread before the apologies were offered. However, official contrition brought the issues back onto the political radar screen and in many cases galvanized conservatives to be more politically active and vocal than they previously had been.

This finding is significant because it casts doubt on the conventional wisdom (prevalent in both academic writing and the popular press) about the utility of contrition—both in the case of Japan's foreign relations and in postconflict reconciliation more broadly. Commentators frequently say, "Japan should just apologize once and for all," implying that if it "finally" did so, Tokyo's relations with its neighbors would improve. But this chapter shows that in a vibrant democracy such as Japan, there is no "once and for all." Relations with South Korea and other countries are tense not because of an *absence* of Japanese contrition but in great part because of the backlash that Japanese contrition provoked. Japan's apologies are not viewed as being "from the Many to the Many";[279] they are viewed (at best) as the gesture of one contrite individual in an overwhelmingly unrepentant country or (at worst) as an effort to deceive the neighbors about Tokyo's true intentions. Thus, yet another Japanese apology seems unlikely to improve relations.

THEORIES OF REMEMBRANCE
AND RECONCILIATION

What does this case study reveal about the theory tested in this book—that is, about the effects of remembrance on perceptions of intentions and threat? As I posited in chapter 1, the "strong" version of the theory—related to the emotions or cognition of observers—holds that denials so enrage observers that unapologetic remembrance will elevate threat perception re-gardless of other signals. The weaker version of the theory, by contrast, posits that countries weigh remembrance just as they evaluate other signals of intentions and threat. This hypothesis might work either because of the link between remembrance and domestic mobilization or because of the link between remembrance and identity.

The Japan–South Korea case does not support the stronger version of the theory. To be sure, the testimony of South Koreans confirms they feel a great deal of emotion on this issue. Although they observe and bitterly re-sent Japanese denials, South Koreans grew less fearful of Japan in the 1960s because they recognized that Japanese power was contained.

Evidence from this case does support the weaker version of the theory. Not only has Korean distrust been congruent with unapologetic remem-brance in Japan, but South Koreans also specifically connect their distrust of Japan's intentions to its unapologetic remembrance. And although Koreans do not currently fear Japan (because it is constrained), their worries that Japan may one day be "uncorked" show the connections between unapolo-getic remembrance and perceptions of threat. Overall, postwar relations be-tween Japan and the ROK lend substantial support to the view that remembrance affects interstate relations and the prospects for reconcilia-tion between former adversaries.

This case offers support for two of the mechanisms posited in chapter 1. In media coverage, scholarly articles, and interviews, South Koreans talk about contrition as a signal of a country's peaceful identity. Frequently praising Germany, they invoke international norms and cite Tokyo's failure to live up to the German standard.

As for the mechanism linking remembrance to a country's level of do-mestic mobilization, this case shows mixed support. Korean observers of-ten discuss Japanese unapologetic statements, visits to Yasukuni Shrine, and so forth as part of an effort to increase domestic nationalism—in order to mobilize the country for a more militarized foreign policy. Importantly, however, this case study does *not* support the view that contrition con-tributes to demobilization. Because of backlash, Japanese contrition ar-guably increased, rather than decreased, Japanese nationalism. Similar dynamics are apparent in Turkey and Austria, where domestic and interna-tional pressure to acknowledge past violence has led to the political em-powerment of the far right.[280]

## OTHER INDICATORS OF THREAT

This chapter also examined other factors that might affect perceptions of intentions and threat: regime type, institutional participation, territorial claims, and capabilities. The evidence suggests that the existence of terri-torial disputes exacerbates mistrust between countries: Japan's claim on the Tokdo/Takeshima Islands reinforces Koreans' suspicions about Japanese intentions. Additionally, national capabilities (power and constraints) powerfully affect threat perception. Although Koreans are extremely wary of Japanese intentions, they do not fear Japan (i.e., perceive a Japanese threat) when they view its power as constrained.

However, evidence for the pacifying effects of mutual democratization is not found in the Japan–South Korea relationship. This variant of democratic peace theory suggests that as South Korean democracy became consolidated, Korean perceptions of Japan's intentions should improve. But this was not the case; Korean distrust remains strong. Moreover, when Koreans discuss their perceptions of Japanese intentions, they do not discuss their neighbor's domestic political institutions. To the contrary, many South Korean observers explicitly argue that remembrance in Japan reveals it to be the same country it was in the 1930s. "It is an illusion," wrote one journalist, "to believe that post-war Japan represents a fresh rebirth with no ties to the past. The truth is that post-war Japan is essentially a continuation of prewar Japan." Another commentator claimed that perceptions of history among Japanese leaders belie "Japan's attempts to prove itself reformed."[281] Democratic peace theorists might, quite reasonably, counter that the period of time in which both countries have been mature democracies (since the 1990s) has been quite short. At this point in time, however, I find no evidence that democratization has built trust between Seoul and Tokyo.

## COMPETING EXPLANATIONS

Critics might raise a number of objections to these findings. One line of argument would question whether Korean statements and policies reflect genuine distrust of Japan or whether Korean elites merely feign distrust—and harp on the inflammatory statements emanating from Tokyo—to capitalize politically on anti-Japanese sentiment in Korea. Given that a core element of Korean nationalism is "anti-Japanism," the tactic of scapegoating Japan should be a politically promising one.[282] In other words, perhaps my evidence does not actually show that Koreans distrust Japan or worry about Japanese remembrance.[283]

Two variants of this argument are possible. One version posits that authoritarian leaders face the greatest incentives to scapegoat neighboring countries and "wave the flag" to rally nationalist support. A second variant suggests that this tendency should be particularly pronounced in countries undergoing political transition from authoritarianism to democracy. Both versions, however, agree that although politicians in mature democracies face some incentives to engage in diversionary and jingoistic behavior, those incentives are less pronounced because elected leaders are less in need of cultivating legitimacy through jingoism and xenophobia. Additionally, mature democracies have a more vibrant "marketplace of ideas" that interferes with mythmaking: even if politicians try to purvey myths, a number of institutions and actors (such as academe and a free press) check such behavior.[284]

There are powerful reasons to believe that Korean distrust of Japan is genuine. First, South Korean responses to Japanese denials have been consistent throughout the postwar period. It is implausible that several generations of South Korean citizens and leaders—with different foreign and domestic policy agendas—have coordinated an effort to pretend to distrust Japan. Second, South Korean outrage and mistrust toward Japan has been consistent through periods in which the ROK was an authoritarian regime, a transitional regime, and a mature democracy.[285] Korean responses to Japanese denials did not grow more muted after the ROK became a mature democracy, as this counterargument would expect.

Third, to guard against the danger that ROK responses to Japanese apologies are crafted for political purposes, I used multiple indicators to assess Korean perceptions. To be sure, some of my evidence is consistent with the domestic posturing hypothesis: symbolic policies (such as canceling a summit or recalling an ambassador) might have been pursued with the domestic audience in mind, and quotes from state-run media or public speeches by South Korean leaders may be evidence of grandstanding rather than of genuine sentiment. However, other evidence that is less susceptible to this criticism also suggests Korean distrust of Japan. For example, the private communications of political leaders—such as their internal memos—echo the same sentiments as their public statements. And in my interviews with South Korean elites, I discovered that former government officials openly disagreed with each other about a broad range of foreign policy issues, but most were wary about Japanese intentions, and much of their wariness stemmed from Tokyo's unapologetic remembrance. My conclusion about these sentiments is supported by the writings of Korean academics, who also express distrust of Japan and connect their distrust to Japanese denials and justifications of war and colonization. Overall, I am confident that Korean distrust of Japan is real, and that it is driven in large part by Japan's unapologetic remembrance.

*Does Remembrance Really Matter?* A second criticism of my analysis of Japan-ROK relations contends that remembrance plays a minor role at best in their political relationship. Because a great deal of the variation in Korean threat perception can be explained by changes in Japan's capabilities (notably the constraint of the U.S.-Japan alliance) one might question the extent to which unapologetic remembrance actually matters. According to this criticism, disputes over remembrance may create some diplomatic noise from time to time, but threat perception is driven primarily by national capabilities.

Although capabilities do powerfully affect threat perception, a narrow "capabilities-only" theory of threat perception cannot explain the most important facts about international relations in East Asia. Had South Korean perceptions of threat been driven entirely by perceptions of capabilities, Koreans (and people in other countries) would have spent the years after World War II worrying about *American* power—not about Japan or the Soviet Union. But, of course, no one assessed threat by looking solely at capabilities; they also considered intentions. Koreans, for example, drew a clear distinction between Japan—which had conquered and colonized them—and the (vastly more powerful) United States, which demonstrated no interest in owning Korea. It is clear that countries assess intentions as they estimate threats: evidence presented in this chapter shows that remembrance (particularly denials of past aggression or atrocities) affects judgments about intentions.

The overriding point is that although Japanese capabilities and Korean perceptions of threat fluctuated in sync during the Cold War, Japan's capabilities do not tell the entire story about how Koreans assess threat. Data from this chapter confirm that Japan's unapologetic remembrance makes Koreans fear it more than they would otherwise. To put this differently, Japan's denials have created a context in which increases in its power are extremely threatening.

*Neglected Issues?* One might also critique this analysis for omitting other factors that are salient to relations between Japan and South Korea. Bound up with the topic of past human rights abuse is the problem of the ethnic Korean minority in Japan and Korean frustration with Japanese discrimination against this group. Another factor that might influence perceptions of Japan's intentions is its "culture of antimilitarism": since World War II, a variety of institutions were created to inhibit military adventurism. Presumably any changes in this would influence Korean perceptions of Japanese intentions.[286] Issues such as these, one might argue, should be discussed in any analysis of the Japan-South Korea relationship.

Such issues probably do play a role in shaping Korean perceptions of Japan; their inclusion would certainly provide a richer description of Japan-Korea relations. However the goal of this analysis is to draw inferences about the link, if any, between remembrance and perceptions of intentions, and omission of these issues does not complicate my ability to draw such inferences. First, these omissions do not interfere with congruence testing because the factors I omitted did not significantly vary over time. As of the mid-1990s, the best research on Japanese antimilitarism concluded that it had not declined significantly since the end of the Second World War.[287] Even today, although many commentators herald that Japan is becoming "normal," Japan has not revised its constitution, renounced its arms export ban, or abandoned its Three Non-Nuclear principles, though these issues remain possibilities for the future. Furthermore, concerns about any potentially neglected issues are mitigated because such issues would have been raised in the archival documents conveying U.S.-ROK discussions about Japan, in the interviews I conducted with Korean elites, or in Korean media coverage; and for the most part this was not the case. In all of these discussions, analyses of the threat posed by Japan were dominated by talk of capabilities, territorial disputes, and remembrance.

*Japan's "Victim Consciousness."* Another competing hypothesis would suggest that Japan's memory of its *own* suffering should convey peaceful intentions to its neighbors. This hypothesis contrasts with the logic of the theory tested in this book: in chapter 1, I laid out the hypothesis that a country's remembrance will reassure former victims if it reflects a candid and remorseful assessment of its past violence against others. However one might instead expect that Japan's mourning of its *own* wartime suffering signaled that it recognized the terrible costs of war, and thus the country would not pursue aggression in the future. Indeed, after the war, there was widespread Japanese agreement that its imperialist policies had been tragic and misguided. The people recalled their starvation, heartbreaking mass suicides, the atomic bombings and fire bombings, and the horrors of the battlefield. Although Japanese textbooks glossed over atrocities on the Asian continent, they did not glorify war: they universally portrayed Japanese imperialism as a tragic mistake. Thus one might argue that despite the fact that the Japanese did not remember foreign victims, its "victim consciousness" (*higaisha ishiki*) might have reassured outside observers that Japan's understanding of the tragedy of war made it less likely to pursue aggression.

Although this hypothesis is a reasonable one, I found no evidence that Japan's memories of its own victimhood reassured Koreans. Contrary to this view, Japan's preoccupation with its own suffering during the war has coincided with six decades of Korean suspicions about Tokyo's regional ambitions. Furthermore, when South Koreans have discussed Japan's war memory, they have not talked about any reassuring signal sent by Japan's memories of its own suffering. Rather, they unanimously lambasted Japan for its unapologetic remembrance of its atrocities.

A final objection to the findings of this chapter concedes that Koreans do indeed distrust Japan, and this distrust is driven in great part by Japan's unapologetic remembrance. However, the extent to which any conclusions can be drawn from this is dubious: perhaps Koreans are uniquely concerned about history, national honor, and apologies. Or, perhaps South Koreans have discounted Japanese apologies more than another country might have because they have some culturally unique expectation about what an apology should be. According to this critique, generalizations from this case are impossible given Korea's unique historical experience and culture. To gain greater confidence that findings from the Japan-Korea case are more broadly applicable, in chapter 4 I examine the cases of Chinese and Australian relations with Japan. There I also discuss the generalizability of the case of Franco-German relations, which is the subject of the next chapter.

# CHAPTER THREE

# Not Your Father's Fatherland

The Germans: unsurpassed both at the crime and at repenting it.
—Daniel Vernet, *Le Monde*

In the years after World War II, first West and then unified Germany engaged in tremendous self-reflection and atonement.* Germans confronted history and Holocaust in their memorials and monuments; they learned about eleven million murdered souls in museums and textbooks; they repented invasion, tyranny, and terror in the haunting speeches and bowed heads of their leaders. The confrontation with the past was, to be sure, imperfect. Germans sometimes flinched from the truth and clung to comforting myths. Nevertheless, their self-reflection was so historically unprecedented, they had to invent a word for it: the German *Vergangenheitsbewältigung* was the most extensive process of national atonement the world had ever seen.

Over this same period, West Germany and France would transform their relations from hereditary enemies to warm friends. The French initially eyed their former conquerors with bitterness and fear; a decade later, however, Franco-German tension relaxed into diplomatic and economic cooperation. By 1960, France viewed West Germany as its closest ally. The expansion of cultural ties bolstered what would develop into a profound reconciliation.

Many scholars have argued that German contrition played an important role in Western European reconciliation. Andrew Kydd comments that Germany successfully repaired its reputation in Europe by "showing repentance, making restitution, and openly investigating the history of the

---

*This chapter evaluates *West* German remembrance and reconciliation with France. Remembrance was strikingly different in East Germany: the German Democratic Republic paid no reparations and offered no apologies. East German politics reflected stark anti-Semitism and hostility toward Israel. Jeffrey Herf, *Divided Memory: The Nazi Past in the Two Germanys* (Cambridge, MA: Harvard University Press, 1997).

period and teaching an internationally approved version in its schools."
Argues Stephen Van Evera: "German hypernationalism has dissipated,
and a powerful barrier against its return has been erected by a strong
movement in Germany for the honest discussion of German history." People urging Tokyo to atone frequently invoke the German comparison:
ROK President Kim Dae-jung said that Koreans might have trusted Japan
if, "like Germany, [it] had reflected upon its past." Nicholas Kristof writes
that only when Japan offers German-style apologies can it "play a part on
the world stage commensurate with its abilities and resources." One newspaper urges Japan to come to terms with its history, "just as Germany repented of its past aggression and reached a reconciliation with France at
the heart of Europe."[1]

This chapter shows, as many analysts have claimed, that Bonn's acknowledgment of Germany's past crimes facilitated reconciliation with its former
enemies. In the 1950s, Bonn took the important step (through reparations
such as the 1952 Luxembourg Agreement) of accepting responsibility for
the war and Holocaust. Unlike in the Japan case, the West Germans
avoided denials, which might have (and which findings from the Japan
case suggest *would* have) torpedoed reconciliation with France and others.
Throughout the postwar era, the French watched West Germany's national
debates. They praised the country's willingness to wrestle with its historical burdens, and they expressed wariness at signs of historical revisionism.

This chapter also shows that contrary to the lessons many people have
drawn from the German case, not much contrition was necessary for the remarkable rapprochement that occurred between West Germany and France.
In the early years after the war, Bonn demonstrated very little contrition. Paying reparations to Israel, it accepted responsibility for Germany's crimes, but
issued only a tepid, self-exculpatory apology. In commemoration, education,
and national discourse, the West Germans mourned their *own* wartime suffering, and forgot the atrocities they had committed against others. Nevertheless, this era witnessed a remarkable rapprochement between France and
West Germany. By the early 1960s, the French were viewing West Germany
as a close friend and security partner. The extensive campaign of contrition
that would distinguish Germany in the world would come later.

## The Bitter Legacy

"We have torn each other apart for a hundred years," lamented Charles de
Gaulle to Konrad Adenauer at a postwar summit.[2] Indeed, in 1945 the
chances for Franco-German reconciliation appeared slim. France under
Napoleon had fought and vanquished Prussia; France then suffered a defeat at the hands of Bismarck in the 1871 Franco-Prussian War. Germany

and France fought again in World War I, when 8 million Frenchmen were mobilized to fight, of whom 1.3 million were killed and nearly 1 million crippled. France's most advanced industrial and agricultural region, the northeast, was devastated; industrial production and economic growth plummeted. After Germany's defeat, France and her allies imposed punishing peace terms in the Treaty of Versailles. Germany was demilitarized and forced to accept responsibility for war damages, including the admission of war guilt and the payment of an impossibly high reparations bill.[3] A disarmed, impoverished, and resentful Germany would eventually bring the Nazi Party into power under Adolf Hitler. After rearming, remilitarizing the Rhineland, and annexing Austria and Czechoslovakia, Hitler conquered Poland in 1939 and then invaded France in May 1940.

The French suffered 92,000 dead and 200,000 wounded in the short campaign. Their leaders debated resistance versus armistice; the undersecretary of war in the fallen Reynaud cabinet, General Charles de Gaulle, fled to London and in a June 18, 1940, radio appeal summoned the French to continue to resist. He continued to lead French resistance throughout the war. The French government, under Philippe Pétain and his deputy Pierre Laval, advocated collaboration: they anticipated a German victory and wanted to safeguard France's colonial possessions. Pétain's government signed an armistice on June 22 in a railway car at Compiègne, where Germany had been forced to accept harsh terms after World War I. The French army was reduced to 100,000 men and the navy disarmed. Armistice allowed for a quasi-sovereign French state; it divided France into an occupied zone (northern France and the western coast), and an unoccupied southern zone. In early July the French Parliament met in Vichy and voted itself and the Third Republic out of existence. The Germans would rely heavily on the Vichy government to administer the occupation.

Relative to German brutality elsewhere, the occupation of France was mild.[4] In other lands, German occupation meant deportation and murder. But Hitler's racial views privileged and even admired the French. Under German occupation they enjoyed some independence in the cultural sphere; schools, publishing houses, theaters, universities, and many newspapers were allowed to continue operations. French construction firms and factories thrived with German military contracts. The Nazis requisitioned, rather than seized, any goods that they needed; the owner received a receipt that, in theory, was redeemable from Vichy or the German authorities. Occupation troops were billeted in French households; personal experiences varied greatly, but in general billeting did not result in violence or looting. Fraternization was commonplace.

The French, however, did suffer a great deal from war, occupation, and chaos after the German surrender. Vichy paid vast sums in occupation costs and reparations to Germany. Towns were forced to designate hostages, to be shot if any harm came to German forces. Later the Germans abandoned the use of hostages and instead deported French dissidents to concentration camps. The Nazis used the 1.5 million French prisoners of war (POW)—in camps in France and Germany—as a large supply of hostages used to extract concessions from Vichy. Vichy instituted forced labor after 1941, deporting 650,000 French people to Germany to work in war industries. Laval presided over the deportation of 76,000 Jews to death camps (only 3 percent survived); he instituted a reign of terror policed by a French militia (*Milice*); and he attempted to eradicate the French Resistance.

Although the majority of the French people accepted the Vichy government, some resisted German rule. Resistors transmitted military intelligence to London, helped downed Allied airmen escape, circulated anti-German leaflets, or sabotaged railways and German installations. Guerilla bands in the hills (*Maquis*) engaged in militant opposition. Resistance increased after the German invasion of the USSR as French Communists joined the opposition, and with the popular outrage that greeted Vichy's decision to conscript labor. In May 1943 several resistance groups were unified by leader Jean Moulin into a National Resistance Council. In London, de Gaulle established an organization called Free France and proclaimed the French National Committee, for which he claimed the status of a government-in-exile.

The Allies liberated Paris in August 1944, and de Gaulle led a triumphant parade into the city. France descended into civil war as Vichy loyalists clashed with de Gaulle's Free France movement; French soldiers fought each other in the colonies in Syria and western Africa. Back home, the postwar power struggle resulted in 10,000 summary executions of accused collaborators carried out by Free French and resistance forces. Pétain and Laval fled eastward with the Germans, claiming to be the exiled rightful French government. After the end of the war, Laval (who had attempted suicide) was executed, and Pétain later died in prison. For decades, the French embraced a myth that exaggerated the size and scope of the resistance. As de Gaulle reassured his countrymen in 1944, "Apart from a handful of wretches the vast majority of us were and are Frenchmen of good faith."[5] Most collaborators were granted amnesty and were fully reinstated into postwar French society.

In sum, as of 1945, France had fought three major wars with Germany since 1871 at astronomical human and financial cost. In World War II—unmistakably caused by German aggression—a total of 600,000 French citizens lost their lives: a third on the battlefield, and the rest in executions, massacres, death camps, or civil war. The German invasion and occupation had unleashed profound terror upon France.

German aggression and atrocities across Europe were also fresh in French minds. This was the most destructive war in history; estimates of casualties range from 50 to 64 million. Seizing Poland, Hitler sought to make room for German settlement by annihilating six million Poles (among them three million Polish Jews). Mobile killing squads (*Einsatzgruppen*) systematically shot Jewish populations on conquered Soviet territory at the rear of the advancing German armies. Eleven million people perished in the Holocaust: six million Jews and five million others, among them political dissidents of all nationalities, Sinti/Roma (gypsies), homosexuals, Christian clergy, Jehovah's Witnesses, the disabled, and the mentally ill. In addition, the Germans conscripted over seven million Europeans into slave labor for German factories, forcing them to work in deplorable conditions that often led to disease and death. Although the French themselves suffered relatively less at German hands, their image of Germany after the war would also be shaped by these atrocities.

The Germans themselves suffered greatly in the maelstrom they had unleashed. In wartime, Allied bombing raids at Dresden, Hamburg, and elsewhere had killed 600,000 Germans and made over three million people homeless.[6] Three and one-half million German men perished in battle, with almost five million wounded. After the war, Stalin—wanting a buffer zone between the Soviet Union and a renewed German threat—seized land from eastern Poland and compensated the Poles with a slice of East Germany. Between 1944 and 1947, before and after the 1945 Potsdam Treaty that codified Stalin's land-grab, fifteen million ethnic Germans living in former Reich territories in Eastern Europe were ethnically cleansed, their properties appropriated by vengeful locals. In their desperate flight to Germany, over two million refugees perished: starving, freezing, or shot. The Soviet army abused and murdered Germans as it swept westward to seize Berlin, raping an estimated two million German women. Nine million German soldiers languished in Soviet POW camps. The armies of Germany's enemies swarmed throughout the country, holding its future in their hands. The campaign to dominate the continent had devastated not only Europe, but the Germans themselves.

## Shaping German Remembrance: The Occupation

From the chaos of war and surrender emerged divided Germany, with the forces of the Soviet Union in the East and Allied forces in the West. The Soviets and Allies began negotiating the future of Germany: the issue that would become the central point of confrontation in the Cold War. After the war, the Allies sought to democratize West Germany, link it to the West through a variety of economic and security institutions, and rebuild it as a vital anti-Soviet ally. Toward these goals, the Allies implemented numerous policies during their occupation of Germany's western zones that would shape later West German remembrance of the war.

First, Allied military governments sought to bring to justice those Germans who had presided over or perpetrated Nazi aggression and atrocities. The International Military Tribunal convened in Nuremberg from November 20, 1945, to October 1, 1946, and held twelve successor trials between 1946 and 1949. These trials convicted 1,517 persons; 324 of whom received the death penalty and 247 of whom received life sentences. The trials "established that Hitler and the Nazi regime had launched World War II as a war of aggression and racism, had ordered and implemented the mass murder of European Jewry and millions of others in the concentration camps and death camps, and in so doing had drawn upon the cooperation of tens of thousands of officials in the Nazi government and army." Allied denazification purged 73,000 people from industry and 150,000 people from government.[7] Between 1946 and 1948, Allied officials required over sixteen million West Germans to fill out questionnaires about their activities during the Nazi era. Less than one percent of these, however, resulted in a guilty verdict. Tribunals were known as a "laundry": one walked in wearing a fascist brown shirt and left in sparkling white.[8]

The German public and political elite resented and resisted trials and denazification. West German leaders successfully pressured Allied officials to commute many death sentences and to overturn convictions. In 1949 one of the first actions of the new West German Bundestag was to pass a general amnesty law, which extended to over 800,000 people.[9] As with legal trials, denazification eventually waned under German pressure.

Because the Nazi regime had been highly effective at cultivating support for its aggression in the schools, Occupation authorities instituted extensive education reforms.[10] Nazi education had been highly centralized and party-controlled, and had indoctrinated the public with hatred toward perceived enemies of the Reich, both foreign and domestic. As Robert Lawson noted, "German language classes became a means of forwarding the particular folk-culture idealized by Hitler, and other languages were de-emphasized. History was especially applicable to the glorification of Germany, abuse of other nations, and intensification of racial issues."[11] After the war, the Allies dispersed administrative control of education to the state level (*Länder*) and made education compulsory and free for all citizens. The Allies expunged Nazi propaganda and sought to instill in West Germans an appreciation of civic responsibility, democracy, and international understanding. Curricula—particularly in the field of history—were revised "to ensure that all traces of National Socialist thinking were removed." Textbooks that contained anti-Semitic, nationalistic, or militaristic propaganda were replaced.[12] In history education, Allied leaders promoted candid discussion of German aggression and atrocities; an education report noted that the German school curricula should reflect "Demonstration of Germany's past errors."[13] Although many Germans viewed education reform with distaste, some scholars supported it and cooperated extensively with

Occupation authorities. In 1946 in Braunschweig, German historians and educators set up a "History Working Party." This group produced the first postwar history curricula and held numerous meetings and discussions with teachers of all levels.[14]

Widespread apathy among Germans regarding Nazi crimes led Allied Occupation authorities to implement a broader publicity campaign. French scholar Alfred Grosser reported: "Listening to the complaints from almost every German they met, foreign visitors were invariably struck with their extraordinary self-centeredness. People in Germany were quite unconcerned at hearing about the meagre rations in occupied France, and were even unaware that the French were still rationed. . . . The Germans could not or would not comprehend the horrible acts of which their misery was the sequel."[15] As a result of German apathy, General Eisenhower ordered the production and broadcast of films about German atrocities. In addition, as Harold Marcuse notes,

> Newspapers printed numerous articles and ran didactic series on the camps; placards showing heaps of corpses with texts such as "YOU ARE GUILTY OF THIS" were posted in cities, towns, and Military Government offices everywhere; picture exhibitions were displayed in storefronts; pamphlets collecting the most shocking images were printed and distributed free and sold; radio reports about the camps were broadcast at regular intervals . . .

Generals Eisenhower and Patton ordered German citizens to tour the death camps and view the horror firsthand. Occupation authorities required Germans—particularly former Nazi Party members—to clean camps and bury corpses. Marcuse comments that this policy "had two primary purposes: to document the atrocities by obtaining reliable German witnesses, and to 'teach a lesson' especially to Nazi Party members singled out for participation."[16] A loudspeaker berated Germans touring Belsen: "What you see here is such a disgrace to the German people that their name must be erased from the list of civilized nations. You stand here judged by what you see in this camp. It is your lot to begin the hard task of restoring the name of the German people to the list of civilized nations." The British showed a film about the camps (*The Mills of Death*) to POWs and to mass audiences in Germany.[17]

In sum, the Occupation implemented several policies that set the stage for later German remembrance. Efforts to bring Nazi planners and perpetrators to justice, though curtailed because of widespread resentment, promoted German awareness of Nazi atrocities. The Allies democratized German education, sought to expunge nationalistic history from West German schools, and forced Germans to confront Nazi atrocities in a massive publicity campaign using all media channels.

## Early Period (1945 to mid-1960s)

EAGER TO FORGET

In the early years after the war, the West German government, under conservative leadership,[†] acknowledged past aggression in key statements and policies. The opposition Left argued powerfully for remembrance and atonement. Early West German remembrance, however, did not yet reflect the soul-searching candor that, decades later, would impress the world. Conservative leaders opposed contrition because they viewed democratization as the most important task at hand; emphasizing German crimes and culpability, they feared, might cause a nationalist backlash and jeopardize German democratic stability. Most people, preoccupied with thoughts of their own suffering, embraced the conservative agenda of limited memory.

Bonn accepted responsibility for the Nazi past through a few key policies and statements. Jeffrey Herf notes that denials of past violence were confined to the political fringe: "No major national political figure in East or West Germany publicly raised doubts about whether or not the Nazi regime had actually carried out a genocide of European Jewry and waged a race war on the Eastern front." Replying to the 1951 Israeli request for reparations, Chancellor Konrad Adenauer told the Bundestag that most Germans "are aware of the immeasurable suffering brought to the Jews in Germany and in the occupied territories in the era of National Socialism." He said, "unspeakable crimes were committed which require moral and material restitution."[18]

West Germany also paid reparations during this period. On September 10, 1952, Bonn signed the Luxembourg Agreement, in which it agreed to pay to the State of Israel and various Jewish organizations DM3.5 billion, which amounts to nearly $5 billion in 2007 U.S. dollars.[19] Between 1954 and 1991, Germany would pay Israel about $US67 billion. In the early years, Bonn also sent key supplies to the young state such as ships, cars, trains, manufacturing and communications technology, and medical equipment: goods amounting to about 10–15 percent of annual Israeli imports at the time.[20]

Bonn also compensated individuals persecuted by the Nazis because of their race, religion, nationality, or ideology. Over time, Germany would pay out over four million claims under the "BEG" laws: 20 percent to German residents, 40 percent to Israelis, and 40 percent elsewhere. Berlin reports that as of 1998, BEG compensation amounted to $US44 billion, and the government anticipated paying an additional $US10 billion.[21] Furthermore, in

---

[†]From 1949 to 1969, the Federal Republic was ruled by the Christian Democratic Union of Germany (*Christlich Demokratische Union Deutschlands*, or CDU) and its sister party, the Christian Social Union of Bavaria (*Christlich-Soziale Union in Bayern*, or CSU). The CDU/CSU ruled in a coalition government with the Free Democratic Party (*Freie Demokratische Partei*, or FDP).

1957 the Bundestag passed the "BRüG" law, which provided guidance for property claims from victims of Nazi persecution. As of 1987, this law settled over 700,000 claims in the amount of $US2 billion (DM 3.9 billion).[22] Bonn's reparations policies thus acknowledged and attempted to atone for German crimes.

In the early postwar years, members of the socialist opposition were passionate advocates of German contrition. Opposition politicians supported Adenauer's reparations policies, and indeed went much further: making frequent, poignant statements about the need to atone. Carlo Schmid of the Social Democratic Party of Germany (SPD) criticized the national tendency to blur distinctions between perpetrators and victims. "People are beginning to forget," he lamented. "Even former SS and SD men are beginning to regard themselves as victims of National socialism."[23] Socialist leader Kurt Schumacher argued that many of his countrymen "still lived in [a] world of illusions" about the Holocaust; he said West Germans were trying to "repress their share of the historical guilt." Schumacher maintained that Germany's "fundamental inner reflection and change of heart must be made apparent."[24] Socialist politician Ernst Reuter similarly emphasized the need to remember: "We cannot make up for the horrors which [the Nazis] inflicted on other countries. But we must, whether we want to or not, atone for them." Theodor Heuss of the Free Democratic Party (FDP), a later Bundestag president, also supported remembrance. He praised Allied reeducation efforts, saying that unlike after World War I, "the German future has been freed from the possibility of a false domestic propaganda." He challenged his countrymen to face the truth of their past in order to "prepare the battle against any kind of emergent Hitler legend."

Commemorative activities of opposition leaders also encouraged remembrance of the Nazi era. Heuss and Nahum Goldmann appeared at a 1952 ceremony at Bergen-Belsen, a wartime concentration camp. Heuss's speech there included a haunting and famous refrain, "No one will lift this shame from us." Ernst Reuter spoke at Plötzensee, (where members of the German resistance had been executed); he also offered a remarkable apology at the Warsaw Ghetto memorial on the tenth anniversary of the Ghetto's destruction. Describing the heroism of the Jewish uprising, Reuter said, "We live in a time that is inclined to forget all too quickly. But in this hour we want to say that there are things which we are not permitted to forget, and which we do not want to forget. As Germans—I speak to you here as well as to my Jewish fellow countrymen as a German—we must not and we cannot forget the disgrace and shame that took place in our German name."[25]

The rest of the West German political elite and society, however, showed widespread amnesia and a reluctance to confront the recent past. Adenauer's reparations package to Israel was highly unpopular, favored by only 11 percent of the public. Parliamentary debates reflected opposition from Adenauer's conservative colleagues, including most of his cabinet. Finance Minister Fritz Schafer doubted the country could afford the reparations. Adenauer's party, the Christian Democratic Union (CDU), included Germans who had suffered in its definition of Nazi "victims." The FDP, his "liberal" coalition partners, were similarly unenthusiastic.[26] CDU politicians negotiating with Israel described the German climate of evasion. As negotiator Franz Böhm bitterly recounted, "No one will admit his guilt for National Socialism, for the Nazi rise to power, or for the terror of the Third Reich." Adenauer's leadership—as well as the support of the Left—was essential to push through the reparations bill against the will of the general public and Adenauer's own cabinet and party. Almost half of the members of Adenauer's CDU/CSU/FDP coalition abstained from the Bundestag vote.

During these early postwar years, Bonn offered occasional vague apologies that emphasized Germany's own suffering. In Adenauer's apology to Israel, the chancellor did note that "unspeakable crimes" required reparations; however, he used the common passive construction of "crimes committed in Germany's name" to describe them and emphasized German resistance efforts and public ignorance of the genocide. "In an overwhelming majority," Adenauer said, "the German people abhorred the crimes committed against the Jews and did not participate in them." He added, "there were many Germans . . . who at their own risk were willing to assist their Jewish fellow citizens." Adenauer's speeches emphasized not Nazi victims but the nine million German POWs in Soviet camps at the end of the war; he lamented that assuming each POW had two concerned relatives, eighteen million Germans were paying the costs of Nazi aggression.

In the judicial realm, Bonn opposed Allied denazification and trials of war criminals, and initially pursued no trials of its own. Adenauer said that it was wrong to divide Germans into "two classes . . . those without political blemishes and those with such blemishes." Adenauer said that Bonn preferred to "put the past behind us" and called for a "tabula rasa," because "many have subjectively atoned for a guilt that was not heavy."[27] His opposition to legal accountability for Nazi crimes was partly rooted in a fear of backlash. "In order to avoid a renewal of German nationalism and Nazism," Adenauer said, "economic recovery and political democratization must take priority over a judicial confrontation with the crimes of the Nazi past." Adenauer preferred measures that were less invasive to most German voters, such as restitution to German Jews and the cultivation of positive relations with Israel. Because of government opposition to denazification, purges of personnel within the West German bureaucracy and higher education were minimal. After the Allies first allowed West German courts to conduct their own trials in 1951, they sentenced only twenty-one people. Bonn passed another general amnesty law in 1954 that expanded its amnesty policies beyond those covered in the 1949 law. In short, as Gerd Knischewski and Ulla

Spittler show, "legal attempts to deal with the legacy of the [Nazi] past were sluggish in this period and soon came to a halt."[28]

Bonn was also slow to provide institutional support for Nazi victims. For example, Adenauer's government did not establish a Ministry for Survivors of Nazi Persecution and Nazi Concentration Camps that could have acknowledged and alleviated the suffering of Germany's victims.[29] Instead, Bonn created an institutional advocate for *German* victims of the war: a cabinet-level office to represent the interests of expellees, refugees, and others. In 1958 Bonn finally created the Central Office for Pursuit of National Socialist Crimes of Violence in Ludwigsburg.

Official commemoration of the period similarly emphasized German suffering. A "Memorial for the expelled ethnic Germans" was erected in Berlin in 1952 at Mehringdamm. Official ceremonies, days of remembrance, and West German monuments did not commemorate Nazi victims. Until the 1980s only six such state-funded monuments or museums had been established in the country.[30] Bonn held no ceremonies remembering the German surrender (May 8, 1945). Jeffrey Olick writes that in the 1950s, "there was no official marking of the occasion, certainly no celebration. In the context of postwar depredations, few saw May 8 as a happy occasion."[31] The ten-year anniversary of the surrender passed in 1955 without official recognition. Rejecting suggestions to preserve the heavily damaged steeple of Gross St. Martin Church—as "a memorial to the wickedness of our time," Adenauer advocated immediate rebuilding to allow the country to move forward.[32] Concentration camp sites and other West German sites of Nazi atrocities were not preserved as memorials. As Knischewski and Spittler describe, "West German society was dominated by utilitarian thinking rather than mourning and commemoration. Places in which [Nazi] atrocities had been committed were either used for different purposes, e.g. as clinics for the mentally ill or as accommodation for refugees, or they were even razed to the ground, as was the case in Dachau."[33] The lakeside villa at Wannsee— site of the historic meeting at which top Nazi officials planned the "Final Solution"—was converted into a youth center.

Two national holidays established during this early period showcased West German amnesia. On July 20, 1944, a group of German army officers had attempted to assassinate Hitler. After the war, Bonn established a July 20 holiday to honor German resistance against the Nazis. The Plötzensee prison (where the conspirators had been housed and then executed) was turned into a memorial and museum about the German resistance. Bonn thus chose to remember a set of victims of whom it could feel proud. Additionally, in 1952 the government established a "people's day of mourning" (*Volkstrauertag*) to honor the victims of war. Socialist leaders had initially suggested commemorating a day in honor of Nazi victims. Adenauer agreed on the need for such a day, but argued that the victims it should honor were "those who lost their lives as victims of National Socialism on the field [of

111

battle] or at home."[34] The Nazi era was further de-emphasized when leaders decided that the day should also honor German victims of World War I and of the East German communist regime. The organization tasked with commemorating the day was the German People's Union for the Care of War Graves (*Volksbund Deutscher Kriegsgraberfürsorge,* or VDK); since 1919 this group had worked to honor the memory and maintain the graves of Germany's war dead. The VDK's World War I focus—as well as its strong Christian identity—would further dilute the holiday's attention to World War II atrocities.[35]

The shame of the recent past inspired Germans to reach farther back into history for events to commemorate. Bonn held large celebrations to honor more distant and glorious events, such as the Frankfurt national assembly's centennial and the 200th anniversary of Goethe's birth, both in 1949. As Rudy Koshar writes, "These events and commemorations marginalized the recent past by establishing heroic continuities, focusing on German survival in the face of insurmountable odds."[36]

Early West German history education (shaped by Allied educational reform) acknowledged Nazi aggression and atrocities but emphasized the innocence and suffering of the German people. Bonn commissioned an eight-volume history, the *Documentation of the Expulsion of Germans from East-Central Europe,*[37] that detailed the experiences of ethnic German expellees and refugees. The project included over 11,000 eyewitness accounts, generally horrific stories of "terror, rape, plundering, the separation of families, forced deportations, starvation, slave labor, and death." Bonn also collected testimonies of German POWs, producing twenty-two books over twenty years that described the imprisonment and brutal treatment they had suffered. "In neither documentation project," argues Robert Moeller, "did the editors elicit testimony about Germany's war of aggression on the eastern front or German rule in Eastern Europe; both projects recorded and sanctioned silence and selective memory."

Selective memory extended into public school textbooks and curricula. Noting that West German education glossed over contemporary history, Alfred Grosser reports that textbooks created an image of a "dream-world." Drawing almost entirely from the works of nineteenth-century authors, textbooks depicted "a romantic and rural Germany, still unsullied by noisy towns and factory chimneys—a land of forest and heath where war and its ruins are unknown." Teachers also emphasized ancient history; judging from most West German curricula, Grosser notes, "one might think that German history ended before Bismarck." Wulf Kansteiner agrees: "Teachers simply opted out of the teaching of contemporary history."[38] Sabine Reichel, author of *What Did You Do in the War, Daddy?* testifies to this point. She commented that as history classes approached the contemporary period, "A shift of mood would creep into the expansive lectures about kings and conquerors from the old ages, and once the Weimar Republic came to an end our teachers lost their proud diction . . . We could feel the impending disaster." Reichel continues,

> There were fifteen pages devoted to the Third Reich, and they were filled with incredible stories about a mass movement called National Socialism which started out splendidly and ended in a catastrophe for the whole world. And then there was an extra chapter, about three-quarters of a page long. It was titled "The Extermination of the Jews" . . . Six million Jews were killed in concentration camps. . . . We never read that chapter aloud with our teacher as we did with so many other ones. It was the untouchable subject, isolated and open to everyone's personal interpretation. There was a subtle, unspoken agreement between teacher and student not to dig into something that would cause discomfort on all sides.[39]

When textbooks did cover contemporary history, discussions were laced with omissions, euphemism, and myths. Of the Holocaust and other atrocities, books emphasized, "Few Germans knew of these terrible things." They assured readers that "a considerable proportion of the German nation had privately turned away from Hitler." Journalist Steve Crawshaw describes West Germany after the surrender as a land of *hinzu kamen* (literally, "in addition came," or an afterthought). A typical book from the period recounted a litany of German misery at home, in POW camps, on the battlefield, and in the expulsions: "*hinzu kamen,* the victims who were killed in the concentration camps, the labour camps, the death chambers etc." Coverage of the war recounted military campaigns "as though this had been a classical military war just like any other."[40]

Although the socialist opposition was arguing for more remembrance, the West German people preferred not to think about the victims of Nazi terror. War correspondent Martha Gellhorn described the national climate: "No one is a Nazi. No one ever was. There may have been some Nazis in the next village . . . that town about 20 kilometres away was a hotbed of Nazism . . . Oh, the Jews? Well, there weren't really many Jews in this neighborhood. Two, maybe, maybe six . . . Ah, how we have suffered. The bombs. We lived in the cellars for weeks." Psychoanalysts later said that German memory during this period reflected an "inability to mourn": Germans adopted the defense mechanisms of amnesia and denial rather than confront the painful reality of their atrocities.[41]

Just as textbooks dodged contemporary history, West German historiography of this period minimized German guilt. Historians argued that because Germany was innocent of instigating the *First* World War, the Second World War was an aberration marring an otherwise proud national tradition. Although most foreign historians concluded that Germany had launched the First as well as the Second World Wars, in Germany "such an interpretation was heretical."[42] As Volker Berghahn and Hanna Schissler write, the Third Reich was deemed "an accident in the works . . . cut out of the mainstream of German history prior to 1933 which was deemed to have been basically 'sound.' " They maintain that German historians "continued to write the history of politics and diplomacy and great men. Of course, Hitler did not qualify as such and came to be portrayed as a demon who had descended upon the German people from another planet."[43] In his book *The German Catastrophe* (*Die deutsche Katastrophe*), historian Friedrich Meinecke argues that Hitler was maneuvered into power, that he actually enjoyed little popular support, and that he alone had been responsible for Nazi crimes. As R. J. B. Bosworth describes, the Hitler myth "was duly seconded and refined by Gerhard Ritter and others. . . . The worst features of Nazism, Ritter explained, were imported—Social Darwinism . . . from England, wayward nationalism from France, gimcrack racism from Austria."[44] Amnesia in 1950s West German historiography was likely exacerbated by the fact that many German academics had either tacitly or overtly supported Hitler's regime and had dodged denazification.

In sum, during the early postwar years Bonn did acknowledge and accept responsibility for Germany's past atrocities and aggression. A critical part of this was the payment of reparations to Israel and Adenauer's accompanying statement. And although West Germans heatedly debated the need for reparations, these discussions elicited no denials or glorifications of Germany's past aggression and atrocities. Aside from this, however, the Federal Republic had yet to begin its soul-searching *Vergangenheitsbewältigung*. Creating a mythology of public innocence and resistance, government policies and broader society focused on German suffering. As Kansteiner and others have concluded, "The culture of the decade is still most appropriately characterized as a period of communicative silence about the most troublesome aspects of the burden of the past."[45]

## COMPETING THEORIES AND PREDICTIONS

As the French evaluated a potential German threat in the early years after World War II, they could have assessed a range of signals of German intentions, as well as German capabilities. Overall, these signals would not have been reassuring. The French would have noticed that the Federal Republic of Germany (FRG) acknowledged and accepted responsibility for Nazi-era crimes; however, they should also have been dismayed by the climate of amnesia and by the focus on Germany's own suffering. Particularly in light of German mythmaking after the First World War, evidence of forgetfulness and self-pity in the FRG should have been disturbing to outside observers.[46]

We might also expect the French to have been wary of German intentions on the basis of unresolved territorial issues. Germany had been divided into the western and eastern zones of occupation, with the Soviet Union ruling the eastern zone. During the 1950s the North Atlantic Treaty Organization (NATO) allies persuaded Bonn to accept division with the promise that they would support future German unification. Traumatized by memories of the 1922 Treaty of Rapallo and the 1939 Nazi-Soviet Non-Aggression Pact, French, British, and American officials lived in continual fear that Bonn would abandon NATO and broker a unification deal with the Soviet Union.

The French could also have worried about a German desire to revise postwar borders. The Allies had agreed at Potsdam that the eastern Oder-Neisse line would constitute a temporary German border until a peace treaty was signed. The German people steadfastly opposed the Oder-Neisse border; a vocal group of refugees from Eastern Europe demanded restitution and exerted pressure on the ruling CDU/CSU Party. Adenauer reassured his allies that the Federal Republic would not resort to force to settle the border issue. But he repeatedly said that Bonn viewed Germany's 1937 borders as the correct borders and contradicted assertions that the matter had been settled in 1945 at Potsdam.[47] Thus the lingering problems of unification and the disputed borders should have elevated French distrust of West Germany.

The democratic peace hypothesis would also predict French skepticism about German intentions during this period. Writes Sabine Lee, "Germany's democratic credentials had been destroyed by twelve years of Nazi dictatorship; by the atrocities which had been committed in the name of the German people; by a lack of effective resistance against the oppressive regime; and by the widespread support which the Nazis had had for many years."[48] Because the Federal Republic in this period was undergoing a democratic transition, a great deal of uncertainty about the future and stability of German democracy remained. From the perspective of democratic peace theory, however, one would expect the French to express the view that Germany's democratization was important for its political stability and for the pacification of its foreign policy.

The French could also assess German intentions by looking at Bonn's support for Western European economic and security institutions. Bonn's early leadership in institution-creation was a positive sign, although it was too soon to tell whether these institutions would take hold or whether they would actually constrain West German behavior. France and the FRG co-founded the European Coal and Steel Community (ECSC), established under the Treaty of Paris in 1951. The ECSC was expanded in 1957 under the Treaty of Rome with the creation of a European atomic energy community, Euratom, and a European Economic Community, or EEC. In 1955 the FRG joined NATO. West German membership in NATO required Bonn's acceptance of several real constraints on its military power: The West Germans agreed to "refrain from any action inconsistent with the strictly defensive character" of the NATO and Brussels treaties and pledged to renounce the right to produce or own weapons of mass destruction.[49] Bonn also agreed not to produce certain conventional weapons such as long-range missiles, strategic bombers, and large battleships. In addition, West Germany accepted verification measures: inspections conducted by officials from the Brussels Treaty Organization (later called the Western European Union, WEU). *All* West German conventional forces would be assigned to NATO's Central European Command (headed by a French general). West Germany was allowed no general staff for its armed forces and no national guard. Furthermore, Germany and its neighbors conducted their primary security policies through NATO (which increased transparency) and established a tradition of consultation and joint training. Institutions theory would thus expect the French to view German intentions as increasingly benign.

To assess a German threat during this time, the French would also have analyzed West German capabilities (defined in chapter 1 as state power and constraints on wielding that power). France and West Germany reflected rough parity in terms of potential power; West Germany had 1.1 to 1.2 times France's population; France had a somewhat higher Gross Domestic Product (GDP).[50] The mobilized power of the two countries was also roughly comparable; they had similarly sized defense budgets (although France had a sizeable advantage over Germany in terms of its numbers of mobilized soldiers).[51] As for nuclear weapons, Bonn had renounced ownership of weapons of mass destruction (WMD), first as a prerequisite for membership in the European Defense Council (an organization that ultimately did not come into existence) and then for NATO membership.[52] The Federal Republic did participate in the nuclear defense of Western Europe; eventually it gained control over nuclear delivery vehicles on West German territory (while American forces controlled the warheads).[53] France, however, acquired an independent nuclear weapons capability after successfully testing a nuclear device in 1960. In sum, French and West German power exhibited rough parity, with France superior in some key respects.

West Germany's ability to project power against France was highly constrained during this period. Bonn faced a severe security threat to the east; the Soviets occupied half of Germany and sought unification under communist leadership. The Soviet army was the largest in Europe, with twenty ground divisions stationed in East Germany.[54] Frequent crises between the two blocs threatened to escalate to all-out war along the German central front (the 1948 Berlin Airlift; the Berlin crises of the late 1950s and early 1960s, and later the 1962 Cuban missile crisis). In addition to the Soviet threat, West Germany was constrained by the presence of 300,000 American troops, as well as troops from France, Britain, and other countries, on its soil. After Germany joined NATO in 1955, one would expect the French to have viewed the NATO constraint as highly credible. France's security was now guaranteed against a Soviet or German threat by the United States and

Great Britain; defense of Western Europe was the cornerstone of each country's security policy after World War II.

Thus, from the end of the war until the mid-1960s, the French should have been wary of West German intentions: although Bonn's acceptance of guilt for the Nazi era was reassuring, its memory was also rife with self-pity and amnesia. Additionally, Bonn had lingering and potentially destabilizing territorial disputes. As West German democracy took hold and as Bonn continued to deepen its involvement in European institutions, France should have felt increasingly reassured. The balance of capabilities should also have lowered France's threat perception: The French had advantages in terms of mobilized power, and West German power was strongly constrained by the existence of both occupying powers and a severe security threat from the east.

FEAR AND LOATHING (1945–LATE 1950S)

In the early postwar years, French perceptions of the Germans were hostile; poll data show that the French distrusted German intentions and perceived an emergent German threat. As Andrei Markovits and Simon Reich have found, most Frenchmen favored "the harshest treatment for Germany, any solution leaving her in a state of inferiority. . . . Prolonged military occupation, transfer of the most harmful elements of population, dismemberment, annexation of the Saar to France, lasting allied control of German industry, international trusteeship of the Ruhr, pastoralization of Germany according to the Morgenthau Plan—any measure seemed acceptable as long as it was radical and severe." When asked by a 1950 poll to rank various nations in order of preference, respondents favored the English and Americans: the Germans came in last, even after the Russians. "The recollections of evil," noted public opinion analyst Jean Stoetzel, "had not been wiped out." A 1951 poll shows that over 60 percent of French viewed Germany with antipathy. When a 1953 survey asked respondents to identify France's enemy, 17 percent picked the Soviet Union, 16 percent picked Germany, and the rest were undecided. Most French agreed that the Germans were "deeply fond of war." A 1956 poll revealed that 66 percent of the public had "not much confidence" or "no confidence" in Germany's future behavior. Scholars agree that survey data from this early period show that the French public was broadly hostile toward Germany.[55]

Elites were similarly wary of German intentions. President Vincent Auriol told American officials, "The Germans were revengeful, nationalistic, and could not be trusted."[56] Germany might be tempted toward "*revanche*" and "bellicose imperialism," claimed French Prime Minister Robert Schuman.[57] Politician Jacques Soustelle predicted that Germany would "inevitably become the most dynamic and dangerous force within the Western Union."[58] Edouard Herriot, the speaker of the National Assembly, said that

France "was certain Germany desired to regain her former grandeur," and "was not so sure the Federal Republic would respect her signed obligations."[59] Former Prime Minister Paul Reynaud said Germany was "a nation that is never static, always in movement, always unsettled"; he predicted, "The militarists, the former Nazis will take the lead in the new independent *Wehrmacht*." As Alfred Grosser summarized in the mid-1950s, the war had caused both the French public and elites to feel "terror and repulsion towards Germany."[60]

The French not only disliked and distrusted Germany, they feared a resurgent security threat. Currently occupied and divided, Germany was not viewed as an immediate threat but as one that would certainly reemerge if French and Allied policy allowed it. The French felt that they had botched the peace after World War I, and must not do so again: this time the possibility of further German aggression must be completely eliminated.[61] Hence French leaders advocated international controls over the coal-rich Ruhr region, a customs union with France for the coal fields of the Saar, permanent military occupation of the Rhineland, the creation of a Military Security Board to preside over German demilitarization, the dismantling of German factories, and the complete dismemberment of the German state into a loosely grouped, decentralized confederation. But facing pressure from the United States to agree to less punitive policies (in order to receive U.S. aid), France had to abandon many of its demands. The Allies did institute numerous safeguards against future German power, but fewer than French leaders would have preferred. After the 1948 foreign ministers conference in London, French Foreign Minister Georges Bidault reported the Allied decisions back to the French National Assembly, where he was lambasted by politicians expressing strong fears of Germany (and later fired as foreign minister).[62]

French diplomacy also reflected fears of a resurgent German threat. France concluded alliances against Germany during the war; the 1944 Franco-Soviet alliance committed the two states to take, noted French official Jules Moch, "all necessary measures to eliminate any new menace coming from Germany," and block "all initiatives liable to make possible a new attempt of aggression on her part."[63] The Treaty of Dunkirk with Great Britain (1947) and the Brussels Pact with Britain and the Benelux countries (1948) provided additional protection.

Perceptions of a German threat led many French to advocate neutrality rather than Western alignment against the Soviet Union. Many regarded the Germans as just as menacing—if not more so—than the Soviets. In 1954, 37 percent said France should be in the Western camp, 39 percent said France should be neutral, and 22 percent were undecided. In the event of war between the United States and Soviet Union, 53 percent said France should be neutral; 23 percent had no opinion, and 22 percent advocated fighting on the American side. As Jean Stoetzel noted in 1957, "The threat from the East does not appear so blinding as to obliterate the dangers run in the recent past from Germany; and these dangers still exist. Committing itself to the West, the public fears, may increase the risks."[64]

## FRENCH REASONING

French fears during the early postwar period were driven by assessments of Germany's intentions and capabilities. French perceptions were influenced by uncertainty about the future of German democracy. The French clearly viewed democracy as necessary to stabilize West German foreign policy, but doubted that democratic reforms had yet had much impact. "No doubt there are men of good faith in Bonn," Schuman said, "but there were also such men in Weimar."[65] Some officials doubted that democratic reforms could pacify what they viewed as the inherently militaristic German national character.[66] However, most French statements and policies reflect the belief that West German democratic institutions would help pacify the Federal Republic.

In French minds, the eradication of German nationalism was essential for promoting democracy and a durable peace. Andrew Barros has chronicled how, after the First World War, the French imposed constraints not only on material power but also undertook Germany's "moral disarmament"; during the interwar years, the French monitored trends in German history education and expressed alarm at signs that Germany did not feel culpable for the war.[67] Similarly after World War II, because German schools were viewed as the laboratory of German nationalism, the French advocated education reform in order to instill a peaceful, democratic national orientation. Scholar Edmond Vermeil wrote that "the concerted aggression of Germany against humanity" required French intervention in German education.[68] During the Occupation, French politician Jean Le Bail said: "We know that nationalistic and chauvinistic currents have a tendency to develop much more quickly in Germany than anywhere else. The present generation, which has seen the war and suffered from it, will be replaced by less cautious generations, that could become, if we do not keep watch, equally dangerous."[69] As French scholar Helen Liddell wrote in the late 1940s, Allied education reform aimed "to change the outlook of the German people" and "to replace an aggressive, militarist, and undemocratic spirit by a co-operative, peace-loving, democratic outlook."[70] German education, argued Vermeil, in the same volume, should be imbued "with a new spirit, oriented toward democratic ideas, and desirous of preparing generations to come for the integration of Germany within the European community."[71]

French educators insisted that German educational materials needed to be fundamentally revised "not only from the angle of denazification but also from all traces of an aggressive spirit."[72] Arthur Hearnden argued that France viewed the reeducation of Germany as a *mission civilisatrice*, which was "designed in this case to awaken in the Germans a love of freedom and individualism."[73] French officials emphasized teaching foreign languages and geography in Germany and sought to instill German curricula with a global rather than parochial and nationalistic outlook. The French also encouraged collaboration on joint history textbook commissions with German historians and educators.

The French advocated candid German remembrance in an effort to eradicate German hypernationalism. "From the earliest days of the new German democracy," wrote Alfred Grosser, "foreigners and Germans alike evaluated [West German] democracy according to the manner in which it interpreted the Nazi past and came to terms with it." He agreed with Adenauer that the Federal Republic "must accept responsibility for Germany's appalling heritage in order to be once again respected among nations and recognized as the true successor to the undivided Reich." Grosser noted that West Germany had many ways of demonstrating its peaceful intentions, but that "acceptance of civil liability for Germany's former commitments and crimes represented a more basic choice than any other." The turning point, argued Grosser, was 1952, when the FRG settled the issue of the Third Reich's external debt and signed the Luxembourg Agreement with Israel that included reparations.[74] More recent French scholarship has echoed Grosser's view on the need for candid German remembrance and its link to the broader effort to prevent the revival of German nationalism and militarism.[75]

French distrust of German intentions in this period stemmed largely from fears of German territorial revisionism. West Germany claimed no part of French territory. However, the French worried that Bonn might one day seek not only reunification with East Germany, but also the territories it formerly controlled beyond the Oder-Neisse line.[76] As de Gaulle had declared, "Only one question will dominate Germany and Europe. Which of the two Reichs will seek unity?"[77]

The French National Assembly's 1953 debate over ratification of the European Defense Community (EDC) reflected intense concern about territorial issues.[78] EDC opponents, who ultimately were able to block the military alliance in the National Assembly, maintained that a revisionist Germany would entrap France in a war against the Soviets. Grosser noted that French elites feared an imminent attack from a rearmed Germany.[79] They feared not only the "old German danger" (i.e., inherent German aggression), but also the "new German danger": namely, that "a rearmed Western Germany is apt to lead the West into war against the East to gain its reunification and to recover the territories beyond the Oder-Neisse."[80] As Defense Minister Jules Moch commented, he "was not prepared to support a crusade for the recovery of Königsberg,"‡ which, he was convinced, was Germany's strongest desire.[81] Opposing the creation of a West German state, Robert Schuman

‡Königsberg had been the capital of East Prussia; the Potsdam convention transferred it to the Soviet Union. The Soviets expelled its German population and renamed it Kaliningrad.

argued, "Any plan which resulted in establishing and authorizing a central power would present to Germany a temptation and to us a permanent and growing threat, first of *revanche* and then of bellicose imperialism."[82] Politician Jacques Soustelle similarly cautioned about the danger to Europe posed by Germany's "territorial ambitions."[83] Territorial claims were thus a major driver of French distrust of West Germany during the early postwar years.

French fears were also strongly influenced by fears of resurgent German capabilities. Political leaders worried that Germany would eventually regain its former power as current constraints fell away. Thus the French strongly opposed German unification. De Gaulle had opposed even the unification of the three zones of occupation, stating bluntly in 1945, "a revived Germany would certainly eventually invade France."[84] The following year he elaborated,

> It is true that Germany is no longer a subject of immediate alarm for the nations that should be building the peace. But after one war of thirty years, one doesn't make peace only for the short-term. Whatever her ordeals, Germany remains Germany: that is to say, a great people in massive numbers installed in the center of Europe, who within the abyss remember their summits. The demon of war could again tempt her one day, if the chance were offered to recover her grandeur. . . . This is why France, facing [Germany] and others, should oppose Germany returning to a unified and centralized state, whose arms and impetus were always the conditions of her warlike enterprises.

De Gaulle said that any German unification "entails the gravest risks for Europe and for peace." "Realize," he said, "that we are the neighbors of Germany, that we have been invaded by Germany three times in one lifetime, and conclude that never again do we want a Reich."[85]

The public also feared an increase in German capabilities and opposed American proposals to rearm the Federal Republic. Poll data from 1953 show that most of the public believed "the existence of German troops constitutes a threat to France" (57 percent of respondents), and in 1954 that "German rearmament is a danger in any form" (56 percent).[86] Jean Stoetzel noted that public opinion in France on the German question was eminently clear; the French were "still hypersensitive after three wars" and "could not think of German rearmament without manifesting the most violent fears."

Such fears were evident in French media coverage. After Dean Acheson in 1950 proposed rearming Germany, the communist newspaper *L'Humanité* reported, "Acheson and the Nazi general Guderian have triumphed: the new *Wehrmacht* is going to be created." A *Le Monde* article warned about "the resurrection of the *Wehrmacht*," noting, "Will one pretend that German rearmament of today, whatever the form, no longer offers the dangers that it presented yesterday? All the evidence points to the danger remaining the same." *L'Humanité* celebrated the failure of the EDC by proclaiming: "Victory to the French people and to peace! The EDC is rejected."[87]

French elites were horrified by American rearmament proposals and referred to Acheson's plan as "La Bombe." Defense Minister Jules Moch reported, "Acheson possesses no supporter within the [French] Cabinet."[88]

Gaullist General Billotte commented that rearmament would create new German divisions that would be the source "from which a new German military supremacy could one day spring."[89] "The Wehrmacht has marched down the Champs Elysées and through all the French towns," warned Paul Reynaud; "Do not allow the great military staff of Germany to be restored, since it would control the German government—for the history of the pressure of the German military forces is too well known, too bloody."[90] Radical Edouard Daladier said, "Bonn would surely go the way of Weimar as soon as a German military caste was allowed to establish itself."[91]

The EDC debate showcased French fears. Both proponents and opponents of the plan feared German rearmament; where they diverged was in their views of how best to contain Germany. EDC proponents—*"les Cedistes"*—argued that German rearmament was inevitable and dangerous for France and that a supranational institution was the best way to contain West Germany. As Pierre Maillard noted in his study of de Gaulle and the German question, "The EDC would permit the 'tying up' of Germany, to prevent its forces from being utilized for purely national ends, to imprison them within a Western system, both military and political, removing all risks of her returning to her past ambitions."[92] *Les Cedistes* characterized the EDC as "the best guarantee against the rebirth of German militarism"; one of their slogans was "EDC or the *Wehrmacht*."[93]

EDC opponents, on the other hand, feared German noncompliance and expected eventual German dominance of the supranational institution. Edouard Herriot said, "guarantees on paper are not enough";[94] the French knew from history that "Germans [do] not have an undue respect for signatures."[95] Gaullists warned that the French army would be divided between the EDC and colonial territories and thus weakened relative to West Germany (which had no colonies). "Germany," cautioned Jacques Soustelle, "will carry more weight in Europe than we do."[96] Gaullists fought the EDC with slogans such as "EDC revives the German Army and destroys the French Army"; "EDC rearms Germany and disarms France"; "Europe would be constructed on the corpse of France"; and "The French Union would be delivered into the hands of Germany and Italy."[97] As scholar Jacques Fauvet notes, EDC opponents feared that "no legal framework would be strong enough to keep Germany's rearmament within limits. The checks would be lifted and France's right of veto would be just as useless as it had proved to be in NATO's councils."[98] *Le Monde* warned about "the renaissance of Prussian militarism" and speculated that the ten leaders of the proposed ten German divisions would form into "a clandestine, underground *Oberkommando*—whose counsel, obligingly channeled to the Supreme Commander, could one day eventually prevail over the viewpoint of officials of the Atlantic Force."[99]

EDC opponents maintained that the only way to contain German power was through British and American defense commitments. Schuman sought assurances from the Americans and British that France would not be left alone "face to face with Germany"; he said that absent such guarantees, the National Assembly would not ratify the EDC. France's strongest aspiration— and one that could not be met—was an American guarantee that Germany would never be able to withdraw from the EDC.[100] Fearing German backlash from discriminatory treatment, the Americans and British refused to issue such guarantees. EDC ratification died in the French National Assembly on November 30, 1954, accompanied by the singing of the *Marseillaise* and shouts of "Down with the *Wehrmacht!*"[101] The French ultimately agreed to a plan to rearm Germany within the Western European Union and NATO because both Britain and the United States agreed to NATO's multilateral security guarantees and to station forces on the continent. West Germany joined NATO in 1955 and was rearmed under its auspices. France's debate about—and rejection of—the EDC revealed intense fears of German resurgence.

The French also sought to contain West Germany within multilateral institutions. Schuman advocated the "integration of a peaceful Germany in a United Europe, a Europe in which the Germans . . . will be able to give up all idea of dominating it." Noting that although the methods were new, he said that "the direction is unchanged: the aim of the system was to control [Germany] much more directly."[102] French moderates believed, commented Fauvet, that "insofar as sufficiently close bonds continue to unite Germany to the West, the poisons which are active in Germany will be neutralized."[103] After the First World War, agreed Socialist Jean Le Bail, "we left her free to act at her own will. . . . and at the end of this long succession of mistakes there was Hitler and the war." Assembly member Alfred Coste-Fleuret argued that the Schuman plan would stabilize Europe because it would "take from the German State, as it does from the French, the disposition over her heavy industry for war-purposes." Schuman declared, "the solidarity in production . . . will make it plain that any war between France and Germany becomes not merely unthinkable but materially impossible."[104] The key motivation behind the European Coal and Steel Community was the French desire to contain German power in a nondiscriminatory manner so as not to inflame German nationalism. "A totally new situation must be created," ECSC architect Jean Monnet wrote. "The Franco-German problem must become a European problem."[105] A French foreign minister later commented, "The 'Fathers of Europe,' French and others, saw within these future European institutions a good instrument for efficiently encasing West Germany within an ensemble, which made the renewal of nationalism out of the question."[106]

In sum, during the early postwar years, the French feared that Germany would break free of constraints on its power and were wary of a German attempt to unify and to recover lost territory. The French clearly valued the creation of a German democracy and a reduction in German nationalism, which was to be achieved in part through candid history education about the recent past.

### THE LATE 1950S: NO FRIEND BUT GERMANY

French perceptions of Germany began to improve markedly in the late 1950s. Grosser wrote that whereas in 1944 the French view had been "no enemy but Germany," by 1960 it had shifted to "no friend but Germany."[107] By 1965 respondents declared that the FRG was "the best friend of France." Scholars of French public opinion note, "The anti-German attitude of the French public and elites immediately after World War II seems to have disappeared almost entirely. Public opinion polls . . . show a reversal of public attitudes."[108]

Perceptions of Germany among French elites also improved. Foreign Minister Maurice Couve de Murville wrote, "The meeting at Colombey-les-deux-eglises marked a new departure in relations between Paris and Bonn."[109] A French ambassador later commented, "The late fifties and early sixties were the turning point, when Adenauer first visited General de Gaulle in 1958, thus starting a process which led to the signature of the Elysée Treaty in January 1963." De Gaulle remarked that between 1958 and 1963, the bilateral meetings and efforts at reconciliation established relations between France and Germany "on foundations and in an atmosphere hitherto unknown in their history."[110]

French policies during this period also evince decreased threat perception. French diplomacy grew less adversarial; the French accepted West German rearmament within NATO and intensified their security cooperation with Germany. Summitry culminated in the 1963 Elysée Treaty, which established semiannual summit meetings between the two heads of state and quarterly meetings of foreign ministers. It created regular bilateral roundtables about defense, education, and human welfare; and it established the Franco-German Youth Office (*Office Franco-Allemand pour la jeunesse*), which instituted numerous youth exchanges between the two countries. The Elysée Treaty also established a framework for extensive security consultation and cooperation; however, these aspects of the agreement stalled until the 1980s.[111] In sum, the late 1950s marked an important shift in French perceptions: Germany was no longer viewed as a threat.

### FRENCH REASONING

The substantial drop in French fears of Germany was caused largely by the establishment of constraints on West German power—constraints that

the French regarded as credible and enduring. Most important, French leaders began to believe that the division of Germany would continue. The French had from the outset opposed any consolidation of German power; "France was not in a hurry for the reunification of Germany," de Gaulle had said, demanding that Adenauer show "unremitting patience as regards unification."[112] Others shared the president's apprehension: a poll of French elites demonstrated that over two-thirds of respondents viewed German unification as "a threat to French security."[113] Such views were pithily captured by French novelist François Mauriac, who famously commented, "I love Germany so much I'm glad there are two of them."[114]

Germany's continued division thus significantly eased French fears. De Gaulle said, "For the first time in her history, [France] was unhampered by any threat from her immediate neighbors. Germany, dismembered, had ceased to be a formidable and domineering power."[115] De Gaulle also told Adenauer, "After the terrible ordeals inflicted on her as a result of Teutonic ambitions in 1870, 1914, and 1939, France now faced a Germany which had been defeated, dismantled, and reduced to a pitiful international position, which entirely altered the circumstances of their relationship." During the 1958–62 summits, the French president noted approvingly that although Adenauer had said Germany would never relinquish the goal of unification, he had agreed not to set a timetable for its achievement.

Diminished French fears also stemmed from Bonn's acceptance of constraints on its military power. Although the French had accepted West German conventional rearmament under NATO command, they firmly opposed the development of nuclear weapons by West Germany. At the 1958 Colombey summit, de Gaulle demanded that Germany forever renounce ownership of weapons of mass destruction. The French president commented in his memoirs, "The right to possess or to manufacture atomic weapons . . . must in no circumstances be granted to her."[116] In 1963, the French foreign minister said that "France was dead set against the idea of a German nuclear force." De Gaulle commented to French ambassador to the United States Herve Alphand, "We have no intention . . . of helping Germany to become a nuclear power, and neither of accepting it if she did."[117] Threat reduction thus required onstraints on West German military power.

Institutional constraints also reassured the French. De Gaulle wrote that France had "bowed to the realities and saw to it that Bonn, contained within a sensible European grouping, remained as closely linked to her as possible." He argued that this strategy would guarantee "the security of all nations between the Atlantic and the Urals."[118] De Gaulle's foreign minister wrote, "It was also necessary to have the courage—or the good sense . . . to know that she was too formidable for us to approach alone; that always it was necessary that we be sheltered behind others or covered by some international combination. . . . Going head to head with Germany is the greatest danger that France should avoid at all costs."[119] A French government spokesman asserted in the National Assembly that the European Community would create "a thousand small linkages" between the FRG and the West and thereby minimize the threat of Franco-German war or German-Soviet rapprochement.[120] One scholar later commented, "The main process of threat reduction in France was due to Europeanization: the Rome Treaty in 1957, the Elysée Treaty in 1963, et cetera. Foundations laid by de Gaulle and Adenauer explain the reduction of threat in both countries."[121]

The French also felt cautious optimism based on West German willingness to table the territorial claims issue. De Gaulle wrote in his memoirs, "On the all-important question of Germany's future, my mind was made up. First of all, I believed that it would be unjust and dangerous to revise the de facto frontiers which the war had imposed on her. This meant that the Oder-Neisse line which separates her from Poland should remain her definitive boundary, that nothing should remain of her former claims in respect of Czechoslovakia, and that a new Anschluss in whatever form must be precluded."[122] As Jeffrey Giaque notes, de Gaulle's views "went directly against Bonn's long-held position that nothing in the outcome of the war could be considered permanent until Germany was reunified and a formal peace settlement was signed."[123] Nevertheless, the West Germans acquiesced in the interest of maintaining good relations with Paris, and the French were greatly relieved. "Devoted as [Adenauer] was to his country," de Gaulle later commented, "he did not intend to make frontier revision the present and principal aim of his policy, knowing full well that to raise the matter would produce nothing but redoubled alarm and fury from Russia and Poland and reproachful anxiety in the West."[124]

To sum up, between 1945 and 1960 French perceptions of Germany underwent a remarkable transformation from loathed conqueror to France's best friend. This reconciliation occurred despite prevalent amnesia in West Germany. Although Bonn had acknowledged Nazi crimes, Germans felt little responsibility for these crimes and were preoccupied with their own suffering. Nonetheless, pressed to partner with Germany by their strategic circumstances in the Cold War, the French enthusiastically effected a reconciliation with their historic enemy.

## Middle Period, 1965–90

### THE AWAKENING OF GERMAN REMEMBRANCE

West German politics and remembrance experienced a profound evolution from the mid-1960s through 1990. Under Social Democratic rule, West Germans began increasingly to admit and atone for past crimes. When conservatives regained power in the 1980s, they sought to restore what they viewed as an upset balance in West German memory. Although no mainstream leaders or intellectuals denied or glorified Nazi crimes, they criticized the Left for emphasizing negative memories of World War II and sought to "draw a line under the past" (*Schlusstrich,* which meant that Germans should move on rather than look back). Out of these national debates eventually emerged a greater national commitment to remembrance and atonement.

West Germany's exploration of the Nazi past began during the "social-liberal era" of the 1960s and 1970s. Political leaders began to give important speeches on the May 8 anniversaries of the surrender. Commemoration of the day began in 1970 with contrite speeches by President Gustav Heinemann and Chancellor Willy Brandt. In his speech, Heinemann clearly stated that the horror of the World War II had occurred prior to 1945, not after 1945, as had been the view in the 1950s.[125] In a speech to the Bundestag, Brandt—in a striking departure from the conventional wisdom—acknowledged that German suffering after the war had been caused by German aggression. President Walter Scheel stated in 1975 that "the German tragedy" began not in 1945, but in 1933 with the election of Hitler. Scheel rebuked those Germans who "want to hear nothing more about our dark past." He asserted, "All words of a national dignity, of self-respect, remain hollow if we do not take on ourselves the entire . . . pressing weight of our history."

On November 9, 1978, Chancellor Helmut Schmidt gave an important speech on the fortieth anniversary of the anti-Jewish pogrom of *Kristallnacht.* Schmidt called the Nazi attack on German Jews and the complaisance of other Germans "a cause of bitterness and shame." He detailed the violence, arson, and arrests of the pogrom, noting that although it occurred "before the very eyes of a large number of German citizens . . . most people, faint of heart, kept their silence." Schmidt said that Germans in the late 1970s were "individually free from blame," but that they too could be considered guilty if they failed to take responsibility for past atrocities.[126]

Commemoration during this period also grew more contrite. Starting in the 1960s, sites from the Holocaust were transformed to serve educational and commemorative functions. In the late-1950s, the theater production of "The Diary of Anne Frank" piqued public interest in the Holocaust; school field trips to Dachau and other camp sites increased rapidly.[127] A large plaque naming concentration camps was installed in 1965 in West Berlin. Exhibitions opened at Neuengamme and Bergen-Belsen in the mid-1960s. Rudy Koshar notes that in 1965, Dachau opened "a more realistic and critical exhibit" that detailed the system of mass killing.[128]

West German politicians commemorated past atrocities against Poland as they sought closer relations. Brandt said that Germany had committed "criminal activities for which there is no parallel in modern history" and had "disgraced the German name in all the world." Recognition of Nazi crimes was essential, wrote Brandt, for eliminating the "underbalance of trust" in postwar Europe.[129] During a 1970 visit to Warsaw (for the purpose of conducting treaty negotiations), Brandt fell to his knees while visiting the memorial for the victims of the Warsaw Ghetto uprising. "Under the burden of millions of victims of murder," he said later, "I did what human beings do when speech fails them." Although Brandt's "Warschauer Kniefall" generated tremendous controversy in the Federal Republic, it became perhaps the most famous act of contrition in the world, then or since.[130]

At Auschwitz-Birkenau in 1977, Chancellor Schmidt became the first West German leader to address a ceremony at an extermination camp. Schmidt said, "The crime of Nazi fascism and the guilt of the German Reich under Hitler's leadership are the basis of our responsibility. We Germans of today are not guilty as individual persons, but we must bear the political legacy of those who were guilty. That is our responsibility."[131]

Judicial proceedings during this period both reflected and promoted greater remembrance of Nazi crimes. Starting in 1963, Nazi personnel from Auschwitz-Birkenau and members of the *Einsatzgruppen* death squads were put on trial. Horrific testimony at these trials shocked the West German population and inspired historical research and literary explorations about the Nazi past. An earlier landmark trial was the Israeli trial of Adolf Eichmann in 1961; Eichmann was a former SS official and architect of the Final Solution. His trial—the first in history to be televised—riveted audiences in Israel, Germany, and all over the world. Ian Buruma reports that it served to "jolt German complacency"; it was "an emotionally explosive event that revealed for the first time to a shocked world audience the Nazi campaign to exterminate European Jewry."[132]

Other important proceedings during this period were four Bundestag debates about extending the statute of limitations on crimes of murder. While in opposition, the SPD had found little or no support from the conservative majority for extending the statute. Later, the socialists enjoyed not only majority status but greater support among conservatives for prosecution of Holocaust-related crimes. One member of the Christian Democratic Union, Ernst Benda, challenged those members of his party who said that trials would harm German honor. Benda said that honor came from demonstrating that "this German people is not a nation of murderers." SPD members Adolf Arndt and Fritz Erler also spoke eloquently in these debates on the need for justice. Arndt invoked the Germans' "historical and moral guilt" for failing to speak out against Nazi persecution of the Jews.[133] Ultimately, the Bundestag twice voted to extend the statue of limitations and then in 1979 abolished it completely. These Bundestag debates both reflected and contributed to greater candor about past violence.

Many scholars note that the West German pursuit of justice at this time was far from comprehensive. Bonn was criticized by the East Germany, Israel, and its own Left for allowing former Nazis to continue in political life. The German Democratic Republic (GDR) published what was known as the "brown book": *War and Nazi Criminals in the Federal Republic* listed over 1,900 former Nazi officials working in influential positions in the FRG. Among the people listed was Hans Globke, chief of staff in the Adenauer administration, who had helped to draft the Nuremberg race laws of 1935. The GDR lambasted Globke as "the Eichmann of Bonn": As Jeffrey Herf has concluded, "The mere mention of his name became shorthand for the failures of denazification in the Federal Republic."[134] Political scandal erupted in 1969 when President Heinrich Lübke of the CDU withdrew from the presidential election after East German charges that during the war his construction business had built concentration camp and slave labor barracks. West German Chancellor Kurt Georg Kiesinger (1966–69) attracted controversy because had worked as a propaganda official in Hitler's Foreign Office. Such controversy reflected that West German postwar justice was imperfect; nonetheless, overall it had grown substantially by the late 1960s relative to the previous era.

Bonn also paid additional reparations during this period. Supplementary legislation expanded both the BEG and BRüG laws, allocating larger payments to a wider set of victims. Bonn also negotiated "global agreements" with eleven Western European nations (Luxembourg, Norway, Denmark, Greece, the Netherlands, France, Belgium, Italy, Switzerland, Great Britain, and Sweden). Between 1959 and 1964, the FRG paid these countries over $US500 million (DM2 billion), which governments then apportioned out to their people.[135] Although the 1970 treaty between West Germany and Poland had reaffirmed Poland's previous renunciation of reparations claims, the Poles later reopened the issue. In 1975 Chancellor Helmut Schmidt and Polish leader Edward Gierek agreed on a settlement of pension claims, Polish assurances of emigration opportunities for its German minority, and a large West German credit package.[136]

West German education also reflected greater coverage of past atrocities. In the late 1950s officials had been alarmed by anti-Semitic vandalism: desecration of synagogues and Jewish cemeteries. Subsequently, local and federal education officials began taking an interest in research by progressive historians, who charged that the public was not being adequately schooled in contemporary history. One report commented, "The 'insufficient knowledge' of the juveniles with respect to the most recent past was frequently deplored. It was emphasized again and again, that for the political education of the citizens of tomorrow a thorough examination of the history of the 20th century and, in particular, of the theory and practice of the totalitarian state, was required." Studies sponsored by the federal and regional governments also found that treatment in school textbooks of Nazism was deplorably inadequate.[137]

As a result, educators and officials undertook several reforms. For example, in October 1959 in Lower Saxony, the Minister of Culture issued guidelines for political education in order to stem the rise of neo-Fascist youth organizations.[138] Ministers in the other Länder issued similar directives. Bonn responded to foreign criticism of German textbooks by participating in multilateral textbook commissions sponsored by UNESCO. One commission participant, German historian Georg Eckert, commented that "after the swastika-smearing incidents, I fully share the opinion of my British colleagues that the analysis of those historical events cannot be left to the discretion of the teacher but must be included in the text books."[139] As a result of these domestic studies and international collaborations, schools made efforts to use books that included greater detail about the Nazi period. Hannah Vogt's *The Burden of Guilt: A Short History of Germany, 1914–1945*—the first West German text to deal openly with the Nazi period—was widely adopted.

As West German education was showing greater candor about the crimes of the Nazi era, within wider society Social-Democratic leadership and social changes provoked interest in exploring the period that many Germans had preferred to forget. Along with the growth in liberal political influence grew the "1968" student and social movement. The "68ers" diverse agenda included calls for greater understanding of German actions during the Third Reich.

Localities across the country began to show greater interest in the Nazi era. Thousands of schoolchildren responded to President Heinemann's proposal for regular nationwide history essay contests. As depicted in the German film "The Nasty Girl," many youths delved into the topic of local history during the Third Reich, unearthing previously unknown sites of Gestapo offices, concentration camps, and other facilities across the country.[140] In Berlin, city officials erected local memorials commemorating the Holocaust. The first official memorial to remember Berlin's devastated Jewish community was installed in 1963 at the site of a former synagogue; two memorials of concentration camps were erected four years later at busy Berlin locations (Wittenberg Square and Kaiser Wilhelm Square) with the heading "Places of terror that we must never forget."[141]

During the social-liberal era, historiography began to focus less on Germany's suffering and more on its guilt. In part this occurred because younger scholars were now receiving more advanced social science training and because the recent Auschwitz and Eichmann trials had sparked scholarly interest in World War II atrocities. As R. J. B. Bosworth has written, "Young historians, like so many others in the Sixties generation, took to asking that simplest of questions: 'What did you do in the war, Daddy?' and the answer which the older generation gave was hedged and unsatisfactory."[142] Whereas previously only foreign scholars had engaged in Holocaust scholarship, now German historians embraced the topic. Research conducted in the earlier tradition that emphasized German victimhood—for example Helmut Diwald's book, *History of the Germans*, which focused on the plight of German expellees and devoted only two pages to Nazi atrocities—was sharply criticized.

During this period, historian Fritz Fischer's studies about the outbreak of the First World War forced a new German confrontation with the Second. As Richard Evans notes, Fischer "broke ranks by presenting a meticulously documented account of Germany's far-reaching plans for European hegemony and world power between 1914 and 1918."[143] If Fischer was correct that Germany deliberately launched World War I, then World War II was not a historical aberration; rather, it was just the most recent German grab for hegemony. Bosworth described Fischer's work as a "time bomb" that exploded a cherished myth about the German past. "Perhaps there was a continuity in German history . . . which ran from 1870 (or 1848) to at least 1945. Whereas, in the Imperial era, Germans had been trained to be proud of their *Sonderweg*, their special way, which was making them ever more rich, powerful, and respected, now the *Sonderweg* was reversed. . . . Maybe there was something wrong with Germany."[144] Fischer's research was complemented by the release of William Shirer's international bestseller, *The Rise and Fall of the Third Reich*.[145] Shirer argued that Nazism—rather than being an accident in an otherwise proud historical tradition—sprang directly out of the German past. As official remembrance of the Nazi era grew apologetic, West German historians, in addition to the rest of society, began to remember and atone for past atrocities.

## CONTROVERSY AND A NEW CONSENSUS: THE 1980S

In 1982 the Free Democratic Party switched its alliance away from the SPD to form a conservative government with the CDU/CSU. This decade witnessed several national debates about the role of the Nazi past in contemporary West Germany. Proponents of contrition decried conservative attempts to "normalize" German memory; by the end of the 1980s, these national debates had coalesced into a bipartisan consensus about the need for contrition.[146]

Reacting to years of social-liberal soul-searching, conservatives argued for less attention to past transgressions and more to postwar accomplishments. In an otherwise contrite statement in 1970, Gustav Heinemann said, "We know today that it does not lead forward to mourn what is lost." Chancellor Schmidt argued on May 8, 1975, that Germans should focus on West Germany's recent achievements. "We Germans," he said, "do not need to go around in hair shirts in perpetuity." He noted that "the great majority of the Germans living today were born only after 1933; they can in no way be burdened with guilt." Returning from a visit to Israel in 1981, Schmidt said that "German foreign policy can and will no longer be overshadowed by Auschwitz."[147] The Minister-President of Bavaria, Franz-Josef Strauss, said that Germans had to get off their knees and learn to "walk tall" once more. Germany must "emerge from the shadow of the Third Reich" and "become a normal nation again." Former FRG president Karl Carstens commented that the younger generation that advocated greater memory was unaware "that many of the National Socialist regime's terrible deeds were not known to the majority of Germans at that time."[148]

Germans should "come out of Hitler's shadow," CDU politician Alfred Dregger urged in 1982; "We must become normal." Dregger contended that the German army had not committed or even known about war crimes. "Responsibility for the crimes of the Third Reich lay with Hitler and the Nazi leadership," he said.[149] During a 1984 visit to Israel, Chancellor Helmut Kohl made a statement regarded by many as an attempt to dodge culpability for Germany's past. Kohl commented that he and his generation enjoyed a "grace of late birth" (die Gnade der späten Geburt), implying that they were innocent and thus not obliged to make amends. The comment triggered international and domestic controversy; for example, the SPD said Kohl "wanted to acquit his cohort and everybody younger of German guilt."[150]

NATO allies supported conservative efforts to "normalize" West German memory. In September 1984 French President François Mitterrand and Chancellor Kohl held a ceremony at the World War I cemetery of Verdun, where both French and German soldiers lay buried. The two leaders were memorably photographed holding hands over the graves. Designing the commemoration in this way served as a great equalizer. Rather than emphasize German crimes and French victimization, it sent the message that two countries that had fought wars were now reconciled and allied. Additionally, by highlighting the First World War rather than the Second, the ceremony shifted the focus away from the German shame of the Holocaust. Verdun symbolized that the root of Franco-German enmity lay not in German aggression, but rather in the turmoil of European power politics.

The 1985 ceremony with U.S. President Ronald Reagan at Bitburg military cemetery also sought to normalize the Federal Republic. President Reagan and Chancellor Kohl laid wreaths at the graves of German soldiers to demonstrate NATO unity and reconciliation (see next page). Shortly before the visit, word leaked out that the cemetery had dozens of graves of the Waffen-SS, an elite German army unit used for "cleansing" operations. This disclosure created global uproar; critics denounced the two leaders for marginalizing the Holocaust and for mourning the perpetrators of Nazi terror. "This planned gesture of reconciliation," said the chairman of the board of the Central Council of Jews in Germany, "overlooks the suffering of millions of Jews in the German concentration camps." Holocaust survivor and author Elie Wiesel declared: "May I . . . implore you to do something else, to find another way, another site. That place, Mr. President, is not your place."[151] Reagan and Kohl responded to criticism by adding a visit to the Bergen-Belsen death camp, but went ahead with the Bitburg ceremony as planned. Reagan commented of the *Waffen-SS:* "Those young men were victims of Nazism also. . . . They were victims, just as surely as the victims in the concentration camps."[152]

During the 1980s, conservative historians also sought to "normalize" German memory. Although they did not deny German aggression or the Holocaust, they challenged the dominant self-critical interpretation of the Nazi era by justifying these policies as self-defense. In the *Frankfurter Allegemeine Zeitung* (FAZ) newspaper in 1986–87, a series of articles discussed the theory that Stalin had planned to invade Germany in 1942 or sooner. The paper depicted World War II as "a war of the dictators" with both sides generally equally culpable. Michael Stürmer, a historian and public intellectual, argued that Germany's difficult geopolitical position between the Soviet Union and France led the country to launch what was essentially a defensive war. Historian Ernst Nolte also argued in a book and in a famous subsequent article, "The Past That Will Not Pass Away," that the Holocaust

Nancy and Ronald Reagan, Hannelore and Helmut Kohl at Bitburg Cemetery, 1985. AP PHOTO.

was a defensive response to the Bolshevik threat. Nolte claimed that because the Soviets had first committed genocide, it would be "permissible, even unavoidable" to ask, "Did the National Socialists or Hitler perhaps commit an 'Asiatic deed,' merely because they and their ilk considered themselves to be potential victims of an 'Asiatic' deed?" Historian Andreas Hilgruber similarly compared the Holocaust to Turkey's genocide of Armenians.[153]

Conservative intellectuals argued that West German memory had moved away from Adenauer's pragmatic policies of limited memory toward excessive self-flagellation. Stürmer and others maintained that the Federal Republic's most important responsibility was not contrition but stable democracy: too much remembrance would threaten democratic stability by creating backlash. Stürmer argued, "We cannot live by making our own past . . . into a permanent sense of endless guilt feelings." The German past was "suspended over the present like an executioner's sword," stated Nolte.[154] He urged the FRG to stop focusing on its past guilt and to educate its people in a more positive history that emphasized West Germany's postwar democratic success.

Such arguments prompted the *Historikerstreit* (Historian's Debate): a condemnation of conservative historiography by the academic and political Left. Scholars and opinion leaders held this debate not in quiet university corridors but across the pages of prominent German newspapers, the conservative FAZ and the liberal Hamburg paper *Die Zeit*. Philosopher Jürgen Habermas lambasted the writings of Stürmer, Nolte, and Hilgruber as revisionist. He accused them of trying to reduce the significance of the Holocaust by "relativizing" it to other mass killings; he argued that the conservative scholars placed "revisionist history in the service of a nationalist renovation of conventional identity." As historian Karl Wilds has noted, liberals viewed these conservative writings as a " 'renationalisation' of West German political culture and a weakening of the social taboo over neo- or post-Fascist positions."[155] The *Historikerstreit* generated over 1,000 articles, mostly from the Left.

Efforts to "normalize" German memory in the 1980s galvanized other elites to call for renewing the national commitment to contrition. Three days after the Bitburg visit by Reagan and Kohl, President Richard Von Weizsäcker (CDU) gave an extraordinary speech on May 8, the fortieth anniversary of the surrender. Rather than emphasize German victimhood, the president mourned "the six million Jews who were murdered in German concentration camps" and the nations who suffered in the war, "especially the countless citizens of the Soviet Union and Poland who lost their lives."[156] Von Weizsäcker invoked victims who had previously gone unmentioned: the Sinti/Roma (gypsies), the handicapped and mentally ill, and homosexuals. In contrast to Adenauer's emphasis on German resistance, Von Weizsäcker described the German response to Nazi persecution of the Jews as ranging "from plain apathy and hidden intolerance to outright hatred." He lamented,

> Who could have remained unsuspecting after the burning of the synagogues, the plundering, the stigmatization with the Star of David, the deprivation of rights, the ceaseless violation of human dignity? Whoever opened his eyes and ears and sought information could not fail to notice that Jews were being deported. . . . There were many ways of not burdening one's conscience, of shunning responsibility, looking away, keeping mum. When the unspeakable truth of the Holocaust then became known at the end of the war, all too many of us claimed that they had not known anything about it or even suspected anything.

Von Weizsäcker exhorted his audience to learn the lessons of history. "We need and we have the strength to look truth straight in the eye—without embellishment and without distortion." Departing from the usual ambivalence surrounding May 8, the president declared the day one of German liberation.

On the fortieth anniversary of Bergen-Belsen's liberation in 1985, Chancellor Kohl also delivered an apologetic speech at the former concentration camp. Kohl enumerated Nazi crimes and singled out the Jewish people as the most victimized. He said, "we are gathered here in memory of the many innocent people who were tortured, humiliated, and driven to their deaths at Bergen-Belsen, as in other camps." He said the Jews "were deprived of their rights and driven out of their country."[157] Kohl rejected the "we didn't know" defense, questioned why so many people remained apathetic, and exhorted Germans to remember their past. "One of our country's paramount tasks," he said, "is to inform people of those occurrences and keep alive an awareness of the full extent of this historical burden." Kohl—along with Von Weizsäcker—expressed further contrition during the 1987 visit of Israeli President Chaim Herzog; the two German leaders apologized and stated their commitment to remembrance. Kohl said the Germans never want to forget that their atrocities were "unique in the history of mankind" and that Germans would "resist every attempt to suppress or play them down." Von Weizsäcker charged successive German generations to remember Nazi terror, declaring, "History never permits us to draw a line under the past."

Another watershed event was the controversial speech given by Bundestag President Philip Jenninger on the fiftieth anniversary of *Kristallnacht* (November 9, 1988). Jenninger's speech admitted and condemned the violence, but it was so awkwardly written and delivered that listeners became confused and thought he was endorsing rather than condemning the pogrom. Jenninger used Nazi terminology. He posed rhetorical questions such as "Didn't the Jews deserve their fate?" and "Didn't Hitler give the

German people back their pride?" Jenninger also questioned whether it wasn't reasonable for Germans to vote for Hitler in 1933. He answered all these in the negative, but the damage had been done. Many Bundestag members left the room in protest. As Elizabeth Domansky has described, "What Jenninger saw was a sea of stony faces intermingled with parliamentarians who buried their faces in their hands. Those who stayed in their seats seemed to do so involuntarily, as if under a spell."[158] Rather than defend Jenninger, the CDU abandoned him; facing strong condemnation from all directions, he quickly resigned. As David Art has written, contrition had become the "third rail" in German politics.

The late 1980s marked a major shift in West German remembrance; no longer was atonement the purview of the Left. As seen in historiography and commemoration, contrition during the social-liberal era had prompted conservative backlash and efforts to "normalize" West German memory. But by the late 1980s, bipartisan condemnation of this trend delineated the boundaries of acceptable public discourse about the war and Holocaust, and established a commitment to remembrance that transcended political party lines.

## COMPETING THEORIES AND PREDICTIONS

Following their initial reconciliation in the late 1950s, we would expect benign French perceptions of West Germany until German unification upset the postwar order. Since the 1960s, apologetic West German remembrance should have reassured the French of the Federal Republic's peaceful intentions. Although West German leaders were divided on the best way to remember, mainstream debates reflected no denials or glorifications of the violence of the Nazi era. Although unification might have called into question whether Germany would continue to atone, decades of contrition should have reassured the French that, under the aegis of the contrite Federal Republic, Germany would remain committed to remembrance and peace.

Franco-German reconciliation should have been further bolstered by the successful consolidation of German democracy. The period from 1965 to 1990 witnessed stable transfers of power among the CDU/CSU, SPD, FDP, and various coalitions thereof. Although scholars measure a democracy's maturity in a variety of ways (see chapter 1), by any accepted standard West Germany qualified as a mature democracy by the 1970s. Upon unification, the incorporation of the GDR into the democratic Federal Republic of Germany should have been very reassuring to the French.

We also would expect the French to have judged Bonn's intentions based on its participation in multilateral institutions. The ECSC had been expanded in 1957 under the Treaty of Rome with the creation of a European Atomic Energy Community, Euratom, and a European Economic Community. All three communities were merged together in 1967 to form the European Community (EC). The Common Agricultural Policy was signed in 1962. Between 1975 and 1982, French President Valéry Giscard d'Estaing and West German Chancellor Schmidt negotiated the European Monetary System, which tied several currencies to the West German deutsche mark and allowed them to fluctuate within defined limits. In 1986, the Single European Act further deepened European institutionalization; the creation of majority voting in some issue areas (as opposed to national vetoes) promised to strengthen the EC by expediting decision-making. Bonn's continued enthusiasm for institutional cooperation should thus have reassured the French. Upon German unification, the French would have been expected to evaluate German intentions based on the Federal Republic's willingness to continue to participate in, and further develop, European institutions.

Some doubts about German intentions may have lingered during this period because of the persistence of the territorial issue. At Colombey in 1958 and in the Elysée Treaty in 1963, Adenauer had reassured de Gaulle that the West Germans had no intention of seeking unification or of using force to recover its lost territory. However, Adenauer also repeatedly stated in the 1950s that the Germans did not accept the postwar borders settled at Potsdam.[159] Germany remained "the European problem," argued French scholar Jacques Vernant, because despite some assurances, "she had not clearly accepted the territorial repercussions of the war."[160] Brandt had signed a treaty with Poland in 1970 confirming the present borders. But France's nightmare of a unification deal between Bonn and Moscow remained a possibility: border issues occasionally sparked controversy and uncertainty about the West German stance.[161] After conservatives regained power in 1982, Chancellor Helmut Kohl denied the legality of the border; in 1985 he attended the annual rally of Silesian expellees in Hanover at which people held banners proclaiming "Silesia Remains Ours."

At the time of unification, uncertainty about Germany's borders should have raised French fears. The large population of German expellees from Eastern Europe who had settled in West Germany after the war was a powerful force in the CDU and particularly the CSU. Pressured by these constituents, Kohl at the time of unification initially hesitated to accept the permanence of the postwar borders.[162] Germany finally settled the matter in a treaty with Poland in November 1990; the German Bundestag ratified the treaty a year later. We would expect the French to have been alarmed about German intentions until the Germans agreed to a settlement.

German capabilities (power and constraints) would also have affected French threat perception. Rough parity between the two countries in terms of potential power (populations and national wealth) would have dampened French fears.[163] In terms of mobilized power, the two countries also reflected approximate parity. The French defense budget ranged from 0.8 to

1.1 times that of Germany's over this period, and the two states fielded similar numbers of troops.[164] West German power continued to be highly constrained during this period; the FRG remained in NATO, with troops from other countries stationed on its soil. Although the severity of the Soviet threat did fluctuate over time with changes in NATO or Warsaw Pact procurement or deployments, on balance it remained a serious threat and a strong constraint. Thus, simply on the basis of capabilities, we would expect French threat perception to have been low for most of this period.

German unification, however, presaged a dramatic upsurge in German capabilities. Its population increasing from 60 to 80 million people, Germany's potential power (population and economy) would grow relative to France's. The addition of the east, though it would initially be costly to develop, promised greater wealth for unified Germany. Furthermore, constraints on German power were disappearing. Unified Germany would no longer face a Soviet threat: the country would be free to build up its military, obtain nuclear weapons, and abrogate the NATO treaty (expelling foreign forces and abandoning troop ceilings). Uncertainty about growing and unconstrained German power should have sent French threat perception of Germany soaring at the time of unification.

## FRENCH PERCEPTIONS OF GERMAN INTENTIONS AND THREAT (1965–89)

The reconciliation that began in the late 1950s developed further into a warm and productive partnership. French polls showed that West Germany was viewed as a close ally. The sense in 1965 that the FRG was "the best friend of France" remained true two decades later; in a 1983 poll, 48 percent of respondents selected West Germany as one of France's most trusted friends. Increasing warmth is evident in growing French support for German unification; whereas in 1960 33 percent of French respondents said they favored German unification, this number had risen to 62 percent by 1987.[165]

Franco-German policies, building on the architecture created by de Gaulle and Adenauer, continued to be cooperative. Security cooperation deepened after 1982, at which time the two sides activated the security consultations established under the 1963 Elysée Treaty. Previously vague about whether they would come to the FRG's defense in the event of a Soviet attack, the French began promising their support, and for the first time began preparing their military for this mission. During the 1980s, France established a rapid reaction force (*Force d'action Rapide*), three divisions of which were intended for West Germany's defense. The French and West Germans staged a major joint military exercise (Bold Sparrow) in 1987. Such increasingly cooperative diplomacy reflects low threat perception.

As noted, French equanimity about West German intentions was based on a variety of factors (the imposition of credible and enduring constraints on German power; Bonn's agreement to respect the postwar borders; participation within European institutions; and German democratization). All of these factors only grew stronger during this period and would contribute to the deepening of Franco-German reconciliation.

Additionally, the French observed West German debates about the past and expressed wariness at perceived revisionism. The French watched the *Historikerstreit* and lauded West Germans who were committed to candid remembrance of past crimes. Many observers expressed concern that efforts of some West Germans to turn away from the past signaled a disturbing backslide toward greater nationalism. An article criticized Kohl as "the spokesperson of a German generation that believes a line should be drawn under the past for once and all." Kohl was called "the man who visited the tombs of SS soldiers in Bitburg" and the man who "tolerates by his side Hans Klein, an admirer of the Waffen SS and author of antisemitic gaffes."[166] An article in *Le Monde* asserted that one must condemn "the Germans who were with Chancellor Kohl in 1985 at the Bitburg Cemetery." Philip Jenninger's awkward speech, argued another *Le Monde* article, was "a scandal of international dimensions that damaged the reputation of his country."[167] Some newspapers pointedly said the trends in German remembrance did not bode well for Germany's future behavior; one noted that people should "be worried about this impatience [to forget] that manifests itself in contemporary German society."[168] Journalist Daniel Vernet wrote, "The recent historian's dispute proves that it is very difficult for Germans to not shift between two extremes" and commented that revisionist historians "want to some extent to minimize Germany's responsibility." Discussing the *Historikerstreit*, another *Le Monde* article speculated about the nature of German patriotism and wondered, "How are relations between German generations, and how are each of them in touch with the Nazi past?"[169] During this period, the French monitored German remembrance as a signal of its intentions; they expressed dismay when they perceived trends toward justification or self-pity.

FRENCH PERCEPTIONS OF GERMANY DURING
UNIFICATION (1989–90)

During the unification period, French perceptions of Germany were highly uncertain. The French people showed tepid support for unification; polls consistently showed that about 60 percent of the public thought it would be a good thing.[170] Views in the French media were even more wary. Newspapers published scores of articles speculating about the implications of the change and whether unified Germany would seek to dominate Europe. "Will German restraint persist? I don't know," worried one article. Vernet wrote that "a nagging question from the Rhine to the Oder was: Should one be afraid of Germany?"[171] Another article queried, "What role will Germany play from now on?" Fearing that Germany's cooperative spirit would not remain, another article warned, "power easily engenders arrogance and the appetite for domination." Another newspaper summarized French unease: "France asks herself, what is her future—prey, or ally?"[172]

The statements and policies of French elites reflected increased fears of Germany during unification. As Philip Zelikow and Condoleezza Rice report in their diplomatic history of unification, "it was made clear that [French] politicians started from the preservation of the realities of the postwar period, including the existence of two German states. All of them will consider raising the question of the unity of Germany as extremely explosive."[173] Stephen Szabo concluded that among Europeans "The French were the most disoriented by changes which began with the opening of the Wall."[174] French diplomacy—notably with the British and the Russians—initially attempted to block or delay unification. Stanley Hoffmann commented that President Mitterrand's trip to meet with Soviet President Mikhail Gorbachev in Kiev in December 1989 "could not but evoke the ghosts of Franco-Russian alliances against the German danger and of German obsessions about encirclement." Mitterrand "also went to London to consult with the Iron Lady [Prime Minister Margaret Thatcher], who was even more, and more openly, upset about a reunified Germany."[175] Eventually, the French president was reconciled to the reality that he could not prevent unification from occurring and thus devoted his energies toward imposing constraints on unified Germany.

## FRENCH REASONING AT THE TIME OF GERMAN REUNIFICATION

The French did not discuss German remembrance during negotiations over unification. Although remembrance was still an issue in French minds, other factors were more significant. As they discussed their perceptions of Germany, the French were the most concerned about the expected increase in German power. Vernet wrote, "Unification gave rise to the fear of one dominant Germany (economically if not politically) within Europe." An article in *Le Monde* argued, "Unified Germany will be the premier economic and demographic power in the EEC, and this worries Europeans." Another commented, "When Germany becomes larger, it is inevitable that this evokes the phantom of a grand Germany whose ambition spilled blood in crimes across Europe."[176] Paris demanded that before it could support unification, Germany must renounce a nuclear weapons capability and accept further institutional constraints. As scholar Michael Baun noted, France was "desperately searching for ways to tie down and keep pace with its more powerful neighbor."[177] Summarized French scholar Edouard Husson: "François Mitterrand's entire European policy can be explained by one simple motive: the obsessive fear of German power."[178]

French fears of unification were also strongly influenced by uncertainties about German intentions. Among these, the issue of territorial claims created the most anxiety. In a February 1990 meeting, Mitterrand told Kohl, "We are building in Europe institutions that are going to attenuate the definition of borders. But it is necessary to settle the problems of borders beforehand." Kohl protested that this would reinforce the extreme Right in his country. Mitterrand insisted that he clarify the territorial issue, arguing, "There is a problem of European equilibrium" concerning "the problem of the eastern border." The French president said, "The treaties of 1919 and 1945 are very unjust, but one lives with them. It is very important not to re-open a collective frenzy in Europe." After Kohl dodged questions about German borders in a March 1 press conference, Mitterrand was "furious with Kohl's behavior" and told an aide "to ask Germany to clarify its position unambiguously." Mitterrand insisted, "The FRG should be very clear on the problem of borders."[179] He was hostile to unification until the territorial issue was settled: not until the issue of the Germany-Poland border was resolved did Mitterrand adopt a more cooperative approach to German reunification.[180] The French media closely monitored the German stance on the territorial issue. One article in *Le Monde* wondered, "What kind of game is Chancellor Kohl playing with the German-Polish border?"[181]

To the French, another litmus test of unified Germany's intentions was its willingness to participate in European institutions. Mitterrand's diplomacy reflected his intense preoccupation with the issue. To West German Foreign Minister Hans-Dietrich Genscher, Mitterrand said bluntly: "German unity will be undertaken after European unity, or you will find against you a triple alliance (France, Britain, and Russia), and that will end in war. If German unity is enacted after European unity, we can help you." Meeting with Gorbachev on December 6, 1989, the French president commented, "I don't want to return to Europe in 1913. . . . We have to make progress with the construction of the European community, so that the German problem will be minimized." Mitterrand said that although France is very friendly with Germany, "I have a responsibility regarding the equilibrium of Europe and peace. I don't want to hurt the Germans, but I told them that the German problem can only be raised after there is resolution on other questions—in the west, the European community."[182] U.S. President George H. W. Bush reported that at a meeting in Kennebunkport, "François did emphasize that what happened in Germany must be linked with NATO and the EC . . .'Otherwise,' [Mitterrand] warned, 'we will be back in 1913 and we could lose everything.' "[183] In an EC summit in Strasbourg in December 1989, the French demanded that the West Germans stop vacillating about European monetary union, and the Germans agreed to schedule a conference on monetary union for the following year. Mitterrand said that the deal at the summit prevented "a rupture" in Franco-German relations.[184] Hoffmann claims that French policy during unification negotiations "aimed at 'smoking out' Bonn, at probing and prodding in order to find out whether the constraints of NATO and, above all, the EC, were still acceptable to the Federal Republic, and indeed whether Chancellor Kohl was willing to tighten the bonds to the community."[185]

Mitterrand was not alone in his preoccupation with Germany's future institutional membership. EC President Jacques Delors similarly wondered whether the Germans were "really interested in economic and military union" and demanded "clear political commitments without ambiguity." Delors argued in 1989 that European federalism was "the only satisfactory and acceptable response to the German question," and in January 1990 called for the acceleration of the political unification of Europe.[186] The French media monitored Germany's stance toward continued European multilateralism; many commentators maintained that continued German willingness to cooperate was vital for European stability. As Le Monde argued, "All efforts should be made to maintain with unified Germany the historic miracle that was the 'marriage'—concluded by Jean Monnet, Robert Schuman, and Adenauer and confirmed by de Gaulle, Schmidt, François Mitterrand, and Kohl—between the two hereditary enemies. With the growing intimacy of common links, national rivalries will become anachronistic." Another article wondered if Germany would continue to be restrained and concluded, "For the moment the commitment of Germany to European construction can be taken in good faith."[187]

French anxieties during German unification were dampened by the perceived strength of German democracy. Observers noted that the Federal Republic was a more stable and durable democracy than the Weimar Republic. "[Germany] is a state of democratic rights," noted an article in Le Monde Diplomatique, "which distinguishes it fundamentally from other united German states in history from 1870 to 1945."[188] Le Monde asserted that the FRG was superior to Weimar because of its strong economy and effective democratic government, and said these factors would stabilize its foreign policies.[189] Former Foreign Minister Couve de Murville agreed: "The FRG is an obviously democratic and highly civilized state, a member of the Western world that is dedicated to liberty; a country that lives with the esteem and friendship of its neighbors." He noted that in contrast to Weimar, "In the FRG, the Germans [gave] themselves a truly and solidly democratic regime for the first time in their history."[190]

In sum, evidence from this period shows that West German capabilities and intentions influenced French threat perception. In particular, the French feared the increase of German power but were reassured by their neighbor's continued acceptance of constraints. Paris worried about Germany's postwar borders and institutional membership and was reassured by Kohl's cooperation on these issues. The French also took solace in the strength of German democracy.

As noted, during unification debates the French did not discuss German remembrance to any noticeable measure. Despite thirty years of the deepest contrition the world had ever seen, even Germany's allies were sent into a panic at the prospect of reunification. The French (and British, as chapter 4 will show) were highly apprehensive about the shift in the balance of power.

This does not mean that remembrance played no role in French perceptions. Consider the counterfactual: If the West Germans had spent the previous thirty years telling themselves tales of Hitler's glory, building monuments to dead expellees and Dresden victims, and denying the Holocaust, this would have sent shockwaves through Europe and would have fundamentally changed the course of the unification debate. It is impossible to prove that this counterfactual is true, but it seems highly plausible given that we know the French and British were watching German remembrance and had expressed concerns about perceived revisionism.

## Late Period (1990s and 2000s)

### THE CULTURE OF CONTRITION

Germans and others worried that unified Germany would begin to forget the Nazi era because of unification euphoria and a new interest in exploring East Germany's authoritarian past.[191] However, such fears were not borne out: German remembrance after unification, both officially and across German society, was extremely apologetic.

Leaders regularly offered apologies for World War II and the Holocaust. Many politicians attended an international commemorative ceremony at the fiftieth anniversary of the liberation of Auschwitz. A statement by Chancellor Kohl said, "The darkest and most horrible chapter of German history was written in Auschwitz" and that "one of our priority tasks is to pass on this knowledge to future generations so that the horrible experiences of the past will never be repeated."[192] A few months later, on May 8, 1995, Germany observed the fiftieth anniversary of its World War II surrender in a ceremony attended by heads-of-state from the former Allied nations. At the occasion, German President Herzog said,

> Germany had unleashed a war that was more terrible than anything that had taken place until then and it suffered the most terrible defeat that one can imagine. Europe was in ruins, from the Atlantic to the Urals and from the Arctic circle to the Mediterranean coast. Millions of members of all European peoples, including the German one, were dead, fallen, torn to shreds in bomb attacks, starved to death in camps, and frozen on the roads during their flight, and other millions—in particular Jews, Romanies, and Sinti,

Poles, and Russians, Czechs and Slovaks—fell victim to the largest operations of eradication that human minds had ever conceived. Millions had lost their relatives, their friends, and their homes, or were in the process of losing them. Millions came from prisoners-of-war camps or were on their way to them. Millions had been maimed. Hundreds of thousands of women had been raped. The stink of the crematories and the smoldering ruins was heavy over Europe.

Herzog also lamented early German amnesia; he said that in the early days Germans were guilty of "finding collective excuses, and collective whitewashing." He noted the importance of commemorating the war's end, "of remembering, and of dealing honestly and relentlessly with our history."[193]

Germany's observance of the sixtieth anniversary of the Allied landings at Normandy also reflects contrition. In a published letter, Chancellor Gerhard Schröder wrote that no one expects Germans of today to feel guilty "for the crimes and genocide of an unspeakable regime, but we carry a responsibility [to acknowledge] our history."[194] Schröder's interpretation of the event was very contrite: Germans should not mourn D-Day because it marked the beginning of Germany's liberation from fascism and "the day that began the liberation of Europe." The Allied victory "was not a victory over Germany, but a victory for Germany." The Chancellor concluded, "It is no longer a question of victory or defeat, but of a day that has become the symbol of the struggle for liberty, democracy, and the rights of man. It is right that we Germans participate in such an event."[195] At the anniversary celebration he laid a wreath at the Ranville war cemetery, where soldiers from eight nations (including Germany) were buried. Avoiding a repeat of Bitburg, the Chancellor refrained from visiting the German cemetery at Cambe, which houses thousands of SS troops.

Germany also expanded its already extensive reparations policy. It compensated victims living in the former East Germany and concluded numerous bilateral agreements that supplemented the earlier BEG and BRüG payments.[196] One was the Czech-German fund, which included a German apology for the conquest of Czechoslovakia and a Czech apology for the expulsion of ethnic Germans after the war that had led to a refugee crisis that killed two million Germans.[197] Berlin concluded a Friendship Agreement with Poland,[198] negotiated accords with successor states to the Soviet Union (Belarus, Russia, and the Ukraine), and extended new benefits to Holocaust survivors in the United States and Israel. In 1996 the Bundestag agreed to set aside funds for foundations yet to be settled with Albania, Bulgaria, Hungary, Slovakia, and the states of the former Yugoslavia.[199]

The government, along with a group of German companies, also compensated victims of wartime forced labor. Seven million slave laborers had worked in deplorable conditions in the German empire. The agreement paid $5 billion in reparations to survivors and established an educational foundation. At a ceremony honoring victims, German President Johannes Rau said, "I pay tribute to all those who were subjected to slave and forced labor under German rule, and, in the name of the German people, beg forgiveness."[200]

German education continued to admit and repudiate Nazi violence. Yasemin Soysal writes that textbooks provide extensive detail about the period, described "as a time of violence, persecution, death, and destruction." In striking contrast to the textbooks of the immediate postwar era, "contemporary history in German textbooks is given a more prominent place. Ancient and medieval history is relatively marginalized in comparison with coverage of the Weimar Republic, the Nazi period, and the Cold War."[201] Textbooks link the lessons of the past to current issues such as integration and multiculturalism; texts prepare German students to be citizens of Europe and a globalized world. As Mark Selden and Laura Hein point out, German national identity today celebrates regional diversity within the country and political, military, economic, and cultural integration with the rest of Europe. Today's integrationist approach in Europe is often seen as a way of avoiding Germany's destructive, nationalist past.[202]

Unified Germany's memorials and museums candidly confront past violence. In the Berlin and the surrounding area, outstanding Holocaust museums and exhibits have taken shape, including the Topographie des Terrors and the Buchenwald and Sachsenhausen exhibits.[203] The Jewish Museum Berlin is an extension of the Berlin Museum for City History, with spectacular architecture in a slashing design inspired by a broken Star of David. Other notable Berlin memorials include the Memorial to the Bookburning at Bebelplatz, the memorial to the deportation of Jews at Grunewald Station, and the "Places of Remembering" (street signs) in the Bavarian Quarter. The latter is a subtle yet pervasive exhibition in a Berlin neighborhood: Through the use of eighty double-sided street signs, it illustrates how Hitler's anti-Jewish laws curtailed Jewish civil liberties as these laws increasingly restricted the daily lives of Jews.

Berlin's most important memorial is its newest: the Memorial to the Murdered Jews of Europe.[204] After a long national debate, the Bundestag voted in June 1999 to build the memorial in a huge plot of land near the Brandenburg Gate. The design consists of more than two thousand columns of irregular height, resembling tombstones, over an awkwardly sloping field (see next page). It includes an information center about the Holocaust.

German days of commemoration established since unification remember and mourn Nazi victims. In June 1995 the Bundestag established Holocaust Remembrance Day, observed on the day Auschwitz was liberated (January 27). German leaders typically commemorate this day by attending official ceremonies at concentration camps. November 9 commemorates the anniversary of the first night of the anti-Jewish pogrom of 1938 (*Kristallnacht,*

The Memorial to the Murdered Jews of Europe, Berlin. AP PHOTO/JOCKEL FINCK.

or *Pogromnacht*). Because the Berlin Wall fell on November 9, 1989, unified Germany might have taken the opportunity to let the pogrom's anniversary slip away in favor of celebrating the far more pleasant event of German unification. However, the government instead chose to protect the pogrom's anniversary by commemorating unification on October 3 (the official first day of unification). This decision reflects a strong commitment to remembrance of past crimes in the face of temptation to obscure them with more uplifting events.

Wider society in unified Germany supports official contrition. In national debates about how and how much the Nazi era should be remembered, moves away from remembrance attract sharp criticism. For example, Helmut Kohl's 1995 refurbishing of the *Neue Wache* memorial provoked charges of whitewashing. The monument was originally built to honor Kaiser Wilhelm III and the 1814 Prussian defeat of Napoleon; over the years it had been adapted and readapted to suit the policy goals of various German regimes. In 1995 it was rededicated as the "Central Memorial of the Federal Republic of Germany for the Victims of War and Tyranny." Critics argued that the monument honored equally the memories of victims and perpetrators and said that its central symbol of a Pietà statue marginalized Jewish victims in the Holocaust.[205] A national outcry led the German government to add two plaques to the memorial that—drawing from von Weizsäcker's 1985 speech—clarified which group constituted the "victims" of the war.

Another controversy arose after a 1998 speech by Martin Walser. The German novelist implored his countrymen to move on from the Nazi past; he lambasted the "instrumentalization" of the Holocaust to achieve political ends and the use of Auschwitz as "a moral cudgel." Walser criticized plans to build the Holocaust memorial in Berlin, saying it represented the "monumentalization of disgrace." In a debate with the novelist, the head of the Central Council of Jews in Germany, Ignatz Bubis, accused Walser of "intellectual arson" and charged Germans to recall the Holocaust in public memory.[206]

The Walser debate became intertwined with deliberations about the Memorial to the Murdered Jews of Europe. After a talk-show host had suggested such a memorial in the 1980s, a lengthy, intense, and very public debate ensued on remembrance and German responsibility. It featured a design competition and a three-part symposium in 1997 among historians, architects, and other experts. Participant James Young argues that one of the memorial's main contributions to German memory was the debate it had inspired. The controversy shaped government policy; politicians who initially had been skeptical about the memorial eventually lent their support as a way of signaling a commitment to remembrance. For example, the initially hesitant Helmut Kohl eventually supported the project after controversy erupted over his refurbishing of the *Neue Wache;* Chancellor Gerhard Schröder signed on after the Walser debate. As scholar Bill Niven writes, "As a result of the far right's enthusiastic response to Walser's criticism of the memorial, Schröder was aware that opposing the project would now appear as support for right-wing extremism."[207] Such debates interacted significantly with government policy and reflected that the German people admitted and sought to atone for the Nazi past.

Controversy over fiftieth anniversary commemorations of the surrender also revealed broad societal support for contrition. At the time, conservative politicians and intellectuals sought a less self-accusatory remembrance of the German past. In their view, the German surrender should mourned, not celebrated: especially the two million dead German expellees from Eastern Europe. A petition signed by 300 political leaders and intellectuals ran as an advertisement (known as the *Aufruf*)§ in the *FAZ* newspaper in April 1995. These conservatives condemned the media's "one-sided" presentation of the German surrender as an act of liberation; May 8, they said,

---

§ *Aufruf gegen das Vergessen,* or "Against Forgetting."

should be seen as the "beginning of the expulsion, terror, and new oppression in the East and the division of our nation." The advertisement claimed, "a conception of history that is silent, represses or relativizes these truths cannot serve as the foundation of the self-understanding of a self-confident nation, something we Germans must become within the family of European peoples if we are to prevent similar catastrophes from occurring in the future."[208]

German society, however, rejected calls to mourn the German surrender. Conservatives and the Left denounced the *Aufruf*; Karl Wilds writes that the response to the *Aufruf* at the party and governmental levels "represented a decisive rebuttal of the thrust of the [New Right]. Whilst one might well have expected left-liberal and critical thinkers to attack the sentiment of the New Right, it was perhaps surprising to note the concerted criticism which emerged from within the *conservative* spectrum." Bundestag President Rita Süssmuth of the CDU lambasted the *Aufruf*. Bavarian Minister-President Edmund Stoiber "made an impassioned speech denouncing those who argued for drawing a line under the German past and stated that the crimes of the Third Reich demanded a sense of historical responsibility from contemporary Germans who, if they succumbed to a culture of amnesia, could enjoy no future."[209] Josef Joffe concludes that the most interesting lesson from the debate was the societal reaction to the efforts of the New Right: "If this was a cancer, the German body politic soon unleashed powerful antibodies."[210]

Another revealing episode occurred upon the release of a book about the Holocaust written by American historian Daniel Jonah Goldhagen. *Hitler's Willing Executioners* sought to debunk the myth that only Hitler and the SS had carried out the Holocaust. It asserted that ordinary Germans had participated energetically in the killing of Jews and that because of deeply rooted German anti-Semitism, they had required no special indoctrination to do so. Reviews of the book across the globe were often critical, but the German people embraced it. Goldhagen became a media star in Germany, booked on major talk shows and speaking to sold-out crowds.[211] Audiences cheered Goldhagen and booed his detractors. A private foundation awarded him the German Democracy Prize. Karl Wilds argues that Goldhagen's popularity showed that "far from promoting the suppression of historical memory of the crimes of the [Nazi] state, the mainstream political culture of reunified Germany is marked by the prominence of open contrition for National Socialism and the Holocaust in particular."[212]

Academic reactions were conditioned by past debates as well as by the German people's embrace of Goldhagen's work. A number of German academics penned critical reviews, but after the effusive public reception, many acknowledged the book's importance in German political development. Methodological critiques came second to the larger goal of acknowledging and condemning the Nazi past. For example, Jürgen Habermas praised the book's contribution to Germany's "ethical-political process of public self-understanding."[213] Many conservative scholars held back criticism because of their experience in the *Historikerstreit*; one noted that moderates and conservatives had learned the lesson that "a 'golden silence' was the safe option during the Goldhagen debate, from which one could only emerge a loser."[214] Goldhagen's reception thus reveals not only the widespread acceptance of contrition in German society; it shows the effects of previous historical debates on establishing norms of acceptable dialogue about the Nazi past.

The myth about the public's innocence in World War II was further attacked by a 1995 museum exhibit. Called "War of Extermination: Crimes of the *Wehrmacht*, 1941–44," the traveling exhibit toured Hamburg, Berlin, Potsdam, and Stuttgart, and by 1999 had attracted 860,000 visitors in thirty-two cities in Germany and Austria.[215] The exhibit challenged the entrenched belief that the SS—not ordinary German soldiers—had perpetrated genocide. It featured photographs and unsent letters collected by the Soviets from captured Germans. "In picture after picture, letter after letter, and report after report, the exhibition detailed the daily participation of all ranks of the German army in executions and hangings of unarmed civilians, and the deportation and mass murder of Jews across the eastern front. These documents made clear beyond doubt that large numbers of Germans from all walks of life had heard and seen firsthand testimony about brown-collar crimes."[216] As liberal politicians promoted the showing of the exhibit, the CDU/CSU and FDP criticized it as one-sided, protested its omission of the role of the army in the July 20, 1944, coup attempt against Hitler, and attempted to block funding and venues. The exhibit prompted a poignant Bundestag debate about German responsibility for the war.[217] After touring Germany and Austria, the *Wehrmacht* exhibit closed in response to criticism about the accuracy of photographs; it reopened in 2001 when errors were corrected and documentation expanded.[218] As with the Goldhagen debate, the *Wehrmacht* exhibit reflects a strong German commitment to contrition.

## COMPETING THEORIES AND PREDICTIONS

French observers assessing unified Germany confronted reassuring signals across the board. Government policy and wider society exhibited a bipartisan, national commitment to contrite remembrance of the Nazi era. The country was a thriving democracy whose institutions had successfully incorporated the GDR. The French would also have been encouraged by unified Germany's continued NATO membership, the creation of the European Union, the founding of the Common Foreign and Security Policy, and the 1999 adoption of the Euro. German unification, and the treaty with Poland, had peacefully resolved the border issue. Thus, in the 1990s through the early 2000s, all signals of German intentions should have reassured the French.

The balance of capabilities between France and Germany also remained stable. Unified Germany has greater potential power, with a larger population and greater wealth (the German GDP in 2007 was $2.6 trillion, compared to France's $1.8 trillion).[219] But despite France's unification nightmares, the two countries remained roughly comparable in terms of mobilized power. Germany steadily reduced its numbers of troops and its defense budget, giving France a slight advantage in military spending (1.4 times the size of Germany's defense budget since 1995).[220] Although the Federal Republic continued to renounce WMD ownership, France retained its nuclear weapons capability, with about 350 strategic nuclear weapons deliverable by aircraft and ballistic missile submarines.[221] Furthermore, France would also have been reassured by constraints on Germany's ability to project power. Although the Soviet threat vanished, Germany remained constrained by American and other foreign military forces on its territory. In sum, after unification, every indicator of Germany's intentions and capabilities predicts low French threat perception.

## THE GERMAN PROBLEM SOLVED: RELATIONS AFTER UNIFICATION

Although Franco-German reconciliation had begun long before, the French media decreed June 6, 2004—the sixtieth anniversary of the Normandy landings—"the last day of World War II."[222] Attending the ceremony in Normandy alongside French President Jacques Chirac and representatives from other Allied nations was German Chancellor Gerhard Schröder, the first German leader ever to attend a Normandy commemoration. The French press effused about the symbolism of Schröder's presence; one newspaper asserted that it showed the world "that reconciliation has guaranteed the peace and prosperity of the continent."[223]

Indeed, in the postunification era, the French perceive no threat from Germany. In a 2004 poll, the French claimed Germany as their closest ally (it received the highest number of votes at 82 per cent of respondents).[224] When another poll asked in 1997, "Is France correct in fearing Germany?" 59 per cent of respondents said no.[225] Elites report high levels of trust in Germany; in interviews, they scoffed at the idea of a German threat. One scholar from the French Institute for International Relations (IFRI) commented, "There is no deep antagonism between France and Germany." An analyst at the Center for International Studies and Research said, "We work together so closely that the idea of conflict between us is absolutely unthinkable."[226] A representative view of French security among elites in the early 2000s was expressed by another IFRI researcher as follows: "Major threats to France are global terrorism and weapons of mass destruction; we need to figure out how best to preserve the Atlantic community, and how France can be a major actor in the world of new threats."[227] French elites said that the "German problem" has been solved; any concerns France has about Germany relate to its influence within the EU, not its military. As one scholar commented, "Germany is no longer a threat, it's a partner. The German problem belongs to the past. Germany no longer wants to dominate Europe by military means." A former defense official commented, "I never attended a meeting in which people said Germany might be a threat to France. The idea of Germany as a threat has disappeared from French political culture."[228]

French policy similarly reflects low threat perception. French officials sit in German ministries and vice-versa—even occasionally representing the other country at international meetings. France also continues to cooperate closely with Germany in the security realm. The two states created the Eurocorps in 1992 and activated the Franco-German brigade in 1993 under the auspices of the Common Foreign and Security Policy. Soldiers from the Eurocorps, including German soldiers, paraded down the Champs d'Elysées on July 14, 1994, to cheering crowds. The two states pursue numerous cooperative efforts in the defense industry, including helicopter and aircraft production and the merger of large defense companies (France's Aerospatiale Matra and Germany's DASA in 1999). The French and Germans also cooperate closely in the cultural realm. They established a Franco-German television channel, Arte, in 1992. Over two million youths from both countries have continued to participate in activities of the Franco-German Youth Office, which was initiated by de Gaulle and Adenauer decades ago.

The French also support an expanded German military role. During the first Persian Gulf War, French commentary noted that Germany lacked the military capability and domestic consensus to participate; media coverage exhibited no fears of German militarism.[229] German military participation has been increasing since 1990. German pilots flew sorties over Kosovo during the 1999 war against Serbia; soldiers provided support in the "out-of-area" mission in Afghanistan. The French support such activities. "The *Bundeswehr*," argued an article in *Le Monde,* should be modernized in order to play a central role in European defense."[230]

In coverage of the Kosovo war—in which German Tornadoes flew sorties over Serbia—the French media reported without a trace of alarm that this was the first time Germany had participated in military operations since World War II. Press coverage focused on German domestic political debates. Coverage was generally favorable, noting the German contribution to the international community. *Le Monde* praised Germany as "a partner like the others at the heart of the Atlantic alliance."[231] Another article quipped, "For the first time in history, Germany fought on the good side!"[232] French government officials similarly praise and encourage German contributions to international security. A former French defense official said that the French government supports greater German military activism. "We always tried to help Germany toward military normalization," he commented. "We view Schroeder's position on Iraq [2002] as a step backward. We welcome progress such as German participation in Kosovo and in counterterrorism."[233]

## FRENCH REASONING SINCE GERMAN REUNIFICATION

Continuing to observe German remembrance, the French have noted that Germany continues to admit its responsibility for the aggression and atrocities of World War II. One French commentator argued, "Within the major parties, left as well as right, there is no question about accepting, clearly and entirely, the German responsibility for past crimes." Scholar Jean-Pierre LeFebvre commented, "Nationalistic themes have not become a major debate within Germany."[234] Another said that in the German debate over the Memorial to the Murdered Jews, "It was difficult for a responsible politician to contest the need for a national commemoration. Those who did so risked situating themselves at the margins of the political arena."[235] The sponsors of the *Aufruf*, maintained Edouard Husson, wanted Germans to "turn the page of confrontation with the Nazi past, . . . but such people were merely "a fringe of the intellectual world" and "if one believes the polls, their call was barely heard."[236]

The French noticed that unification had not distracted the Germans from *Vergangenheitsbewältigung*. French observers were particularly impressed by the construction of the Memorial to the Murdered Jews of Europe. Irène Kruse commented, "At the moment of reformulating its national identity," Germany built "a monument at the center of its capital to the memory of the most heinous crime in its history: an enterprise without precedent that is taking place under the vigilant watch of world opinion." *Le Monde* praised "the acceptance within Germany of its historic responsibility vis-à-vis the victims of Nazism." On the memorial's dedication, a *La Croix* article noted that Germany showed that "she observes her past squarely, and that her democracy rests on the conscience of the Shoah."[237]

The French also paid a great deal of attention to—and indeed were somewhat mystified by—German enthusiasm for the work of Daniel Jonah Goldhagen.[238] According to Husson, "All in all, one will make the case for the utility of the [*Wehrmacht*] exhibition and for the Goldhagen debate, which bear witness to the incessant progress of the critical examination of the past within democratic Germany. Contrary to those who might have thought otherwise, the end of the Cold War signified the intensification of studies about the Third Reich."[239] The media reported on the "Crimes of the *Wehrmacht*" museum exhibition and approvingly quoted Schröder's contrite statements at the 2004 Normandy commemoration.[240] All in all, as commentator Lorraine Millot argues, "The manner in which Germany assumes culpability of its Nazi past and the Holocaust could be the most positive chapter of its history."[241]

Although the French praised Germany's willingness to confront its past, they simultaneously worried that it was growing increasingly forgetful. "This seems to be the hour," wrote Daniel Vernet, "in which Germans rediscover themselves as victims, as if the period of mourning and contrition were over."[242] Others worried that Schröder's ascent signaled a tilt toward amnesia, for in 1998 Schröder had declined to join Jacques Chirac in commemoration ceremonies of the World War II armistice. Schröder said, "We have to remember the past so the bad things will not be repeated, but it is also a mistake to live in the past." The French media at the time criticized Schröder as less committed to German contrition than his predecessors, speculating, "Has Schröder the nationalist succeeded Kohl the European?" Scholar Nicholas Weill wondered, "Will the end of German partition and the accession of the 'Republic of Berlin' under the new Chancellor Gerhard Schröder coincide with the end of the culpability for the genocide of the Jews?" According to a Sorbonne scholar, "We were concerned when Schröder succeeded Kohl; he doesn't think he needs to be constrained by Germany's past. . . . As a result there was a revival of concern about Germany."[243]

Similarly, in French coverage of debate about Martin Walser's remarks, many people asserted that the German novelist's comments signaled a new historical revisionism. Commentators argued that the debate was really about "how to define the German identity." Joseph Mace-Scaron asserted that the episode showed "the fragility of that which would appear more solid within the conscience of the former West Germany: the consensus over the relationship to the Nazi past."[244] One scholar argued that the debate reveals the "fissures within the façade of normality claimed by reunified Germany and raises some fundamental questions over the form and the place of memory within Germany." Worrying that Germans were becoming impatient with endless self-criticism, Nicholas Weill contended that Germany was "a nation squashed by a half-century of culpability, of reparations of every kind, of commemoration and the education of the Holocaust." He warned, "This nation finally wishes, at the start of the twenty-first century, to shake off the yoke of a memory become oppressive and intends to make itself normal."[245]

As the French evaluated German intentions, they were also reassured by the strength of German democracy. Vernet wrote, "Germany is reunified. . . . It has democratic institutions that have proven themselves by weathering political and economic crises." Vernet maintained that democratic Germany is "impervious to any expansionist impulses."[246] As Gilles Martinet commented in Le Monde, "[France] knows Germany is resolutely pacifist and has established a tried and true democratic system."[247] A scholar argued: "It's clear that Germany has changed a great deal—it's a democratic nation that we can work with. It suffered a terrible defeat, and was totally destroyed. The German people won't forget that."[248]

Another important indicator for the French of Germany's benign intentions is the country's continued participation in European institutions. Upon unification, one article noted, "Germany's leaders resolutely chose Europe."[249] Scholar Stephan Martens argued, "The position of the West German leaders was perfectly clear. The fundamentals of German foreign policy since Chancellor Konrad Adenauer remained indisputably the integration of the Federal Republic within the Western community."[250] According to another analyst, "Germany's pro-Europe stance has been key in making it look unthreatening to France." "The EU has changed everything," one scholar commented, noting that the shock of unification absent the EU would have been too much for France. With the EU, however, "No one can think of a military conflict between France and Germany."[251] As Jèrôme Vaillant asserted in *Le Monde Diplomatique,* Germany "recovered her sovereignty and was reconstituted as a nation-state when . . . she consented to important transfers of sovereignty within the European Economic Community."[252]

Low French threat perception since reunification also depends on the balance of capabilities. One scholar notes that since unification "Germany has had falling defense budgets and is very weak." He commented, "The nightmare postunification scenarios did not come true. Germany hasn't become an economic or political giant. There is still a balance of military power."[253] Echoing a very common sentiment, another analyst said, "We're not trying to keep Germany down; it's the reverse. We're trying to get them to do more, to increase their defense budget."[254] He noted, "Germany is no longer a threat because its military capabilities are low. There was fear after German unification that Germany would become a great power, but then we saw that not only did they not want to be a hegemon, they were terrified of even being thought of as a threat." Scholars also commented that French fears of German military power have been erased by France's nuclear arsenal and by Germany's renunciation of WMD. One analyst asserted, "With French security ultimately guaranteed by nuclear weapons, the 'German question' moved from one of 'security' to 'influence'—that is, the realm of competition moved from questions about how much military power Germany had to how much *influence* Germany had within the EU."[255]

The French no longer view the U.S. military presence in Germany as an important constraint on German power. Former NATO Secretary General Lord Ismay once famously said that the purpose of NATO was "To keep the Americans in, the Russians out, and the Germans down." In interviews, French elites dismissed the idea that Ismay's statement remained relevant. "NATO is not needed to keep Germany down," one scholar argued. "NATO's only purpose is to keep the U.S. in. We like relying on U.S. capabilities."[256] Another analyst commented, "Some people thought after German unification that NATO would be even more important to keep the Germans down, but this simply didn't pan out." He noted, "If the U.S. pulled out its troops, I wouldn't see this as a problem at all, so long as we find a way to maintain U.S.-European security ties." According to another scholar, "We don't need the United States as a balancer within Europe. Competition within Europe is about influence, not about security. The Germans have no stomach for adventure."[257] This perception is both dramatically different from French perceptions in earlier periods and from the East Asian case, in which Koreans remain petrified of a U.S. departure from the region. The French view also appears to be more than cheap talk; the diversion of large numbers of American forces from Germany to the Persian Gulf has caused no insecurity.

In sum, the French perception of threat from Germany since reunification has fallen to its lowest level since World War II. The French assess German power as low and constrained; German intentions are judged as benign on every indicator. As one scholar commented, "they have told us in all practical terms that they would never wage war against us."[258]

## Findings, Counterarguments, and Conclusions

Many commentators cite German atonement as they urge countries (particularly Japan) to assuage the fears of former enemies by coming to terms with past violence. Indeed, the Federal Republic's avoidance of denials or glorification about past aggression and atrocities *did* facilitate reconciliation: both initially and throughout the postwar era. In the 1950s, although they preferred to discuss Dresden rather than Dachau, mainstream elites admitted German responsibility for the war and Holocaust and did not tolerate justifications or denials. The French were concerned about West German remembrance; in their postwar occupation they encouraged candid history education to prevent the rise of German nationalism, and throughout the postwar era they were wary of revisionist trends. Unlike Tokyo—which denied and even glorified past violence—Bonn avoided the denials that might have thwarted its rapprochement with France and others.

Germany's extraordinary atonement, and its remarkable reconciliations with its neighbors, might suggest that one is necessary for the other. Although Bonn's acknowledgment of past violence was a significant step, this case study shows that West Germany's remarkable *Vergangenheitsbewältigung* followed, rather than preceded, Franco-German rapprochement. France's image of West Germany was transformed from loathed enemy to trusted ally at a time when the Germans had taken responsibility for past crimes, yet were emphasizing their own suffering and forgetting the terror they had unleashed on others.

A puzzle emerges from the comparison of the German and Japanese cases. In Japan, even modest efforts to apologize and pay reparations triggered Japanese conservatives to justify or deny past atrocities. In the end, Japan's contrition thus alarmed foreign observers because of the nature of the debates it triggered. Germany, by contrast, pursued far more contrition than did Japan, yet domestic backlash to contrition was rare and far more muted. German conservatives did not deny or glorify Nazi violence. Watching German debates, the French saw a country that accepted its guilt but was attempting to decide what kind of remembrance—and how much remembrance—was appropriate. Thus the French praised Germany's national debates as a remarkably cathartic and useful enterprise: as a testament to the strength of German democracy. The utility of contrition as a tool in international reconciliation thus seems to pivot on the question of whether contrition is likely to trigger a domestic backlash. Addressing this issue in the conclusion of this book, I discuss reasons for Germany's relatively muted debates and discuss broader implications for the role of contrition in international reconciliation.

SKEPTICS might raise at least two counterarguments to my findings from this case. First, one might agree with my interpretation of Franco-German relations but doubt that these findings will be borne out elsewhere. Perhaps the French case is idiosyncratic: there is something about French culture, its specific experience with Germany, or its postwar circumstances that made it willing to reconcile with the Federal Republic in the 1950s despite very little German contrition. Perhaps France is exceptional, and countries generally require much more contrition as they reconcile after wars.

The Franco-German rapprochement in the 1950s is not a unique example: many formerly bitter enemies have been able to restore productive and friendly relations without contrition. After World War II, the United States and Japan achieved not only reconciliation not only as defined by this book (i.e., trust and a lack of threat perception), but a strong alliance and warm relations between peoples. This was possible despite an absence of Japanese apologies for Pearl Harbor or for brutality toward American POWs, and an absence of American apologies for the bloody counter-civilian bombing campaigns against Japanese cities. The Japanese teach their children that they launched an ill-advised attack on Pearl Harbor; the Americans acknowledge that they dropped atomic bombs on Japan and killed hundreds of thousands of people in bombing raids. However, neither side has apologized, and both continue to justify their actions as warranted by the circumstances of the time.[259] The absence of contrition has not interfered with the creation of friendly relations.

Many other countries have been similarly forgiving of their bitter enemies. Britain and Germany achieved productive relations despite an absence of British contrition for fire bombings, such as Dresden, that killed hundreds of thousands of Germans.[260] Italy's neighbors have embraced it in close economic and security partnerships despite its national mythology that few Italians supported Mussolini and most fought in the resistance (instead of the other way around). Austria's former enemies allowed it to forget its complicity in the crimes of the Third Reich. Reconciliation between France and West Germany is thus far from an isolated example: many other countries that fought devastating wars have managed to repair their relations without contrition.

## CONCLUSIONS

What do these findings suggest for the theory outlined earlier—that is, about the effects of remembrance on perceptions of intentions and threat? This case study provides evidence for the "weak" version of the theory, which states that observers will evaluate remembrance along with several other indicators as they assess another country's intentions. In addition to remembrance, the French paid great attention to the other indicators highlighted in this book: capabilities, territorial claims, institutional membership, and democracy. Although these other factors indeed figured more prominently in French assessments, the French since the early days after the war were concerned about West German remembrance and from time to time have expressed wariness about revisionist trends. Their attention to German national debates supports the following counterfactual: had Germany engaged in denials or justifications about the past, the French would have been extremely alarmed about what this portended for German intentions.

And what does this case suggest for the mechanisms posited in chapter 1? One mechanism posited that a country's remembrance shapes perceptions of its image and identity among other countries; the other hypothesized a link between remembrance and domestic mobilization. Indeed, both of these mechanisms resonate with French reasoning. French diplomats believed that, for European unity to succeed, German nationalism and xenophobia needed to be replaced with a more internationalist and European identity. French Occupation reforms and the early coordination of textbooks (as early as 1950) were pursued with this goal in mind. Throughout the postwar era, the French saw Germany's willingness to remember and atone as a sign of its cooperative and peaceful foreign policy.

As for domestic mobilization, the French (and British, as the next chapter will show) strongly believed in the link between mythologized, nationalistic history and domestic mobilization. Advocates of education reform invoked the example of World War I, after which the Germans had been free to purvey myths about the war that empowered Hitler's rise. But, interestingly, many Occupation officials after World War II warned of the backlash that would be sure to follow should Germany's conquerors interfere too much in its domestic affairs. As I will argue in the conclusion to this book, their concerns—while not borne out—were quite justified.

This case study also provides evidence relevant to the debate within international relations theory about the role of capabilities versus intentions in threat perception. The French discussed both as they assessed a potential

German threat. The role of capabilities was certainly significant: French fears were elevated when they viewed German power as unconstrained (1945 to the mid-1950s; also at the time of unification). They viewed West Germany as less threatening when they believed its capabilities to be low (after NATO admission in 1955; again after unification in 1990).

This case, however, also lends substantial support for the role of intentions in threat perception. The French observed remembrance among several other signals. At a time when German capabilities were expected to increase—for example, during rearmament in the 1950s and after unification—the French keenly watched for signals of German intentions. They were reassured by Germany's continued participation in European institutions and by its agreement to abandon its territorial claims. Germany's vibrant democracy was also another encouraging sign. Although testing for the influence of these alternate variables was not the central aim of this study, the Franco-German case supports scholars who argue that these factors shape perceptions of a country's intentions—and, more broadly, that intentions shape threat perception.

CHAPTER FOUR

# The Soul of a People Can Be Changed

It is a good rule in life never to apologize. The right sort of
people do not want apologies, and the wrong sort take a mean
advantage of them.

—P. G. Wodehouse, *The Man Upstairs*

In this book I argue that denials of past aggression and atrocities fuel distrust and elevate threat perception. Chapter 2 shows the link between
Japan's unapologetic remembrance and South Korean distrust of its intentions. This finding is further supported in chapter 3. Although the West
Germans did not justify or deny past atrocities, chapter 3 shows that the
French both carefully watched West German debates for signs of revisionism, and were reassured by its absence.

This chapter turns to additional cases to determine whether the link between remembrance and perceptions of intentions appears to be borne out
elsewhere. Is unapologetic remembrance really so damaging, or is there
something about South Korea—its culture, domestic politics, or specific experience with Japan—that makes Koreans particularly sensitive to Japanese
denials? I examine Chinese and Australian relations with Japan to determine whether they, like the South Koreans, reacted with anger and mistrust. I also turn to the case of British-German relations, to determine
whether or not the British paid attention to West Germany's remembrance
as they assessed its intentions.

Evidence from these cases indicates that, like the South Koreans, the
Chinese and Australians observe Japanese remembrance and specifically
connect their distrust of Japan to its denials of past violence. In the European case, although West Germany did not deny or glorify the Nazi era,
the British—like the French—watched its national debates and expressed
trepidation at even hints of historical revisionism.

Chapter title from Lord Robert Vansittart advocating German reeducation, *Black Record*
(1941).

159

## Remembrance in Sino-Japanese Relations

In April 2005 Chinese riot police watched passively as angry protestors hurled stones and bottles at Japan's embassy in Beijing and its consulate in Shanghai, defacing walls and shattering windows. Crowds of chanting, fist-shaking demonstrators took to the streets to vent their anger over Tokyo's approval of a textbook that glossed over past Japanese atrocities. Although order was eventually restored, Chinese resentment about Japan's remembrance continues to hang heavy over relations between Asia's two great powers.

Encouraged by Chinese Communist Party (CCP) propaganda, the Chinese people recall with vivid clarity a past that the Japanese remember only vaguely. Japan invaded and occupied China after 1931, turning Manchuria into the colony known as "Manchukuo." Chinese forces (of various factions in an ongoing civil war) battled the Japanese from 1931 to 1945. Casualty figures are murky, but scholars agree that anywhere between ten and twenty million Chinese people perished.

In this war, Japan committed horrific atrocities. Its air forces killed more than 250,000 civilians in bombing raids against Chinese cities.[1] Its army used chemical and biological weapons, and Japanese army doctors and scientists conducted macabre medical experiments on Chinese civilians and prisoners of war. Many such experiments were done by the infamous army laboratory called Unit 731. After the war's end, this unit cruelly and pointlessly released plague-infected rats into the population, killing 30,000 people. Japanese soldiers terrorized and massacred civilians in occupied territories. To deter people from aiding Chinese forces, the Japanese army slaughtered whole villages and destroyed livestock in its "three-alls" policy: "Kill all, burn all, destroy all." During the 1937 Nanjing Massacre, Japanese soldiers slaughtered inhabitants and raped innumerable girls and women; estimates of casualties range widely from 40,000 to 300,000 Chinese dead. As in Korea, Chinese people were mobilized to work in war industries: 37,000 were sent to Japan where they toiled unpaid, starved, and beaten. Girls and women were conscripted into sexual slavery as "comfort women." The Japanese thus committed staggering violence against the Chinese people during the war and occupation.[2]

Following the war, the first time that Tokyo and Beijing focused significant attention on issues of memory and war guilt was upon their diplomatic normalization in 1972. The People's Republic of China (PRC) requested a Japanese apology. Accordingly, the two sides issued a joint communiqué that said, "The Japanese side is keenly aware of Japan's responsibility for causing enormous damages in the past to the Chinese people through war and deeply reproaches itself."[3] Beijing accepted this statement graciously, assuring Tokyo that with respect to war guilt, "The Chinese people make a strict distinction between the very few militarists and the broad masses of the Japanese people." Other Chinese statements from the 1970s noted that although China "endure[d] tremendous disasters" during the war, "the Japanese people, too, suffered a great deal."[4] Upon normalization, Tokyo also gave Beijing a low-interest loan, which—although not linked to wartime misdeeds—was viewed by many people in both countries as reparations. China agreed to renounce any further reparations claims. Normalization was followed by a productive period of expanding trade ties and trilateral U.S.-Japanese-Chinese alignment against the Soviet Union.

## CHERISHING THE SPIRIT OF MILITARISM

Sino-Japanese relations began to sour in the 1980s because of history-related issues. Controversy over history textbooks was a major factor. After the Japanese and international media reported revisions to Japan's textbooks in 1982, Beijing protested the changes to Tokyo.[5] The Chinese media picked up the story; as scholar Allen Whiting notes, "A full-scale campaign ensued, recapitulating the story of Japanese aggression and atrocities in vivid detail. Photographs, films, reminiscences, and political cartoons accompanied dramatically worded captions, headlines, and commentaries that specifically warned against the danger of renewed Japanese militarism."[6]

The Chinese lambasted Japan's history education as "cherishing the spirit of Japanese militarism." The Chinese media said the "distortion" of textbooks evinced "a hostile attitude toward China and its people." The books were said to "signal a very serious danger" that should be carefully watched: they represented "an attempt by some people to revive militarism because historically, Japanese militarist education began at primary school."[7] As *Renmin Ribao* editorialized, "Memory of the past is the teacher for the future." *Beijing Review* criticized the Japanese Ministry of Education for attempting to "obliterate" history and "lay the basis for reviving militarism in Japan." Urging the Japanese people to "prevent a resurgence of militarism," *Beijing Review* also asserted that this was only possible "if they refuse to forget that period of history and [to] use its concrete facts as a lesson for successive generations." Commentator Liu Zheng excoriated "a handful of militarists who refuse to draw lessons from the wars of aggression and instead try to prettify them."[8] In Whiting's study of Chinese perceptions of Japan, his interlocutors stressed the importance of Japanese history books for bilateral relations. Whiting quotes one person as saying that the Chinese "want to make certain that the younger generation is properly taught the true lessons of history"; the author concludes that the Chinese perceive that a group in Japan is "capable of totally transforming public opinion over time through such indirect means as textbook revisions of history."[9]

The Chinese also expressed concern about the new significance of the Ya-sukuni Shrine. Japan's Prime Minister Miki Takeo had visited the shrine to Japan's war dead in 1975 without eliciting a major response from Beijing. But Yasukuni took on new meaning after 1978, when 1,068 convicted war criminals (including Prime Minister Tojo Hideki and thirteen other Class-A criminals), were enshrined there: thereafter Beijing and others viewed the shrine as glorifying the architects of war and atrocities.

By visiting the shrine in 1985, Japanese Prime Minister Nakasone Ya-suhiro sparked uproar among Chinese and other neighbors. Nakasone went to the shrine on August 15 (the anniversary of Japan's World War II surren-der); he was the first postwar prime minister to visit Yasukuni in an official capacity. *Renmin Ribao* decried Yasukuni as "the spiritual pillar of Japanese military ideology," arguing that "to officially visit the shrine and to worship the dead including the Class-A criminals implies that Japan has made a pub-lic announcement of its refusal to admit its war responsibility to the world." Asians should be "on their guard once again." Xinhua editorialized, "China hopes that the Japanese government will bow to the historical facts" to pre-vent "the renewal of militarism and the recurrence of any such crime." In September (on the anniversary of Japan's invasion of Manchuria in 1931), large anti-Japanese student demonstrations broke out in Beijing and other cities. Marching in Beijing's Tiananmen Square, students shouted "Down with Japanese militarism" and "Down with Nakasone."[10]

Chinese observers also expressed distrust of Japan when prominent lead-ers denied past atrocities. After the highly controversial remarks by Educa-tion Minister Fujio Masayuki in 1986 (see chapter 2), articles exhorted the Chinese people to "exercise vigilance to ensure historical truth and prevent a resurgence of militarism." Reacting to Okuno Seisuke's comments in 1988, one article said, "There really exists an extremely dangerous force and trend of thought in Japan." The article noted that this strain of Japanese na-tionalism "contains elements . . . of racial superiority and expansionism." Japan's neighbors, said the article, must be vigilant "to prevent a repeat of the war." Japanese denials and amnesia testified "to the existence of Japa-nese people still dreaming to create the Greater East Asia Co-prosperity Sphere planned by Japanese militarists during World War II."[11]

In the next two decades, the Chinese continued to distrust Japanese inten-tions, and continued to link their distrust to Japan's unapologetic remem-brance. Media coverage of the 1995 Diet Resolution debate included long feature articles about Japanese atrocities.[12] An article in Xinhua condemned remarks made by Education Minister Shimamura Yoshinobu and argued that politicians' "perceptions of history are often taken as attitudes of their nation over relations with other members of the international community." De-nouncing "right-wing forces" who were "clamoring for the spirit of mili-tarism," another article warned, "Countries in Asia and the rest of the world" could not possibly "rest assured" about Japan because of controversy there about its World War II crimes. The article rebuked Japanese conservatives for refusing to "admit their guilt" and for trying "to reverse the verdict on the 'Greater East Asia Co-prosperity Sphere.' "[13] The *China Daily* lambasted, "Denials of past atrocities . . . attest to the fact that [Japan is] unwilling to face its past and repent wrongdoing." In another article it concluded that Japan's "wish to distort the facts and rewrite its notorious history" showed it "has not and will never take responsibility" for its aggression.[14] In 2003, after Chinese construction workers were killed and wounded while excavating Japanese chemical weapons from World War II, a commentator writing in *Ming Pao* excoriated Japan for its "successive and increasingly more eager attempts to reverse the verdict [on Japanese aggression]."[15]

JAPANESE leaders since Nakasone had avoided Yasukuni Shrine for several years. The resumption of prime ministerial visits dismayed and angered the Chinese. The media condemned Prime Minister Koizumi Junichiro's 2001 visit. The newspaper *Jiefanjun Bao* stated, "To worship and pay respect to those war criminals is tantamount to an official sanction of Japan's past aggression and beautifies Japan's militarism." According to the *People's Daily*, "It is well known that the Shrine is a tool used to manipulate the feelings of the Japanese people, and to stir up militaristic spirit"; the shrine was a "symbol of Japan's overseas aggression and expansion in modern history." After Koizumi's January 2003 visit, Beijing complained to the Japanese ambassador. Vice Foreign Minister Yang Wenchang asserted, "Only a correct understanding of history can avoid a replay of historical tragedies" and "ensure the peace and development of the Asia-Pacific region." Beijing rejected a proposed summit between the two countries, issuing a statement that said "Koizumi's official visit to China is contingent on the Japanese premier not paying homage at Yasukuni Shrine."[16]

Recurring disputes about history textbooks showcased Chinese suspicions of Japan. In the spring 2005 dispute, in addition to the violence directed at the Japanese embassy in Beijing, protestors organized a boycott of Japanese products and vandalized Japanese stores and automobiles. "The protesters sang China's national anthem, 'March of the Volunteers,' and chanted slogans such as 'Down with Japanese imperialism!' and 'Rejuvenate China and raise our national prestige!' Some ripped down advertisements for Japanese products, and others carried a large banner that read, 'Selling Japanese products is shameful! Buying Japanese products is shameful!' "[17]

Chinese elites charged that Tokyo's "whitewashing" of textbooks signaled its remilitarization. During the initial debate about the controversial Fusosha textbook in 2001, the Chinese foreign minister said that history was a mirror to the future and that Japan's misleading of its younger generation "could lead to endless trouble." Foreign Ministry spokesman Zhu Bangzao said

Anti-Japanese protests in Beijing, 2005. AP PHOTO/GREG BAKER, FILE.

that the episode "reveals once again that in Japan there exist ultra-rightist forces who have been trying to deny and whitewash that country's history of aggression, and who are still bent on aggression," and that "their actions call for a high state of vigilance from peace-loving people around the world." As a Chinese Education Ministry spokesman argued, "textbooks should reflect true history, so as to cultivate the correct history perspectives of the youth and prevent the recurrence of historical tragedies." During the 2005 dispute, Foreign Ministry spokesman Qin Gang said that the protestors were motivated by "Japan's wrong attitude and actions on the history of the [Chinese] invasion." The PRC opposed Japan's bid for UN Security Council membership, declared Premier Wen Jiabao: "Only a country that respects history, takes responsibility for history and wins over the trust of peoples in Asia and the world at large can take greater responsibilities in the international community." Minster of Commerce Bo Xilai attributed the crisis to "the failure of the Japanese side to correctly deal with historical issues." The Fusosha textbook, said scholar Bu Ping, resembled books used by Japan's prewar governments to mobilize the population: it emphasized pride, service to the nation, and "the obligation of national defense." "The book is dangerous," he commented, because "it will mobilize Japanese people and children to future war."[18]

The Chinese media also continue to express concern about Japanese textbooks. Tokyo was "trying to shirk the blemishes and shadows caused by the war before the new millennium," complained one article, "erasing" them from the memory of younger generations. *China Daily* asserted that "ever-growing Japanese rightist forces" had "pushed the government to take action from time to time to distort historical facts." Tokyo's certification of this book reflected "conscious ignorance of the truth" and "paraded the strong influence of Japanese rightist forces." As a commentator warned, Tokyo was "stepping further on the road to militarism." The textbooks "cannot but arouse profound concerns among the public in Japan and the countries that fell victim to these wars and the international community at large." According to the *People's Daily*, "In recent years, Japanese rightists, though small in number, have been using the sluggish economy to drum up nationalism and militarism." In the 2005 dispute, a *China Daily* editorial slammed the Fusosha text because it "reasserts the wartime ideology that Japan's invasions of China, the Korean Peninsula and Southeast Asia were justified acts of self-defense." The editorial approvingly cited efforts by Seoul and Beijing to block Japan from obtaining a permanent seat on the UN Security Council; it said, "Without a consensus on the history issue and other disputes, the Asian peoples cannot place their trust in Japan's desire to play a bigger role in world affairs."[19] An article argued that approval of the Fusosha book "will undoubtedly further strain Japan's relations with Asian neighbors, which have been uneasy over Japan's reluctance to acknowledge its war crimes and apologize for its atrocities. Japan is losing trust among its Asian neighbors." In sum, like the South Koreans, the Chinese observed Japan's unapologetic remembrance and linked it to their distrust of Japan's intentions.

## IS THIS JUST DOMESTIC POLITICS?

One might question whether the Chinese statements quoted here are true reflections of distrust. Scholars have argued that—particularly since the 1980s—the CCP has deliberately cultivated nationalism in order to respond to growing threats to its legitimacy, and that anti-Japanese sentiment is a core component of Chinese nationalism.[20] Indeed, skeptics might dismiss much of the evidence referenced here (particularly leaders' public statements or quotes from state-controlled media) as domestic political theater. Perhaps all of this outcry among officials and the media is not a reflection of true distrust, but rather of the CCP's effort to whip up nationalism among the Chinese people.

The data cited here, however, align with evidence from private interviews with Chinese foreign policy elites: evidence that is less vulnerable to the charge of domestic political posturing. In his seminal study, *China Eyes Japan*, Allen Whiting described "the mixture of suspicion, cynicism, anger and hostility" toward Japan evident in his 1980s interviews with Chinese elites. Whiting commented on the "singular and strong negative attitude" toward the Japanese, whom the Chinese said showed a "pernicious tendency toward future militarism." He noted, "as became repetitively clear, a powerful consensus . . . viewed Japan with mistrust and suspicion. This view became more heatedly expressed the longer and more intensive the discussion, or, alternatively, the more informal and alcoholic the ambience, suggesting that it genuinely reflected personal feelings."[21]

Nearly two decades later, Thomas Christensen commented that his numerous interviews reflected "historically based mistrust and animosity" toward Japan. Christensen discussed the possibility that concerns about Japan expressed by Chinese leaders might be a "spin" strategy pursued cynically to justify increased military spending. But he argued that "given the large number of interlocutors, the diversity of opinions expressed on various issues over the five years of my discussions, and the controversial positions I sometimes heard expressed on issues such as the Tiananmen massacre or the Chinese missile exercises near Taiwan, I find it difficult to believe that Beijing, or any other government, could manufacture such complex theater over such an extended period of time."[22]

Not only do scholars conclude from interviews that their interlocutors genuinely distrust Japan, they say that this stems in large part from Japan's unapologetic remembrance. As Whiting reported, many Chinese leaders fear that Japanese textbook revisionism shows that some Japanese nationalists are trying to transform public opinion so that it supports a more militarily assertive posture. That is, "The Chinese see the Japanese desire to avoid discussion of their aggressive record as a deliberate effort to justify behavior that can one day be repeated more successfully." Christensen maintained that animosity toward Japan has been fed by "Tokyo's refusal to respond satisfactorily to Chinese requests that Tokyo recognize and apologize for its imperial past." Yinan He agrees: "The shadow of war history has intensified the Chinese perception of Japan's negative intention," making China increasingly sensitive to the bilateral balance of power.[23]

In sum, critics might be tempted to question whether evidence from the Chinese case reflects genuine mistrust. It is true that the Chinese government relies on, and consciously manipulates, anti-Japanese sentiment for its domestic political legitimacy. But at the same time—as evident from private communications—Japan's unapologetic remembrance has indeed fueled Chinese distrust of its intentions.

## Remembrance in Australian-Japanese Relations

Aso Taro, a powerful figure in Japan's Liberal Democratic Party, was foreign minister under both Koizumi and Abe Shinzo. Known for his nationalist views—such as exhorting the emperor to visit Yasukuni Shrine—Aso is a controversial figure who lost the prime ministership in 2007 to the tamer Fukuda Yasuo. He remains a serious contender to be a future prime minister.

During World War II, when Aso was a four-year-old boy, Australian and other POWs labored in the mines owned by his family company, Aso Mining. Mick Kildey describes the conditions he and other Allied POWs endured in Aso's Yoshikawa coal mine. "We were beaten half to death, starved and covered with vermin you could never get rid of. . . . We never had enough to eat, not enough clothes to keep warm . . . [and were] sent down to dangerous pit levels where the Japanese would not go." John Hall, another Australian survivor, recalls: "If you slipped or failed you were beaten with rifle butts or fists. Once I was smashed in the face with a rifle butt for stealing an onion and I still wake at nights sweating and see that guard." Max Venables was a POW at Changi camp in Singapore who was beaten, starved, and worked to near-death by the Japanese. Writing shortly after the announcement of deeper military ties between Japan and Australia, the 85-year-old veteran acknowledged, "For those who welcome the 'normalization' of Japan, that may seem a long time ago. But if I close my eyes, I can see, hear and smell a different Japan—a country I still can't trust."[24]

Many Australians remember their terrible war with Japan. At sixtieth anniversary observances of the end of the war in 2005, in an emotional speech Prime Minister John Howard bluntly recalled the "barbarity" of Australia's "cruel enemy."[25] Japan neither invaded nor occupied Australian territory during the war. However, for the first time in their history, Australians feared an invasion, particularly after Japanese advances in New Guinea. The war came to Australian shores with the Japanese strategic bombing of Darwin in February 1942. Japanese air forces also attacked Broome and other coastal towns; Sydney Harbor was raided in May 1942 by Japanese midget submarines. Australian naval forces fought alongside the Allies in the Pacific, and Australian "Diggers," as their soldiers are nicknamed, battled in the savage island-hopping campaigns. Important Australian efforts occurred in Milne Bay in Papua, in which the Japanese suffered their first defeat on land, and in the Kokoda campaign, which halted the advance on Port Moresby. During the war, Japanese held over 20,000 Australian POWs, who suffered horrendous abuse, starvation, and often execution. Many POWs were forced to work in Japanese factories (such as Aso Mining) or on the frontlines digging trenches and performing other hard labor. An astonishing one-third of them perished in captivity.[26] Mistreatment of POWs, and the high fatality rate in Japanese camps, fueled a loathing of Japan that many Australians harbor to this day.

Thrown together by their mutual American ally and mutual Soviet adversary, Japan and Australia began to reconcile in the 1950s. A signatory of the San Francisco Peace Treaty, Australia normalized relations with Japan much earlier than non-signatories China and South Korea. The apology issue arose in the context of diplomatic normalization, a process that featured summits in both countries. Visiting Australia in 1957, Japanese Prime Minister Kishi Nobusuke laid a wreath at the National War Memorial. He said, "It is my official duty, and my personal desire, to express to the people of Australia our heartfelt sorrow for what occurred in the war." Australian Prime Minister Robert Menzies received the statement graciously; he acknowledged that World War II created "the most bitter of feelings" between the two states and said that enthusiasm about Kishi's visit showed "that we have reached the wise conclusion it is sometimes better to hope than always to remember." Australia and Japan, he said, should "concentrate our minds on peace."[27] Wider reactions to Kishi's visit were also positive. Upbeat press coverage detailed the various stops on his tour (for example, one newspaper ran on its front page a picture of a smiling Kishi holding a Koala bear). There were some stirrings of controversy: Some veterans sought to prevent Kishi from attending the wreath-laying ceremony, and the event was disrupted by a man shouting that it was "an infamous day for Australia." However, the Returned and Services League (RSL) veterans' group was supportive. Its leadership squelched internal dissent about the visit and called the ceremony "a respectful salute to Australians who perished in all theatres of war" and "a sign of the growing awareness of the need for a strong mutual link between our two countries." Overall, the trip was a success. Some anti-Japanese sentiment lingered in subsequent years, but in general, Australians accepted Kishi's apology and did not pay much attention to Japanese remembrance for several decades.[28]

The issue of war memory reappeared in the headlines when the Japanese Emperor died in January 1989. Australians debated Hirohito's war responsibility and Japan's record of contrition.[29] They discussed history textbooks and visits to the Yasukuni Shrine (examined below); they followed the evolution of the "comfort women" issue and recalled wartime atrocities after the release of a film about a women's POW camp.[30]

During these debates, Australians expressed concerns about Japan's denials of its wartime misdeeds. Tokyo "has shown a doggedness in refusing to acknowledge responsibility for some of the worst atrocities in human history," asserted one article in the *Canberra Times*.[31] Criticizing the "unapologetic interpretation of the past" in history textbooks, another article maintained that Japan "has failed to decry the excesses of its imperial rule." Tokyo was condemned for its "policy of downplaying Japan's guilt for the sufferings of other Asians during World War II." An article condemned the "inconsistency in the Japanese approach to history," noting that textbooks and Koizumi's shrine visits contradict his apologies. Australian citizens' groups also criticized Japan's failure to pay reparations. RSL members staged protests against Tokyo's policies, including turning their backs on Emperor Akihito while he passed by in a parade and successfully lobbying to remove the word "Peace" from a "Japanese Peace Park" built in Canberra. They declared the park's name "inappropriate" given that "Japan had not fully apologized for the war."[32]

Australian prime ministers regularly pressure Tokyo to atone for its past atrocities. In 1991 Bob Hawke "urged Japan to acknowledge its guilt for war-time horrors"; the following year Paul Keating did the same. Visiting Tokyo in 1995, Keating raised the issue again, saying, "We believe that Japan should not allow these events to be forgotten." In 1998 acting Prime Minister Tim Fischer said, "An appropriate gesture would be sought" from Tokyo in the next state visit. "I think there is a problem in Japan in relation to history," said John Howard in 2002, which is "understandably a problem with many people in Australia." Howard added, "I do hope that they face the realities of their past as all societies must."[33]

Although the two countries enjoy peaceful and productive relations, Australian doubts about Japan linger because of its unapologetic remembrance. "Lack of atonement and reparations for war crimes in Asia," argued one article, "has become the chief obstacle to normal relations between Japan and its neighbours." Tom Uren, a government minister and former POW, commented that distrust persists because Tokyo has not acknowledged its war crimes and because many ultranationalists want to restore the country to a major military power. "There is a large element in Japan," he said, "that wants to return to the position before the last war." Several articles described omissions in history textbooks and visits to the Yasukuni Shrine as nascent signs of militarism. Japan was criticized for emphasizing its own victimhood in the annual remembrance ceremonies on August 15.

An article in the *Australian Financial Review* reflected the these concerns: "There is no recognition of Japan as an aggressor nation, the 1937 [Nanjing Massacre], forced prostitution of the 'comfort women,' forced labour of two million Koreans, the murders of millions of Asians and thousands of European POWs." Citing the "drumbeat" of nationalism in Japan, one commentator argued, "We can never be entirely comfortable about a partner which has failed conspicuously to come to terms with its past."[34]

Australians regularly discuss Japan's unapologetic remembrance as they contemplate its increasing military activism. An article in the *Australian Financial Review* pointed out trepidation among East Asians about the 1996 Guidelines for Defense Cooperation, maintaining that "few nations in the region are willing to forget Japanese aggression in World War II partially because not too many of Japan's post-war leaders" have been willing to apologize for the war. Another article mentioned various signs of Japanese nationalism (school textbooks, the Yasukuni Shrine, statements of denial) and argued, "What must be of concern to Japan's neighbors, including Australia, is the possibility that the ghosts of wartime past are increasingly able to influence developments in Japan." The article supported greater Japanese burden sharing, but invoked the example of the United States arming Afghanis against the Soviets in the 1980s and cautioned about empowering an ally that one might later have to fight. A bilateral agreement for joint exercises and training of Japanese troops in Australia prompted controversy in 2007: While Canberra embraced closer security ties, the national debate reflected great uncertainty. Although ultimately arguing that Japan is a "totally different country," one commentator noted that many Australians have doubts because the "barbarity of the Japanese Imperial Army is not easily forgotten" and because the Japanese were reluctant "to deal with the demons of the past, warts and all." Journalist Shane Green lamented that although Australians were taught about Japanese aggression as an "unchallenged fact of recent history"—the same is not true in Japan: "At the Yasukuni museum, there is a different story." Green asserted that the "lack of real contrition has now assumed an even greater importance," because Japan—facing threats from North Korea—was contemplating major changes in its security strategy. It questioned, "Should we worry about Japan's new defense posture? Probably not. But as long as Japanese prime ministers continue to make visits to Yasukuni, it is an assurance that must be qualified."[35]

In July 2006, Japanese Foreign Minister Aso Taro visited the Juganji Temple near Osaka, which once housed the remains of over a thousand Allied POWs who perished as forced laborers. As mentioned above, Aso's family owns the company formerly known as Aso Mining, which during World War II relied on forced labor. Aso's younger brother runs the company. At the ceremony, Aso thanked the temple priests, who hold an annual ceremony to honor the memory of the POWs. He said he "would like to pray for the souls of the people who passed away." The Australian government called Aso's private visit "a genuine gesture of reconciliation which we understand and appreciate."[36]

Not long thereafter, however, Tokyo issued a curt denial about wartime forced labor. In response to a *New York Times* article, the government of Japan said it was "not in a position to comment on employment forms and conditions of a private company, Aso Mining, at that time. However our government has not received any information the company has used forced laborers. It is totally unreasonable to make this kind of judgmental description without presenting any evidence." Denials such as these have not prevented Australia and Japan from establishing a cooperative relationship that, in the days of China's rise, appears to be moving closer. However, Japan's unapologetic remembrance has contributed to lingering Australian wariness about Tokyo. As one article put it, "How can other nations trust a Japan that appears increasingly determined to forget and ignore its past aggression?"[37]

EVIDENCE from the cases of Sino-Japanese and Australian-Japanese relations substantiates my findings from chapter 2 that a country's unapologetic remembrance sustains distrust among its former adversaries. As in South Korea, both Chinese and Australians argue that Japan's denials make them wary of its intentions. Whereas critics might dismiss findings from the Japan-Korea case as idiosyncratic, support for these findings in the cases of China and Australia suggests their broader applicability. In particular, the Australian case bolsters the argument that concerns about Japanese remembrance should not be dismissed as political posturing: a mature democracy, Australia has no need to fan anti-Japanese nationalism to prop up its regime. Because Australia is an Anglo-Saxon culture, its perspective also suggests that concerns about denials transcend cultures.

South Korean, Chinese, and Australian reactions to Japanese remembrance or assessments of Japanese intentions are far from uniform. National differences certainly appear: for example, disputes between Japan and its neighbors over historical memory resonate far more in Korean and Chinese politics than in Australia.[38] Japan's relations with South Korea, and with Australia, are far more productive than the Sino-Japanese relationship. However despite differences in their cultures, political systems, and levels of victimization, all three countries observe Japanese remembrance and express alarm about its denials.

## Remembrance in British-German Relations

"I awoke to hear a roar and a thundering," one Londoner wrote in her diary, "to feel that horrible 'got you' thud of a heavy bomb and the sound of half the world raining down on us. My mother and sister were both giving little screams; I put my arms round my sister and said 'It's all right' several times. Mother got off her bed, crying 'The house has been hit' as she ran to the stairs." Emerging from the house timidly, this London family looked around the chaos to see that two nearby houses had been destroyed and a third "seemed to have its roof sliced off." The family panicked as once again "suddenly shells started bursting overhead." "We heard Jerry feeling his way back—I suppose looking to see what he had done."[39]

Having just fought "Jerry" from 1914 to 1918, the British found themselves at war again: this time fearing an invasion made possible by the fall of France. Once again they experienced the carnage of continental battlefields, losing another 300,000 British soldiers in World War II. At home they endured the Blitz: the Luftwaffe bombed British cities in 1940–41 to attempt to coerce London to withdraw from the war. Millions of people evacuated to the countryside. In those two years, over 44,000 British civilians were killed and approximately 250,000 wounded.[40]

After the war, traumatized by bombings and European battlefields, the British felt great hostility toward the Germans. This only intensified as the liberation of concentration camps revealed the extent of German barbarity. In 1941 Robert Vansittart authored a best-selling book, *Black Record: Germans Past and Present*, which argued that the German "race" was "vicious and guilty." Views of Germany's wicked national character were common among both the public and elites. Historian Donald Cameron Watt observed that at war's end, most British scholarship reflected "a deep and enduring antipathy to Germany and all things German." Prime Minister Clement Atlee remarked that he had never met a good German, except perhaps a housemaid his family had once employed. Foreign Minister Ernest Bevin, in his Cockney accent, made what would later be a famous statement to Sir Brian Robertson, the British Military Governor in Germany: "I tries 'ard, Brian, but I 'ates 'em."[41]

## TILL THEN WE WILL NOT BE SAFE AGAIN

As the British discussed their distrust of the Germans, they frequently expressed concerns over the direction of German remembrance. After the war, British elites worried that—as after World War I—the Germans would craft a mythology of their victimhood that would nurture German nationalism and militarism. To combat this, many officials argued in favor of "reeducation." Others were skeptical, arguing that such an effort would be futile or counterproductive. "We cannot re-educate Germany," wrote British official T. H. Marshall. A Foreign Office report concluded, "Any scheme for the reeducation of Germans, young or old, by means of textbooks, teachers, censors, or advisors, may be ruled out as futile." Other British officials—who had allies among many German conservatives—opposed reeducation because, they argued, British interference in Germany's domestic affairs would prompt a nationalist backlash and jeopardize democratic stability. Ultimately, proponents of education reform invoked a simple but powerful argument: look what happened last time. After World War I, Britain and its allies had contemplated education reform but had rejected it because of similar arguments about ineffectiveness or backlash. As a British Occupation official later noted, "In 1918 we had pretty well left it to the Germans" to decide how to change their society, and "There was general agreement that they had made a pretty inadequate job of it."[42]

Thus, British plans to democratize and denationalize West Germany won out, and Occupation authorities embarked on education reform. Scholar E. H. Carr held that Germany's defeat would usher in "a state of moral and intellectual exhaustion and chaos" and that the Allies had to introduce "a new European perspective." Occupation authorities sought "to help build up in Germany an education which will make it a country of free men, ready to live at peace with its neighbors, and to use its immense gifts for the benefit of the world and not for its destruction . . . ." Together with their allies, the British planned "to build up democracy 'from the bottom upwards' with the help of new democratic forces which were to emerge in Germany with the help of re-education." Lord Vansittart—who had argued that Europe faced an eternal threat from "a deep-seated flaw in the German 'national character' "—nonetheless believed, "the soul of a people *can* be changed." Vansittart advocated "drastic" interventionism by the Allies in German education, and speculated that it would take "at least a generation" to succeed. Conservative member of Parliament Sir George Cockerell discussed the need to "eradicate" those "deep-rooted traditions that glorify physical force, assert a claim to racial superiority, justify territorial aggrandizement, and challenge all the liberties for which democracies are fighting." He contended, "There can be no place in a sane world for German untutored independence." Clement Atlee, drafting plans for the Occupation, asserted, "Everything that brings home to the Germans the completeness and irrevocability of their defeat is worthwhile in the end."[43]

As part of reeducation, the British encouraged "German atonement and 'guilt mobilization.' "[44] Education official Michael Balfour wrote, "The question of guilt was fundamental to Britain's relationship with the German people." "With one eye clearly on the experiences of Versailles," he continued, unless justice and an accurate history of the war were established, "it will remain (in German eyes) merely the kind of settlement which the victorious side imposes by force of arms at the end of the war."[45] Foreign Minister Gordon Walker, who had visited Belsen after the surrender, said that the only hope for future peace was "if the German people admits and recognises, both openly and in its heart, that these 12 years have been the blackest in the whole of Europe's history. If this becomes part of the German conscience and tradition, there is some hope, if not, none." Walker argued that Britain must "purge the German soul" by teaching the truth "in German schools, in

German history, in literature, in sermons, in cinemas, in conversation, beyond chance of reversal. Till then we will not be safe again."[46]

The British emphasized a few key lessons in reeducation. First, they wanted to prevent the emergence of myths such as the "stab-in-the-back" legend that the German government purveyed after the First World War. This *Dolchstosslegende* held that Germany had not lost the war on the battlefield, but rather on the home front: Leftists, foreigners within Germany, gypsies, and the Jews had caused the German defeat by undermining unity and morale. After World War II, rather than have the Germans emerge from the war making excuses and pointing fingers, the British wanted to encourage them to confront the bald truth of their military defeat "for the purpose of teaching the Germans that war does not pay."[47] Second, the British wanted Germans to know about the atrocities they had committed. Understanding the need to balance reeducation with the establishment of order, Occupation authorities said that they would "emphasize German war guilt, as long as it was 'considered to be psychologically desirable.' " In their Occupation zone, the British launched a publicity campaign to educate people about the death camps, saying that "the moral responsibility for these crimes must be laid wholly and solely on the German nation."[48] One of the centerpieces of the British effort was the POW reeducation program at Wilton Park, where German prisoners were tutored about democracy and had to sit through a film about the liberation of Belsen. In sum, after the war the British feared the revival of German nationalism and militarism: to forestall the rise of German nationalism, they implemented policies to shape remembrance of the war.

## WHO ARE THE GERMANS, AND WHAT IS GERMANY?

Throughout the postwar era, the British observed West Germany's national debates about its past and expressed wariness at signs of historical revisionism. They noted Bonn's amnesia during the early postwar years. "For most of the past 20 years," contended the *Times* in 1965, "they wanted merely to forget." The article characterized controversy about the May 8 anniversary of the surrender as a German "awakening" after twenty years of dodging the past. An article in the *Guardian* that same year commented on Bonn's inability to deal with its past as follows: "It is no easy thing for a nation to admit that it is capable, as it were, of committing murder . . . and the Germans, for the most part, have failed to do so."[49]

In the 1980s the British watched with interest Bonn's struggles with war memory. British media criticized Helmut Kohl's "clumsy" attempts to move Germany forward. Kohl's Bitburg visit, said one article, "has reopened the deepest wounds in their society, stimulated angst and let loose a torrent of recrimination." During the Historian's Debate in Germany, some commentators expressed fears of a German nationalist resurgence. "Four decades later," one *Guardian* article lamented, "the Germans still haven't come to terms with 'the whole truth' "; German historians, the author asserted, were making excuses for the Holocaust. The article noted the recent Jenninger gaffe, which was called "the tip of the iceberg" of German revisionism.[50] West German remembrance was explicitly linked to its intentions; another *Guardian* article commented that Kohl's actions represented "an ambitious and controversial step towards answering the question that has long tormented historians and philosophers: Who are the Germans, and what is Germany?" While following the Historian's Debate, the press noted that this was not merely an academic dispute: "The Historian's Quarrel about the Nazi period is really about the future" and the kind of people the Germans would be in the 1990s.[51]

For the most part, the British were reassured by West Germany's engagement with its past. Although sometimes rebuked in the British press, Kohl was often portrayed sympathetically: as spearheading a national effort to "gain confidence" or to craft "a sense of identity."[52] "To be fair," one article noted, "Kohl doesn't want the Holocaust forgotten or excused. To clear any doubt on that he went to Auschwitz to make the point." The media also reported Kohl's speech at Bergen-Belsen concentration camp. Covering the Bitburg Cemetery visit, the British, like the French, castigated Reagan far more than Kohl for the blunder. An article critical of the Bitburg visit nonetheless praised West German contrition, noting that a "sense of guilt has entered deeply into the West German character. It is kept there in the classroom, where schoolchildren are taught about Nazism, and in school outings to the sites of extermination camps. A close watch is kept on extreme right-wing groups, even though their following is negligible."

British observers pondering the prospect of German unification discussed—among other things—German remembrance. Their debates reflect conflicting views. Some people praised Germany's willingness to confront its past as grounds to trust its future intentions. In March 1990 Margaret Thatcher held a meeting at her estate at Chequers in which she discussed with advisors the implications of German reunification. As transcribed in the leaked minutes of the meeting, many of the British intellectuals who attended urged Thatcher to recognize that the Germans had changed and linked their optimism to German contrition. As transcribed in the meeting's notes: "There was . . . no more militarism. Education and the writing of history had changed. There was an innocence of and about the past on the part of the new generation of Germans. We should have no real worries about them." Scholars Timothy Garton Ash, Hugh Trevor-Roper (Lord Dacre), and Gordon Craig argued that the British should be reassured about the Germans because of their willingness to admit and atone for their past violence. Participant George Urban commented, "No one would wish to deny the Nazis' guilt, least of all the Germans themselves."

Urban said that most participants agreed that although there could be no guarantee of benign German behavior in the future, "the record of the Federal Republic had been very good. German attitudes, both private and public, had fundamentally changed since 1945. The teaching of history in German schools was so thoroughly reformed that we need not fear a return of extreme nationalism, much less any kind of Nazi mentality."[53]

A second view, however, dismissed German remembrance as an unreliable or irrelevant signal. Thatcher's advisors commented that it had apparently never occurred to her to pay attention to German memory. Urban wrote, "She seemed to have no knowledge of the strength of the anti-Nazi element in German politics, or of the power of self-incrimination in the whole of post-war German political culture." Thatcher and others argued that although West Germany may have pursued deferential policies, *unified* Germany would be different. "Could the Germans be trusted?" she queried. "What about those Prussians and Saxons who were now joining West Germany but had had no experience, since 1933, of any political system other than Nazism and Stalinism? How did we know what they might do or think?"[54] Others also maintained that Germany—having attained its goal of unification—could now abandon its deferential Cold War policies and would be free to embrace nationalism. Noted journalist Conor Cruise O'Brien commented, "Reunification will be celebrated with an explosion of nationalist enthusiasm, and rejection of everything thought to have been imposed on Germany." He argued that the Germans would soon change their historical interpretations; that "Germans have spent too long groveling to foreigners"; and that "now Germany will get off its knees." Cruise O'Brien noted that "nationalist intellectuals will explain that true Germans should feel not guilt but pride about the Holocaust . . . . The self-awarded 'not-guilty' verdict will be welcomed by the German public."[55]

Many skeptics believed in an unchanging German national character (the view most associated with Robert Vansittart's writings from the 1940s). Scholar Nile Gardiner summarized the view of many people from the wartime generation who rejected any argument that the Germans had "changed their spots." He wrote, "There is a populist, age-old suspicion of the German race, coupled with resentment mixed with fear, which has resurfaced in the 1990s in reaction to German unification and Chancellor Kohl's vision of a unified Europe." Thatcher herself repeatedly echoed Vansittart: "I do believe in national character," she wrote in her autobiography; "Since the unification of Germany under Bismarck . . . Germany has veered unpredictably between aggression and self-doubt." Thatcher told advisors, "We know perfectly well what the Germans are like . . . and how national character basically doesn't change." Urban wrote that at Chequers, Thatcher had listened to scholars who discussed postwar German contrition and democratization: "I'm not sure that MT was swayed by any of this," he commented, "because she went on and on telling us, 'Yes, yes, but you can't *trust* them.' "[56]

The British, like the French, continued to observe German remembrance in the years after German unification. The media reported and expressed concern about revisionist trends. For example, the press described the activities of German conservatives on the fiftieth anniversary of Germany's surrender and followed the controversy sparked by Martin Walser's statements that Germany should no longer emphasize its shameful past.[57] However, for the most part the British praised Germany's candor. The media reported a myriad of German remembrances: the memorial to the 1933 book burning; the opening of a museum at the Wannsee villa about the "Final Solution"; German reactions to the film *Schindler's List;* and the charitable activities of German youths abroad.[58] One article said that the German media "have flooded the public with recollections of the war years. Every town has felt obliged to mount lectures and exhibitions. Berlin alone is staging more than 40 war exhibitions or performances. 'Never again' has been the signature to this deluge." In the wake of controversies over the Goldhagen book and the Memorial to the Murdered Jews of Europe, an article in the *Financial Times* noted that such debates "always focus on the past and the issue of coming to terms with the Third Reich" and were "therapeutic" for German political culture.[59]

In sum, evidence from the British case supports my claim that acknowledgment of past atrocities facilitates international reconciliation. Like the French, the British imposed education reforms within their zone of occupation, seeking to prevent German mythmaking and nationalist resurgence. In subsequent years, the British watched German national debates about the past for signs of revisionism: They were reassured by Bonn's willingness to confront it past crimes, and by the absence of nationalist themes.

Also like the French, the British evaluated other indicators of West German intentions or threat: particularly capabilities. Initially loath to accept West German conventional rearmament, London eventually acquiesced, but warned about excessive increases in German military power and demanded that Bonn accept tight constraints on its military capabilities.[60] Afraid of a "German finger on the nuclear trigger," as Prime Minister Harold Wilson put it, London rebuffed any diplomatic effort that might lead Germany to an independent nuclear weapons capability.[61] While capabilities were significant in British threat assessment, evidence from this case also shows that the British were deeply concerned about West Germany's remembrance of the war and what it signaled about its intentions.

## Denials and Mistrust

Chapter 2 concluded from the Japan-South Korea case that unapologetic remembrance sustains mistrust between former adversaries. Because critics might wonder whether this finding is idiosyncratic to Korea, I examined additional cases to see if it appears to be borne out elsewhere. The cases of British-German relations and Japan's relations with China and Australia provide further support that countries observe each other's remembrance and regard denials as a signal of hostile intentions.

Concerns about the pernicious effects of denials extend beyond the cases of postwar Germany and Japan. Israeli alarm about possible Iranian nuclear weapons acquisition has been heightened by a number of malevolent signals from Iran, not the least of which is President Ahmadinejad's Holocaust denial. Israelis and the international community alike decry the Iranian president's claim that the Jews "invented a myth that the Jews were massacred." An Israeli Foreign Ministry spokesman responded, "What the Iranian president has shown us today is that he is clearly outside the international consensus, he is clearly outside international norms and international legitimacy, and in so doing he has shown the Iranian government for what it is—a rogue regime opposed to peace and stability and a threat to all its neighboring countries." Israelis also expressed pessimism about peace with the Palestinian Authority upon the release of Palestinian textbooks that whitewashed the Holocaust and taught a Middle East geography that omitted the presence of an Israeli state. A report to the Knesset issued by a media watch organization said that the textbooks "glorify terror and teach their children to hate Israel, vilify Israel's existence, and define the battle with Israel as an uncompromising religious war." The *Jerusalem Post* called the books "a tragic recipe for incessant war," because they portray Israel as "an illegitimate enemy to be hated, fought and destroyed."

Similarly, Turkey's denial of the Armenian genocide fuels distrust among its former victims. The Armenian foreign minister notes "a lingering security concern about a neighbor that has not repudiated such state violence." The European Union has demanded Turkish acknowledgment of the genocide before it is willing to approve Turkey's application for EU membership.[62] All over the world, countries fear their neighbors who fail to acknowledge past violence.

# Conclusion

Look not mournfully into the past. . . . Wisely improve the
present. It is thine. Go forth to meet the shadowy future,
without fear.

— Henry Wadsworth Longfellow

The sixtieth anniversary of the end of World War II showcased a striking difference between Europe and Asia. In Europe, relations among the major powers have never been better—highlighted by Germany's dramatic reconciliation with its former enemies. Germans spent decades confronting and atoning for the terrible crimes of the Nazi era. Today, the Federal Republic is welcomed as a leader in international diplomacy and trade; its military forces now fight alongside those of its allies in UN and NATO operations. The warmth of European relations was felt in 2004, when the former Allies invited German Chancellor Gerhard Schröder to attend the sixtieth anniversary commemoration of the Normandy invasion. Standing alongside the leaders of countries that had been Germany's bitter adversaries, Schröder celebrated the anniversary as a day that marked Germany's liberation from fascism. French newspapers, decorated with photos of the German chancellor and French president in a warm embrace, proclaimed "the last day of World War II."[1]

In Asia, by contrast, sixty years have not soothed the jangled nerves of Japan's neighbors. They watch in dismay as Tokyo apologizes for war and colonization amid a chorus of domestic acrimony and even denials. In 2005, Japan's education ministry approved textbooks widely perceived as whitewashing past atrocities, triggering violent protests in Beijing: demonstrators overturned and torched Japanese cars, vandalized Japanese-owned businesses, and threw rocks and bottles at the Japanese embassy. Embraces between heads of state were not an option: summit visits had been cancelled amid rancor over textbooks and shrine visits. Relations between Japan and its neighbors remain fraught with distrust.

The stark difference between relations in Europe and Asia suggests a simple lesson about international politics: Contrition is vital for postwar reconciliation, and the more deeply countries repent their past violence, the more they will improve relations with their former adversaries. Germany, after all, has done more to atone for its historical crimes than any country in history, and it has warm relations with its neighbors; Japan has been far less apologetic, and its neighbors harbor deep mistrust about Tokyo's intentions.

This book both supports and challenges this common view. First, my analysis of the Japanese and German cases substantiates the claim that denying and glorifying past violence fuels distrust and impedes reconciliation. Japan's unapologetic remembrance—for example, repeated denials by high-ranking leaders and efforts to whitewash Japan's history textbooks—fans Korean suspicions of Japanese intentions and elevates threat perception. Koreans are not unique in their anger about Japanese denials. Chinese and Australians also distrust Japan and link their distrust to its failure to acknowledge past violence. In Europe, Bonn's acceptance of responsibility for Germany's crimes facilitated reconciliation with former adversaries. After the war, France and Britain worried greatly about the resurgence of German nationalism. In their Occupation policies they sought to contain this danger by preventing Germany from engaging in nationalist mythmaking about the war. French and British concerns lingered: throughout the postwar era, they carefully watched West Germany's national debates. They were reassured by Bonn's repudiation of its past, and were worried when they perceived even hints of revisionism. These findings all show that avoiding denials and glorification of past violence is an important step for moving relations forward.

Many analysts have pointed to the German model to argue that international reconciliation requires countries to "come to terms with the past." But my second finding overturns this claim. Countries do not need to model Germany's *Vergangenheits-bewältigung* in order to soothe relations with former adversaries. Many bitter enemies—including West Germany and France—successfully reconciled with only modest contrition. In the early years after the war, Bonn demonstrated very little. While it offered a tepid apology and paid reparations to Israel, West German commemoration, education, and public discourse ignored the atrocities Germany had committed, and instead mourned *German* suffering during and after the war. Surprisingly, this era of minimal contrition witnessed a profound reconciliation between France and West Germany. By the early 1960s, the French viewed the West Germans as a close friend and ally. Bonn had not yet begun the major campaign of atonement that would later distinguish it in the world: the formal and repeated apologies, the memorials to Germany's victims, and the textbooks filled with candid descriptions of the war and Holocaust.

Other World War II adversaries were able to repair their relations with even fewer expressions of remorse. Neither the British nor the Americans have apologized for fire-bombing German cities, yet both countries successfully restored peaceful and cooperative relations with West Germany after the war. Japan and the United States have extremely friendly relations and a solid military alliance, despite the fact that Washington has repeatedly refused to apologize for killing nearly a million civilians while burning down the sixty-eight largest Japanese cities. Tokyo has not apologized for Pearl Harbor or the abuse of American POWs.[2] Both governments continue to justify their actions as necessary given the strategic situation at the time.[3] Furthermore, Vienna's European partners sang along with the *Sound of Music* myth that Austria was a country of steadfast Hitler opponents victimized by the Nazis. Italy's postwar allies similarly indulged its mythology of victimization and resistance. Although a basic acknowledgment of past violence appears to be an important step toward reconciliation, the Franco-German and other cases show that countries have successfully restored their relations with little, if anything, beyond this.

Finally, my analysis draws attention to an issue that has been neglected in debates about contrition and international justice: the potential dangers of contrition. The media, NGOs, scholars, and governments have been increasingly vocal in demanding that countries offer apologies and reparations for past human rights abuses. However, the Japan case shows that contrition can spark a domestic backlash that poisons the very relations it intends to soothe.

## Contrition and Backlash

The comparison of the Japanese and German cases raises a puzzle. On the one hand, Japanese efforts to apologize repeatedly triggered justifications and denials from influential mainstream conservatives. For example, the statements by Prime Ministers Hosokawa and Murayama and the 1995 Diet Resolution prompted high-level officials to decry what they called unpatriotic distortions of Japanese history. The conservative backlash seems partly motivated by ideology and partly by a desire to score political points with constituents. Because of the backlash, the result of Japan's contrite gestures was perverse: it angered and alarmed neighbors.

The German case appears in stark contrast to the Japanese experience. Although Bonn offered the most contrition the world has ever seen, mainstream political leaders never made a concerted effort to justify or deny Germany's past crimes. Rare efforts by some conservatives to justify past aggression—or to "draw a line under the past" and move forward—were resoundingly rejected by a society committed to atonement. As a result, West German contrition provided a measure of justice and solace to individual victims, and reassured Germany's former adversaries about its peaceful intentions.

What explains the vast discrepancy between these two cases? Will contrition generally trigger backlash as it did in Japan, or will the German experience be closer to the norm? Perhaps backlash is an unusual response to contrition, and there is something unique about Japan—its domestic politics, culture, wartime experience, or occupation—that makes apologies particularly controversial there. If the Japanese experience is exceptional, then apologies, reparations, and other gestures of atonement can be helpful tools in international reconciliation. But if the Japanese experience is the norm, then contrition is a less promising—indeed, potentially counterproductive— instrument of international reconciliation.

Further research about the domestic and international conditions that affect the occurrence of backlash is needed. But three powerful reasons suggest that the Japanese experience—in which contrition triggers backlash— will be more common. First, the lack of German backlash can be understood by considering the strategic constraints facing West Germany during the Cold War. Second, evidence from around the world suggests that backlash is the frequent response to apologies. Finally, even a cursory consideration of the domestic politics of contrition reveals the powerful incentives that apologies create for politicians to oppose "unpatriotic" history. In sum, in most cases contrition will spark domestic controversy featuring denials and justification of past misdeeds.

## THE CURIOUS INCIDENT OF WEST GERMANY

Germany has atoned for its past more than any other country in history. And although German contrition did elicit some calls to look forward rather than back, and to emphasize a more patriotic historical narrative,[4] West Germans did not deny or justify past atrocities. One thinks of Sherlock Holmes's "curious incident of the dog in the night-time": why didn't West German politicians denounce contrition and counter it with justifications and denials? What explains why West German conservatives "didn't bark"?

One might argue that the restrained German backlash was unique because of the Holocaust; that the Holocaust was too terrible and too well documented, and that Germans after the war were so thoroughly educated about it that the Germans could not oppose contrition for a crime of this magnitude. However, even if Germans accepted a policy of contrition for the Holocaust, they still could have found plenty to criticize; for example, they might have rejected the interpretation of World War II as a war of German aggression. After all, debate over responsibility for the outbreak of World War I (*Kriegsschuldfrage*) had been intense during the interwar years.[5] Following World War II, West German conservatives might have parroted Hitler's claims about the Poles starting the war. (In Japan, for example, "Chinese terrorists" have been blamed for starting the war in China.) Or Germans might have maintained that with Stalin's military machine on the rise, Germany in the 1930s needed to increase its military power and create a buffer zone between itself and the Red Army. But mainstream conservatives almost never made such arguments. Attempts to introduce such views into the national debate (notably in the *Historikerstreit*) were squelched by a broad consensus committed to admitting and expressing remorse both for the Holocaust and for German aggression.

What factors, then, muted German backlash, and are they likely to be present elsewhere? Evidence suggests that Germany's strategic situation after the war was a major factor. The group most likely to protest contrition and offer a more "patriotic" interpretation of Germany's recent history—West German conservatives—faced a strong *dis*incentive to do so. German conservatives were committed to three paramount foreign policy goals: reunification, rearmament, and integration with the West. Even after Bonn's new allies reluctantly agreed to West German rearmament (because of the Soviet threat), German leaders understood the need to demonstrate that the FRG was "not your father's Fatherland." If Bonn appeared revisionist, its new allies would never support German unification. As Adenauer explained to other German leaders, reparations to Israel were necessary to reassure the West and clarify that the FRG did not "agree" with "what was done to the Jews."[6] Thus, Bonn's strategic conditions dissuaded conservatives from justifying, denying, or glorifying Nazi violence.

It is worth noting that many people feared the German backlash that did not occur. Many Allied Occupation officials feared that policies of reeducation would incite nationalist resentment and, in doing so, empower West Germany's far right. Today, the French worry about the possibility that resentment over contrition—particularly among younger Germans who feel no connection to the war—will have similar effects and will move Germany in a less cooperative direction. As journalist Daniel Vernet wrote, "The risk is that the Germans would abandon self-flagellation to fall into self-pity, to feel sorry for themselves and for the fate reserved for them."[7] Indeed, even the Germans themselves have worried about domestic backlash. In the early postwar years, such concerns led Bonn to prohibit neo-Nazi political parties and motivated Adenauer's approach of acknowledging past violence but emphasizing the future.[8] More recently, Germany criminalized Holocaust denial. People pursuing historical revisionism can be charged with incitement or slander; the *Auschwitz-Lüge*, or Auschwitz lie, is punishable by up to five years in prison. We now know that German conservatives ranked reunification and rearmament as higher priorities than crafting a "patriotic" historical narrative, but, as Adenauer and others recognized, muting nationalist backlash was by no means a foregone conclusion.

## A PEOPLE CONDEMNED TO RUIN

Evidence from all over the world shows that contrition often triggers backlash. In Austria, the onset of debates about the past led Joerg Haider to champion a more "patriotic" version of Austrian history, and to defend the country's war heroes—among them convicted war criminals. "A people that does not honor earlier generations," Haider said, "is a people condemned to ruin." Haider's activism propelled his Austrian Freedom Party from the political fringe into national coalition governments. In France, Jacques Chirac's historic 1995 apology for French complicity in the Holocaust—Vichy's deportation of 75,000 Jews—was denounced by rightists and the socialist opposition. Conservatives in Switzerland, Italy, and Belgium also mobilized against recent attempts to confront past collaboration.[9] In Britain, the Archbishop of York's call for the country to apologize for slavery prompted a national outcry; critics argued that Britain should be proud—not ashamed—because of its leadership in ending the slave trade. Earlier, apologies by Tony Blair to the people of Ireland for the Potato Famine and for the 1972 Bloody Sunday massacre led many British and Northern Irish unionists to denounce the gestures, dismiss British culpability, and criticize the Irish for their "victim mentality."[10] In the United States, a proposed Smithsonian exhibit that discussed the horrors of Hiroshima and questioned the necessity of the bombing unleashed a storm of protest, including statements of justification from Congress, veterans' groups, and the media. The U.S. Senate *unanimously* passed a resolution that declared the museum script "revisionist, unbalanced, and offensive."[11] The exhibition was rewritten. Apologies and reparations proposed for domestic victims are no less divisive. As Melissa Nobles has pointed out, proposals for reparations to Black Americans for slavery and apologies to indigenous peoples in Australia and New Zealand provoke intense and often polarizing domestic controversy.[12]

The frequency of backlash should be no surprise from the standpoint of domestic politics: conservatives might oppose contrition for either ideological or purely opportunistic reasons. Ideologically, many conservatives argue that a strong polity requires that citizens have a deep sense of national identity and love of country. Patriotism, according to this view, is undermined by emphasizing past atrocities and other failings. Thus history education—while it should not deny the country's past actions—should be presented in a "tone of affirmation" that will promote national pride within citizens.[13]

Objections to contrition might also be purely opportunistic. In a postwar setting, politicians face strong incentives to oppose contrition to foreign victims. Many people in the country will have endured great hardship during wartime. Family members will have perished in battle; people back home may have endured bombings, starvation, rape, or ethnic cleansing. Their houses—even cities—may have been destroyed. People will want to honor their war dead and receive government funds to help them rebuild. Politicians, bureaucrats, and soldiers who planned military aggression or perpetrated atrocities during the war will want to protect their jobs and pensions and shield themselves from prosecution.

In this setting, apologies or reparations to foreigners will be highly unpopular. They impugn wartime leaders (some of whom may still be in power), veterans, and the war dead. Reparations to foreign victims compete with domestic demands for government assistance. Apologies are (by definition) admissions of guilt, and hence they open the possibility for criminal prosecution. Contrition will not only be generally unpopular, it will be unpopular among groups who, in many cases, are politically mobilized and influential (e.g., war victims and veterans).

Because contrition will be controversial, political leaders have incentives to oppose it. Politicians will jump at the opportunity to score gains among dissatisfied constituencies. As they protest contrition, elites are likely to justify past violence ("that's how the world was back then"; or "we had to do it because of the threat facing our nation"), to deny it, or to glorify it ("what about all the *good* things we did for the lands we colonized?").

The depth of anger displayed against those who support contrition reveals how opposed many people are to revisions of history that cast their country's actions in a critical light. Advocates of contrition have been targeted for assassination. In Japan, rightists attempted to assassinate the mayor of Nagasaki, Motoshima Hitoshi, after he commented that the emperor was partly to blame for World War II. Prominent LDP Diet member Kato Koichi was targeted after he criticized Koizumi's visits to Yasukuni Shrine. Kato's home—where he lived with his aged mother—was burned down by rightists (no one was killed). In Turkey, prominent journalist Hrant Dink was gunned down by a Turkish nationalist because Dink advocated Turkish recognition of the Armenian genocide.[14] More broadly, Israeli Prime Minister Yitzak Rabin, Egyptian President Anwar Sadat, and Mahatma Gandhi were all assassinated by rightists for advocating conciliation toward foreign adversaries. In general, contrition is likely to cause political outcry because of the domestic political climate after wars and the incentives politicians face to denounce such gestures.

Further exploration of the conditions that mute or exacerbate backlash is necessary. Follow-up studies should be constructed to confirm whether the relationship is as strong as it appears, or whether the examples of backlash in Japan, Austria, the United States, France, Britain, and Australia are atypical. In particular, scholars should investigate whether there are circumstances (domestic and international) that dampen the link between contrition and backlash.

What is clear, however, is that activists, commentators, scholars, and political leaders are urging countries to apologize for past crimes without considering the potential for triggering counterproductive backlash and for damaging the very relations they intend to repair. Those who urge greater contrition are like physicians prescribing a drug without a clear understanding of the possible side effects. And in fact, we have clear evidence that this drug has made some "patients" sicker than before. Before contrition should be prescribed, we need to better understand the conditions under which it is likely to heal rather than hurt.

## Addressing Counterarguments

In previous chapters I presented my findings from various cases of reconciliation (and nonreconciliation) in Europe and Asia; I also addressed critiques about that evidence and the conclusions drawn from it. Here I focus on four broader critiques of the book's overall findings.

First, one might question my causal claim—that remembrance affects threat perception—by raising the issue of endogeneity. In other words, perhaps the causal arrows are actually reversed, and that perceptions of the threat posed by another state affect how a state remembers one's past relations with it.

Concerns about endogeneity should be mitigated for two important reasons. First, had my empirical findings shown a strong correlation between remembrance and threat perception, the possibility that threat perception was driving remembrance would have to be taken very seriously. Indeed, the correlation could mean that apologetic remembrance reduces threat, *or* it could mean that periods of low threat are conducive to more apologetic remembrance. However, my study does not find a strong positive correlation between remembrance and threat perception. To the contrary, I find that while modest gestures of contrition (e.g., a basic acknowledgment of past misdeeds) reduces threat, greater contrition has no reliable beneficial effect, and can in fact worsen relations if it triggers domestic backlash.

I do argue that denials elevate threat perception, and thus that some contrition is necessary for reconciliation. On this point, I address the potential problem of endogeneity through process tracing. I do *not* draw my conclusions merely on the basis of a correlation between contrition and improved relations (or denials and mistrust). Rather, I draw conclusions on the basis of interviews, documents, newspaper accounts, and so forth that specifically connect remembrance to perceptions of intentions. Neither my findings about the soothing effects of acknowledgement, nor my findings about the poisonous consequences of denials, are artifacts of endogeneity in my research design.

### DOES REMEMBRANCE REALLY MATTER?

In response to the finding that denials promote mistrust and elevate fear, critics might raise two different concerns. First, as I discussed in chapter 4, one might argue that this finding stems largely from the Japan-Korea experience and can be explained by Korean idiosyncrasies. That is, perhaps the ROK's culture, politics, or specific experience with Japan makes issues of historical memory particularly salient there and Japanese denials particularly upsetting. If this is true, then denials may be less harmful to relations between countries than this book argues.

With this critique in mind, I examined additional case studies in chapter 4. Both the Chinese and the Australians—very disparate cultures and regimes—reacted angrily to Japanese denials and explicitly connected those denials to their ongoing mistrust of Japan. Chapter 4 also looked at the case of British-German relations. I found that the British carefully watched West Germany's debates about its past and expressed significant concern about even a hint of German historical revisionism. Denials appear to harm relations; not just for Koreans but for former victims generally.

Skeptics might also challenge the significance of remembrance from a different angle, arguing that although unapologetic remembrance does indeed stir up acrimony, it ultimately has little effect on the "high politics" of national security. In other words, denials and glorification do not damage relations between states in any real way. After all, chapter 3 demonstrated that most of the fluctuations in Korean threat perception of Japan during the Cold War resulted from changes in Japanese capabilities rather than Japanese remembrance. Thus, a simpler theory of threat perception adequately explains the case: Koreans fear a powerful and unconstrained Japan; they feel safe when Japan is weak or contained. According to this view, neither apologies nor inflammatory denials affect threat perception much, because threat is simply a function of capabilities.

Capabilities do have a powerful effect on threat perception, but a capabilities-only theory of threat—which ignores remembrance and other indicators of intentions—is implausible. It is difficult to imagine that during the Cold War West Germany could have begun denying the crimes of the Nazi era without sending shock waves throughout Europe. This does *not* suggest that Germany's extensive contrition was essential for Franco-German reconciliation: indeed, as I argued in chapter 3, it was not. But by avoiding denials—similar to those that repeatedly emanated from Tokyo—the FRG made it possible for Europeans to stop worrying about a return of German militarism. In fact even today, after more than six decades of good behavior, a major German effort to recast its history and deny or glorify its Nazi era crimes would change the strategic situation in Europe overnight. It is impossible to prove that this counterfactual is true—that Europe would shudder if Germany began denying its past—but it is hard to imagine that it is false.

Beyond the counterfactuals about German denials, additional reasons exist to reject a capabilities-only theory of threat perception: it cannot explain the most important facts about international relations in East Asia. Had Korean perceptions of threat been driven entirely by perceptions of capabilities, they (and everyone else in the region) would have spent the decades since the end of World War II worrying about *American* power—not about

Japan or the Soviet Union. Whether one measures power by looking at existing military forces, military potential, or wealth, U.S. power dwarfed everyone else in the region. But, of course, no one estimated threat by looking solely at capabilities; they also assessed intentions. Koreans, for example, drew a clear distinction between Japan—which had conquered them—and the vastly more powerful United States, which demonstrated no interest in colonizing Korea. It is clear that countries assess intentions as they estimate threats, and the evidence presented in this book shows that remembrance (particularly denials) plays an important role in their judgments about intentions.[15]

A clear illustration of how assessments of intentions and capabilities interact in threat perception can be seen in the different views in Asia and Europe about the possibility of American military withdrawal. In Asia, the United States is seen as the "cork in the bottle"[16] that keeps poisonous Japan from pouring out. Because Japanese intentions are so deeply mistrusted (in great part because of their repeated denials about the past), Japan's neighbors would worry about the growth of Japan's freedom and power if the United States were to leave the region. But in Europe the prospect of U.S. withdrawal is no longer a worry. Even though an American withdrawal would increase Berlin's relative power on the continent, the French say they no longer fear Germany because they trust its intentions. Power in the hands of a country with hostile intentions generates intense fear; power in the hands of a country that appears benign causes, at most, caution.

The overriding point is that although Japanese capabilities and Korean perceptions of threat fluctuated in sync during the Cold War, Japan's capabilities do not tell the entire story about how Koreans assess threat. The reasoning data in chapter 2 confirms that Japan's unapologetic remembrance makes Koreans fear it more than they would otherwise, and is one powerful reason why Koreans would fear Japanese power were the United States to withdraw from the region. To put this differently, Japan's denials have created a context in which increases in its power are extremely threatening. The fact that capabilities also powerfully contribute to threat assessment does not negate this finding.

## SELECTION BIAS

As discussed in chapter 1, one might argue that these cases of egregious violence are not representative of most cases in which contrition might play a healing role. The principal cases in this book focus on crimes that are both extraordinary in their barbarity and thoroughly documented: this introduces bias into the study and reduces the broader applicability of its findings.

This objection is correct in that examining such cases biases the findings. I maintain, however, that the direction of this bias strengthens two of the findings and only weakens one. One of my central arguments is that reconciliation can occur without contrition. This finding was demonstrated by the Franco-German rapprochement in the 1950s. The fact that France was willing to reconcile prior to significant German contrition, despite Nazi Germany's heinous crimes, suggests that reconciliation with very little contrition is even more feasible in cases in which the crimes have been less severe. The selection bias therefore reinforces my finding.

A second claim is that apologies cause backlash. This argument was principally derived from the Japanese experience but, as noted above, is reinforced by evidence from many other cases. What is striking is that backlash occurs in these cases despite broad historical consensus about the basic nature of the crimes. For example, the nature of Japan's actions in China are well understood (even if exact casualty figures are disputed); the inhumanity of the slave trade is beyond question; the American civilian bombardment of Japanese cities is acknowledged on both sides of the Pacific. But even in these cases, efforts to atone trigger backlash. We should expect that in more typical cases, in which there is greater historical uncertainty, denials will be more prevalent. The direction of bias thus strengthens this argument as well.

Finally, the one finding that the direction of bias *weakens* is the claim that unapologetic remembrance fuels distrust of intentions. After horrendous violence, observers should be particularly surprised and alarmed by denials and glorifications of such atrocities. It is thus fair to argue that denials of less egregious acts may not be so damaging to bilateral relations. At the same time, however, this finding is the least controversial. To the extent that scholars and analysts are skeptical about the pernicious effects of denials, they should build on the theoretical setup of this study and examine the effects of denials in a wider range of cases.

## ACHIEVING A TRUE RECONCILIATION

A final critique holds that although West Germany's atonement was clearly not necessary for its initial rapprochement with France, the two countries would not have achieved the level of reconciliation they now enjoy without it. According to this view, it might be true that countries can cease hostilities and regain functional relations without offering contrition. But perhaps the development of a true reconciliation among both polities and peoples requires countries to confront and atone for their past atrocities.[17]

The significance of the Franco-German rapprochement in the 1950s must not be minimized. The poll data—which shows that a majority of French considered West Germany their "best friend" only fifteen years after the end of the occupation of France—is striking. From the perspective of international politics, scholars should be greatly interested in the conditions that lead to such transformations from hated enemy to friendly neighbor.

Even more important, the idea that a stable peace requires contrition is contradicted by substantial evidence. Both chapters 2 and 3 show that acknowledging past violence facilitates reconciliation and that a failure to do so can poison bilateral relations. But creating a sense of warmth between peoples does not require confronting the past and apologizing for crimes. As discussed above, many countries have experienced a profound reconciliation without any soul-searching about past violence. The United States conducted a massive counter-civilian bombing campaign that killed hundreds of thousands of Germans and has barely offered an ounce of remorse. But despite this, German and American relations are warm not only between governments, but among peoples. The same pattern was evident in the U.S-Japan relationship. It is surprising and strange that people can put such terrible crimes behind them, but they do.

## Policy Implications

This book argues that the kind of remembrance that will be the most helpful for international reconciliation is a middle ground between whitewashing and contrition. Whitewashing alarms foreign observers, while contrition risks triggering domestic backlash. Where exactly this middle ground lies will depend on the circumstances of each case. Depending on domestic and international factors, victims will have varying levels of interest in contrition; perpetrators will have varying ability to offer it without inciting backlash. For example, French disinterest in German contrition after World War II may have stemmed partly from the growing Soviet threat; similarly, West Germany's strategic dilemmas may have allowed Bonn to be unusually contrite without triggering backlash. This study cannot identify the ideal amount of contrition to repair relations. It does, however, draw attention to the need for countries to balance the demands of internal and external audiences, and the goals of justice and international reconciliation.

### NEGOTIATING MEMORY

Leaders trying to strike this balance can choose among a few strategies. Countries that seek to reconcile can construct a shared and nonaccusatory vision of the past. Rather than frame the past as one actor's brutalization of another, their leaders can structure commemoration to cast events—as much as possible—as shared catastrophes. Countries can remember past suffering as specific examples of the tragic phenomena that afflict all countries, such as war, militarism, or aggression. This kind of remembrance does not blame individual countries but instead focuses attention on the problems of international politics, or of human nature, that vigilance and cooperation can mitigate.

This approach—which privileges international reconciliation over justice—raises painful dilemmas. Constructing a nonaccusatory version of the past necessarily downplays terrible crimes. By casting terrible events as being mere examples of the tragedy of world politics, this strategy risks moral equivocation and diverts attention from the people and governments who commit heinous acts. This nonaccusatory approach is both deeply unsatisfying and a wise strategy for international reconciliation.

France and West Germany frequently employed this nonaccusatory approach to remembrance. Their leaders attempted to create positive new focal points to demonstrate their mutual commitment to reconciliation and cooperation. In 1962, Charles de Gaulle and Konrad Adenauer carefully chose the location for a symbolic ceremony: they attended a joint mass at Reims Cathedral (see next page). Reims evoked the long Franco-German struggle: the town and cathedral were the site of fighting in the Franco-Prussian War and the First World War. As de Gaulle explained, Reims symbolized "our age-old traditions"; it was "the scene of many an encounter between the hereditary enemies, from the ancient Germanic invasions to the battles of the Marne. In the cathedral, whose wounds were not fully healed, the first Frenchman and the first German came together to pray that on either side of the Rhine the deeds of friendship might forever supplant the miseries of war."[18]

France and West Germany continued to choose nonaccusatory symbols when they met to commemorate the past. In 1984, François Mitterrand and Helmut Kohl attended a ceremony at Verdun Cemetery. Verdun—where 700,000 French and Germans lost their lives in 1916—evoked the shared tragedy of World War I, rather than German aggression in World War II. The two leaders were photographed holding hands over the graves of French and German soldiers (see page 193). This haunting image decorated French newspapers and magazines, which enthused about Franco-German reconciliation. One article noted, "François Mitterrand and Helmut Kohl, hand-in-hand, sealed Franco-German reconciliation." An editorial commented, "the silent meditation of President Mitterrand and Chancellor Kohl standing hand-in-hand in front of the Verdun graves last fall was an emotional symbol for the French and German people." As France's former Foreign Minister Hubert Védrine later said, "From De Gaulle and Adenauer at Reims cathedral, to Mitterrand and Kohl at Verdun, symbolism has been essential to remind us of our history, its excesses, and joint action we have taken to rebuild the Franco-German relationship from the top down."[19] The location of this important symbolic event did not emphasize German crimes but rather the mutual suffering that war and militarism brought to both peoples.

The ceremonies at Reims and Verdun contrast starkly with the view that reconciliation occurs when an aggressor clearly admits and repudiates past crimes. Franco-German commemoration blamed Franco-German strife not

Konrad Adenauer and Charles de Gaulle at Reims Cathedral, 1962. AP PHOTO.

on German aggression but on the tumult of European great-power politics. Rather than hold ceremonies at a concentration camp or at Oradour-sur-Glane (the site of a German massacre in France), they were held at a cathedral repeatedly caught in the middle of European wars and at a World War I cemetery. This strategy was not without its drawbacks, and indeed at the time drew criticism for forgetting Germany's atrocities.[20] Although the Franco-German approach did obscure Germany's World War II crimes, it is a promising strategy for reducing the risk of backlash and promoting reconciliation.

Because these strategies require major compromises on both sides, leaders in both countries will need to have a strong mandate for bilateral reconciliation if they are to survive politically. On the victim's side, imagine the potential domestic political vulnerability of a leader holding out the olive branch to a hated enemy. (Backlash, in other words, works both ways.) Thus this approach is only likely to be feasible in countries facing a strong imperative to reconcile, such as West Germany and France in 1945. It will be unlikely to succeed in countries such as contemporary China and Japan.

François Mitterrand and Helmut Kohl at Verdun Cemetery, 1984. AP PHOTO/POOL/FILE.

These countries confront no powerful forces pushing them toward reconciliation: Quite the opposite, with the rise of Chinese power, they are more likely to emerge as strategic competitors. Moreover, the Chinese Communist Party traditionally has reaped domestic political gains from anti-Japanese sentiment, so even has incentives to keep acrimony alive.[21]

FOUND IN TRANSLATION

Leaders have other tools to use for promoting international reconciliation while minimizing the risk of domestic backlash. They can use linguistic differences to their advantage. For example, they might negotiate a Joint Communiqué that can be translated in a way that permits each side to save face to constituents back home. In 2001, the uproar caused when an American EP-3 military aircraft collided with a Chinese fighter jet was resolved in this manner. Washington and Beijing negotiated a letter in English only, which the Chinese government and media translated for the Chinese audience. Although the Americans had not offered an "apology," the Chinese people were told that the United States had apologized.[22] A similar strategy resolved the dispute over the U.S.S. *Pueblo*, a naval intelligence ship seized by North Korea in 1968 in disputed waters. Ultimately Washington secured the release of the crew by giving Pyongyang the written apology it had demanded. As American negotiator Major General Gilbert Woodward was about to sign the statement, he announced that it was inaccurate and had been written by the North Koreans: "I will sign the document," he said, "to free the crew and only to free the crew." Nonetheless, Pyongyang accepted the written apology, publicized it to the North Korean people, and ignored the verbal repudiation. The crisis ended.[23] Furthermore, chapter 2 noted that when Seoul and Tokyo normalized relations, Seoul demanded that the compensation it received be called "reparations," while Tokyo refused to refer to the funds in this manner. Ultimately Tokyo described the compensation as "congratulatory funds for independence," while Seoul triumphantly reported that it had extracted "reparations" from Japan. Scholars have argued that the most intractable disputes are those over indivisible goods.[24] Diplomats have shown that apologies can be quite "divisible," and have used them cleverly to end international disputes.

STRATEGIES FOR THE INTERNATIONAL
COMMUNITY

In January 2007, U.S. Congressman Mike Honda (D-CA) proposed House Resolution 121, which urges Tokyo to apologize to the "comfort women." Testifying to a congressional subcommittee, he spoke earnestly and eloquently for justice. "I learned that Japan's Ministry of Education sought to omit or downplay the comfort women tragedy in its approved textbooks," the former educator recalled. "As a teacher interested in historical reconciliation, I knew the importance of teaching and talking about tragedy and injustice without flinching from the details. Without honesty and candor," Honda said, "there could be no foundation for reconciliation."[25]

Honda's words are stirring, and the proposed bill certainly did raise awareness of the atrocities endured by the "comfort women." Moreover, the strategy of "naming and shaming" has worked in the past: the international community has embarrassed countries into to upholding higher standards of conduct in human rights.[26] The problem, however, is that a public shaming strategy risks triggering backlash in the targeted country. Backlash seems particularly likely when the namers and shamers have not confronted their own past violence. (Tokyo might ask Beijing why—if it is so concerned about candid remembrance—it omits Tiananmen Square, and the 30 million victims of Mao Zedong, from its own history textbooks; Ankara might wonder why Washington pressures Turkey to remember its genocide of Armenians while forgetting its own genocide of Native Americans).

Indeed, the debate over H.R. 121 unfolded in the lamentable fashion that this book expects. Discussion of the proposed bill led Japan's prime minister, Abe Shinzo to deny that the "comfort women" had been coerced: a significant backtrack from Tokyo's previous admissions. Once again, Japan's neighbors expressed outrage and alarm.[27]

External pressure may have other domestic political consequences that are undesirable from the standpoint of the international community. Foreign pressure may empower—rather than discredit—nationalists and deniers. They will attempt to paint themselves as the defenders of the country's honor against foreign interference, and in doing so will deride advocates of truth and conciliation as unpatriotic. This pattern is evident in Turkey and Austria, where calls for atonement caused a backlash that increased the political power of the nationalist Right.[28]

The good news is that the international community can encourage remembrance in less inflammatory ways. Institutions such as UNESCO have sponsored international textbook commissions in order to help countries negotiate their historical narratives. Since World War II, this strategy has been used to great success by Germany, France, Poland, and many other European countries. More recently, it has also been used productively in East Asia, where Japan, South Korea, and China co-authored a history textbook for joint use.[29] Furthermore, East Asian leaders and activists who want to raise awareness about World War II sex slaves, for example, might organize a multinational inquiry about violence against women in wartime—widening the focus beyond Japan's crimes to consider the atrocities committed by many countries in many wars. Because such multilateral strategies do not wag a finger at Tokyo in particular, Japanese nationalists and deniers will have less ammunition to use against moderates and liberals who favor participation.

Even these less ambitious strategies will still elicit criticism—probably from both sides. Victims will understandably say they deserve justice, not some UN meeting designed to promote a version of history based on moral equivalency. And nationalists will denounce foreign interference and protest what they see as unpatriotic self-abnegation. (Imagine, for example, the hurdles to Turkish participation in an inquiry about genocide in world history.) However, many conservatives might support such an approach; the more moderate among them often oppose contrition not because they deny or glorify the acts in question, but because they object to their country being the only one asked to atone for them. In sum, the international community can and should encourage remembrance of past atrocities. As it does so, however, activists should keep the risk of backlash in mind.

## Theoretical Implications

This book also offers several contributions to political science theory. First, it informs theoretical debates about how countries perceive threats. Many scholars expect both intentions and capabilities to influence threat perception;[30] however, international relations theory has yet to sufficiently explore (1) what factors shape perceptions of intentions and (2) how capabilities and intentions interact in threat perception. I find that capabilities weigh heavily in threat perception, but a state's capabilities will appear more or less threatening depending on whether its intentions appear hostile or benign.

On the question of which factors shape perceptions of intentions, this analysis demonstrates the importance of a previously under-studied signal of intentions—remembrance—and yields evidence for the significance of ideational factors more generally. Until recently, the power of ideas in international security affairs was asserted in a largely theoretical literature. By showing the link between unapologetic remembrance and mistrust, this book contributes to a growing body of work that has begun to test empirically the effects of ideas on international outcomes. It also pushes the debate in a direction encouraged by many critics: toward exploring not only the pacifying effects of ideas, but also the destabilizing effects that they may have.[31]

In addition, this book contributes to the study of political memory and international justice. It creates an analytic framework for conceptualizing and measuring the intangible and elusive concepts of remembrance and contrition. This framework can be applied to numerous research questions about memory in international relations, ethnic politics, and transitional justice. My findings about the counterproductive effects of backlash bear on an important debate within the transitional justice literature: this book supports "pragmatists" who argue that legal prosecutions prolong conflicts and imperil stability in transitioning states. These scholars contend that amnesties and "golden parachutes" for repressive leaders—however repugnant—promote democratic consolidation and stability and, most important, put an end to conflicts that might otherwise drag on to kill thousands or even hundreds of thousands of people.[32]

## A New Research Program on Remembrance and Reconciliation

Findings from this book suggest that perpetrator countries wishing to reconcile with former adversaries should search for a middle ground that is contrite enough to placate former adversaries abroad, but not so much that it triggers backlash from nationalists at home. The first question for scholars is thus, "How contrite can a government be without triggering backlash?" Contrition may in some cases be a promising tool; if nationalists support goals that would be difficult to achieve without it, they will be less likely to denounce efforts to apologize. More broadly, scholars should investigate what conditions make backlash more or less likely.

In seeking this middle ground, a second question to answer is, "How much contrition is needed to satisfy foreign audiences?" The Japan case shows the harmful influence of denials and whitewashing: clearly, avoiding these poisonous denials is an important step toward reconciliation. How much contrition a victimized country might need, however, will vary.

It may depend on the nature of the atrocities committed or, as noted earlier, on the two countries' strategic situation after the war. For example, countries desperate for financial, diplomatic, or military support against a security threat will probably settle for little or no contrition. (Anarchy, in other words, means never having to say you're sorry.) Cultural or domestic political circumstances may also play a role: for example, a leader with a tenuous claim to power might not have the luxury of offering his country's forgiveness if he knows it would empower his political rivals.

Future research should investigate the fuller range of domestic and international conditions that help restore relations: the wider set of conditions that make guilty countries willing to offer contrition and the conditions that make victims willing to forgive.

The circumstances that shape countries' historical narratives is a second important area for research. As noted above, calls for national atonement make political leaders vulnerable to electoral defeat (or worse). This begs the question: Why do some states pursue contrition at all? The above interpretations noted the influence of a country's strategic environment: although this clearly plays a role, factors related to international norms, domestic politics, and individual leadership probably do as well.

A common hypothesis about what encouraged German contrition (and what muted it in Japan) is cultural: for example, the view that certain cultures are more inclined than others to apologize. Culture undoubtedly affects how a country remembers, and scholars should build on existing work to explore its influence.[33] However, a crude cultural argument saying "Japan didn't apologize because of its culture" and "West Germany apologized because of its culture" is clearly unsatisfying. It fails to explain, for example, the substantial variation in remembrance among the three Germanic peoples (postwar West Germany, East Germany, and Austria); only one of them was apologetic. It also fails to explain the dramatic evolution in West German remembrance over time (i.e., the onset of self-reflection in the mid-1960s after twenty years of evasion and self-pity). My argument draws attention to the international political factors that muted denial and glorification in West Germany. However, the issue of why the West Germans later chose the historically unprecedented course of confronting their war guilt still requires explanation. Future studies should investigate this specifically in the German case and should explore more generally how and why countries' historical narratives evolve.

ALTHOUGH this book has uncovered many areas for future research, it has advanced our understanding of remembrance and international relations in several ways. It creates a framework for the study of remembrance in international (or intergroup) politics, and develops a theory that connects a country's remembrance to its ability to reconcile with its former adversaries. Through empirical testing it substantiates the common view that justifying, denying, or glorifying past violence sustains mistrust and inhibits reconciliation. However, I show that countries have been able to reconcile with very little in the way of contrition, and that offering more risks provoking domestic backlash. If individual leaders or international institutions want to promote remembrance of past violence, they should do so in ways that are mindful of backlash: in ways that support—rather than stigmatize—advocates of remembrance and justice.

# Notes

## Introduction

1. Quoted in The Korean Council for Women Drafted for Military Sexual Slavery by Japan et al., eds., *The True Stories of the Korean "Comfort Women"* (London: Casell, 1995). Interviews with Kim Hak-soon and other former "comfort women" appear in the 1999 documentary *Silence Broken*, directed by Dai Sil Kim Gibson.

2. Martin Gilbert, *The First World War: A Complete History* (New York: Henry Holt, 1994), 510.

3. Nicholas D. Kristof, "The Problem of Memory," *Foreign Affairs* 77, no. 6 (November/December 1998): 37–49; "Japan's Burden," *Financial Times*, April 8, 2005; "So Hard to Be Friends," *Economist*, March 23, 2005; Iris Chang, *The Rape of Nanking* (New York: Penguin Books, 1998); Christine Chinlund, "Should We Call It a Massacre or a Genocide?" *Boston Globe*, May 5, 2003; "Iran's Holocaust Denial Advances Another Agenda," *USA Today*, December 13, 2006.

4. On the United States and France, see *New York Times*, March 6, 2007; *New York Times*, October 13, 2006. On the EU and UN, see *Financial Times*, October 17, 2006; *New York Times*, January 27, 2007.

5. Interview with Author, Centre d'Etudes et des Recherches Internationales, October 2002. On German remembrance see Nicholas Kulish, "Germany Confronts Holocaust Legacy Anew," *New York Times*, January 29, 2008.

6. Thomas J. Christensen, "China, the U.S.-Japan Alliance, and the Security Dilemma in East Asia," *International Security* 23, no. 4 (Spring 1999): 49–80; Richard Ned Lebow, "Memory, Democracy, and Reconciliation," in *The Politics of Memory in Postwar Europe*, ed. Richard Ned Lebow, Wulf Kansteiner, and Claudio Fogu (Durham: Duke University Press, 2004); Andrew Kydd, "Sheep in Sheep's Clothing: Why Security Seekers Do Not Fight Each Other," *Security Studies* 7, no. 1 (Autumn 1997): 114–54; Stephen Van Evera, "Primed for Peace: Europe after the Cold War," *International Security* 15, no. 3 (Winter 1990/91): 7–57; Thomas U. Berger, "The Construction of Antagonism: The History Problem in Japan's Foreign Relations," in *Reinventing the Alliance: U.S.-Japan Security Partnership in an Era of Change*, ed. G. John Ikenberry and Takashi Inoguchi (New York: Palgrave, 2003), 63–90.

7. Some prominent works in the voluminous literature on transitional justice include James L. Gibson, "Does Truth Lead to Reconciliation? Testing the Causal Assumptions of the South African Truth and Reconciliation Process," *American Journal of Political Science* 48, no. 2

(2004): 201–17; Martha Minow, *Between Vengeance and Forgiveness: Facing History after Genocide and Mass Violence* (Boston: Beacon Press, 1998); Priscilla B. Hayner, *Unspeakable Truths: Confronting State Terror and Atrocity* (New York: Routledge, 2001).

8. The British constructed a monument to the memory of "Bomber Harris," the commander of the Dresden raids. *New York Times,* January 6, 1992, A6. On American refusals to apologize, see *Washington Post,* April 20, 1995; *New York Times,* April 8, 1995; *New York Times,* December 2, 1991.

9. *South China Morning Post,* June 10, 2005.

10. Emilie Hafner-Burton, "Sticks and Stones: Naming and Shaming the Human Rights Enforcement Problem," *International Organization,* forthcoming. On U.S. Congressional resolutions pressuring Japan and Turkey see, respectively, *New York Times,* March 6, 2007; *Los Angeles Times,* February 4, 2007; on EU pressure toward Austria see *Financial Times,* October 17, 2006.

11. See, for example, C. William Walldorf, Jr., *Just Politics: Human Rights and the Foreign Policy of Great Powers* (Ithaca: Cornell University Press, forthcoming 2008); Mark Haas, *The Ideological Origins of Great Powers Politics, 1789–1989* (Ithaca: Cornell University Press, 2005); Martha Finnemore, *The Purpose of Intervention: Changing Beliefs about the Use of Force* (Ithaca: Cornell University Press, 2003).

12. On memory in intergroup conflict, see Stuart J. Kaufman, *Modern Hatreds: The Symbolic Politics of Ethnic War* (Ithaca: Cornell University Press, 2001). Leslie Vinjamuri and Jack Snyder survey the transitional justice literature in "Advocacy and Scholarship in the Study of International War Crime Tribunals and Transitional Justice," *Annual Review of Political Science* (2004).

13. For discussion of how legalist strategies provoke backlash, see Gary Jonathan Bass, *Stay the Hand of Vengeance: The Politics of War Crimes Tribunals* (Princeton: Princeton University Press, 2000). "Legalists" include M. Cherif Bassiouni, "Searching for Peace and Achieving Justice: The Need for Accountability," *Law and Contemporary Problems* 59, no. 4 (1996); Christopher C. Joyner, "Arresting Impunity: The Case for Universal Jurisdiction in Bringing War Criminals to Accountability," *Law and Contemporary Problems* 59, no. 4 (Autumn 1996): 153–72. "Pragmatists" include Leslie Vinjamuri and Jack L. Snyder, "Trials and Errors: Principle and Pragmatism in Strategies of International Justice," *International Security* 28, no. 3 (Winter 2003/04): 5–44; Samuel P. Huntington, *The Third Wave: Democratization in the Late Twentieth Century* (Norman: University of Oklahoma Press, 1991).

## 1. Remembrance and Reconciliation

1. On contrition and "deep interstate reconciliation," see Yinan He, "Overcoming Shadows of the Past: Post-Conflict Interstate Reconciliation in East Asia and Europe," Ph.D. diss., Department of Political Science, Massachusetts Institute of Technology, 2004 manuscript, 2007. Also see Arie M. Kacowicz, Yaacov Bar-Siman-Tov, Ole Elgstrom, and Magnus Jerneck, eds., *Stable Peace among Nations* (Lanham, MD: Rowman and Littlefield, 2000); Kenneth Boulding, *Stable Peace* (Austin: University of Texas Press, 1978).

2. John J. Mearsheimer, *The Tragedy of Great Power Politics* (New York: Norton, 2001); Kenneth N. Waltz, *Theory of International Politics* (Reading, Mass.: Addison-Wesley, 1979).

3. Stephen Walt, *The Origins of Alliances* (Ithaca: Cornell University Press, 1987); David M. Edelstein, "Managing Uncertainty: Beliefs about Intentions and the Rise of Great Powers," *Security Studies* 12, no. 1 (Autumn 2002): 1–40; Charles L. Glaser, "The Security Dilemma Revisited," *World Politics* 50 (October 1997): 171–201.

4. John M. Owen, "How Liberalism Produces Democratic Peace," in *Debating the Democratic Peace,* ed. Michael E. Brown, Sean M. Lynn-Jones, and Steven E. Miller (Cambridge, Mass.: MIT Press, 1996), 124. Also see Bruce Russett, *Grasping the Democratic Peace: Principles for a Post–Cold War World* (Princeton: Princeton University Press, 1993); Russett, "The Fact of Democratic Peace," in *Debating the Democratic Peace,* 58–81; Michael E. Doyle, "Kant, Liberal Legacies, and Foreign Affairs," in *Debating the Democratic Peace,* 3–57.

5. Thomas Risse-Kappen, "Collective Identity in a Democratic Community," in *The Culture of National Security,* ed. Peter J. Katzenstein (New York: Columbia University Press, 1996), 367;

Ted Hopf, "The Promise of Constructivism in International Relations Theory," *International Security* 23, No. 1 (Summer 1998): 171–200.

6. Edward D. Mansfield and Jack Snyder, *Electing to Fight: Why Emerging Democracies Go to War* (Cambridge, Mass.: MIT Press, 2005).

7. Celeste Wallander, *Mortal Friends, Best Enemies: German-Russian Cooperation after the Cold War* (Ithaca: Cornell University Press, 1999), 26. Also see Janice Gross Stein, "Deterrence and Reassurance," in *Behavior, Society, and Nuclear War*, ed. Philip E. Tetlock, J. L. Husbands, R. Jervis, P. C. Stern, and C. Tilley (New York: Oxford University Press, 1989), 1:9–72; Robert O. Keohane and Lisa M. Martin, "The Promise of Institutionalist Theory," *International Security* 20, no. 1 (1995): 39–51; John Gerard Ruggie, ed., *Multilateralism Matters: The Theory and Praxis of an Institutional Form* (New York: Columbia University Press, 1993);

8. On territorial claims and war see, for example, John Vasquez and Marie T. Henehan, "Territorial Disputes and the Probability of War, 1816–1992," *Journal of Peace Research* 38, no. 2. (2001): 123–38; Stephen A. Kocs, "Territorial Disputes and Interstate War, 1945–1987," *The Journal of Politics* 57, no. 1 (1995): 159–75.

9. Major works in this economic literature include Vincent P. Crawford and Joel Sobel, "Strategic Information Transmission," *Econometrica* 50, no. 6 (1982): 1421–51; Joseph Farrell and Matthew Rabin, "Cheap Talk," *Journal of Economic Perspectives* 10, no. 3 (1996): 103–18. On costly signaling see Andrew Kydd, *Trust, Reassurance, and Cooperation* (Cambridge, Mass.: MIT Press, 2000); James Fearon, "Signaling Foreign Policy Interests: Tying Hands versus Sinking Costs," *Journal of Conflict Resolution* 41, no. 1 (February 1997): 68–90; Robert Jervis, *The Logic of Images in International Relations* (New York: Columbia University Press, 1970), 18.

10. Andrew Kydd, "Sheep in Sheep's Clothing: Why Security Seekers Do Not Fight Each Other," *Security Studies* 7, no. 1 (Autumn 1997): 134.

11. Hans Morgenthau, *Politics among Nations: The Struggle for Power and Peace*, 5th ed. (New York: Knopf, 1973); Barry R. Posen, "Nationalism, the Mass Army, and Military Power," *International Security* 18, no. 2 (Fall 1993); Stephen Van Evera, "Hypotheses on Nationalism and War," *International Security* 18, no. 4 (Spring 1994); Thomas J. Christensen, *Useful Adversaries: Grand Strategy, Domestic Mobilization, and Sino-American Conflict, 1947–1958* (Princeton: Princeton University Press, 1996).

12. Jack L. Snyder, *From Voting to Violence: Democratization and Nationalist Conflict* (New York: Norton, 2000); Stuart J. Kaufman, *Modern Hatreds: The Symbolic Politics of Ethnic War* (Ithaca: Cornell University Press, 2001).

13. On this point see David A. Mendeloff, "Truth-telling and Mythmaking in Post-Soviet Russia: Pernicious Historical Ideas, Mass Education, and Interstate Conflict" (Ph.D. diss., Department of Political Science, Massachusetts Institute of Technology, 2001), chap. 1; on Yugoslavia see Gagnon, "Ethnic Nationalism and International Conflict: The Case of Serbia," *International Security* 19, no. 3 (Winter 1994/95): 130–166;" on Imperial Japan see Saburo Ienaga, *The Pacific War: 1931–1945* (New York: Pantheon, 1978), 19–32; on Nazi Germany see Heinz Sunker and Hans-Uwe Otto, *Education and Fascism: Political Identity and Social Education in Nazi Germany* (London: Falmer Press, 1997); on Rwanda see African Rights, *Rwanda: Death, Despair, and Defiance* (London: African Rights, 1995), 69–85.

14. Michael Ignatieff uses the term "permissible lies" in "Articles of Faith," *Index on Censorship* 5 (1996): 113.

15. Stephen Van Evera, "Primed for Peace: Europe after the Cold War," *International Security* 15, no. 3 (Winter 1990/91): 7–57; Mansfield and Snyder, *Electing to Fight*.

16. Jervis, *Logic of Images*, 28.

17. Supporting this view is Chaim Kaufman, "Threat Inflation and the Marketplace of Ideas: The Selling of the Iraq War," *International Security* 29, no. 1 (Fall 2004): 5–48.

18. Quoted in Lothar Kettenacker, "The Planning of 'Re-Education' during the Second World War," in *The Political Re-Education of Germany and Her Allies after World War II*, ed. Nicholas Pronay and Keith Wilson (Totowa, NJ: Barnes and Noble Books, 1985), 46. Gary Jonathan Bass discusses the backlash from legal trials in *Stay the Hand of Vengeance: The Politics of War Crimes Tribunals* (Princeton: Princeton University Press, 2000), 285–86.

19. Alexander Wendt, *Social Theory of International Politics* (Cambridge: Cambridge University Press, 1999); Jeffrey Checkel, "The Constructivist Turn in International Relations Theory," *World Politics* 50, no. 2 (January 1998); Hopf, "The Promise of Constructivism"; Risse-Kappen, "Collective Identity in a Democratic Community."

20. John G. Ruggie, "What Makes the World Hang Together? Neo-Utilitarianism and the Social Constructivist Challenge," *International Organization* 52, no. 4 (October 1998): 883.

21. Robert Jervis, "Perceiving and Coping with Threat," in *Psychology and Deterrence*, ed. Robert Jervis, Richard Ned Lebow, and Janice Gross Stein (Baltimore: Johns Hopkins University Press, 1985), 13–33.

22. Thomas Berger, "The Construction of Antagonism: The History Problem in Japan's Foreign Relations," in *Reinventing the Alliance: US-Japan Security Partnership in an Era of Change*, ed. G. John Ikenberry and Takashi Inoguchi (New York: Palgrave Macmillan, 2003), 63–88; Lebow, "The Memory of Politics in Postwar Europe," in *The Politics of Memory in Postwar Europe*, ed. Richard Ned Lebow, Claudio Fogu, and Wulf Kansteiner (Durham: Duke University Press, 2004).

23. Consuelo Cruz, "Identity and Persuasion: How Nations Remember Their Pasts and Make Their Futures," *World Politics* 52 (2000): 311, 277.

24. On interpersonal reconciliation, see Aaron Lazare, "Go Ahead: Say You're Sorry," *Psychology Today* 28, no. 1 (1995): 40; Michael E. McCullough, Everett Worthington, and Kenneth C. Rachal, "Interpersonal Forgiving in Close Relationships," *Journal of Personality and Social Psychology* 73 (1997); Nicholas Tavuchis, *Mea Culpa: A Sociology of Apology and Reconciliation* (Stanford: Stanford University Press, 1991).

25. On these diverse theoretical strands, see Peter J. Katzenstein and Rudra Sil, "Rethinking Asian Security: A Case for Analytical Eclecticism," in *Rethinking Security in East Asia: Identity, Power, and Efficiency*, ed. J. J. Suh, Peter J. Katzenstein, and Allen Carlson (Stanford: Stanford University Press, 2004), 15.

26. Neta C. Crawford, "The Passion of World Politics: Propositions on Emotion and Emotional Relationships," *International Security* 24, no. 4 (Spring 2000): 134–135; also see Richard Ned Lebow, Between Peace and War: the Nature of International Crisis (Baltimore: Johns Hopkins University Press, 1981); Jervis, "Perceiving and Coping with Threat," 13–34; Jonathan Mercer, "Rationality and Psychology in International Politics," *International Organization* 59 (Winter 2005): 77–106; Roger D. Petersen, *Understanding Ethnic Violence: Fear, Hatred, Resentment in Eastern Europe in the Twentieth Century* (New York: Cambridge University Press, 2002).

27. On a similar distinction between official and "vernacular" realms, see John Bodnar, "Public Memory in an American City," in *Commemorations: The Politics of National Identity*, ed. John R. Gillis (Princeton: Princeton University Press, 1994), 74–89.

28. For clarification of such mechanisms see David A. Mendeloff, "Truth-Seeking, Truth-Telling, and Post-Conflict Peacebuilding: Curb the Enthusiasm?" *International Studies Review* 6 (2004): 355–80.

29. Peter Novick, *The Holocaust in American Life* (Boston: Houghton Mifflin, 1999).

30. Bodnar, "Public Memory in an American City."

31. Ernest Gellner, *Nations and Nationalism* (Oxford: Blackwell, 1983), 26–35; E. J. Hobsbawm, *Nations and Nationalism since 1780: Programme, Myth, Reality* (Cambridge: Cambridge University Press, 1990), 91–96; Boyd Shafer, *Faces of Nationalism: New Realities and Old Myths* (New York: Harcourt, Brace, Jovanovich, 1972), 198.

32. Charles Merriam, *The Making of Citizens* (Chicago: University of Chicago Press, 1931; reprint, New York: Teachers College Press, 1966), 125.

33. David A. Mendeloff, "Truth-telling and Mythmaking in Post-Soviet Russia," 6.

34. Ibid., chap. 1; Michael W. Apple and Linda K. Christian-Smith, *The Politics of the Textbook* (New York: Routledge, 1991); Elie Podeh, "History and Memory in the Israeli Educational System: The Portrayal of the Arab-Israeli Conflict in History Textbooks (1948–2000)," *History & Memory* 12, no. 1 (2000): 65–100.

35. Lebow, "The Memory of Politics in Postwar Europe," 15; David Art, *The Politics of the Nazi Past in Germany and Austria* (Cambridge: Cambridge University Press, 2006), 23.

36. Jervis, *The Logic of Images*, 27.

37. On collective memory see Art, *The Politics of the Nazi Past,* chap. 2; Jeffrey K. Olick and Joyce Robbins, "Social Memory Studies: From 'Collective Memory' to the Historical Sociology of Mnemonic Practices," *Annual Review of Sociology* 24 (1998): 105–140.

38. For example, see Lazare, "Go Ahead: Say You're Sorry"; McCullough et al., "Interpersonal Forgiving in Close Relationships"; Tavuchis, *Mea Culpa;* Carl D. Schneider, "What It Means to Be Sorry: The Power of Apology in Mediation," *Mediation Quarterly* 17, no. 3 (Spring 2000): 265–280; Barry O'Neill, *Honor, Symbols, and War* (Ann Arbor: University of Michigan Press, 1999).

39. Quoted and analyzed in Lazare, "Go Ahead: Say You're Sorry."

40. Sasa Grubanovic and Lovorka Kozole, "Apologies All Around," *Transitions Online,* September 15, 2003, http://www.tol.cz.

41. Quote from Tony Judt, "The Past Is a Different Country: Myth and Memory in Postwar Europe," *Daedalus* 221, no. 4 (Fall 1992): fn 15. Stephen Van Evera writes that countries purvey "self-glorifying" and "other-maligning" myths. Van Evera, "Hypotheses on Nationalism and War." An alternative hypothesis would hold that focusing on one's own victimhood might actually signal benign intentions if doing so led the country to reject war. I address this issue in chapter 2.

42. Judt, "The Past Is a Different Country," 97; "Iranian Leader: Holocaust a 'Myth,' " CNN .com, December 14, 2005. On the long tradition of nationalistic history writing, see Paul M. Kennedy, "The Decline of Nationalistic History in the West, 1900–1970," *Journal of Contemporary History* 8, no. 1 (January 1973): 77–100; on Russia see Peter Finn, "New Manuals Push A Putin's-Eye View in Russian Schools," *Washington Post,* July 20, 2007, A1.

43. Media coverage slants in the direction of its audience's beliefs. Matthew Aaron Gentzkow and Jesse M. Shapiro, "What Drives Media Slant? Evidence from U.S. Daily Newspapers," NBER Working Paper, No. 12707 (November 13, 2006).

44. Christensen, *Useful Adversaries.*

45. Alexander L. George and Timothy J. McKeown, "Case Studies and Theories of Organizational Decision Making," in *Advances in Information Processing in Organizations,* vol. 2 (Greenwich, CT: JAI Press, 1985); Stephen Van Evera, *Guide to Methods for Students of Political Science* (Ithaca: Cornell University Press, 1997). On multiple within-case observations, see Gary King, Robert O. Keohane, and Sidney Verba, *Designing Social Inquiry: Scientific Inference in Qualitative Research* (Princeton: Princeton University Press, 1994).

46. For regime type, I rely on the Polity III dataset's classification of regime type and adopt Mansfield and Snyder's measurement of a period of political liberalization as a five-year period. Mansfield and Snyder, *Electing to Fight,* 74–79.

47. See Mearsheimer, *The Tragedy of Great Power Politics,* 78; Jeremy Pressman, "Leashes or Lemmings: Alliances as Restraining Devices" (Ph.D. diss., Department of Political Science, Massachusetts Institute of Technology, 2002).

48. On the role of historical memory in ethnic conflict, see Kaufman, *Modern Hatreds;* Daniel L. Byman, *Keeping the Peace: Lasting Solutions to Ethnic Conflicts* (Baltimore: Johns Hopkins University Press, 2002).

## 2. An Unhappy Phase in a Certain Period

1. Howard W. French, "Seoul Drawing Closer to Tokyo as Anger Fades," *New York Times,* September 20, 1999, A1.

2. "ROK President Addresses Liberation Day Ceremony," Seoul Korea.net, in Foreign Broadcast Information Service (FBIS) South Korea, August 15, 2001.

3. This invasion is far from a dim memory to Koreans. When I discussed Japan with Korean interlocutors, *every person* cited this invasion. For historical accounts of Korea-Japan relations, see Carter J. Eckert, *Korea, Old and New: A History* (Seoul: Ilchokak Publishers, 1990); Gregory Henderson, *Korea: The Politics of the Vortex* (Cambridge, Mass,: Harvard University Press, 1968).

4. On Japanese colonization in Asia, see Ramon Hawley Myers, Mark R. Peattie, and Ching-chih Chen, *The Japanese Colonial Empire, 1895–1945* (Princeton: Princeton University

Press, 1984). On the occupation of Korea, see Michael E. Robinson, *Cultural Nationalism in Colonial Korea, 1920–1925* (Seattle: University of Washington Press, 1988); Chong-Sik Lee, *The Politics of Korean Nationalism* (Berkeley: University of California Press, 1963).

5. A useful survey of the extensive literature on the "comfort women" is Yoshiko Nozaki, "The 'Comfort Women' Controversy: History and Testimony," *Japan Focus* (July 2005). Also see Yoshiaki Yoshimi, *Comfort Women: Sexual Slavery in the Japanese Military during World War II,* trans. Suzanne O'Brien (New York: Columbia University Press, 2002); C. Sarah Soh, "Japan's National/Asian Women's Fund for 'Comfort Women,' " *Pacific Affairs* 76, no. 2 (2003): 209–33. For victims' testimony, see Korean Council for Women Drafted for Military Sexual Slavery by Japan et al., eds., *True Stories of the Korean Comfort Women* (London: Cassell Academic, 1996).

6. On Unit 731, see John W. Powell, "Japan's Germ Warfare: The U.S. Cover-up of a War Crime," *Bulletin of Concerned Asian Scholars* 12 (Oct./Dec. 1980): 2017; and Special Report, *Bulletin of Atomic Scientists* (October 1981). Bombing casualty figures from Robert A. Pape, *Bombing to Win: Air Power and Coercion in War* (Ithaca: Cornell University Press, 1996), 337.

7. John W. Dower, *Embracing Defeat: Japan in the Wake of World War II* (New York: Norton, 1999), 22.

8. Steven T. Benfell, "Why Can't Japan Apologize? Institutions and War Memory since 1945," *Harvard Asia Quarterly* (Spring 2002).

9. Quoted in Toshio Nishi, *Unconditional Democracy: Education and Politics in Occupied Japan, 1945–1952* (Stanford: Stanford University Press, 1982), 152. Also see Herbert P. Bix, *Hirohito and the Making of Modern Japan* (New York: HarperCollins, 2000), 32.

10. MacArthur issued the directive, "Administration of the Educational System of Japan," on October 22, 1945. Teachers deemed unacceptable were all career military staff, active nationalists, and enemies of the Occupation.

11. Quoted in Yoshiko Nozaki and Hiromitsu Inokuchi, "Japanese Education, Nationalism, and Ienaga Saburo's Court Challenges," *Bulletin of Concerned Asian Scholars* 30, no. 2 (1998): 38. This law was revised in 2006 to re-emphasize patriotism. See *New York Times,* December 15, 2006.

12. MacArthur quoted in Nishi, *Unconditional Democracy,* 165. The textbooks were *Kuni no Ayumi* [Footsteps of the nation], *Nihon Rekishi* [Japanese history], and *Minshushugi* [Democracy]. For discussion see James J. Orr, *The Victim as Hero: Ideologies of Peace and National Identity in Postwar Japan* (Honolulu: University of Hawai'i Press, 2001), chap. 4. On public information campaigns, see Rikki Kersten, *Democracy in Postwar Japan* (New York: Routledge, 1996), 22–23; Yuki Tanaka, "Crime and Responsibility: War, the State, and Japanese Society," *Japan Focus,* August 22, 2006.

13. Nishi, *Unconditional Democracy,* 148, 214.

14. Orr, *Victim as Hero,* chap. 4; Dower, *Embracing Defeat;* Benfell, "Why Can't Japan Apologize?"

15. For the Potsdam Declaration, see http://www.isop.ucla.edu/eas/documents/potsdam.htm.

16. Powell, "Japan's Germ Warfare," 2017. On the limitations of the Tokyo Trials, see Dower, *Embracing Defeat;* Richard Minear, *Victor's Justice: The Tokyo War Crimes Trial* (Princeton: Princeton University Press, 1971).

17. Howard B. Schonberger, *Aftermath of War: Americans and the Remaking of Japan, 1945–1952* (Kent, Ohio: Kent State University Press, 1989), 165–66, 313; John Welfield, *An Empire in Eclipse: Japan in the Postwar American Alliance System* (London: Athlone Press, 1988), 50.

18. John W. Dower, "Occupied Japan and the Cold War in Asia," in Dower, *Japan in War and Peace* (New York: New Press, 1993), 187.

19. Declassified Documents Collection, "Report of the Van Fleet Mission to the Far East, Chapter 13: Inventory of Commitments and Problems—Korea," The White House, April 26, 1954, 29; Takasaki Soji, *Mogen no genkei* (Tokyo: Mokuseisha, 1990), 224–51.

20. Won-Deog Lee, "Perception of History and Korea-Japan Relations," in *Korea and Japan: Past, Present and Future,* ed. Young-sun Ha (Seoul: Nanam, 1997), 83. Also see Kwan Bong Kim, *The Korea-Japan Treaty Crisis and the Instability of the Korean Political System* (New York: Praeger, 1971).

21. Quotes in this paragraph from Won-Deog Lee, "Perception of History," 84; Kwan Bong Kim, *The Korea-Japan Treaty Crisis*, 43; Yoshibumi Wakamiya, *The Postwar Conservative View of Asia: How the Political Right Has Delayed Japan's Coming to Terms with Its History of Aggression in Asia* (Tokyo: LTCB International Library Foundation, 1999), 33–36, 69.

22. James Morley, *Japan and Korea* (New York: Walker, 1965). Deflators from Bureau of Economic Analysis, U.S. Department of Commerce.

23. Declassified Documents Collection, Department of State, Office of Intelligence Research, Intelligence Report No. 7331, "The Recent and Prospective Foreign Relations of Japan (1956–61)," Prepared by Division of Research for Far East, September 12, 1956, 10.

24. William Underwood, "Mitsubishi, Historical Revisionism, and Japanese Corporate Resistance to Chinese Forced Labor Redress," *Japan Focus*, February 11, 2006, 5–6. Available at http://www.zmag.org/content/showarticle.cfm?ItemID=9703.

25. *Daily Yomiuri*, April 29, 2007.

26. Bix, *Hirohito*, 652, 660.

27. Nozaki and Inokuchi, "Japanese Education," 40. The Hatoyama Administration succeeded in passing this bill only by bringing police into the Diet.

28. See Nozaki and Inokuchi, "Japanese Education," 40; Orr, *Victim as Hero*, 73; Saburo Ienaga, "The Historical Significance of the Japanese Textbook Lawsuit," *Bulletin of Concerned Asian Scholars* 2, no. 4 (Fall 1970): 8.

29. Hyun Sook Kim, "History and Memory: The Comfort Women Controversy," *Positions* 5 (1997): 79.

30. Ienaga, "Historical Significance," 3, 8.

31. Orr, *Victim as Hero*, 90, 94.

32. Quotes in this paragraph from Won-Deog Lee, "Perception of History," 87, 85.

33. Orr, *Victim as Hero*, 139, 137. This service had been conducted since 1958 unofficially by the Japan Veterans Friendship League and the Japan War-Bereaved Families Association, who celebrated the day in order to "enshrine the heroic spirits of all those who died for the country in the War of Greater East Asia." Bix, *Hirohito*, 658.

34. Dower, *Embracing Defeat*, 493–94. On later renovations to the Hiroshima museum, see Agence France-Presse, July 27, 1995.

35. Thomas U. Berger, *Cultures of Antimilitarism: National Security in Germany and Japan* (Baltimore: Johns Hopkins University Press, 1998).

36. Benfell, "Why Can't Japan Apologize?"; Orr, *Victim as Hero*, chap. 4; Dower, *Embracing Defeat*.

37. Orr, *Victim as Hero*, 2–3; Dower, *Embracing Defeat*, 505.

38. Bix, *Hirohito*, 657.

39. The books, entitled *The Twenty-Year Whirlwind: Exposing the Inside Story of the Showa Period*, were authored by a team of Mainichi newspaper reporters. Dower, *Embracing Defeat*, 491.

40. Bestsellers included *Kike Wadatsumi no Koe* [Listen to the Voices from the Sea] (1949); Takeyama Michio, *Biruma no Tategoto* [The Harp of Burma]; other popular works included Ooka Shohei's *Furyoki* [Prisoner of War] (1948) and *Nobi* [Fires on the Plain] (1951).

41. Quoted in Orr, *Victim As Hero*, 26.

42. Cho Fumitsura, *Haisen hishi senso sekinin oboegaki* [A Secret History of the War Defeat: A Note on War Responsibility] (Tokyo: Jiyu Shobo, 1946). Quoted in Utsumi Aiko, "Changing Japanese Views of the Allied Occupation of Japan and the War Crimes Trials," *Journal of the Australian War Memorial* 30 (April 1997). Utsumi also details early Japanese scholarly efforts with respect to the Tokyo Trials.

43. Maruyama Masao, "Words for Thought" [Shiso no Kotoba] *Shiso* 381 (March 1956): 322–25. Reprinted as "Senso Sekinin ron no moten" [Blindspots in the Debate over War Responsibility], in Maruyama Masao, *Senchu to sengo no aida, 1936–1957* [Between War and Postwar, 1936–1957] (Tokyo: Misuzu Shobo, 1976); Maruyama Masao, "Gunkoku shihaisha no seishin keitai," [The Psychological State of Militarist Leaders] in *Gendai seiji no shiso to koudou* [Thought and Behavior of Contemporary Politics] (Tokyo: Miraisha, 1964), chap. 3.

44. Toyama Shigeki, Imai Seiichi, and Fujiwara Akira, *Showa-shi* [A History of Showa] (Tokyo: Iwanami Shoten, 1955). For discussion see Utsumi, "Changing Japanese Views."

45. Telegram from the Embassy in Japan to U.S. Department of State, September 8, 1964, *Foreign Relations of the United States*, Korea, 1964–68, vol. 29, doc. 349. (This publication is hereafter cited as FRUS.)

46. On the weakness of East Asian institutions, see Aaron L. Friedberg, "Ripe for Rivalry: Prospects for Peace in a Multipolar Asia," *International Security* 18, no. 3 (Winter 1993/94): 5–33; Avery Goldstein, "Great Expectations: Interpreting China's Arrival," *International Security* 22, no. 3 (Winter 1997/98): 69.

47. Japan's population in 1960 numbered 94 million compared to South Korea's 25 million. Population figures from International Institute of Strategic Studies (IISS), *The Military Balance* (London: IISS, various years). In 1960 Japan and the ROK spent $3.2 billion and $737 million on defense, respectively (data in 2007 constant U.S. dollars). South Korea's GDP was $42 billion in 1960; Japan's was $999 billion (figures in 2007 constant U.S. dollars). See World Bank, World Development Indicators database, 2003; deflators from Bureau of Economic Analysis, U.S. Department of Commerce, 2008.

48. George Packard, *Protest in Tokyo: The Security Treaty Crisis of 1960* (Princeton: Princeton University Press, 1966).

49. Until border disputes with the Chinese in 1962, the Soviets maintained 12–14 divisions in the Far Eastern Military Districts out of 160 total divisions (the rest were deployed along the Central Front in Western Europe, in Eastern Europe, or in Central Russia). Lowell Dittmer, *Sino-Soviet Normalization and Its International Implications, 1945–1990* (Seattle: University of Washington Press, 1992), 193. Information on Soviet divisions from IISS, *The Military Balance, 1963–62* and *The Military Balance, 1970–71*.

50. Rhee letter to President Eisenhower, December 29, 1954, in FRUS Korea, 1952–1954, vol. 15, part 1 (1984), pp. 1937–41.

51. Rhee quoted in Chae-Jin Lee and Hideo Sato, *U.S. Policy toward Japan and Korea: A Changing Influence Relationship* (New York: Praeger, 1982), 26; also Declassified Documents Collection, U.S. Department of State, Office of Intelligence and Research, Intelligence Report No. 7331, "The Recent and Prospective Foreign Relations of Japan (1956–61)," prepared by Division of Research for Far East, September 12, 1956, 10.

52. Pyun Yong-tae, *Korea: My Country* (Washington, D.C.: Korea Pacific Press, 1953), 64.

53. Pyun Yong-tae, Memorandum of Conversation, October 17, 1952, FRUS Korea, 1952–1954, vol. 15, part 1 (1985).

54. Hui-sung Lee, "An Open Letter to Japanese Intellectuals," *Sasangge* (December 1961), 49.

55. Chong-Sik Lee, "Japanese-Korean Relations in Perspective," *Pacific Affairs* 35, no. 4 (Winter 1962/63): 321–22.

56. Hae Kyoung Cho, "South Korea's Relations with Japan, 1951 to 1987: From Hostility to Accommodation," Ph.D. diss., University of Tennessee, 1988, 82.

57. Rhee quote from Sung-hwa Cheong, *The Politics of Anti-Japanese Sentiment in Korea: Japanese-South Korean Relations under American Occupation, 1945–1952* (New York: Greenwood Press, 1991), 27–28; U.S. official's statement in Memorandum by Assistant Secretary of State for Far Eastern Affairs (Robertson) to the Secretary of State, FRUS China/Japan, 1952–1954, vol. 14, part 2, (1985), doc. 665, 1465–69.

58. Victor D. Cha, "Bridging the Gap: The Strategic Context of the 1965 Korea-Japan Normalization Treaty," *Korean Studies* 20 (1996): 123–60.

59. Kwan Bong Kim, *The Korea-Japan Treaty Crisis*, 43.

60. Quoted in Chong-Sik Lee, *Japan and Korea: The Political Dimension* (Stanford, Calif.: Stanford University Press, 1985), 37.

61. *Mainichi Shinbun*, December 21, 1955.

62. File of American diplomat Robert T. Oliver, quoted in, *Japan and Korea*, 204.

63. Chong-Sik Lee, "Japanese-Korean Relations in Perspective," 321.

64. Quoted in Declassified Documents Collection, "Current Korean Problems," Department of State, Memorandum of Conversation, March 22, 1965, 5. U.S. Ambassador to Japan Edwin Reischauer also argued that a Japanese apology to Korea would improve Korean attitudes toward Japan. See Telegram from the Embassy in Japan to U.S. Department of State, September 8, 1964, FRUS Korea, 1964–68, vol. 29, doc. 349.

65. Quoted in Kwan Bong Kim, *The Korea-Japan Treaty Crisis*, 45.

66. Kwan Bong Kim, *The Korea-Japan Treaty Crisis*, 48.

67. Telegram: Chargé in the Republic of Korea (Lightner) to Department of State, September 25, 1952, FRUS China/Japan, 1952–54, vol. 14, part 2 (1985), doc. 601, 1336–37.

68. Quotes from Cheong, *The Politics of Anti-Japanese Sentiment*, 27–28.

69. Telegram: Chargé in the Republic of Korea (Lightner) to Department of State, September 25, 1952, FRUS China/Japan, vol. 14, 1952–54, part 2 (1985), doc. 601, 1336–37.

70. Quotes from Cheong, *The Politics of Anti-Japanese Sentiment*, 45, 40.

71. One ROK diplomat had a creative solution to the Tokdo/Takeshima dispute. In a meeting with the U.S. secretary of state, Kim Jong-pil, director of the Korean CIA, dismissed the island chain as "a place for sea gull droppings" and "suggested to the Japanese that it be blown up." (The American secretary of state replied that this thought had occurred to him as well.) See Memorandum of Conversation, October 29, 1962, in FRUS Northeast Asia, 1961–63, vol. 22 (1996), 611.

72. Quotes from Memorandum by Assistant Secretary of State for Far Eastern Affairs (Robertson) to the Secretary of State, FRUS China/Japan, vol. 14, 1952–54, part 2 (1985), doc. 665, 1465–69.

73. Rhee letter to President Eisenhower, December 29, 1954, FRUS Korea, vol. 15, 1952–54, part 2 (1984), pp. 1937–41.

74. Quotes from Pyun, *Korea: My Country*, 64, 83.

75. Victor D. Cha, *Alignment despite Antagonism: The U.S.-Korea-Japan Security Triangle* (Stanford, Calif.: Stanford University Press, 1999), 32.

76. Memorandum of Conversation, October 9, 1962, FRUS China/Japan/Korea, 1961–63, vol. 22, doc. 21.

77. Memorandum of Conversation, January 21, 1964, FRUS Korea, 1964–68, vol. 24, doc. 333. Reflecting Korean popular fears is "We Watch the Conference between the U.S. and Japan," *Shinhan Minbo*, October 26, 1961.

78. *Choson Ilbo*, March 18, 1965.

79. State Department quote in Report of John M. Allison, December 5, 1952, FRUS China/Japan, 1952–54, vol. 14, part 2 (1985), doc. 620, 1367; Eisenhower quote in Memorandum of Conversation, July 29, 1954. FRUS Japan, 1952–54, vol. 14, doc. 781, 1688.

80. Rusk quote from Airgram from the Embassy in Korea to the Department of State, February 5, 1964, FRUS Korea, 1964–68, vol. 24, doc. 3. State Department quote in Telegram from the Department of State to the Embassy in Korea, May 12, 1964, FRUS Korea, 1964–68, vol. 24, doc. 341; also see Cha, *Alignment despite Antagonism*, 33.

81. On remarks by Acheson and Senator Tom Connally, see Acheson, *Present at the Creation* (New York: W. W. Norton, 1969), 355–58; FRUS 1950, vol. 7, 64–66. "Stepchild" phrase used in Memorandum from Robert W. Komer to President Johnson, National Security Council, July 31, 1964, Declassified Documents Collection, Johnson Library, document no. CK3100018376. On American plans for Japanese responsibility for Korea, see FRUS 1950, vol. 7, 627–29; Michael Schaller, *The American Occupation of Japan: The Origins of the Cold War* (New York: Oxford University Press, 1985).

82. Rhee statements from Cheong, *The Politics of Anti-Japanese Sentiment*, 27–28; Memorandum of Conversation, October 17, 1952, FRUS 1952–54, vol. 15, Korea, part 1 (1984). Rhee to President Eisenhower, July 11, 1953, FRUS Korea, 1952–54, vol. 15, part 2 (1984), 1368–69.

83. Editorial Note, Department of State, FRUS China/Japan, 1952–54, vol. 14, part 2 (1985), 1465–69.

84. Memorandum by Assistant Secretary of State for Far Eastern Affairs (Robertson) to the Secretary of State, FRUS 1952–54, vol. 14, China/Japan, part 2 (1985), doc. 665, 1465–69.

85. Memorandum of Conversation, November 14, 1961, FRUS China/Korea/Japan, 1961–63, vol. 22, doc. 246.

86. Central Intelligence Agency, Office of Current Intelligence, "The Future of Korean-Japanese Relations," March 18, 1966, Declassified Documents Collection, document no. CK3100015406.

87. Airgram from the Embassy in Korea to the Department of State, February 5, 1964, FRUS, 1964–68, vol. 24, Korea, doc. 3.

88. Wakamiya, *The Postwar Conservative View of Asia*, 194.

89. See, for example, *Asahi Shinbun*, February 18, 1965, 1. This article comments that Shiina offered a statement of deep remorse (*fukai hansei*) which Korean diplomats interpreted as an apology in their spin to the Korean public.

90. The $300 million in grants is equivalent to $1.6 billion in 2007 U.S. dollars; $500 million in loans is equivalent to 2007 $US 2.6 billion. Deflators from Bureau of Economic Analysis, U.S. Department of Commerce, 2008.

91. Memorandum of Conversation, October 29, 1962, FRUS 1961–63, vol. 22, China/Korea/Japan, doc. 282.

92. Quotes in this paragraph from *A New Era in Korea-Japan Relations* (Seoul: Korean Overseas Information Service, 1984). Hirohito's apology was drafted explicitly from Shiina's 1965 statement.

93. Chun-Nakasone Joint Communiqué, September 8, 1984. For text see Lee, *Japan and Korea*, appendix C.

94. Quoted in Nicholas Tavuchis, *Mea Culpa: A Sociology of Apology and Reconciliation* (Stanford, Calif.: Stanford University Press, 1991), 106.

95. *Asahi Shinbun*, August 10, 1982.

96. Published in *Bungei Shunju*, October 1985; also see Won-Deog Lee, "Perception of History," 107.

97. Byung-il Lee, "Kuranari Delivers Japanese Gov't Apology to Choi," *Korea Times*, September 11, 1986, 1; "Nakasone Makes Apology to Chun over Fujio Case," *Korea Times*, September 21, 1986.

98. Lisa Martineau, "Outspoken Tokyo Minister Resigns," *Guardian*, May 14, 1988; *New York Times*, April 27, 1988; Wakamiya, *The Postwar Conservative View of Asia*, 11; *Asahi Shinbun*, April 26, 1988, 2.

99. Ienaga, "Historical Significance," 3; also see Nozaki and Inokuchi, "Japanese Education," 42.

100. Orr, *Victim as Hero*, 97–99. Orr comments that interest in Asian liberation movements "probably reflect[ed] the growing interest in Asian history that followed the official policy of rapprochement with mainland China."

101. See Masanori Nakamura, "The History Textbook Controversy and Nationalism," *Bulletin of Concerned Asian Scholars* 30, no. 2 (1998), 26.

102. Chong-Sik Lee, *Japan and Korea*, 150, 145.

103. *Japan Times*, October 1, 1986.

104. Wakamiya, *The Postwar Conservative View of Asia*, 177–78.

105. "Japan Clarifies Ministers' Remarks on Textbooks," Yonhap Wire Service, August 3, 1982, in FBIS South Korea, same date; "Education Ministry: 'No Intention to Change' Textbooks," Kyodo News Agency, August 5, 1982, in FBIS Japan, same date.

106. Iris Chang, *The Rape of Nanking* (New York: Penguin Books, 1998), 208.

107. Ian Buruma, "Japanese Lib," *New York Review of Books* 33, no. 4 (March 13, 1986).

108. Quoted in Allen S. Whiting, *China Eyes Japan* (Berkeley: University of California Press, 1989), 62.

109. "Beheiren" is short for "Betonamu ni Heiwa o Shimin Rengo" [Citizen's League for Peace in Vietnam]. See Oda Makoto, *Nanshi no Shiso* [Thoughts on Hard Death] (Tokyo: Iwanami Shoten, 1991); translated by Tanaka Yuki in "Oda Makoto, Beiheiren and 14 August 1945: Humanitarian Wrath Against Indiscriminate Bombing," *Japan Focus*, September 30, 2007. Available at http://www.zmag.org/content/showarticle.cfm?ItemID=13923. For Konaka quote and discussion of the greater prominence of "victimizer" theme see Orr, *Victim as Hero*, 4–6.

110. On the Fujio episode, see *Asahi Shinbun*, September 6–7, 1986; on the Okuno controversy see *Asahi Shinbun*, April 23 and 26, 1988. Also see Otake Hideo, *Sengo nihon no ideology tairitsu* [Ideological Confrontation of Postwar Japan] (Tokyo: Sanichi Shobo, 1996); Hosaka Masayasu, *Sengo Seijika Bougenroku* [Record of Gaffes Made by Postwar Politicians] (Tokyo: Chuo Koron Shinsho, 2005).

111. *Asahi Shinbun*, August 15, 1986, 1; and August 16, 1989, 2.

112. The ROK did not begin its democratic transition until 1987 and cannot be considered a mature democracy until still later. See Monty G. Marshall and Keith Jaggers, *Polity IV Project: Political Regime Characteristics and Transitions, 1800–2003*, University of Maryland, Center for International Development and Conflict Management, 2003.

113. On Korean development, see David C. Kang, *Crony Capitalism: Corruption and Development in South Korea and the Philippines* (Cambridge: Cambridge University Press, 2002); Stephan Haggard, *Pathways from the Periphery: The Politics of Growth in the Newly Industrializing Countries* (Ithaca: Cornell University Press, 1990).

114. Defense budget data in constant 2007 U.S. dollars, from World Bank, World Development Indicators Database, 2003; adjusted with dollar deflators from Bureau of Economic Analysis, U.S. Department of Commerce, 2007. Troop figures from IISS, *The Military Balance*, various years.

115. "Joint Communiqué Issued by ROK President Park and President Johnson of the U.S.," *Chronology of the Foreign Affairs of the Republic of Korea, 1965* (Seoul: Ministry of Foreign Affairs and Trade, 1966), 155. Also see "Cooperation for the Pacific Community: No Reduction of U.S. Armed Forces in Korea," *Dong-a Ilbo*, November 2, 1966, 1.

116. Nixon clarified in a November speech that the United States would continue to respect its treaty obligations, to provide a nuclear umbrella, and come to the aid of an ally that was attacked; but that allies were expected to furnish most of the necessary manpower for their defense. On the proposed Carter withdrawal, see Cha, *Alignment despite Antagonism*, chap. 5.

117. In an August 1969 joint statement, both the U.S. and ROK reaffirmed their cooperation against North Korean aggression. Nixon said the United States had no intention of weakening U.S. efforts to support South Korean security. See "The Maintenance of U.S. Armed Forces in Korea and Adherence to the Defense Treaty," *Chosun Ilbo*, August 22, 1969, 1. For Carter's statements, see "Joint Statement of the Seventh Annual U.S.-ROK Security Consultative Meeting," in *Chronology of the Foreign Affairs of the Republic of Korea, 1975*; "Joint Statement by Prime Minister Fukuda and President Carter," quoted in Hang Young-gu and Yun Deok-min, *The Source of the Modern Relationship between Korea and Japan* (Seoul: Oreum, 2003). Carter himself reiterated the continued U.S. commitment to maintaining a high degree of combat readiness to deter a North Korean threat. See "Joint Communiqué between Park Chung-hee and Jimmy Carter," trans. Kim Jung-hae from *Chronology of the Foreign Affairs of the Republic of Korea, 1979*.

118. One of the architects of American Cold War strategy, George Kennan, identified Japan as one of the seven global industrial regions that the United States must defend from entering the Soviet orbit. See John Lewis Gaddis, *Strategies of Containment* (Oxford: Oxford University Press, 1982).

119. As Japan improved its relations with North Korea, this soured its relations with the ROK. See Cha, *Alignment despite Antagonism*, 104–6.

120. Jennifer M. Lind, "Pacifism or Passing the Buck? Testing Theories of Japanese Security Policy," *International Security* 29, no. 1 (Fall 2004): 92–121.

121. 1975 poll from *Chungang Ilbo*, August 14, 1975. This newspaper is Korea's second-largest daily, with moderate political inclinations. Quoted in Hong N. Kim, "Japanese-South Korean Relations in the Post-Vietnam Era," *Asian Survey* (October 1976): 981–95. 1972 poll from Kong Dan Oh, "Japan-Korea Rapprochement: A Study in Political, Cultural, and Economic Cooperation," Ph.D. diss., University of California, 1986, 130–31. 1978 poll from "Japan Is an Unreliable Country," trans. Kim Jung-hae from *Chosun Ilbo*, December 29, 1978, 1.

122. 1985 poll in Oh, "Japan-Korea Rapprochement," 137. 1982 poll in *Kyonghyang Sinmun*, October 6, 1982, quoted in Hong N. Kim, "Japanese-South Korean Relations after the Park Assassination," *Journal of Northeast Asian Studies* 1 (December 1982), 86.

123. "Epoch in Korea-Japan Ties," *Korea Times*, September 9, 1984; Chong-Sik Lee, *Japan and Korea*, 1–2.

124. Defense Ministry official is Yong-Ok Park, "Japan's Defense Buildup and Regional Balance," *Korea Journal of Defense Analysis* 3, no. 1 (Summer 1991): 98. Also see idem, "Korean-Japanese-American Triangle: Problems and Prospects," RAND Report P-7138 (September 1985); "Government to Watch Japan's Naval Maneuvers," Yonhap, January 26, 1983, in FBIS Asia/Pacific, South Korea, same date.

125. Chongwhi Kim, "Korea-Japan Relations and Japan's Security Role," *Korea and World Affairs* 12, no. 1 (Spring 1988): 115.

126. Soong-Hoom Kil, "South Korean Policy toward Japan," *Journal of Northeast Asian Studies,* no. 2 (Spring 1983): 43.

127. Foreign Minister Lee Dong-won noted that Shiina had been the first Japanese official to ever apologize and that "his statement had had a most helpful effect." Declassified Documents Collection, "Current Korean Problems," Department of State, Memorandum of Conversation, March 15, 1965, 5, document no. CK3100006064. On reaction to Hirohito's apologies, see Chongwhi Kim, "Korea-Japan Relations and Japan's Security Role," 108; also see *Korea Herald,* September 7, 1984, 4; and extensive coverage in *A New Era in Korea-Japan Relations.*

128. Among the bilateral disputes during this period were the controversy over the rights of ethnic Koreans living in Japan, resentment over Japan's trade surplus with the ROK, the Korean CIA's kidnapping of dissident Kim Dae-jung from a Japanese hotel, and the assassination of President Park by a Korean living in Japan. See Cha, *Alignment despite Antagonism,* chap. 4.

129. "Foreign Ministers' Meeting with Japan Postponed," Yonhap, September 8, 1986, in FBIS South Korea, same date; *Korea Times,* September 11, 1986; "No Sing-yong, NKDP Discuss Fujio Remarks," Yonhap, September 11, 1986, in FBIS South Korea, same date.

130. *Korea Times,* September 9, 1986, in FBIS South Korea, same date; *Korea Times,* September 10, 1986, in FBIS South Korea, same date.

131. "Education Minister Views Textbook Issue," Yonhap, August 2, 1982, in FBIS South Korea, same date.

132. " 'Stronger' Reaction Urged," Yonhap, August 3, 1982, in FBIS South Korea, same date; Chong-Sik Lee, *Japan and Korea,* 2; Hong N. Kim, "Japanese-South Korean Relations after the Park Assassination," 83, 85.

133. *Kyongjyang Shinmun,* August 5, 1982; *Hankook Ilbo,* August 5, 1982. (The *Hankook Ilbo* is a medium-sized, moderate, independent daily.) "Rallies Protest Textbooks," Yonhap, August 5, 1982, in FBIS South Korea, same date; *Korea Herald,* August 11, 1982; *Korea Times,* August 11, 1982.

134. On Japan's maritime buildup, see Lind, "Pacifism or Passing the Buck?" The $5.5 billion Force Improvement Program emphasized ground forces, with some improvements of naval and air forces. See Korean Overseas Information Service, *A Handbook of Korea* (Seoul: 1978), 451. The naval improvements were a response to fast boats used by North Korean infiltrators.

135. Quotes from "Japan's Nuclear Allergy," *Korea Herald,* May 23, 1981; *Korea Herald,* May 10, 1981; "The Plan for Blockade of the Korea Strait and Our Stand," *Kyonghyang Sinmun,* January 26, 1983, in FBIS Asia/Pacific, South Korea, January 28, 1983.

136. Quoted in Soong-hoom Kil, "South Korean Policy toward Japan," 38.

137. "Government to Watch Japan's Naval Maneuvers," Yonhap, January 26, 1983, in FBIS Asia/Pacific, South Korea, same date.

138. Articles translated by Kim Jung-hae from *Dong-a Ilbo,* January 11, 1977, 2, and *Dong-a Ilbo,* May 4, 1978, 4;, Yong-Ok Park, "Korean-Japanese-American Triangle: Problems and Prospects," 14.

139. "Regional Security," *Korea Times,* July 26, 1979.

140. "Trilateral Military Ties Urged," *Korea Herald,* September 6, 1983, 1.

141. Soong-Hoom Kil, "Two Aspects of Korea-Japan Relations," *Korea and World Affairs* 8, no. 3 (Fall 1984): 509.

142. *Chosun Ilbo,* May 21, 1960, 3; Sheen Sang-Cho, "The Automatic Extension of the U.S.-Japan Security Treaty and the Security of East Asia," *See Dea* [The Times] 83 (August 1970), 23. Both translated by Kim Jung-hae.

143. Quotes in this paragraph from Sang-il Han, "Japan's Defense Capability and Defense Policy," *Korea and World Affairs* 7, no. 4 (Winter 1983), 677–709; Chongwhi Kim, "Korea-Japan Relations and Japan's Security Role"; *Dong-a Ilbo,* July 12, 1976, 2; *Kyonghyang Sinmun,* January 26, 1983, in FBIS Asia/Pacific, South Korea, January 28, 1983; *Korea Herald,* May 10, 1981.

144. Chongwhi Kim, "Korea-Japan Relations and Japan's Security Role," 115. See also Soong-Hoom Kil, "Japanese Defense Posture in the 1980s," *Korea and World Affairs* 3, no. 4 (Winter 1979): 496.

145. Cha, *Alignment despite Antagonism*, chaps. 3–5.

146. Quotes from: "Remarks by Foreign Minister Lee Dong-won at the Signing Ceremony of the Status of Forces Agreement," *Chronology of the Foreign Affairs of the Republic of Korea, 1967,* 131; "Statement by the ROK Prime Minister, His Excellency Chung Il-kwon," in *Chronology of the Foreign Affairs of the Republic of Korea, 1968;* "Inauguration of General Headquarters of the Korea-U.S. Allied Forces," *Chosun Ilbo,* November 8, 1978, 1. Also see "Speech by President Chun Doo Hwan at the Luncheon in Honor of Vice President George Bush of the U.S.," in *Chronology of the Foreign Affairs of the Republic of Korea, 1982;* "Joint Communiqué of 15th Annual ROK-U.S. Security Consultative Meeting," in *Chronology of the Foreign Affairs of the Republic of Korea, 1983.* All quotes translated by Kim Jung-hae.

147. Laura Hein and Mark Selden, "The Lessons of War, Global Power, and Social Change," in *Censoring History: Citizenship and Memory in Japan, Germany, and the United States,* ed. Hein and Selden (Armonk, N.Y.: M. E. Sharpe, 2000), 21.

148. *Asahi Shinbun,* May 25, 1990. The emperor's apology was the product of intense negotiations between Seoul and Tokyo; Roh had demanded that Akihito offer a clearer apology than Hirohito, who, he complained, had "used ambiguous expressions." See "Seoul Presses for Clear-Cut Akihito Apology for Past," *Korea Herald,* May 16, 1990.

149. Kaifu apology in Norma Field, "The Stakes of Apology," *Japan Quarterly* 42, no. 4 (October–December 1995): 413; Miyazawa apology quoted in Won-Deog Lee, "Perception of History."

150. *Asahi Shinbun,* November 7, 1993; Wakamiya, *The Postwar Conservative View of Asia,* 254.

151. Wakamiya, *The Postwar Conservative View of Asia,* 254.

152. "LDP Holds up Wartime Apology in Diet," *Daily Yomiuri,* December 6, 1991.

153. *Daily Yomiuri,* November 27, 1998. Text of Joint Declaration from *Asahi Shinbun,* October 8, 1998.

154. Speech given August 13, 2001, Foreign Press Center Translation. http://www.kantei.go .jp/foreign/koizumispeech/2001/0813danwa_e.html.

155. Speech by Minister for Foreign Affairs Makiko Tanaka at the Ceremony in Commemoration of 50th Anniversary of the Signing of the San Francisco Peace Treaty, San Francisco Opera House, September 8, 2001. http://www.mofa.go.jp/region/n<->america/us/fmv0109/010908 .html.

156. After Koizumi visited the site, he said "When I looked at things put on display [at the park], I strongly felt . . . regret for the pains Korean people suffered during Japanese colonial rule. As a politician and a man, I believe we must not forget the pain of [Korean] people." See "PM Koizumi Visits ROK President Kim Dae-Jung; Protesters Rage," *Mainichi Shinbun,* October 15, 2001; Aya Igarashi, "PM Koizumi Meets ROK President Kim at Blue House; Visits 'Prison' Museum," *Daily Yomiuri,* October 16, 2001.

157. "Japanese PM Apologises for War," BBC News, April 22, 2005; http://news.bbc.co.uk/ 2/hi/asia-pacific/4471495.stm.

158. *China Post,* April 24, 2005.

159. Ministry of Foreign Affairs of Japan, "Statement by Chief Cabinet Secretary Koichi Kato on the Issue of the so-called 'Wartime Comfort Women' from the Korean Peninsula," http:// 210.163.22.165/policy/postwar/state9207.html.

160. *Asahi Shinbun,* January 11, 1992; Yoshimi, *Comfort Women.* Shimizu quoted in George Hicks, *The Comfort Women: Sex Slaves of the Japanese Imperial Forces* (New York: Norton, 1995), 168. For more sources on the sex slaves, see note 5.

161. "Miyazawa Leaves only Words," *Korea Times,* January 14, 1992; T.R. Reid, "Japan Apologizes to Sex Slaves: Premier Cites WWII Abuse of Captive Women," *Washington Post,* August 5, 1993.

162. "Hosoda Apologizes to Former Sex Slaves," Kyodo News Service, December 3, 2004.

163. Murayama quote from http://www.awf.or.jp/01_e.html. In Japanese, the Asian Women's Fund is known as *Josei no tame no Ajia Heiwa Kokumin Kikin.* For discussion see C. Sarah Soh, "Japan's National/Asian Women's Fund for 'Comfort Women,' " *Pacific Affairs* 76, no. 2 (2003): 209–33.

164. For quotes, see O'Herne testimony to U.S. Congress, February 15, 2007, available at

http://www.internationalrelations.house.gov/110/ohe021507.htm; *New York Times*, April 25, 2007; Norma Field, "War and Apology: Japan, the Fiftieth, and After," *Positions* 5 (Spring 1997).

165. Underwood, "Mitsubishi, Historical Revisionism," 15.

166. *International Herald Tribune*, April 28, 2007.

167. Underwood, "Mitsubishi, Historical Revisionism," 15.

168. Koizumi statement given August 13, 2001, Foreign Press Center Translation, available at http://www.kantei.go.jp/foreign/koizumispeech/2001/0813danwa_e.html. On Koizumi's other visits see *New York Times*, October 17, 2005; *Yomiuri Shinbun*, April 22, 2002.

169. *Daily Yomiuri*, October 19, 2005. Also see "Japanese Lawmakers Visit Yasukuni Shrine," BBC Worldwide Monitoring, April 21, 2006, which noted the visit of ninety-six Diet members. Takebe quote from *Daily Yomiuri*, August 5, 2006.

170. *Japan Times*, November 5, 2005; *Asahi Shinbun*, November 11, 2005. On the 2006 visit, see "Japanese Lawmakers Visit Yasukuni Shrine," BBC Worldwide, April 21, 2006.

171. *Sankei Shinbun*, August 14, 2001. Translation by Foreign Press Center of Japan.

172. Roger B. Jeans, "Victims or Victimizers? Museums, Textbooks, and the War Debate in Contemporary Japan," *Journal of Military History* 69 (January 2005), 149–95; *New York Times*, October 30, 2002.

173. *New York Times*, October 30, 2002; *New York Times*, May 21, 1995. The museum's refurbishing was funded largely by the War Bereaved Families Association. Criticism of the tone of the exhibits has led to plans for "softening" their language. See *New York Times*, December 21, 2006.

174. Jeans, "Victims or Victimizers?" 158; *Washington Post*, October 31, 1996, 7.

175. Jeans, "Victims or Victimizers?" 159.

176. For comparisons of textbook discussions, see *New York Times*, April 17, 2005 and *Japan in Modern History* (Tokyo: International Society for Educational Information, 1996). Chinese casualty figures from Pape, *Bombing to Win*, 337.

177. *Osaka Shoseki*, quoted in *Japan in Modern History: High School*, vol. 1 (Tokyo: International Society for Educational Information, 1996), 337. Also see the textbooks *Nihonshi* and *Gendai no Nihonshi*, quoted in *Osaka Shoseki*, 140, 141.

178. *Atarashii Shakai Rekishi*, quoted in *Japan in Modern History: Junior High School* (Tokyo: International Society for Educational Information, 1996).

179. See *Asahi Shinbun*, September 13, 2000, 37; "Japan Fails to Learn from the Past," Yonhap Wire Service, September 14, 2000, in FBIS South Korea, same date; Kitazawa Takuya, "Textbook History Repeats Itself," *Japan Quarterly* 48, no. 3 (July–September 2001): 55.

180. On the 2001 textbook dispute, see Frank Ching, "Japan Still Haunted by Its Past," *Far East Economic Review*, March 29, 2001; "Japan's Sins of Omission," *Economist*, April 14, 2001, 38. On the books' adoption, see *New York Times*, August 16, 2001; Mari Yamaguchi, "Criticized History Textbook at Center of Japan-China Rift Rarely Used in Classrooms," Associated Press, April 14, 2005.

181. On the revision of the Fundamental Law, see *New York Times*, December 16, 2006.

182. Tawara Yoshifuni, *"Ianfu" Mondai to Kyokasho Kogeki* [The "comfort women" issue and the textbook controversy] (Tokyo: Tobunken, 1997). The lawsuit regarding Unit 731 coverage had been brought against the Japanese government thirty years before by Ienaga Saburo; in the 1997 verdict, the court ruled that although the full scope of events was not clearly understood, its existence was generally accepted within academia. *Globe and Mail* (Toronto), August 30, 1997.

183. Quoted in *Japan in Modern History: High School*, 392, 391.

184. Textbooks quoted in *Japan in Modern History: Junior High School*, 461, 463.

185. For descriptions of the textbook, see Irene Wang, " 'Truthful' Account of a Painful Shared Past," *South China Morning Post*, June 10, 2005. The textbook was published in Japan as *Mirai o hiraku rekishi: Higashi Ajia sangoku no kingendaishi* (Tokyo: Kobunken, 2005).

186. Christine M. Chinkin, "Women's International Tribunal on Japanese Military Sexual Slavery," *American Journal of International Law* 95, no. 2 (April 2001) 335–41.

187. For Okuno's statement, see *Sydney Morning Herald*, June 6, 1996; on Abe's statement, see *San Francisco Chronicle*, March 13, 2007.

188. Underwood, "Mitsubishi, Historical Revisionism."

189. William Underwood, "NHK's Finest Hour: Japan's Official Record of Chinese Forced Labor," *Japan Focus* (August 2006).

190. *Daily Yomiuri*, April 29, 2007.

191. "Partners Give Final Pitch on Yasukuni," Asahi News Service, August 11, 2001.

192. Brian Bremner, "In Japan, Dead Soldiers Never Fade Away," *Business Week Online*, July 24, 2001; "Koizumi Faces Conflicting Calls over Shrine Visit," Japan Economic Newswire, August 9, 2001; *Financial Times*, April 10, 2006; Xinhua News Agency, August 15, 2006; Kyodo News Service, August 8, 2001; *Daily Yomiuri*, October 19, 2005; Japan Economic Newswire, July 3, 2006; and *Asahi Shinbun*, November 11, 2005.

193. Quotes from Japan Economic Newswire, November 17, 2006; Xinhua News Agency, August 15, 2006; Nobumasa Tanaka, "What Is the 'Yasukuni Problem'?" *Sekai*, 679 and 680 (September and October 2000). Translation by Gavan McCormack available at http://www.iwanami.co.jp/jpworld/text/yasukuni01.html.

194. September 2006 Nikkei Emergency Telephone Opinion Poll, available at http://www.mansfieldfdn.org/polls/poll-06-12.htm.

195. See Xiaohua Ma, "Constructing National Memory of War: War Museums in China, Japan, and the United States," in *The Unpredictability of the Past: Memories of the Asia-Pacific War in U.S./East Asian Relations*, ed. Marc Gallicchio (Durham: Duke University Press, 2007); Agence France-Presse, July 27, 1995.

196. Quotations from Ma, "Constructing National Memory of War."

197. *Mainichi Shinbun*, May 5, 1994. Nagano was a former army captain and a former chief of staff of Japan's Ground Self-Defense Forces.

198. *Asahi Shinbun*, August 13, 1994; quoted in Chang, *The Rape of Nanking*, 204. Sakurai was the director of Japan's environmental agency at the time.

199. For the politics of the Diet resolution, see John Dower, "Japan Addresses Its Wartime Responsibility," *Journal of the International Institute*, University of Michigan, vol. 3, no. 1 (Fall 1995); "Murayama Threatens to Quit Coalition over War Apology, with Little Effect," *Daily Japan Digest*, June 1, 1995, 1.

200. Gavin McCormack, "The Japanese Movement to 'Correct' History," *Bulletin of Concerned Asian Scholars* 30, no. 2 (1998), 17. The Dietmembers' League had 212 members, chaired by Okuno Seisuke (the former education minister forced out in 1988 for his statements about the war). The opposition Shinshinto Party formed a similar group with forty-one members led by Nagano Shigeto called the "Dietmembers League for the Passing on of a Correct History."

201. Quoted in Wakamiya, *The Postwar Conservative View of Asia*, 14.

202. *Asahi Shinbun*, August 10, 1995. Also see Wakamiya, *The Postwar Conservative View of Asia*, 13.

203. Eto was the director-general of the Management and Coordination Agency. "Reportage on Results of Japan's Eto Remarks Seoul Considers Envoy Recall," Yonhap, November 11, 1995, in FBIS South Korea, same date.

204. For Norota comments, see Rose Tang, "Japanese Politician Condemned for WWII Remarks," www.cnn.com, February 19, 2001. On Nakayama, see *Dong-a Ilbo*, November 30, 2004. On Aso, see Japan Economic Newswire, June 2, 2003.

205. See *The Restoration of a National History* (Tokyo: Japanese Society for History Textbook Reform, 1998). The books were entitled, *Kyokasho ga oshienai rekishi* [The history that textbooks do not teach] (Tokyo: Sankei Shinbun News Service, 1996, 1997, 1998).

206. Authors interview with the vice chairman of *Atarashii Rekishi Kyokasho wo Tsukuru-kai*, October 2001.

207. Quoted in *New York Times*, March 25, 2001.

208. Quotes in this paragraph from: "Intellectuals Protest Nationalist-Authored History Text," Kyodo News Service, March 16, 2001; *International Herald Tribune*, May 4, 2001; "Deeply Concerned about Regressive History Textbooks," *Sekai*, 688 (May 2001).

209. Jim Frederick, "Respect and Resentment," *Time International*, November 29, 2004.

210. *Dong-a Ilbo*, March 30, 2005; *New York Times*, March 22, 2005, A3; *Washington Post*, March 20, 2005, A17.

211. The ASEAN Regional Forum and Asia-Pacific Economic Cooperation (APEC) forum

have deliberately rejected greater formalization. Miles Kahler, "Legalization as Strategy: The Asia-Pacific Case," *International Organization* 54, no. 3 (Summer 2000): 549–71. On East Asian institutional development, see Amitav Acharya, "Ideas, Identity, and Institution-Building: From the 'ASEAN Way' to the 'Asia-Pacific Way'?" *Pacific Review* 10, no. 3 (1997): 319–46.

212. Coding of transition timing according to Marshall and Jaggers, *Polity IV Project.* Predictions about elevated risk of conflict from Edward D. Mansfield and Jack Snyder, *Electing to Fight: Why Emerging Democracies Go to War* (Cambridge, Mass.: MIT Press, 2005).

213. Japan's population in 2000 was 127 million compared to South Korea's 47 million; Japan's GDP was $7 trillion compared to the ROK GDP of $784 billion. In 2000 Japan spent $54 billion on defense; the ROK spent $15.2 billion. Data in constant 2007 U.S. dollars. See World Bank, World Development Indicators Database, 2003. Deflators from Bureau of Economic Analysis, U.S. Department of Commerce, 2008. Population data from IISS, *Military Balance, 2000–2001.* On Japan's maritime capabilities, see Lind, "Pacifism or Passing the Buck?"

214. For example, *Daily Yomiuri,* April 26, 2004; *New York Times,* October 17, 2003.

215. On the China-Japan military balance, see Christopher P. Twomey, "Japan, the Circumscribed Balancer: Building on Defensive Realism to Make Predictions About East Asian Security," *Security Studies* 9, no. 4 (Summer 2000), 178–219.

216. 1996 RAND-*Chungang Ilbo* survey. Quoted in Sook-jong Lee, "Korea and Japan: Engaged but Distant," in *The Future of Korea-Japan Relations,* ed. Robert Dujarric, Proceedings of the Hudson Institute/East Asian Security Study Group Conference, 1997, 102.

217. *Chungang Ilbo* poll, September 21, 2001, at http://bric.postech.ac.kr/bbs/daily/krnews. Also see Harris Poll *Dong-a Ilbo* newspaper poll, January 2001, at http://www.harrisinteractive.com/harris_poll/printerfriend/index.asp?PID=218.

218. "The Survey of Public Opinion on the Korea-Japan Relationship," *Chosun Ilbo,* October 22, 2001, 7. Translated by Kim Jung-hae. See also "The Joint Survey of Public Opinion of Hankook Ilbo and Yomiuri," *Hankook Ilbo,* June 10, 2005, 1.

219. Nam Si-uk, "Future of Korea-Japan Relations," *Korea Focus* 3, no. 6 (1995), 28; Rhee Kyu-ho, "A Review of Korea-Japan Relations," *Shin Dong-a Monthly,* February 1995, translated in *Korea Focus* 3, no. 2 (1995), 16–23. The *Dong-a Monthly* is a publication put out by South Korea's large and second-oldest daily, *Dong-a Ilbo,* which has moderate political leanings.

220. "Japan's View of History," *Korea Herald,* May 7, 1994; " 'Apology' by Japan's Prime Minister," *Hankook Ilbo,* August 16, 1995.

221. *Dong-a Ilbo,* August 5,1999, in FBIS South Korea, same date; Ch'ae Myong-sok, "Ever Increasing Self-Defense Forces—Everyone, Except the United States, Come and Fight," *Sisa Journal,* September 9, 1999, in FBIS South Korea, same date.

222. *Korea Herald,* August 16, 1999; *Dong-a Ilbo,* May 5, 2000, in FBIS South Korea, same date.

223. From author's interviews conducted at Korea University, Yonsei University, Ministry of National Defense (MND), Korea Institute for Defense Analyses (KIDA), and Institute of Foreign Affairs and National Security (IFANS), October 2000.

224. *The Military Balance* 107, no. 1 (February 2007).

225. David Ibison, "S. Korea Halts Military Links with Japan," *Financial Times,* July 13, 2001; "Korea, Japan Resume Naval Exercise," *Korea Times,* September 12, 2002. See also articles in Ralph Cossa, ed., *U.S.-Korea-Japan Relations: Building toward a "Virtual Alliance"* (Washington, D.C.: CSIS Press, 1999).

226. In Korean, "21 Segiui Gukka Anbowa Gukbangbi," translated for the author by LTC Jiyul Kim, KIDA. Portions of the document were published in *Dong-a Ilbo,* August 19–20, 2000.

227. Author's interview, MND, October 2000.

228. *Korea Times,* October 3, 2000. One ship was named the "Yi Sun-shin" in honor of the famous Korean admiral who defeated the Japanese fleet; the other "Ahn Yong-bok" after a fisherman who fought for the Korean claim to Tokdo/Takeshima Island. See Yonhap Wire Service, March 28, 2005.

229. Robert Wall, "Korea Détente No Bar to Military Buys," *Aviation Week and Space Technology,* September 18, 2000, 38.

230. "New Interests Spur Force Development," *Jane's Defence Weekly,* May 22, 1996, 23. Roh quoted in John Feffer, "Asian Arms Race Gathers Speed," *Asia Times Online,* February 14, 2008.

231. Avery Goldstein, *Rising to the Challenge: China's Grand Strategy and International Security* (Stanford, Calif.: Stanford University Press, 2005), chap. 3.

232. Seo-hang Lee, "Naval Power as an Instrument of Foreign Policy: The Case of Korea," *Korea Focus* 5, no. 2 (1997): 31.

233. Kim Min-sok argues that the 1996 dispute with Japan "brought a flood of self-criticism that our Navy was hopelessly behind Japan's Maritime Self-Defense Forces. For Mr. An, it was like acquiring an ally." Kim Min-sok, "Drifting Next-Generation Submarine Project: Too Busy Reading the Feelings of Strong Conglomerates and Big Powers," *Wolgan Chungang*, May 8, 1999, in FBIS South Korea, same date. Also see *Sisa Journal*, April 30, 1998, 50–53, in FBIS South Korea, May 7, 1998. On KDX-III see "Korea Launches Aegis Warship," *Korea Times*, May 25, 2007.

234. Author's interview, October 2000.

235. Seo-hang Lee, "Naval Power as an Instrument of Foreign Policy," 29.

236. *Korea Times*, May 1, 1998.

237. Author's interview, KIDA, October 2000.

238. Of those surveyed, 53 percent identified Japan as the most threatening country in the future; 24 percent indicated China; 15 percent indicated the United States; and 8 percent indicated Russia. Sook-jong Lee, "Korean Perceptions and National Security," *Korea Focus* 3, no. 4 (July/August 1995): 17, 19.

239. *Chungang Ilbo*, September 21, 2001.

240. Norman D. Levin, *The Shape of Korea's Future: South Korean Attitudes toward Unification and Long-Term Security Issues* (Santa Monica: RAND, 1999), 18; for the Hankook Ilbo/Yomiuri Shinbun poll see "South Korean Mistrust of Japan: Poll," *Yomiuiri Shinbun*, June 10, 2005, available at http://www.japanfocus.org/products/details/1556 .

241. "Foreign Minister Writes on ROK-Japan Summit," *Hankook Ilbo*, November 10, 1993, in FBIS South Korea, same date; Yi Dong-min, "Korea-Japan Summit Help Close Book on Unhappy Past," in Yonhap, FBIS South Korea, November 7, 1993, same date; *Korea Times*, October 9, 1998. For other laudatory coverage of the Obushi-Kim summit, see "Japan's Apology," *Korea Herald*, October 9, 1998; *Korea Herald*, October 9, 1998.

242. Author's interviews, October 2000, Seoul, Korea; "Poll: S. Koreans Dissatisfied By Akihito's Apology," *Stars and Stripes*, May 30, 1990.

243. Quotes in this paragraph from: *Korea Times*, January 16, 1992; "Ministry Issues Statement on 'Comfort Women,' " Yonhap, April 21, 1998; *Korea Times*, January 19, 1992; Kim Kyong-min, "Why Is Japan Distrusted?" *Dong-a Ilbo*, May 8, 1995; *Hankook Ilbo*, April 29, 1998, translated in *Korea Focus* 6, no. 3 (1998). Poll data from "60th Anniversary after the War, 40th after Friendship: The Perception of Japan," *Seoul Shinmun*, August 2, 2005, 5. For earlier poll results, see "The Confirmation of Complete Distrust against Japan and Public Opinion regarding the Comfort Women," *Segye Ilbo* 13 (July 13, 1992), 3, translated for the author by Kim Jung-hae.

244. *Dong-a Ilbo*, September 12, 1994; " 'Apology' By Japan's Prime Minister," *Hankook Ilbo*, August 16, 1995.

245. *Hankook Ilbo*, June 6, 1995, quoted in "Watanabe Remarks on Japan Colonial Rule Decried," in FBIS South Korea, June 7, 1995; "Japan's Resolution Minus No-War Pledge," *Hankook Ilbo*, June 6, 1995. Translated in *Korea Focus* 3, no. 3 (1995): 125–28; Kim quoted in *Asahi Shinbun*, August 9, 1995, 8.

246. Quotes in this paragraph from: Hahnkyu Park, "Between Caution and Cooperation: The ROK-Japan Security Relationship in the Post Cold War Period," *Korean Journal of Defense Analysis* (Summer 1998), 9; Nam Si-uk, "Future of Korea-Japan Relations," *Korea Focus* 3, no. 6 (1995): 28; "Roh Moo-hyun: Actions Speak Louder Than Words," *China Daily*, May 8, 2005.

247. "Japanese Minister Defends Colonial Annexation Remarks to 'Negatively Affect Ties,' " Yonhap Wire Service, in FBIS South Korea, June 5, 1995. Foreign minister's quote in "Japanese Minister's Remark on WWII Criticized by Political Parties," Yonhap, August 10, 1995, FBIS South Korea, same date.

248. Lee Chul-seung, "Review of Korea-Japan Basic Treaty," *Seoul Shinmun*, October 30, 1995, translated in *Korea Focus* 3, no. 6 (1995). The *Seoul Shinmun* (name subsequently changed to *Taehan Maeil*) is a progovernment daily. Also Author's interview, KIDA, October 2000.

249. Quotes in this paragraph from: "Watanabe Remarks on Japan Colonial Rule Decried," in FBIS South Korea, June 7, 1995; *Dong-a Ilbo,* May 7, 1994, translated in *Korea Focus* 2, no. 3 (1994): 142–43; *Korea Herald,* May 7, 1994; *Korea Times,* June 8, 1995.

250. *Korea Herald,* August 12, 1999; Kim Young-ho, "South Korea-Japan Relations Still Mired in Snowy Weather," *Munhwa Ilbo,* August 14, 1999, 105.

251. Quotes in this paragraph from: "Scars of Japan's Colonialism Unhealed in Korea," *Asia Pulse,* December 30, 2004; *Chosun Ilbo,* December 1, 2004; "South Korea Raises Japan Textbook Issue at UN Rights Meeting," BBC Monitoring International Reports, April 7, 2005; *China Daily,* April 6, 2005; Lee statement from *Chungang Ilbo,* April 22, 2005. For poll data, see "More Than 9 of 10 People Oppose the Advance of UNSC of Japan," Yonhap Television News, April 15, 2005, translated for the author by Kim Jung-hae.

252. "ROK President Addresses Liberation Day Ceremony," Seoul Korea.net, in FBIS South Korea, August 15, 2001.

253. Author's interview, Yonsei University, October 2000; Won-Deog Lee, "Perception of History," 100.

254. Quotes in this paragraph from: *Korea Herald,* September 15, 2000; *Korea Herald,* February 22, 2001; *Dong-a Ilbo,* June 8, 2001, translated in *Korea Focus* 9, no. 4 (2001): 15–16; *Chungang Ilbo,* July 9, 2001, quoted in FBIS South Korea, July 10, 2001, same date.

255. *Korea Herald,* October 17, 2005; *Chungang Ilbo,* April 22, 2002, in FBIS South Korea, April 23, 2002.

256. "Lawmakers Adopt Resolution Calling for Japan's Apology," Yonhap, October 17, 2001, in FBIS Korea, same date; "Legislators Hold Various Meetings to Mark Aug. 15 Liberation Day," Yonhap, August 14, 2001, in FBIS South Korea, same date; "S. Korea's Ruling Party Holds Rally to Protest Yasukuni Visit," Kyodo News Service, August 17, 2001, in FBIS Japan, same date; Han Sung-joo, "Japanese Textbooks: Stop Being Offensive to the Neighbors," *International Herald Tribune,* July 18, 2001.

257. "Civic Groups Voice Opposition to Koizumi Visit," Yonhap, February 24, 2003; *Guardian* (London), August 14, 2001.

258. *Dong-a Ilbo,* October 16, 2001; *Choson Ilbo,* October 15, 2001.

259. "Legislators Hold Various Meetings to Mark August 15 Liberation Day," Yonhap, August 14, 2001, in FBIS South Korea, same date.

260. *New York Times,* March 22, 2005.

261. Author's interviews, KIDA and IFANS, October 2000.

262. *Defense White Paper* (Seoul: Ministry of National Defense, 1990); *Korea Times,* October 13, 1997.

263. *Dong-a Ilbo,* February 11, 1996, translated in *Korea Focus* 4, no. 1 (1996), 97–98; *Chosun Ilbo,* March 30, 2005.

264. "Civic Group Calls for Mori's Apology for His Remarks on Tokdo," Yonhap, October 6, 2000, in FBIS South Korea, same date; "Pan-National Headquarters for Protecting Tokdo Opens Sat.," Yonhap, December 1, 2000, in FBIS South Korea, same date.

265. This saying was made famous by the statement of U.S. Major General Henry C. Stackpole. Stackpole, commander of the U.S. Third Marine Division in Japan, commented in an interview that U.S. forces were like a "cork" that keeps "a rearmed, resurgent Japan . . . in the bottle." *Washington Post,* March 20, 1993.

266. Author's interview, Korea Institute for Defense Analysis, October 2000; and Author's interview, ROK Ministry of Foreign Affairs and Trade (MOFAT), October 2000.

267. *Defense White Paper* (Seoul: Ministry of National Defense, 1990).

268. Yong-Ok Park, "Japan's Defense Buildup and Regional Balance," 98; Choon Kun Lee and Jung Ho Bae, "Korean Perspectives on Security in the Post Cold War Era: Analysis through the Selected Writings of Korean Scholars on International relations," presented at Korean Association in International Studies/Japanese Association of International Relations Conference, September 11, 1999, Tokyo, Japan.

269. Author's interview, MOFAT, October 2000.

270. Yong-Ok Park, "Japan's Defense Buildup," 99; Rhee Kyu-ho, "A Review of Korea-Japan Relations," *Shin Dong-a Monthly,* February 1995, translated in *Korea Focus* 3, no. 2 (1995): 21.

271. Sang-woo Rhee, "Korea-Japan Security Cooperation: A Prescriptive Design," in *Korea-Japan Security Relations: Prescriptive Studies*, ed. Sang-woo Rhee and Tae-hyo Kim (Seoul: New Asia Research Institute, 2000), vi.

272. In-taek Hyun and Masao Okonogi, "Coping with the North Korean Nuclear Nightmare," in *Korea and Japan: Searching for Harmony and Cooperation in a Changing World*, ed. Hyun and Okonogi (Seoul: Sejong Institute, 1995), 253.

273. Woosang Kim, "Northeast Asia Regional Security Order and the Importance of Alliance Structures," in Rhee and Kim, eds., *Korea-Japan Security Relations*, 3–22; Byung-joon Ahn, "Korea and Japan in Asia and the Pacific after the Cold War," in Hyun and Okonogi, eds. *Korea and Japan*, 17; Author's interview, MOFAT, Asia-Pacific Affairs section, October 2000.

274. "ROK Foreign Ministry Welcomes U.S.-Japan Security Declaration," Yonhap, April 18, 1996, in FBIS South Korea, same date; Yu quoted in "ROK Has Mixed Feelings on U.S.-Japan Military Guidelines," Yonhap, September 24, 1997, from FBIS, same date.

275. This paragraph's quotes from: Han Sung-joo, "New U.S.-Japan Security Ties," *Dong-a Ilbo*, April 28, 1996; Kim Woo-sang, "New U.S.-Japan Defense Guidelines," *Chungang Ilbo*, June 12, 1997, translated in *Korea Focus* 5, no. 4 (1997); author's interview, Sejong Institute, October 2000.

276. Roh quoted in Frank Davies, "Japan Denies 'Comfort Women,' " *San Jose Mercury News*, March 2, 2007.

277. Wakamiya, *The Postwar Conservative View of Asia*, 180.

278. *San Francisco Chronicle*, March 13, 2007.

279. Phrase from Tavuchis, *Mea Culpa*, 99.

280. On Austria, see David Art, *The Politics of the Nazi Past in Germany and Austria* (Cambridge: Cambridge University Press, 2006), chap. 6. On Turkey, see Jennifer Dixon, "Changing the Story: Understanding the Sources of Change and Continuity in States' Official Narratives," paper prepared for presentation at the American Political Science Association Annual Meeting, Chicago, Illinois, 30 August–2 September 2007, 19–20.

281. *Chosun Ilbo*, August 16, 1999; *Chosun Ilbo*, December 1, 2004.

282. Cha, *Alignment despite Antagonism*, 20–23.

283. Sung-jae Choi, "The Politics of the Dokdo Issue," *Journal of East Asian Studies* 5 (2005): 465–94. On Korean nationalism, see Cha, *Alignment despite Antagonism*, 20. My claim that the territorial dispute elevates Korean distrust is equally susceptible to this critique: perhaps Korean statements and policies regarding Tokdo/Takeshima are also just domestic political theater.

284. Kurt Taylor Gaubatz, *Elections and War: The Electoral Incentive in the Democratic Politics of War and Peace* (Stanford, Calif.: Stanford University Press, 1999); Jack Levy and Lily Vakili, "Diversionary Action of Authoritarian Regimes: Argentina in the Falklands/Malvinas Case," in *The Internationalizaton of Communal Strife*, ed. M. Midlarsky (London: Routledge, 1992). On nationalism in transitioning states and the "marketplace of ideas," see Mansfield and Snyder, *Electing to Fight*.

285. Although definitions vary, by most accepted standards South Korea became a mature democracy in the late 1990s. Before then, the country was ruled by a series of dictators who at different times would pursue liberal reforms. South Korea experienced three democratic transitions: two of them incomplete (1962–67 and 1980–84) and one culminating in full democracy (1987–92). Keith Jaggers and Ted Robert Gurr, "Tracking Democracy's Third Wave with the Polity III Data," *Journal of Peace Research* 32, no. 4 (1995): 469–82.; Jennifer Lind, "Democratization and Stability in East Asia," paper presented at the Annual Meeting of the American Political Science Association, Philadelphia, August 2006.

286. Berger, *Cultures of Antimilitarism*.

287. Berger, *Cultures of Antimilitarism*; Sun-Ki Chai, "Entrenching the Yoshida Defense Doctrine: Three Techniques for Institutionalization," *International Organization* 51, no. 3 (Summer 1997): 389–412; Peter J. Katzenstein, *Cultural Norms and National Security: Police and Military in Postwar Japan* (Ithaca: Cornell University Press, 1996).

### 3. Not Your Father's Fatherland

1. "Truth of Massacre Cannot Be Denied," *China Daily*, December 14, 2002. Previous quotes from Andrew Kydd, "Sheep in Sheep's Clothing: Why Security Seekers Do Not Fight Each Other," *Security Studies* 7, no. 1 (Autumn 1997): 134; Stephen Van Evera, "Primed for Peace: Europe after the Cold War," *International Security* 15, no. 3 (Winter 1990–91): 7–57; Kim Dae-jung quoted in *Daily Yomiuri,* August 12, 2001, 5; Nicholas D. Kristof, "The Problem of Memory," *Foreign Affairs* 77, no. 6 (November/December 1998): 45. For other comparisons of Japanese and German memory, see "At War with History," *Newsweek,* August 27, 2001; Frank Ching, "A Tale of Former Allies," *Far Eastern Economic Review,* March 2, 2000, 35.

2. Quoted in Alfred Grosser, *French Foreign Policy under de Gaulle,* trans. Lois Ames Pattison (Boston: Little Brown, 1967), 70.

3. The population and territory of Germany were reduced by about 10 percent; France inherited the provinces of Alsace and Lorraine to the west (lost to the Germans in the Franco-Prussian War), and other nations received other pieces of German territory. The coal-rich German Saarland was placed under international supervision. The "war guilt" clause of the treaty identified Germany as the aggressor in the war and held it liable for an enormous $33 billion in reparations. As Germany fell behind on payments, French and Belgian forces occupied the Ruhr valley to extract reparations. Furthermore, the Versailles treaty placed strict limitations on future German military power.

4. This discussion draws on Philippe Burrin, *France under the Germans: Collaboration and Compromise* (New York: New Press, 1996), 133, 187; Robert Gildea, *Marianne in Chains: In Search of the German Occupation, 1940–1945* (London: Macmillan, 2002), 49, 79, 84.

5. Quoted in Robert Gildea, *France since 1945* (Oxford: Oxford University Press, 1996), 60. On the "resistantialist myth," see Henry Rousso, *The Vichy Syndrome: History and Memory in France since 1944,* trans. Arthur Goldhammer (Cambridge, Mass.: Harvard University Press, 1991).

6. This discussion draws on W. G. Sebald, *On the Natural History of Destruction* (New York: Random House, 2003); Anthony Beevor, *The Fall of Berlin, 1945* (New York: Viking, 2003).

7. Jeffrey Herf, *Divided Memory: The Nazi Past in the Two Germanys* (Cambridge, Mass.: Harvard University Press, 1997), 206.

8. John Ramsden, *Don't Mention the War: The British and the Germans since 1890* (London: Little, Brown, 2006).

9. Norman Frei, *Adenauer's Germany and the Nazi Past,* trans. Joel Golb (New York: Columbia University Press, 2002), 24.

10. Arthur Hearnden, *Education in the Two Germanies* (Oxford: Basil Blackwell, 1974), 29.

11. Robert F. Lawson, *Reform of the West German School System, 1945–1962* (Ann Arbor: University of Michigan School of Education, 1965), 26.

12. This and the following draws on Arthur Hearnden, "The Education Branch of the Military Government of Germany and the Schools," in *The Political Re-Education of Germany and Her Allies after World War II,* ed. Nicholas Pronay and Keith Wilson (Totowa, N.J.: Barnes and Noble Books, 1985), 100–102.

13. Lawson, *Reform of the West German School System,* 46.

14. Hearnden, "The Education Branch of the Military Government," 102.

15. Alfred Grosser, *The Colossus Again: Western Germany from Defeat to Rearmament,* trans. Richard Rees (New York: Praeger, 1955), 82.

16. Harold Marcuse, *Legacies of Dachau: The Uses and Abuses of a Concentration Camp, 1933–2001* (Cambridge: Cambridge University Press, 2001), 56, 61.

17. Ramsden, *Don't Mention the War,* 227–28.

18. Herf, *Divided Memory,* 207, 282.

19. Otto R. Romberg and Heiner Lichtenstein, *Thirty Years of Diplomatic Relations between the Federal Republic of Germany and Israel* (Frankfurt: Tribune Books, 1995). DM3.5 billion is then US$800 million. US$1=DM4.195 in 1952. Historical exchange rates from PACIFIC Exchange Rate Service, obtained at http://fx.sauder.ubc.ca; deflators from Bureau of Economic Analysis, U.S. Department of Commerce, 2008.

20. Herf, *Divided Memory*, 288.

21. "BEG" is short for *Bundesentschädigungsgesetz*, or the Supplementary Federal Law for the Compensation of the Victims of National Socialist Persecution, passed October 1, 1953. See German Information Office website, http://www.germany-info.org.

22. "BRüG" is short for *Bundesrückerstattungsgesetz*, or the Federal Restitution Law. 1987 exchange rate of US$1=DM 1.79. Source: PACIFIC Exchange Rate Service, obtained at http://fx.sauder.ubc.ca.

23. Jeffrey Herf, "Legacies of Divided Memory for German Debates about the Holocaust in the 1990s," *German Politics and Society* 17, no. 52 (Fall 1999): 18.

24. This and subsequent quotes in the next two paragraphs appear in Herf, *Divided Memory*; the quote from Schumacher, p. 251; from Reuter, p. 263; from Heuss, pp. 231, 233, 319.

25. Herf, "Legacies of Divided Memory," 16.

26. Poll data from Michael Wolffsohn, *Eternal Guilt? Forty Years of German-Jewish-Israeli Relations*, trans. Douglas Bokovoy (New York: Columbia University Press, 1993). Quotes from this and the next paragraph are from Herf, *Divided Memory*, 223, 282–85; also see David Art, *The Politics of the Nazi Past in Germany and Austria* (Cambridge: Cambridge University Press, 2006), 54.

27. This and subsequent quotes from Herf, *Divided Memory*, 271, 209; "Tabula rasa" quote appears in Frei, *Adenauer's Germany*, 6.

28. Gerd Knischewski and Ulla Spittler, "Memories of the Second World War and National Identity in Germany," in *War and Memory in the Twentieth Century*, ed. Martin Evans and Ken Lunn (Oxford: Berg, 1997), 241.

29. Robert G. Moeller, "War Stories: The Search for a Usable Past in the Federal Republic of Germany," *American Historical Review* 101, no. 4 (October 1996): 1032.

30. Art, *The Politics of the Nazi Past*, 86.

31. Jeffrey K. Olick, "Genre Memories and Memory Genres: A Dialogical Analysis of May 8, 1945 Commemorations in the Federal Republic of Germany," *American Sociological Review* 64, no. 3 (1999): 387.

32. Adenauer quoted in Rudy Koshar, *Germany's Transient Pasts: Preservation and National Memory in the Twentieth Century* (Chapel Hill: University of North Carolina Press, 1998), 219.

33. Knischewski and Spittler, "Memories of the Second World War," 242.

34. Adenauer quoted in Herf, *Divided Memory*, 224.

35. Knischewski and Spittler, "Memories of the Second World War," 242.

36. Koshar, *Germany's Transient Pasts*, 208.

37. Entitled *Dokumentation der Vertreibung der Deutschen aus Ost-Mitteleuropa*, this series was published by the Bundesministerium für Vertriebene, Flüchtlinge und Kriegsgeschädigte. The first volume appeared in 1954. This paragraph draws on Moeller, "War Stories," 1023–26.

38. Grosser, *The Colossus Again*, 166–67; Wulf Kansteiner, "Losing the War, Winning the Memory Battle: The Legacy of Nazism, World War II, and the Holocaust in the Federal Republic of Germany," in *The Politics of Memory in Postwar Europe*, ed. Richard Ned Lebow, Wulf Kansteiner and Claudio Fogu (Durham: Duke University Press, 2006), 111.

39. Sabine Reichel, *What Did You Do in the War, Daddy? Growing up German* (New York: Hill and Wang, 1989).

40. Quotes in this paragraph from Steve Crawshaw, *Easier Fatherland: Germany and the Twenty-First Century* (London: Continuum, 2004), 28–30.

41. Alexander and Margarete Mitscherlich, *The Inability to Mourn: Principles of Collective Behavior*, trans. Beverley R. Paczek (New York: Grove Press, 1975). Gellhorn quoted in Crawshaw, *Easier Fatherland*, 23.

42. R. J. B. Bosworth, *Explaining Auschwitz and Hiroshima: History Writing and the Second World War, 1945–1990* (London: Routledge, 1993). The case for German guilt was supported by the massive study by Italian historian Luigi Albertini, *The Origins of the War of 1914*, trans. and ed. Isabella M. Massey (London: Oxford University Press, 1952–57).

43. Volker R. Berghahn and Hanna Schissler, "History Textbooks and Perceptions of the Past," introduction to *National Identity and Perceptions of the Past: International Textbook Research in Britain, the United States, and West Germany*, ed. Volker R. Berghahn and Hanna Schissler (Oxford: Berg, 1987), 11.

44. Bosworth, *Explaining Auschwitz*, 62.

45. Kansteiner, "Losing the War," 108.

46. Holger Herwig, "Clio Deceived: Patriotic Self-Censorship in Germany after the Great War," *International Security* 12, no. 2 (Fall 1987).

47. Walther Hubatsch, ed., *The German Question* (New York: Herder Book Center, 1967), 307–9.

48. Sabine Lee, *Victory in Europe: Britain and Germany since 1945* (Harlow: Pearson Education Ltd., 2001), 8.

49. Quoted in Paul B. Stares, *Allied Rights and Legal Constraints on German Military Power* (Washington, D.C.: Brookings, 1990), 3–9.

50. West Germany's population in 1960 was 54 million compared to France's 45 million. International Institute of Strategic Studies (IISS), *The Military Balance* (London: IISS, various years). In 1960 France's GDP was $625 billion and West Germany's $411 billion. Data in 2007 constant U.S. dollars from World Bank, World Development Indicators Database. Dollar deflators from Bureau of Economic Analysis, U.S. Department of Commerce, 2008.

51. France had over one million troops in 1960 compared to West Germany's 330,000. France demobilized a substantial portion of its army after the withdrawal from Algeria in the early 1960s. By 1965 the French had 557,000 and West Germany 438,000 troops. Data from International Institute of Strategic Studies, *The Military Balance, 1961–62;* IISS, *The Military Balance, 1965–66.* West Germany's defense budget for 1970 was $24 billion and France's was $26 billion. Data in 2007 constant U.S. dollars from World Bank, World Development Indicators Database, 2003. Deflators from Bureau of Economic Analysis, U.S. Department of Commerce, 2008.

52. James L. Richardson, *Germany in the Atlantic Alliance* (Cambridge, Mass.: Harvard University Press, 1966), 23.

53. Marc Trachtenberg, *A Constructed Peace: The Making of the European Settlement, 1945–1963* (Princeton: Princeton University Press, 1999).

54. International Institute of Strategic Studies, *The Military Balance,* various years.

55. Andrei S. Markovits and Simon Reich, *The German Predicament: Memory and Power in the New Europe* (Ithaca: Cornell University Press, 1997), 125; 1950 and 1953 surveys quoted in Jean Stoetzel, "The Evolution of French Opinion," in *France Defeats EDC,* ed. Daniel Lerner and Raymond Aron (New York: Praeger, 1957), 73–74, 88; 1951 poll from "L'Europe et l'Allemagne," *Sondages,* no. 1 (1951), 20–21; 1956 poll from "Les relations avec les pays étrangeres," *Sondages* 18, no. 3 (1956).

56. Quoted in Dean Acheson, *Present at the Creation: My Years in the State Department* (New York: Norton, 1969), 552.

57. Quoted in Edgar S. Furniss, Jr., *France, Troubled Ally: De Gaulle's Heritage and Prospects* (New York: Harper Brothers, 1960), 41.

58. Quoted in Alexander Werth, *France, 1940–1955* (London: Robert Hale, 1956), 406.

59. Quoted in Robert McGeehan, *The German Rearmament Question: American Diplomacy and European Defense after World War II* (Urbana: University of Illinois Press, 1971), 211.

60. Grosser, *The Colossus Again,* 231. Reynaud quoted in Alfred Grosser, "Germany and France: A Confrontation," in *France Defeats EDC,* ed. Lerner and Aron, 69.

61. Robert Gildea, *France since 1945* (Oxford: Oxford University Press, 1996), 11.

62. Ibid, 12.

63. Jules Moch, *Histoire Du Rearmement Allemand Depuis 1950* (Paris: Robert Laffont, 1965).

64. This paragraph draws on Stoetzel, "The Evolution of French Opinion," 76–78.

65. Minutes of private conference of Foreign Ministers, September 14, 1950, FRUS, 1950, vol. 3, 293–301.

66. On this debate, see Raymond Schmittlein, "Briser les chaines de la jeunesse allemande," *France-Illustration,* September 17, 1949, 18. Also see Roy F. Willis, *The French in Germany, 1945–1949* (Stanford: Stanford University Press, 1962), 93.

67. Andrew Barros, "Disarmament as a Weapon: Anglo-French Relations and the Problems of Enforcing German Disarmament, 1919–28," *Journal of Strategic Studies* 29, no. 2 (April 2006): 312.

68. Edmond Vermeil, "Les Allies Et La Rééducation Des Allemands," in *L'education De L'allemagne Occupée*, ed. Helen Liddell, Edmond Vermeil, and Bogdan Suchodolski (Paris: Librairie Marcel Riviere et Cie, 1949), 28.

69. Quoted in Alfred Grosser, "Germany and France: A Confrontation," in *France Defeats EDC*, ed. Lerner and Aron, 70.

70. Helen Liddell, Introduction to *L'education De L'allemagne Occupée*, ed. Liddell et al.

71. Vermeil, "Notes Sur La Rééducation En Zone Française," in *L'education De L'allemagne Occupée*, ed. Liddell et al., 58.

72. Liddell, Introduction to *L'education De L'allemagne Occupée*, ed. Liddell, et al.

73. Hearnden, *Education in the Two Germanies*, 37.

74. Quotes in this paragraph from Alfred Grosser, *Germany in Our Time*, trans. Paul Stephenson (New York: Praeger, 1970), 210, 301; Jean Solchany, *Comprendre le nazisme dans l'Allemagne des annees zero, 1945–1949* (Paris: Presses Universitaires de France, 1997), XXI; Edouard Husson, *Une culpabilite ordinaire? Hitler, les Allemands, et La Shoah* (Paris: François-Xavier de Guibert, 1997), 13.

75. See, for example, Solchany, *Comprendre le nazisme dans l'Allemagne des Annees zero, 1945–1949*, XXI; Edouard Husson, *Une culpabilite ordinaire?* 13.

76. Raymond Aron, "Historical Sketch of the Great Debate," in *France Defeats EDC*, ed. Lerner and Aron, 13.

77. Quoted in Pierre Maillard, *De Gaulle et l'Allemagne: Le rêve inacheve* (Paris: Plon, 1990), 89.

78. In French, CED. The EDC would have consisted of a fifty-year treaty envisioning twenty divisions of 600–700,000 soldiers. It would have included a "range of supranational institutions such as a European executive authority, ministerial council, parliamentary assembly, and court of justice, to be supplied and financed through a single common system and fund." McGeehan, *The German Rearmament Question*, 138. The FRG would have committed twelve divisions but would have had no decision-making authority (i.e., no General Staff or Minister of Defense). See Lerner and Aron, *France Defeats EDC*; Trachtenberg, *A Constructed Peace.*

79. Grosser, *The Colossus Again*, 238.

80. Grosser, "Germany and France: A Confrontation," 67.

81. David Clay Large, *Germans to the Front: West German Rearmament in the Adenauer Era* (Chapel Hill: University of North Carolina Press, 1996), 92.

82. Quoted in Furniss, *France, Troubled Ally*, 41.

83. Quoted in Werth, *France, 1940–1955*, 706.

84. Quoted in Caffrey to Byrnes, November 3, 1945, FRUS, 1945, vol. 3, 890–91.

85. De Gaulle quoted in Maillard, *De Gaulle et l'Allemagne*, 87, 89.

86. This paragraph draws on Stoetzel, "The Evolution of French Opinion," 82, 89.

87. *L'Humanité*, September 27, 1950, and August 31, 1954; *Le Monde*, November 4, 1954.

88. Quoted in Moch, *Histoire du rearmement allemand depuis 1950*, 132.

89. Quoted in Large, *Germans to the Front*, 141–42.

90. *Journal Oficiel*, 4478. Quoted in Grosser, "Germany and France," 69.

91. Quoted in Large, *Germans to the Front*, 142.

92. Maillard, *De Gaulle et l'Allemagne*, 136.

93. *Rapport de la Délégation Francaise au Gouvernment* (Paris: Imprimerie des Journaux Officiel, 1952), 28.

94. Quoted in Large, *Germans to the Front*, 142.

95. Quoted in McGeehan, *The German Rearmament Question*, 211.

96. Werth, *France, 1940–1955*, 705.

97. Aron and Lerner, *France Defeats EDC*, 11; Jacques Fauvet, "Birth and Death of a Treaty," in *France Defeats EDC*, ed. Aron and Lerner, 142. For de Gaulle's own passionate denunciations of the EDC, see Maillard, *De Gaulle et l'Allemagne*, 133.

98. Fauvet, "Birth and Death of a Treaty," 192.

99. *Le Monde*, October 5, 1950.

100. McGeehan, *The German Rearmament Question*, 200, 204.

101. Gildea, *France since 1945*, 15.

102. Quoted in Simon Serfaty, *France, de Gaulle, and Europe* (Baltimore: Johns Hopkins University Press, 1968), 11; Mark Sheetz, "Responses to Cresswell and Trachtenberg," in *Journal of Cold War Studies*, 5, no. 3 (2003): 41.

103. Fauvet, "Birth and Death of a Treaty," 187–88.

104. Le Bail and Cost-Fleuret quoted in Grosser, "Germany and France: A Confrontation," 70, 65; Schuman quoted in Trevor Salmon and Sir William Nichol, eds., *Building European Union: A Documentary History and Analysis* (Manchester, UK: Manchester University Press, 1997), 44.

105. Quoted in Edwina S. Campbell, *Germany's Past and Europe's Future* (Washington, DC: Pergamon-Brassey's, 1989), 61.

106. Maurice Couve de Murville, *Le Monde en face* (Paris: Plon, 1989), 50.

107. Alfred Grosser, *French Foreign Policy under De Gaulle*, 6.

108. Karl W. Deutsch, Lewis J. Edinger, Roy C. Macridis, and Richard L. Merritt, *France, Germany, and the Western Alliance: A Study in Elite Attitudes on European Integration and World Politics* (New York: Charles Scribner's Sons, 1967), 66. 1965 poll data from *France Soir*, March 18, 1965.

109. Maurice Couve de Murville, *Une politique etrangere, 1958–1969* (Paris: Plon, 1971), 238.

110. Ambassador's statement from Speech by François Bujon de l'Estang, French Ambassador to the United States, February 26, 1998, Berkeley, California. Charles de Gaulle, *Memoirs of Hope: Renewal and Endeavor*, trans. Terence Kilmartin (New York: Simon and Schuster, 1971), 181.

111. The French had envisioned the Elysée Treaty as the establishment of a Franco-German "third force" to balance the U.S.-Soviet conflict. In the early 1960s the Soviets had developed a second-strike nuclear capability, thus calling into question the credibility of the U.S. nuclear guarantee to its Western European allies. The French effort was accepted by Konrad Adenauer but rejected by the German Bundestag, which voted unanimously to insert a preamble to the treaty reaffirming the FRG's commitment to NATO.

112. De Gaulle quoted in Jeffrey Glen Giaque, *Grand Designs and Visions of Unity: The Atlantic Powers and the Reorganization of Western Europe, 1955–1963* (Chapel Hill: University of North Carolina Press, 2002), 92; de Gaulle, *Memoirs of Hope*, 176.

113. Deutsch et al, *France, Germany, and the Western Alliance*, 67.

114. Quoted in the *Times* (London), October 14, 1978.

115. Quotes in this paragraph from de Gaulle, *Memoirs of Hope*, 164–77.

116. de Gaulle, *Memoirs of Hope*, 173.

117. Trachtenberg, *A Constructed Peace*, 392; de Gaulle quote appears in Herve Alphand, *L'étonnement d'être: Journal 1939–1973* (Paris: Fayard, 1977), 445.

118. de Gaulle, *Memoirs of Hope*, 227, 177.

119. Couve de Murville, *Une Politique Etrangere*, 236.

120. Quoted in Andrew Moravcsik, *The Choice for Europe: Social Purpose and State Power from Messina to Maastrict* (Ithaca: Cornell University Press, 1998), 104.

121. Author's interview, Sorbonne, October 2002.

122. de Gaulle, *Memoirs of Hope*, 173.

123. Giaque, *Grand Designs*, 89.

124. de Gaulle, *Memoirs of Hope*, 173.

125. Quotations in this section from Olick, "Genre Memories," 389.

126. Herf, *Divided Memory*, 347.

127. Marcuse, *Legacies of Dachau*, 430.

128. Koshar, *Germany's Transient Pasts*, 246.

129. Quoted in Herf, *Divided Memory*, 344–345.

130. On the domestic controversy see Knischewski and Spittler, "Memories of the Second World War," 243. Brandt quoted in Crawshaw, *Easier Fatherland*, 39. Invoking Brandt are Timothy Ryback, "Japan May Have to Bend Its Knee," *International Herald Tribune*, April 26, 2005; and Republika Srpska President Dragan Cavic, who said in 2003 that Bosnia needed "three Willy Brandts" for apologies to improve relations. See "Marovic Apologizes to Bosnians," November 17, 2003, Balkan Reconstruction Report Newsletter, http://balkanreport.tol.cz.

131. Quoted in Herf, "Legacies of Divided Memory," 25.

132. Ian Buruma, *The Wages of Guilt* (New York: Farrar Straus Giroux, 1994), 148.

133. Quoted in Herf, *Divided Memory*, 338–39.

134. Herf, *Divided Memory*, 184.

135. Claus Hofhansel, "The Diplomacy of Compensation for Eastern European Victims of Nazi Crimes," *German Politics* 8, no. 3 (December 1999): 109. Also see http://www.germany-info.org. US$1=DM4 in 1964; found at http://fx.sauder.ubc.ca.

136. Hofhansel, "The Diplomacy of Compensation," 107.

137. Quote from Helmuth Leichtfuss, "A Study of the Present Situation Regarding Contemporary History Instruction in the High School of Land Hesse," in *Education for Democracy in West Germany: Achievements, Shortcomings, Prospects*, ed. Walter Stahl (New York: F. A. Praeger, 1961), 140; Marcuse, *Legacies of Dachau*, 210. Also see Olick, "Genre Memories," 388.

138. Leichtfuss, "A Study of the Present Situation," 142–44

139. Stahl, ed. *Education for Democracy in West Germany*, 117.

140. Bill Niven, *Facing the Nazi Past: United Germany and the Legacy of the Third Reich* (London: Routledge, 2002), 24.

141. Ibid., 205–6.

142. Bosworth, *Explaining Auschwitz*, 62. Also see Saul Friedlander, "Some German Struggles with Memory," in *Bitburg in Moral and Political Perspective*, ed. Geoffrey Hartman (Bloomington: Indiana University Press, 1986), 26–42.

143. Richard J. Evans, *In Hitler's Shadow: West German Historians and the Attempt to Escape from the Nazi Past* (New York: Pantheon Books, 1989), 113; Fischer's book *Griff nach der Weltmacht* [Grab for world power] was published in 1961 in English under the title, *Germany's Aims in the First World War*. Fischer later published a more explicit version of his argument in a 1969 published monograph, *Krieg der Illusionen* [War of illusions].

144. Bosworth, *Explaining Auschwitz*, 60.

145. William L. Shirer, *The Rise and Fall of the Third Reich: A History of Nazi Germany* (New York: Simon and Schuster, 1960).

146. Art, *The Politics of the Nazi Past*.

147. Heinmann quoted in Olick, "Genre Memories," 389. A "hair shirt" is a garment woven of coarse cloth and often goat's hair; it is designed to maximize discomfort, as a gesture of penance by Christians. Schmidt quotes from Ibid., 392; and Siobhan Kattago, "Representing German Victimhood and Guilt: The *Neue Wache* and Unified German Memory," *German Politics and Society* 16, no. 3 (Fall 1998): 96.

148. Strauss and Carstens quoted in Evans, *In Hitler's Shadow*, 19.

149. Quoted in Evans, *In Hitler's Shadow*, 55.

150. Dennis L. Bark and David R. Gress, *A History of West Germany*, vol. 2., 2nd ed. (Oxford: Blackwell, 1989), 424.

151. See Foreign Broadcast Information Service (hereafter cited as FBIS), Western Europe, Federal Republic of Germany, May 3, 1985, "Jewish Council Chairman's Remarks on Bitburg Visit." On the controversy, see David B. Morris, "Bitburg Revisited: Germany's Search for Normalcy," *German Politics and Society* 13, no. 4 (Winter 1995): 92–109.

152. Quoted in Olick, "Genre Memories," 394.

153. Evans, *In Hitler's Shadow*, 42, 104; Jerry Z. Muller, "German Neoconservatism and the History of the Bonn Republic, 1968 to 1985," *German Politics and Society* 18, no. 1 (Spring 2000): 22. Nolte quotes from *Forever in the Shadow of Hitler? Original Documents of the Historikerstreit, the Controversy Concerning the Singularity of the Holocaust*, trans. James Knowlton and Truett Cates (Atlantic Highlands, N.J.: Humanities Press International, 1993), 21–22. Hilgruber cited in Evans, *In Hitler's Shadow*, 52.

154. Stürmer quoted in Evans, *In Hitler's Shadow*, 104; Nolte quoted in *Forever in the Shadow of Hitler*, 18–20.

155. Karl Wilds, "Identity Creation and the Culture of Contrition: Recasting 'Normality' in the Berlin Republic," *German Politics* 9, no. 1 (April 2000): 85. For a useful collection of *Historikerstreit* writings translated into English, see *Forever in the Shadow of Hitler*. For analysis, see Charles S. Maier, *The Unmasterable Past: History, Holocaust, and German National Identity* (Cambridge, Mass.: Harvard University Press, 1988).

156. Quoted in Herf, *Divided Memory,* 262–65. Full text of Von Weizsäcker's speech can be found in Hartman, *Bitburg,* 262–73.

157. Quotes in this paragraph from Hartman, *Bitburg,* 244–50. Von Weizsäcker quoted in Bark and Gress, *A History of West Germany,* 446.

158. Elizabeth Domansky, "Kristallnacht, the Holocaust, and German Unity: The Meaning of November 9 as an Anniversary in Germany," *History and Memory* 4, no. 1 (Spring/Summer 1992): 66. See also Marcuse, *Legacies of Dachau,* 367–68.

159. Hubatsch, ed., *The German Question* 307–9.

160. Jacques Vernant, "Le Général de Gaulle et la politique extérieure," *Politique Étrangère* 35, no. 6 (1970): 627.

161. A thaw in inter-German relations during the "German Spring" led Moscow to launch a propaganda campaign in the mid-1980s in which it accused Bonn of territorial ambitions in Europe. See Morris, "Bitburg Revisited." For other territorial controversies, see Susan J. Smith, "Soviet Bloc Storm over Interior Minister's Remarks," Associated Press, February 2, 1983. On the Silesian rally, see Moeller, "War Stories," 1041.

162. Glenn Frankel, "France Presses Kohl on Border Pact," *Washington Post,* March 2, 1990; Ian Davidson, "Old European Ghosts Return to Haunt Germany," *Financial Times,* March 22, 1990; Thomas L. Friedman, "Evolution in Europe; 2 Germanys Vow to Retain Border with the Poles," *New York Times,* July 18, 1990.

163. In 1970 France's GDP was about $1 trillion and West Germany's was $819 billion; in 1980 France's GDP was $1.4 trillion and Germany's was $1.3 trillion; in 1990 the respective figures were $1.2 trillion and $1.5 trillion. Data in 2007 constant U.S. dollars, from World Bank, World Development Indicators Database, 2003; adjusted with dollar deflators from Bureau of Economic Analysis, U.S. Department of Commerce, 2008.

164. For example, France had 557,000 troops and the FRG had 438,000 in 1965; by 1985, France had 476,500 and Germany had 478,000. International Institute of Strategic Studies, *Military Balance,* various years.

165. 1965 poll from *France Soir,* March 18, 1965; 1983 poll appears in "L'image compareé de la France et l'Allemagne de l'Ouest," *Sofres* (May 1983): 1. Polls regarding unification appear in *Sondages,* no. 3 (1960): 71; "La Reunification Allemande?" *Geopolitique* (1987): 6–9.

166. In French, "grâce de naissance tardive." Luc Rosenzweig, *Le Monde,* January 22, 1987 and October 5, 1990.

167. On Bitburg, see Jean Lesieur, "D'Auschwitz à Hiroshima," *L'Express,* February 2, 1995, 57; on Jenninger, see *Le Monde,* November 12, 1988. Also see Daniel Vernet, *Le Monde,* November 14, 1988.

168. Luc Rosenzweig, *Le Monde,* January 22, 1987.

169. Daniel Vernet, "Le scandale Jenninger en RFA L'ombre portée du nazisme," *Le Monde,* November 14, 1988; Jean-Jacques Guinchard, "Passé Nazi, Passé Allemand?" *Le Monde Diplomatique,* July 1987.

170. In November 1989, *Paris Match* reported that 61 percent of respondents said that German unification would be "a good thing for France," and a Figaro-Louis Harris poll that month found a similar result (60 percent). *Paris Match,* November 23, 1989; Figaro-Harris poll in *Le Figaro,* November 13, 1989. Two months later, in January 1990 the *Economist* also reported that 61 percent of French favored German unification. Published in *Le Monde,* January 27, 1990, 34.

171. *Le Monde,* October 12, 1990, 1; Daniel Vernet, *Le Monde,* January 9, 1991.

172. Jèrôme Vaillant, *Le Monde Diplomatique,* October 1990, 1–3; Andre Fontaine, "Plus fort que Bismarck," *Le Monde,* October 3, 1990; Bruno Frappant, "Puissants voisins," *Le Monde,* October 13, 1990, 31.

173. Philip Zelikow and Condoleezza Rice, *Germany Unified and Europe Transformed: A Study in Statecraft* (Cambridge, Mass.: Harvard University Press, 1995), 88.

174. Stephen F. Szabo, *The Diplomacy of German Unification* (New York: St. Martin's Press, 1992), 48.

175. Stanley Hoffmann, "French Dilemmas and Strategies in the New Europe," in *After the Cold War: International Institutions and State Strategies in Europe, 1989–1991,* ed. Robert O. Keohane, Joseph S. Nye, and Stanley Hoffmann (Cambridge, Mass.: Harvard University Press,

1993), 130. Margaret Thatcher describes Mitterrand's fears of German unification in her memoirs. Thatcher, *The Downing Street Years* (New York: HarperCollins Publishers, 1993), 797.

176. Quotes appear in Daniel Vernet, *Le Monde,* January 9, 1991; Jèrôme Vaillant, *Le Monde Diplomatique,* October 1990, 1–3; Bruno Frappant, "Puissants Voisins," *Le Monde,* October 13, 1990, 31. For summaries of French media reports, see Nicholas Moll, "L'Allemagne de nos obsessions," *Documents,* no. 2 (June 1990): 11–17. See also Stephan Martens, "Le Traité 2+4: L'anti-Versailles ou l'intelligence multilatérale," *Allemagne d'Aujourd'hui,* no. 146 (October–December 1998): 286–307.

177. Michael J. Baun, "The Maastrict Treaty as High Politics: Germany, France, and European Integration," *Political Science Quarterly* 110, no. 4 (Winter 1995/96): 622.

178. Edouard Husson, *L'Europe contre l'amitié franco-allemande* (Paris: François-Xavier de Guibert, 1998), 36.

179. Quotes in this paragraph from Jacques Attali, *Verbatim,* vol. 3 (Paris: Fayard, 1995), 424, 436, 377.

180. Szabo, *The Diplomacy of German Unification,* 50. On Mitterrand's stance on the border question, see FBIS Western Europe, June 15, 1990, and April 24, 1990.

181. Claire Trean, "La controverse sur la frontiere germano-polognaise," *Le Monde,* March 3, 1990.

182. Quotes from Attali, *Verbatim,* 364.

183. George Bush and Brent Scowcroft, *A World Transformed* (New York: Knopf, 1998), 201.

184. Baun, "The Maastrict Treaty as High Politics," 613–14.

185. Hoffmann, "French Dilemmas," 135.

186. Quoted in Andre Fontaine, "Plus fort que Bismarck," *Le Monde,* October 3, 1990; *Economist,* October 21, 1989, 50.

187. Fontaine, "Plus fort que Bismarck"; "L'Allemagne au Singulier," *Le Monde,* October 12, 1990.

188. Jèrôme Vaillant, *Le Monde Diplomatique,* Oct 1990, 1–3.

189. Maurice Duverger, "Allemagne—Une Seconde République de Weimar?" *Le Monde,* September 11, 1990.

190. Couve de Murville, *Le Monde en face,* 48.

191. The phrase "culture of contrition" is from Wilds, "Identity Creation." On the confrontation with the East German past, see Anne Sa'adah, *Germany's Second Chance: Trust, Justice, and Democratization* (Cambridge, Mass.: Harvard University Press, 1998).

192. Quoted in Marcuse, *Legacies of Dachau,* 379. Marcuse comments, "This unequivocal statement of acceptance of Germany's brown-collar past was a far cry from Kohl's homage to German victimhood at Bitburg a decade earlier."

193. "Herzog Addresses 8 May Ceremony in Berlin," Munich ARD Television, May 8, 1995, in FBIS Germany, same date.

194. Charles M. Sennott, "Germans Also Participate, With a New Perspective," *Boston Globe,* June 7, 2004, A1. See also *Le Temps,* June 7, 2004.

195. Sennott, "Germans Also Participate"; Schröder quoted in *Le Monde,* June 5, 2004.

196. In 1992 the Bundestag passed the "Law on Compensation for Victims of National Socialism in the Regions Acceding to the Federal Republic." This law recognized that persons had been denied compensation by the GDR and invited them to submit new applications to the unified German government. German Information Office, http://www.germany-info.org.

197. In the 1996 agreement, Germany contributed DM140 million, and the Czech government provided DM25 million (equivalent to $119 million and $22 million in 2007 $US, respectively). Hofhansel, "The Diplomacy of Compensation." Deflators from Bureau of Economic Analysis, U.S. Department of Commerce, 2008.

198. This treaty established the "Foundation for German-Polish Reconciliation." The German government paid DM500 million toward this foundation. Recipients of compensation were 40,000 former concentration camp inmates, 30,000 victims who as children had been imprisoned or had served as forced laborers, and about 500,000 former forced laborers. Hofhansel, "The Diplomacy of Compensation," 111. The two nations signed a border treaty as well as this friendship treaty in 1991.

199. Hofhansel, "The Diplomacy of Compensation," 118.

200. Quoted in *New York Times,* January 28, 2000, A3.

201. Yasemin Nuhoglu Soysal, "Identity and Transnationalization in German School Textbooks," *Bulletin of Concerned Asian Scholars* 30, no. 2 (1998), 56–57.

202. Laura Hein and Mark Selden, "The Lessons of War, Global Power, and Social Change," in *Censoring History: Citizenship and Memory in Japan, Germany, and the United States,* ed. Hein and Selden (New York: M. E. Sharpe, 2000), 13; Yasemin Nuhoglu Soysal, Teresa Bertilotti, and Sabine Mannitz, "Projections of Identity in French and German History and Civics Textbooks," in *The Nation, Europe, and the World: Textbooks and Curricula in Transition,* ed. Hanna Schissler and Yasemin Nuhoglu Soysal (New York: Berghahn Books, 2005), 23.

203. James A. Young, "Berlin's Holocaust Memorial," *German Politics and Society* 17, no. 3 (Fall 1999): 55.

204. Bertrand Benoit, "Vast Holocaust Memorial Opens in Central Berlin," *Financial Times,* May 11, 2005, 8. For background, see Young, "Berlin's Holocaust Memorial"; John Grimond, "The Burden of Normality," *Economist,* February 6, 1999, S3.

205. Kattago, "Representing German Victimhood."

206. FAZ, November 16, 1998. The Walser episode is discussed in Niven, *Facing the Nazi Past,* chap. 7.

207. Niven, *Facing the Nazi Past,* 230.

208. Quoted in Heilbrunn, "Germany's New Right," 91.

209. Wilds, "Identity Creation," 94.

210. Joffe, "Mr. Heilbrunn's Planet," *Foreign Affairs* 76, no. 2 (March/April 1997): 155.

211. Marcuse, *Legacies of Dachau,* 381. The book is Daniel Jonah Goldhagen, *Hitler's Willing Executioners: Ordinary Germans and the Holocaust* (New York: Knopf, 1996). For reviews see Josef Joffe, "Goldhagen in Germany," *New York Review of Books* 43, no. 19 (November 28, 1996): 18–21; Omer Bartov, "Ordinary Monsters," *New Republic,* April 29, 1996; *Economist,* July 20, 1996, 45; Fritz Stern, "The Goldhagen Controversy: One Nation, One People, One Theory?" *Foreign Affairs* 75, no. 6 (November/December 1996): 138.

212. Wilds, "Identity Creation," 94. On the "Goldhagen debate," see Atina Grossmann, "The 'Goldhagen Effect': Memory, Repetition, and Responsibility in the New Germany," in *The "Goldhagen Effect": History, Memory, Nazism—Facing the German Past,* ed. Geoff Eley (Ann Arbor: University of Michigan Press, 2000), 89–129; Max Frankel, "Willing Executioners?" *New York Times,* June 28, 1998; Josef Joffe, "Mr. Heilbrunn's Planet," 152–57.

213. Quoted in Marcuse, *Legacies of Dachau,* 381.

214. Ulrich Herbert, "Academic and Public Discourses on the Holocaust: The Goldhagen Debate in Germany," *German Politics and Society* 17, no. 3 (Fall 1999): 46.

215. Marcuse, *Legacies of Dachau,* 380. The English-translation catalog of this exhibit is Hannes Heer, *The German Army and Genocide: Crimes against War Prisoners, Jews, and Other Civilians in the East, 1939–1944* (New York: New Press, 1999).

216. Marcuse, *Legacies of Dachau,* 380.

217. Niven, *Facing the Nazi Past,* chap. 6; Art, *The Politics of the Nazi Past,* 90–92.

218. Michael Adler, "Exhibition on Nazi Army War Crimes Opens in Berlin," Agence France-Presse, November 28, 2001.

219. CIA World Factbook, 2008 (PPP adjusted). Accessed at https://www.cia.gov/library/publications/the-world-factbook/index.html.

220. International Institute of Strategic Studies, *The Military Balance,* various years. In unification negotiations, Germany had agreed to a troop ceiling of 370,000 soldiers and pledged not to develop WMD. France troop size in 2000 was 90 percent that of unified Germany's: 294,000 to Germany's 321,000. IISS, *The Military Balance,* 2000–2001.

221. Data on French nuclear weapons stockpile from Natural Resources Defense Council, http://www.nrdc.org/nuclear/nudb/datab16.asp.

222. *Libération,* June 6, 2004.

223. *Le Figaro,* June 7, 2004; *Le Temps,* June 7, 2004.

224. *Le Figaro,* June 5, 2004. French praise for its Germany ally had increased since a 1993 poll, in which Germany was declared France's closest ally by 56 percent of respondents. This

had in turn risen since 1989, when 44 percent of respondents gave this answer for West Germany. See *Le Monde,* January 23, 1993, 7. In another poll, 61 percent called Germany "the principal ally of France." *L'Evenement du Jeundi,* no. 639 (January 30, 1997): 446.

225. 9 percent were undecided. Source: *L'Evenement du Jeundi,* no. 639 (January 30, 1997): 446.

226. Personal interviews with author, L'Institut Français des Relations Internationales (IFRI), October 2002; Centre d'Etudes et des Recherches Internationales (CERI), October 2002.

227. Personal interview with author, Institut Français des Relations Internationales, October 2002.

228. Personal interview with author, Institut Français des Relations Internationales, October 2002; Personal interview with author, Fondation pour la Recherche Stratégique, October 2002.

229. See, for example, Luc Rosenzweig, "Espace Europeen," *Le Monde,* November 14, 1992.

230. Arnaud Leparmentier and Daniel Vernet, "L'Armee allemande sans sabous," *Le Monde,* June 21, 1999.

231. Ibid. See also Lorraine Millot, *Libération,* June 15, 1999; Michel Colomès, "Kosovo: le sans-faute des Allemands" [Kosovo: So far so good, Germans], June 11, 1999.

232. Colomès, "Kosovo: le sans-faute des Allemands."

233. Personal interview with author, Fondation pour la Recherche Stratégique, October 2002.

234. Marc Semo, *Libération,* September 26, 1998; Jean-Pierre LeFebvre, "La rêve de la normalité," *Esprit,* no. 221 (May 1996): 114.

235. Irène Kruse, "Le Mémorial de l'Holocaust de Berlin," *Vingtiéme Siecle* 67 (2000): 26.

236. Edouard Husson, "Les Allemands et l'Holocauste," *Documents,* no. 3 (1997): 8; *Le Monde Diplomatique,* June 1995, 20.

237. Quotes from Kruse, "Le Mémorial de l'Holocaust de Berlin," 5; *Le Monde,* June 5, 2004; *La Croix,* May 10, 2005, 5.

238. Among voluminous coverage is Henry Rousso, "De Nuremberg à Goldhagen," *L'Express,* no. 2376 (January 16, 1997); Alfred Grosser, "La mémoire et le pardon," *La Croix,* October 6, 1999; Alfred Grosser, "Allemagne: Goldhagen et la vérité," *L'Express,* October 14, 1999.

239. Edouard Husson, "Les Allemands et l'Holocauste," *Documents,* no. 3 (1997): 14.

240. Wehrmacht exhibition coverage includes Bernard Henri Levy, "Les Damnés et les autres," *Le Monde,* February 8, 1999; Eric Roussel, "L'honneur perdu de la Wehrmacht," *Le Figaro,* March 4, 1999; Olivier Vieviorka, "Wehrmacht=SS," *Libération,* March 25, 1999; Lorraine Millot, "A Berlin, dits et non-dits de l'Holocauste," *Libération,* January 28, 2002. Coverage of the Normandy anniversary in *La Croix,* June 4, 2004; *Le Monde,* June 5, 2004; *Le Temps,* June 7, 2004; *Le Figaro,* June 7, 2004; *Libération,* June 6, 2004.

241. Lorraine Millot, *Libération,* January 28, 2002.

242. Daniel Vernet, *Le Monde,* January 16, 2003.

243. Schröder quoted in BBC Special Report, November 4, 1998, electronic version; *Le Monde,* September 17, 1999; Nicholas Weill, "La Culpabilité Allemande, entre mythe et réalités," *La Revue Internationale et Stratégique* 33, 70; Personal interview with author, Sorbonne, October 2002.

244. Joseph Mace-Scaron, "L'Allemagne contre son passe," *Le Figaro,* December 18, 1998. See also interview with Anne-Marie LeGloannec in Joseph Mace-Scaron, "Un renforcement identitaire," *Le Figaro,* December 18, 1998. Extensive coverage of the Walser debate includes Lucas Delattre, "L'Allemagne décomplexée face au passé," *Le Monde,* November 9, 1998; Pascale Hugues, "Faut-il oublier le passé?" *Le Point,* no. 1373, January 9, 1999; Bernard Henri Levy, "La tentation de l'oubli," *Le Monde,* February 6, 1999; Alain-Gérard Slama, "Faut-il avoir peur de l'Allemagne?" *Le Figaro,* June 14, 1999.

245. Marcel Tambarin, "L'Avenir du passé: la polémique Walser-Bubis," *Allemagne d'Aujourd'hui,* no. 149 (July–September 1999): 32; Weill, "La Culpabilité Allemande," 70.

246. Daniel Vernet, *Le Monde,* December 9, 2000.

247. Gilles Martinet, "Europe faut-il avoir peur de l'Allemagne?" *Le Monde,* January 15, 1992.

248. Personal interview with author, L'Institut Français des Relations Internationales, October 2002.

249. Bernard Bosson, *Le Monde,* September 11, 1990.

250. Stephan Martens, "Le Traité 2+4: L'anti-Versailles ou l'intelligence multilatérale," *Allemagne d'Aujourd'hui,* no. 146 (October–December 1998), 286–307; quote on p. 290.

251. Personal interviews with author, L'Institut Français des Relations Internationales, October 2002; Centre d'Études et de Recherches Internationales, October 2002.

252. Jèrôme Vaillant, *Le Monde Diplomatique,* October 1990.

253. Personal interview with author, L'Institut Français des Relations Internationales, October 2002.

254. Personal interview with author, L'Institut Français des Relations Internationales, October 2002.

255. Personal interview with author, L'Institut Français des Relations Internationales, October 2002.

256. Personal interview with author, L'Institut Français des Relations Internationales, October 2002.

257. Personal interview with author, L'Institut Français des Relations Internationales, October 2002; Personal interview with author, L'Institut Français des Relations Internationales, October 2002.

258. Personal interview with author, L'Institut Français des Relations Internationales, October 2002.

259. On Bill Clinton's and George H. W. Bush's refusals to apologize for the atomic bombings, see *Washington Post,* April 20, 1995; *New York Times,* April 8, 1995; *New York Times,* December 2, 1991. In 1991 liberal Japanese politicians advocated an apology for Pearl Harbor. This was blocked by LDP conservatives. *New York Times,* December 7, 1991, 9. Tokyo eventually apologized to the *Japanese* people for attacking Pearl Harbor in the absence of a declaration of war. *Washington Post,* November 22, 1994, A23.

260. The British constructed a monument to the memory of "Bomber Harris," the commander of the Dresden raids. Stephen Kinzer, "Honor to R.A.F. Leader Wakes Dresden's Ghosts," *New York Times,* January 6, 1992, A6.

## 4. The Soul of a People Can Be Changed

1. Strategic bombing figures from Robert Pape, *Bombing to Win* (Ithaca: Cornell University Press, 1996), 337–38.

2. Joshua A. Fogel, ed. *The Nanjing Massacre in History and Historiography* (Berkeley: University of California Press, 2000); Peter Williams and David Wallace, *Unit 731: Japan's Secret Biological Warfare in World War II* (New York: Free Press, 1989).

3. *China Quarterly,* no. 52 (1972): 782–83. As part of the normalization agreement, Japan also recognized Taiwan as part of China. On the history issue in Sino-Japanese relations, see Yinan He, "History, Chinese Nationalism, and the Emerging Sino-Japanese Conflict," *Journal of Contemporary China* 16, no. 50 (February 2007): 1–24; Daqing Yang, "Reconciliation between Japan and China: Problems and Prospects," in *Reconciliation in the Asia-Pacific,* ed. Yoichi Funabashi (Washington, D.C.: United States Institute of Peace Press, 2003), 61–90.

4. *Peking Review* 15, no. 39 (September 29, 1972): 7. See also the editorial in *People's Daily,* August 13, 1978, which similarly commented, "The Japanese people, too, suffered much."

5. On these disputes see Caroline Rose, *Interpreting History in Sino-Japanese Relations: A Case Study in Political Decision-making* (London: Routledge, 1998), chaps. 5–6; Hidenori Ijiri, "Sino-Japanese Controversy since the 1972 Diplomatic Normalization," in *China and Japan: History, Trends, Prospects,* ed. Christopher Howe (Oxford: Clarendon, 1996), 60–82.

6. Allen S. Whiting, *China Eyes Japan* (Berkeley: University of California Press, 1989), 146.

7. Quotes from Chen Tiquiang, "Conclusions Confirmed by History," *Beijing Review* 25, no. 35 (August 30, 1982): 28; "We Must Bear in Mind This Lesson," *Renmin Ribao,* July 20, 1982; Ren Yan, "Friendship Grows Only by Respecting History," *Beijing Review* 25, no. 32 (August 9, 1982): 10.

8. *Renmin Ribao*, August 15, 1982; "Japanese Government Should Be True in Word and Deed," *Beijing Review* 25, no. 38 (September 20, 1982); Liu Zheng, "Japan Should Draw a Lesson from History," *Beijing Review* 25, no. 34 (August 23, 1982).

9. Whiting, *China Eyes Japan*, 146–47.

10. Quotes from Whiting, *China Eyes Japan*, 147; Xin Zong, "Nakasone's Shrine Visit Draws Fire," *Beijing Review* 28, no. 35, 12; Ijiri, "Sino-Japanese Controversy since the 1972 Diplomatic Normalization," 70. On the demonstrations, see also Whiting, *China Eyes Japan*, chap. 4. Nakasone abstained from a planned visit to the shrine during an October festival. Ijiri, "Sino-Japanese Controversy since the 1972 Diplomatic Normalization," 71.

11. Quotes from "The Trend of the Times Is Irresistible," *People's Daily*, September 10, 1986, in FBIS China, same date; Mei Zhenmin, "Background to Okuno's Defense of Aggression," *Liowang* 21, May 23, 1988, in FBIS China, June 2, 1988 [Liaowang is the weekly journal of Xiaohua news service]; Liu Wenyu, "What Can Be Learned from Okuno's Resignation," Xinhua News Service, May 13, 1988, in FBIS China, May 16, 1988; "Friendship Group's Reaction," Kyodo News Service, April 28, 1988, in FBIS China, April 29, 1988.

12. See Yinan He, "Politicization of History-Making and Sino-Japanese Relations," Paper prepared for the Annual Meeting of the Association of Asian Studies, Chicago, Ill., March 2001, 26; "Unforgettable Aggression: Time to Ponder Two Sino-Japanese Wars," *Beijing Review*, no. 34 (August 21–27, 1995): 8–15, in FBIS China, August 21, 1995; "People Never to Forget Japanese 'War Crimes,'" Xinhua News Service, August 16, 1995, in FBIS China, same date.

13. Quotes from Tan Jianrong, "Politicians Should Face Up to the Past," Xinhua News Service, August 16, 1995, in FBIS China, same date); Wang Guotai, "Resolution That Fails to Distinguish Right From Wrong," Xinhua News Service, August 16, 1995, in FBIS China, same date.

14. Jing Xian, "China: To the Point," *China Daily*, January 26, 2000.; "China: Japan's 'No' to Apology Rooted Deeply," *China Daily*, June 2, 2001; "Truth of Massacre Cannot Be Denied," *China Daily*, December 14, 2002; "Japanese PM Apologizes to Chinese People," Xinhua News Service, October 9, 2001; Xi Mi, "China: Never Forget Infamous History," *China Daily*, February 26, 2000.

15. "Japan's Attitude Is So Contemptuous That China Should Get Tough On It," *Ming Pao*, October 21, 2003. For the Japanese apology, see *New York Times*, August 14, 2003; also see Lin Zhibo, "Doubts of 'The New Idea on Relations with Japan'," *Renmin Wang*, July 22, 2003 in FBIS China, same date.

16. Quotes in this paragraph from *Jiefanjun Bao*, May 12, 2001, quoted in Xiaohua Ma, "Security Multilateralism and Conflicting Memories in East Asia: The Promise of a Multilateral Dialogue for Confidence Building," Paper prepared for the Annual Meeting of the International Studies Association, Portland, Oregon, February 25-March 1, 2003, 5; Xinhua News Service, "Article Slams Japanese PM's Shrine Visit," August 14, 2001; Shrine Visit Jeopardizes Relations," *China Daily*, January 15, 2003; Takeshi Sato, "No Progress on Koizumi's Trip to China: Officials," Kyodo Wire Service, April 1, 2003.

17. Philip P. Pan, "Youth Attack Japan's Embassy in China," *Washington Post*, April 10, 2005, A20.

18. Quotes in this paragraph from "Chinese FM Stresses Significance of Sino-Japanese Ties," Xinhua News Service, July 10, 2001; "Japan's Decision on Textbook Unacceptable: Chinese Education Ministry Spokesman," Xinhua News Service, July 9, 2001; Joseph Kahn, "China Pushing and Scripting Anti-Japanese Protests," *New York Times*, April 15, 2005; Philip P. Pan, "Chinese Step Up Criticism of Japan," *Washington Post*, April 13, 2005, A14; "Prolonged Disharmony 'To Hurt' Trade Growth," *China Daily*, April 23, 2005; "Experts Slam Japan's Incendiary School Book," *China Daily*, April 7, 2005. See also "Textbook Sanction Negates Truth of War, Is Political Provocation," *China Daily*, April 6, 2005.

19. "Japan Dodges War Crimes," *China Daily*, November 12, 1999; "Japan Tarnishes Its International Image," *China Daily*, February 12, 2003; Xinhua News Service, April 4, 2001; Xinhua News Service, April 5, 2001; Jing Xian, "China: To the Point," *China Daily*, January 26, 2000; "Textbook Sanction Negates Truth of War," *China Daily*, April 6, 2005; "Written Lies Can Never Cover Up Bloody Facts," Xinhua News Service, April 6, 2005.

20. He, "History, Chinese Nationalism," 6–8; Zhao, *A Nation-State by Construction*, chap. 6. I thank Robert Ross for discussions about this issue.

21. Whiting, *China Eyes Japan*, 144.

22. Quotes in this paragraph from Whiting, *China Eyes Japan*, 144; Thomas J. Christensen, "China, the U.S.-Japan Alliance, and the Security Dilemma in East Asia," *International Security* 23, no. 4 (Spring 1999): 50 and 53, n. 8; He, "History, Chinese Nationalism," 51.

23. Quotes in this paragraph from Whiting, *China Eyes Japan*, 187; Christensen, "China, the U.S.-Japan Alliance, and the Security Dilemma," 52; He, "History, Chinese Nationalism," 21.

24. Quotes from Christopher Reed, "Japan's Shame," *Australian*, July 4, 2006, 11; Max Venables, "For Some, Wounds Will Never Heal," *Sunday Mail*, March 18, 2007.

25. Doug Conway, "Howard Remembers Brutal Enemy," *Hobart Mercury*, August 16, 2005.

26. Gavan Daws, *Prisoners of the Japanese* (New York: Morrow, 1994).

27. For Kishi's apology, see *Canberra Times*, December 5, 1957, 1; *The Age*, December 5, 1957, 5. In a visit to Tokyo that year, Menzies had also made a gesture of forgiveness that surprised and gratified his Japanese hosts. Menzies called Japan a "great" and "proud" country and commented, "It is part of the tradition in British countries that when you have had a fight you shake hands and have friendly relations." Quoted in Alan Rix, *The Australia-Japan Political Alignment: 1952 to the Present* (London: Routledge, 1999), 31.

28. Photo in "Japanese PM Arrives," *The Age*, November 30, 1957, 1; "No Support of 8th Div. Protests," *The Age*, December 2, 1957, 7; "Protest on Kishi Visit at National Shrine," *The Age*, December 5, 1957, 3. In general the public denounced the disruption: see, for example, "A Protest at Canberra," *The Age*, December 7, 1957, 2.

29. See, for example, Candace Sutton and Julie Power, "Hirohito: Fury over Funeral," *Sydney Morning Herald*, January 8, 1989, 1; "Sympathy and Praise and Not a Little Bitterness," *The Age*, January 9, 1989, 8; Sophie Arnold and Hugo Kelly, "Boycott Hirohito Funeral, Says Halfpenny," *The Age*, January 7, 1989, 1.

30. "Comfort Women Haunt Summit," *The Australian* (Sydney), January 27, 1997; "Japan Apologizes," *The Australian*, June 24, 1996; "Comfort Women Accused," *The Australian*, June 7, 1996; D. D. McNicoll, "Film-maker Rejects Japan-bashing Charge," *Weekend Australian* (Sydney), April 12, 1997; Richard Jinman, "Too Tough? These Men Stole My Youth, Says Camp Victim," *Sydney Morning Herald*, April 17, 1997; K. D. Sligo and Narelle Pasco, "Survivors of Paradise Road are Proof of Film's Accuracy," *Weekend Australian*, April 19, 1997.

31. Quotes in this paragraph from "Time to End this Deafening Silence," *Australian Financial Review* (Melbourne), June 1, 2001, 83; Jonathan Este, "POW's Hard Road to Forgiveness," *The Weekend Australian*, June 14, 2002. On Koizumi's visit, see Matt Price, "Koizumi Moved by Images of War Dead," *The Australian*, May 2, 2002; Christopher Bantick, "Playing Politics with History," *Hobart Mercury*, May 17, 2005, 18; "Sino-Japanese Dispute Driven By Cynicism," *Canberra Times*, April 26, 2005, 9.

32. Under the terms of the Treaty of Peace with Japan signed at San Francisco in 1951, signatories (including Australia) renounced the right to further reparations claims from Japan. With this in mind, the Australian government has not sought reparations from Japan, but rather has compensated former POWs on its own. They received reparations and free health care from the Australian government. For details, see "Department of Veterans' Affairs Budget Factsheet—POW," May 22, 2001, available at www.dva.gov.au. On RSL actions, see *Sydney Morning Herald*, April 23, 1998; *The Australian*, January 31, 2001, 1.

33. Quotes in this paragraph from *Australian Financial Review*, March 20, 1991; *Courier-Mail* (Brisbane), February 20, 1992; Keating quoted in Rix, *The Australia-Japan Political Alignment*, 39; "Japan War Apology Tipped," *The Australian*, January 14, 1998, 3; Christopher Bantick, "Playing Politics with History," *Hobart Mercury*, May 17, 2005, 18.

34. Reed, "Japan's Shame"; "Japanese Troops' Reported Plans to Train in Australia Upset WW II Veterans," Agence France-Presse, December 11, 2004; Neil Wilson, "Japanese Struggle with Truth," *Herald Sun* (Melbourne), July 23, 2005, 24; Brian Victoria, "Right Face! The Return of Wartime Ghosts," *Australian Financial Review*, August 9, 2002, 3; "Time to End this Deafening Silence," *Australian Financial Review*, June 1, 2001, 83.

35. Quotes from Victoria, "Right Face!"; Russell Skelton, "Asia Casts Wary Eye on Wartime Aggressor," *The Age*, September 25, 1997, 17; *Advertiser* (Adelaide), March 13, 2007, 16; Shane

Green, "Japan's Lack of Remorse Troubling as It Moves to Rearm," *Sydney Morning Herald,* June 19, 2003, 15.

36. *Weekend Australian,* July 1, 2006, 13.

37. Statement available at http://www.ny.us.emb-japan.go.jp/en/q/japan_policies23.html (accessed May 26, 2007); Victoria, "Right Face!"

38. Paul Midford has argued that national reactions to contrition and to increases in Japanese military power and roles hinge on a country's wartime experiences with Japan. Paul Ian Midford, "Making the Best of a Bad Reputation: Japanese and Russian Grand Strategies in East Asia," Ph.D. diss., Department of Political Science, Columbia University, 2001.

39. Quoted in Tom Harrison, *Living through the Blitz* (London: Collins, 1976), 88.

40. Pape, *Bombing to Win,* 343.

41. Robert Vansittart, *Black Record: Germans Past and Present* (London: Hamish Hamilton, 1941); for discussion and quotes by Atlee and Bevin see John Ramsden, *Don't Mention the War: The British and the Germans since 1890* (London: Little, Brown, 2006), 184, 273–75, 265–66.

42. On German mythologizing after World War I, see Holger Herwig, "Clio Deceived: Patriotic Self-Censorship in Germany after the Great War," *International Security* 12, no. 2 (Fall 1987). Quotes in this paragraph from Lothar Kettenaker, "The Planning of 'Re-Education' during the Second World War," in *The Political Re-Education of Germany and Her Allies after World War II,* ed. Nicholas Pronay and Keith Wilson (Totowa, N.J.: Barnes and Noble Books, 1985), 60–63; Michael Balfour, "In Retrospect: Britain's Policy of 'Re-Education,' " in *The Political Re-Education of Germany,* ed. Nicholas and Wilson, 141.

43. Quotes from Kettenacker, "The Planning of 'Re-Education,' " 63; Robert Birley, education advisor to the military governor in the British zone, quoted in Kurt Jürgensen, "British Occupation Policy after 1945 and the Problem of Re-Educating Germany," *History* 68, no. 223 (June 1983), 239; Barbara Marshall, "British Democratization Policy in Germany," in *Reconstruction in Postwar Germany: British Occupation Policy and the Western Zones, 1945–55,* ed. Ian D. Turner (Oxford: Berg, 1989), 191; Ramsden, *Don't Mention the War,* 184, 199.

44. David Welch, "Priming the Pump of German Democracy: British 'Re-Education' Policy in Germany after the Second World War," in *Reconstruction in Postwar Germany,* ed. Turner, 219.

45. Welch, "Priming the Pump," 220.

46. Quoted in Ramsden, *Don't Mention the War,* 209.

47. Kettenacker, "The Planning of 'Re-Education,' " 71. On the "stab-in-the-back" myth, see Herwig, "Clio Deceived."

48. ISC policy directive, quoted in Welch, "Priming the Pump," 220–21.

49. *Times* (London), May 6, 1965, 15; *Guardian* (London), May 19, 1965.

50. Quotes from Michael White, "History—Or Living Horror?" *Guardian,* May 8, 1985 ; Walter Schwarz, "A History That Won't Go Away," *Guardian,* December 27, 1988.

51. Anna Tomforde, "History Lesson Raises a Storm," *Guardian,* October 29, 1987; Walter Schwarz, "Tell It Like It Was," *Guardian,* December 28, 1988.

52. White, "History—Or Living Horror?"; John Ezard, "Hopes for the Future on May 8, 1985," *Guardian,* May 8, 1985; Anna Tomforde, "Kohl Says Belsen Is Never-Ending Shame," *Guardian,* April 22, 1985; Alan Travis, "Cemetery Visit Disowned: British Premier Thatcher Critical of US President Reagan's Visit to Bitburg, West Germany," *Guardian,* April 26, 1985; "Sensitivities Tend to Outweigh Commemoration," *Guardian,* April 22, 1985; Tomforde, "Kohl Says Belsen Is Never-Ending Shame"; "Biting the Bitburg Bullet," *Guardian,* May 1, 1985; "Reagan Balm Washes Bitburg Scars," *Guardian,* May 6, 1985; "The Past Is Not Prologue," *Economist,* May 4, 1985.

53. See Charles Powell, "What the PM Learned About the Germans," in *When the Wall Came Down: Reactions to German Unification,* ed. Harold James and Marla Stone (New York: Routledge, 1992), 234; Timothy Garton Ash, "The Chequers Affair," *New York Review of Books,* September 27, 1990; George R. Urban, *Diplomacy and Disillusion at the Court of Margaret Thatcher: An Insider's View* (London: I. B. Tauris Publishers, 1996), 134, 142.

54. Margaret Thatcher's remarks at the March 1990 Chequers meeting, chronicled in Urban, *Diplomacy and Disillusion,* 133.

55. Conor Cruise O'Brien, "Beware, the Reich Is Reviving," *Times* (London), October 31, 1989. O'Brien was former editor of the London *Observer* newspaper.

56. Nile Gardiner, "Forever in the Shadow of Churchill? Britain and the Memory of World War II at the End of the Twentieth Century," Occasional Paper, no. 9, International Security Studies, Yale University, January 1997, 30; Margaret Thatcher, *The Downing Street Years* (New York: Harper Collins, 1993), 791; Urban, *Diplomacy and Disillusion,* 104, 134.

57. "Historical Dilemma Sparks Strong Reactions," *Financial Times,* June 1, 1999; "Holocaust Debate Highlights a Divided Germany," *Financial Times,* December 15, 1998; "German Right Puts Fresh Gloss on Nazi History," *Guardian,* May 9, 1995.

58. "Berlin at Last Opens Memorial to Holocaust," *Guardian,* January 20, 1992; "Testimony to Shame," *Evening Standard* (London), January 21, 1992; " 'Library' Recalls Berlin's Shame," *Guardian,* March 22, 1995; "Schindler's List Taxes Germans," *Guardian,* March 2, 1994; "Volunteers: The Guilt Trip," *Guardian,* June 19, 1996.

59. Quotes from "German Right Puts Fresh Gloss on Nazi History"; "Historical Dilemma Sparks Strong Reactions"; "Do Mention the War," *Financial Times,* November 1, 2003; "Ritual Rows That Are Running Out of Steam," *Financial Times,* December 16, 2000. On the Goldhagen debate, see "Book Ignites Holocaust Row," *Guardian,* April 16, 1996; "Holocaust Historian Brought to Book," *Guardian,* August 23, 1997; "German Guilt Brought to Book," *Guardian,* September 11, 1996. On Berlin's Jewish memorial, see "Blank Page in National History Book," *Financial Times,* August 31, 1998; "German MPs Back Jewish Memorial," *Guardian,* June 26, 1999.

60. On British fears of West German rearmament see Saki Dockrill, *Britain's Policy for West German Rearmament, 1950–1955* (Cambridge: Cambridge University Press, 1991), 6–7; Spencer Mawby, *Containing Germany: Britain and the Arming of the Federal Republic* (New York: St. Martin's Press, 1999), 17, 18, 27.

61. Wilson quoted in Susanna Schrafstetter, "The Long Shadow of the Past: History, Memory and the Debate over West Germany's Nuclear Status, 1954–69," *History & Memory* 16, no. 1 (Spring/Summer 2004): 124; also see Susanna Scrafstetter and Stephen Twigge, "Trick or Truth? The British ANF Proposal, West Germany and U.S. Nonproliferation Policy, 1964–68," *Diplomacy & Statecraft* 11, no. 2 (July 2000): 161–84.

62. Quotes in this paragraph from "Iranian leader: Holocaust a 'Myth,' " CNN.com, December 14, 2005; *Jerusalem Post,* March 20, 2007, 4; *Jerusalem Post,* February 25, 2007, 13; *International Herald Tribune,* October 20, 2006, 8.

## Conclusion

1. *Libération* (Paris), June 6, 2004.

2. Robert A. Pape, *Bombing to Win: Air Power and Coercion in War* (Ithaca: Cornell University Press, 1996), 106.

3. The British constructed a monument to the memory of "Bomber Harris," the commander of the Dresden raids. Stephen Kinzer, "Honor to R. A. F. Leader Wakes Dresden's Ghosts," *New York Times,* January 6, 1992, A6. On American refusals to apologize see *Washington Post,* April 20, 1995; *New York Times,* April 8, 1995; *New York Times,* December 2, 1991. On Japan's aborted 1991 apology, see *New York Times,* December 7, 1991, 9.

4. On German debates about contrition see Art, *The Politics of the Nazi Past,* chap. 3; Charles S. Maier, *The Unmasterable Past: History, Holocaust, and German National Identity* (Cambridge, Mass.: Harvard University Press, 1988).

5. Holger Herwig, "Clio Deceived: Patriotic Self-Censorship in Germany after the Great War," *International Security* 12, no. 2 (Fall 1987): 5–44.

6. Jeffrey Herf, *Divided Memory: The Nazi Past in the Two Germanys* (Cambridge, Mass.: Harvard University Press, 1997), 285–86.

7. Daniel Vernet, *Le Monde,* January 16, 2003. The fear that contrition would trigger a German backlash was expressed in numerous personal interviews with author: Centre d'Etudes et des Recherches Internationales (CERI), October 2002; L'Institut Français des Relations Internationales (IFRI), October 2002.

8. Kurt Jürgensen, "British Occupation Policy after 1945 and the Problem of Re-educating Germany," *History* 68, no. 223 (June 1983): 242; Lothar Kettenaker, "The Planning of "Re-Education"

During the Second World War," in *The Political Re-Education of Germany and Her Allies after World War II*, ed. Nicholas Pronay and Keith Wilson (Totowa, NJ: Barnes and Noble Books, 1985), 63–67. On Adenauer's fears of backlash, see Herf, *Divided Memory*, chap. 8.

9. Haider quoted in *Time Europe* 155, no. 6 (February 14, 2000); also on Austria, see David Art, *The Politics of the Nazi Past in Germany and Austria* (Cambridge: Cambridge University Press, 2006), chap. 6. Other European cases are discussed in Art, "The Politics of the Past in Western Europe," paper prepared for delivery at the Annual Meeting of the International Studies Association, February 28, 2007, 13. On France, see "Europe Socialists Reject Chirac Apology," *Globe and Mail* (Toronto), July 18, 1995.

10. On the slavery apology issue, see *Guardian*, March 26, 2007. On the Ireland apologies, see *New York Times*, June 3, 1997; "Blair Walks into Mire of Controversy over Famine," *Belfast News Letter*, June 9, 1997. On the Bloody Sunday apology, see *Evening Standard* (London), January 16, 1998; *Irish Times*, January 19, 1998; *Evening Standard*, January 19, 1998.

11. "Senate Prods Museum on Enola Gay Exhibit," Associated Press, September 24, 1994; *Washington Post*, September 26, 1994.

12. Melissa Nobles, "Official Apologies in Domestic Politics: Do They Matter?" Paper prepared for the Annual Meeting of the American Political Science Association, September 2005. In polls, 80 percent of Australians agreed: "Everyone should stop talking about the way Aboriginal people were treated in the past, and just get on with the future."

13. Lynn E. Cheney, "History Lessons," *Wall Street Journal*, October 20, 1994, A22. For broader debates about education content see Martha Nussbaum, *For Love of Country: Debating the Limits of Patriotism* (Boston: Beacon Press, 1996); William Galston, *Liberal Purposes: Goods, Virtues, and Diversity in the Liberal State* (Cambridge: Cambridge University Press, 1991); James Bernard Murphy, "Against Civic Schooling," *Social Philosophy and Policy* 21, no. 1 (Winter 2004): 221–265.

14. *New York Times*, January 20, 2007, A3.

15. The seminal work on the role of intentions in threat perception is Stephen Walt, *The Origins of Alliances* (Ithaca: Cornell University Press, 1989).

16. Phrase from U.S. Major General Henry C. Stackpole, the former commander of the U.S. Third Marine Division in Japan. Stackpole famously commented in an interview that American military forces were like a "cork" that keeps "a rearmed, resurgent Japan . . . in the bottle" (*Washington Post*, March 20, 1993). Every Korean I interviewed used this expression or a similar analogy.

17. On different levels of reconciliation see Kenneth Boulding, *Stable Peace* (Austin: University of Texas Press, 1978); Arie M. Kacowicz, Yaacov Bar-Siman-Tov, Ole Elgstrom and Magnus Jerneck, eds., *Stable Peace among Nations* (Lanham, Md.: Rowman and Littlefield Publishers, Inc., 2000); Yinan He, "Overcoming Shadows of the Past: Post-Conflict Interstate Reconciliation in East Asia and Europe," Ph.D. diss., Department of Political Science, Massachusetts Institute of Technology, 2004.

18. Charles de Gaulle, *Memoirs of Hope: Renewal and Endeavor*, trans. Terence Kilmartin (New York: Simon and Schuster, 1971), 180.

19. Quotes from Agence-France Presse, September 22, 1984; "France-Allemagne: la paix de Verdun," *Quotidien de Paris*, September 24, 1984; *Le Monde*, April 18, 1985; *Libération*, November 24, 1998.

20. Alfred Grosser, "Célébrer le 8 mai," *Le Monde*, April 30, 1985. For a similar reaction, see Marcel Fourier, ". . . Mais il a oublié d'aller a Dachau!" *Libération*, September 10, 1962.

21. Suisheng Zhao, *A Nation-State By Construction* (Stanford, Calif.: Stanford University Press, 2004).

22. Erik Eckholm, "Chinese Claim a Moral Victory, Describing a Much Bigger Battle," *New York Times*, April 12, 2001; David E. Sanger and Steven Lee Meyers, "Delicate Diplomatic Dance Ends Bush's First Crisis," *New York Times*, April 12, 2001; William Safire, "Dipolingo Discovers Apologrets," *New York Times Magazine*, April 29, 2001, 34.

23. Quoted in Bradley K. Martin, *Under the Loving Care of the Fatherly Leader: North Korea and the Kim Dynasty* (New York: St. Martin's, 2004), 130.

24. See, for example, Ron E. Hassner, "To Halve and to Hold: Conflicts over Sacred Space and the Problem of Indivisibility," *Security Studies* 12, no.4 (Summer 2003): 1–33; Stacie E. Goddard,

"Uncommon Ground: Indivisible Territory and the Politics of Legitimacy," *International Organization* 60, no. 1 (Winter 2006): 35–68.

25. http://foreignaffairs.house.gov/110/hon021507.htm (Aaccessed June 2007); also *New York Times,* March 6, 2007.

26. Martha Finnemore and Kathryn Sikkink, "International Norm Dynamics and Political Change," *International Organization* 52, no. 4 (Autumn 1998): 887–917; also Emilie Hafner-Burton, "Sticks and Stones: Naming and Shaming the Human Rights Enforcement Problem," *International Organization,* forthcoming.

27. Norimitsu Onishi, "Denial Reopens Wounds of Japan's Ex-Sex Slaves," *New York Times,* March 8, 2007, A1; Shi Jingtao, "China Urges Japan to Face 'Comfort Women' Issue," *South China Morning Post,* March 7, 2007, 1.

28. Art, *The Politics of the Nazi Past;* on Turkey, see Jennifer Dixon, "Changing the Story: Understanding the Sources of Change and Continuity in States' Official Narratives," Paper prepared for presentation at the American Political Science Association Annual Meeting, Chicago, Illinois, 30 August–2 September, 2007, 19–20.

29. *South China Morning Post,* June 10, 2005.

30. Walt, *The Origins of Alliances;* Charles L. Glaser, "Realists as Optimists: Cooperation as Self-Help," *International Security* 19, no. 3 (Winter 1994/95): 50–90; David M. Edelstein, "Managing Uncertainty: Beliefs about Intentions and the Rise of Great Powers," *Security Studies* 12, no. 2 (Autumn 2002): 1–40.

31. Some important empirical works in this literature are C. William Walldorf, Jr., *Just Politics: Human Rights and the Foreign Policy of Great Powers* (Ithaca: Cornell University Press, 2008); Mark Haas, *The Ideological Origins of Great Power Politics, 1789–1989* (Ithaca: Cornell University Press, 2005); Martha Finnemore, *The Purpose of Intervention: Changing Beliefs about the Use of Force* (Ithaca: Cornell University Press, 2003); Elizabeth Kier, *Imagining War: French and British Military Doctrine between the Wars* (Princeton: Princeton University Press, 1997); Audie Klotz, *Norms in International Relations: The Struggle against Apartheid* (Ithaca: Cornell University Press, 1994). On the need to focus on the destabilizing effects of ideas, see Jeffrey T. Checkel, "The Constructivist Turn in International Relations Theory," *World Politics* 50 (January 1998): 339.

32. For the legalist point of view see, for example, Martha Minow, *Between Vengeance and Forgiveness: Facing History After Genocide and Mass Violence* (Boston: Beacon Press, 1998); M. Cherif Bassiouni, "Searching for Peace and Achieving Justice: The Need for Accountability," *Law and Contemporary Problems* 59, no. 4 (1996). A pragmatist approach is offered in Jack Snyder and Leslie Vinjamuri, "Trials and Errors: Principle and Pragmatism in Strategies of International Justice," *International Security* 28, no. 3 (Winter 2003): 5–44; Samuel P. Huntington, *The Third Wave: Democratization in the Late Twentieth Century* (Norman: University of Oklahoma Press, 1991), 211–31. For the legalist point of view see, for example, Martha Minow, *Between Vengeance and Forgiveness: Facing History after Genocide and Mass Violence* (Boston: Beacon Press, 1998); M. Cherif Bassiouni, "Searching for Peace and Achieving Justice: The Need for Accountability," *Law and Contemporary Problems* 59, no. 4 (1996).

33. Akiko Hashimoto, "Japanese and German Projects of Moral Recovery: Toward a New Understanding of War Memories in Defeated Nations," Occasional Paper in Japanese Studies, 1999–01, Weatherhead Center for International Affairs, Harvard University, 1999. Arguing that cultural influences encouraged German self-examination and muted such tendencies in Italy is Richard Ned Lebow, "Memory, Democracy, and Reconciliation," in *The Politics of Memory in Postwar Europe,* ed. Richard Ned Lebow, Wulf Kansteiner, and Claudio Fogu (Durham: Duke University Press, 2004).

# Index

*Figures and tables are indicated by italicized page numbers.*

CPSIA information can be obtained
at www.ICGtesting.com
Printed in the USA
LVHW09s1836110918
589816LV00004B/279/P

9 780801 476280